D0869927

STUDIES IN INTERNATIONAL POLITICAL ECONOMY
Stephen D. Krasner, Editor
Ernst B. Haas, Consulting Editor

Scientists and World Order: *The Uses of Technical Knowledge in International Organizations*
Ernst B. Haas, Mary Pat Williams, and Don Babai

Pollution, Politics, and International Law: *Tankers at Sea*
R. Michael M'Gonigle and Mark W. Zacher

Plutonium, Power, and Politics: *International Arrangements for the Disposition of Spent Nuclear Fuel*
Gene I. Rochlin

National Power and the Structure of Foreign Trade
Albert O. Hirschman

Congress and the Politics of U.S. Foreign Economic Policy, 1929–1976
Robert A. Pastor

Natural Resources and the State: *The Political Economy of Resource Management*
Oran R. Young

Resource Regimes: *Natural Resources and Social Institutions*
Oran R. Young

Managing Political Risk Assessment: *Strategic Response to Environmental Change*
Stephen J. Kobrin

Between Dependency and Autonomy: *India's Experience with the International Computer Industry*
Joseph M. Grieco

The Problems of Plenty: *Energy Policy and International Politics*
Peter F. Cowhey

Standing Guard: *Protecting Foreign Capital in the Nineteenth and Twentieth Centuries*
Charles Lipson

Structural Conflict: *The Third World Against Global Liberalism*
Stephen D. Krasner

Liberal Protectionism: *The International Politics of Organized Textile Trade*
Vinod K. Aggarwal

The Politicized Market Economy: *Alcohol in Brazil's Energy Strategy*
Michael Barzelay

From Marshall Plan to Debt Crisis: *Foreign Aid and Development Choices in the World Economy*
Robert Wood

The Power of Ideology: *The Quest for Technological Autonomy in Argentina and Brazil*
Emanuel Adler

Ruling the Waves: *The Political Economy of International Shipping, 1945–1985*
Alan Cafruny

Banker to the Third World: *Latin America and U.S. Capital Markets, 1900–1980*
Barbara Stallings

From Marshall Plan to Debt Crisis

FROM MARSHALL PLAN TO DEBT CRISIS

Foreign Aid and Development Choices
in the World Economy

ROBERT E. WOOD

UNIVERSITY OF CALIFORNIA PRESS
Berkeley · Los Angeles · London

University of California Press
Berkeley and Los Angeles, California

University of California Press, Ltd.
London, England

© 1986 by
The Regents of the University of California

Library of Congress Cataloging-in-Publication Data
Wood, Robert Everett, 1944–
    From Marshall Plan to debt crisis.
    (Studies in international political economy)
    Includes index.
    1. Economic assistance.   2. Economic assistance,
American—Europe.   3. Economic development.
4. Economic assistance—Developing countries.
5. Debts, External—Developing countries.   I. Title.
II. Series.
HC60.W62   1986   338.9′009172′4   86–6934
ISBN 0–520–05526–8 (alk. paper)
ISBN 0–520–05868–2 (pbk.: alk. paper)

Printed in the United States of America

1 2 3 4 5 6 7 8 9

For Joy

CONTENTS

TABLES AND FIGURES

Tables

Figure

ACKNOWLEDGMENTS

Sociology colleagues and students have commonly expressed surprise upon learning that I was writing a book about foreign aid. In a discipline that lumps all papers dealing with the Third World into a single session on "developing societies" at its professional meetings, foreign aid can appear to be an esoteric subject indeed.

My boldness in tackling a subject generally the preserve of economists and to a lesser extent political scientists has had several sources. My belief in the virtue—in fact, the necessity—of transgressing disciplinary boundaries developed early in my undergraduate career as a social studies major at Harvard in a pioneering interdisciplinary program whose leading light was Stanley Hoffman. During my sophomore year, I had the extraordinary good fortune to participate in a tutorial led by Allen Graubard and Ted Marmor, which I still look back to as a model of teaching and learning. By a quirk of fate, Allen Graubard later became one of my editors at the University of California Press and helped me along in a second of life's passages.

Coming of intellectual and political age during the Vietnam War, I, like many of my generation, turned to history to try to make sense of United States foreign policy. The work of William Appleman Williams and Gabriel and Joyce Kolko had a particularly profound impact on me; the Kolkos' influence is particularly evident in my treatment of the Marshall Plan.

Teaching and research experience in East Africa and Southeast Asia broadened my awareness of external constraints on Third World development choices and deepened my conviction that the traditional disciplinary boundaries of the social sciences too often stand in the way of an understanding of development. It convinced me of the sociologist's obligation to address the larger structural forces behind the patterns of dependent development observable in most of the Third World.

In studying foreign aid, I have not felt that I have left my sociologist's craft behind. Substantively, it has become increasingly apparent to me that foreign aid plays a significant role in shaping those aspects of the social world that sociologists commonly look at: social inequality, class structure, politics, gender relations, rural-urban relations, and so forth. Methodologically, my training as a sociologist in the tradition of Marx, Weber, and Durkheim has made me particularly sensitive to the existence of structures behind processes that on the surface seem without "rhyme or reason." As I explain in the Introduction, I have found it useful to pull together two contemporary structural perspectives, world systems and international regime analysis, in making sense of the role of aid in the world economy.

There are many ways to trace the impact of foreign aid; I have chosen one both ambitious and simple. I have sought to identify the overall way that access to concessional external financing is structured and to link that structure to the issue of development options and choices in the Third World. One cannot deduce outcomes in Third World countries from this structure, but one can gain a better understanding of basic contours of world development and of the complex combination of opportunity and constraint that foreign aid presents to Third World countries. And as I argue, an analysis of the major aid institutions sheds light on both the origins and consequences of the devastating debt crisis in the Third World.

My indebtedness to many scholars who have studied various facets of the complex realities of aid will be evident as I proceed. Here I would like to acknowledge a broader debt to friends and colleagues whose intellectual stimulation, support, and encouragement have been critical for me. These include Fred Block, Harry Brill, Steven Cohn, Susan Eckstein, Gonzalo Falabella, Linda Falstein, Roz Feldberg, Keitha Fine, Ann Froines, Sheila Grinell, Susan Gore,

David Hunt, Carole Joffe, Bruce Johnson, Karl Klare, Magali Sarfatti Larson, Arthur MacEwan, Susanne Morgan, Ann Popkin, Jack Spence, and Ann Swidler. Sheila Grinell gets special thanks for copy-editing the original draft of this book. I also consider myself unusually blessed to be able to cite the genuine stimulation and support from my colleagues in the Department of Sociology and Anthropology at Camden College of Arts and Sciences, Rutgers University: Myra Bluebond-Langner, Sheila Cosminsky, Ted Goertzel, Meredith Gould, Drew Humphries, and Arthur Paris.

Some of the research and costs of manuscript preparation were supported by the Rutgers Research Council and by the Office of the Provost at Rutgers University, Camden.

My wife Joy and my sons Nicholas and Timothy have mostly found ways of lending support other than observing claims of the sanctity of my study or releasing me from household chores. Their challenge and delight is the best contribution of all.

LIST OF ABBREVIATIONS

ADB	Asian Development Bank
AfDB	African Development Bank
BIS	Bank for International Settlements
CABEI	Central American Bank for Economic Integration
CDB	Caribbean Development Bank
CIP	Commodity Import Program
CMEA	Council for Mutual Economic Assistance
DAC	Development Assistance Committee
DFC	Development Finance Company
DLF	Development Loan Fund
EADB	East African Development Bank
ECA	Economic Cooperation Administration
EDF	European Development Fund
EEC	European Economic Community
ERP	European Recovery Program
ESF	Economic Support Fund
IBRD	International Bank for Reconstruction and Development
IDA	International Development Association
IDB	Inter-American Development Bank
IFC	International Finance Corporation
IGP	Investment Guaranty Program
IMF	International Monetary Fund
LDC	Less developed country
LIBOR	London interbank offering rate

LIC	Low-income country
LLDC	Least developed country
MDB	Multilateral Development Bank
MIC	Middle-income country
MIGA	Multilateral Investment Guarantee Agency
MSA	Mutual Security Agency
NIC	Newly industrializing country
ODA	Official development assistance
OECD	Organization for Economic Cooperation and Development
OEEC	Organization for European Economic Cooperation
OOF	Other official flows (non-ODA)
OPEC	Organization of Petroleum-Exporting Countries
OPIC	Overseas Private Investment Corporation
SAL	Structural adjustment loan
SSE	Small-scale enterprise
SUNFED	Special United Nations Fund for Economic Development
UNCTAD	United Nations Conference on Trade and Development
UNDP	United Nations Development Program
USAID	United States Agency for International Development

INTRODUCTION: ECONOMIC AID, DEVELOPMENT, AND THE WORLD ECONOMY

In 1955, at the close of his account of the origins of the Marshall Plan, ex–U.S. State Department official Joseph Jones paused to ask: "What, indeed, are the limits of United States power? And what are the limits of United States foreign policy?" He replied: "The answer is that the limits of our foreign policy are on a distant and receding horizon; for many practical purposes they are what we think we can accomplish and what we think it is necessary to accomplish at any given time." The experience of the Marshall Plan's creation suggested "not the limits but the infinite possibilities of influencing the policies, attitudes and actions of other countries by statesmanship in Washington."[1] A few years earlier, Paul Hoffman, the former Studebaker executive who administered Marshall Plan aid in its formative years, had expressed similar sentiments: "We have learned in Europe what to do in Asia, for under the Marshall Plan, we have developed the essential instruments of a successful policy in the arena of world politics."[2]

Disillusionment about the efficacy of aid replaced Jones's and Hoffman's certitude within a few years, although it took the Vietnam War to undermine seriously the vision of a limitless foreign policy.[3] By the 1980s, popular disenchantment with aid was such that one survey found the U.S. public's desire to reduce foreign aid outranking its fear of nuclear war.[4] Eighty-two percent of respondents in a 1980 poll said foreign economic assistance should be cut.[5] U.S. foreign aid was funded by continuing resolutions six out of seven times between 1979 and 1985 as a result of the failure of new aid bills in Congress. Combined liberal and conservative opposition came close

1

to defeating the U.S. quota increase in the International Monetary Fund (IMF) in 1983.

Yet foreign economic aid has remained a fixture of international relations, and virtually all developed countries, and even a few underdeveloped ones, administer substantial aid programs and/or contribute to international or multilateral institutions providing aid. Aid occupies a central and institutionalized role in the world economy, not only financing a significant proportion of imports and projects but also often certifying good behavior that "unlocks," as IMF Managing Director Jacques de Larosière is fond of saying, vast other resources.[6] A world without aid would be a very different world.

This book traces the evolution of concessional financing to Third World countries from its postwar origins in the Marshall Plan to the debt crisis that engulfed virtually the entire Third World in the early 1980s. It documents the evolution of a system of aid provision, of structured access to concessional external financing. The central focus is on how this structure of access to aid has changed over time and shaped development options and choices in the Third World. From this perspective, the emergence of the debt crisis is closely connected to the role of aid in the world economy. Although the debt crisis had other roots as well, this book elucidates an important set of determinants, generally overlooked, within the system of aid provision itself. It further seeks to show that the debt crisis defines a new era, not simply a set of discrete and extraordinary events between, say, Mexico's request for rescheduling in August 1982 and Argentina's coming to terms with the International Monetary Fund in September 1984. The debt crisis has profoundly altered the international environment that Third World countries face, and the legacy of debt will continue to be a central focus of international relations and development choices for years to come.

Aid and Development: Reconceptualizing the Issue

More than thirty-five years of aid programs in Third World countries have not yielded any firm conclusions about the relationship between aid and development. Statistical studies of the relationship between aid and development have produced inconsistent and inconclusive results. Indeed, the Development Assistance Committee (DAC) of the major advanced capitalist countries, which exists in part to drum up support for continued aid, conceded in 1980 that "there can be no rigorous scientific proof that in the past the aggregate of everything officially designated as official development assistance has had an identifiable, assignable, positive and cost-effective impact on Third World development."[7]

The DAC attributed this inconclusiveness to the variety of donor purposes and to the complexity of donor-recipient "interface." But there are also methodological and theoretical problems in measuring aid's impact. For one thing, the activity financed by aid may not be the true measure of aid's impact because the recipient government might have carried out such activity in the absence of aid. This problem is usually referred to as "fungibility" or "substitutability." The real impact of aid in such cases may be to finance some alternative government activity or simply to underwrite higher domestic (often luxury) consumption.[8]

Determining aid's impact is further complicated by its relationship to other types of capital flows, particularly private loans and foreign investment. Access to aid is generally inversely related to the availability of private foreign capital and to the security of existing investments by foreign capital. If lower levels of aid are associated with higher levels of other capital flows, aid is unlikely to be statistically associated with economic growth, even if its impact on individual countries is indeed developmental.

In addition, economic aid is always but one of a variety of factors, both domestic and international, impinging on decisions about development strategy. In many cases, these factors mutually reinforce one another, making outcomes "overdetermined." Isolating the distinctive role of aid in such cases can be very difficult.

However, the most fundamental problem in linking aid to development involves the concept of development itself. Development is often treated as something that takes place purely at the national level and that is identified narrowly with economic growth. Accordingly, because per capita aid flows fail to be statistically associated with common measures of economic growth, a number of observers deny any determinate relationship between aid and development. By the same logic, self-interested and "political" motivations on the part of donors (for example, promotion of exports and foreign investment, and suppression of insurgent social movements) are interpreted as representing the intrusion of "nondevelopmental" considerations into the aid process.[9] Attention is thereby shifted away from the relationship between aid and development to the relationship between aid and allegedly alternative economic and political goals—on the assumption that these latter represent "nondevelopmental" objectives.

What this type of analysis fails to grasp is aid's relationship to the *nature* of the development that has occurred both within individual Third World countries and within the world economy as a whole. There is indeed no necessary relationship between levels of aid and rates of growth. But there is a profoundly important relationship between aid, conceptualized as structured access to concessional external financing, and the basic features of the kind of development that has characterized most Third World societies and the overall world economy over the past thirty years. A basic thesis of this book holds that this structure of aid financing has fundamentally affected the viability of alternative development choices open to Third World countries. This structure, which I shall subsequently call the aid regime, has posed a complex combination of possibilities and constraints for Third World societies and thereby played a central role in shaping the nature of development strategies and processes.

From its origins in the Marshall Plan, access to aid has been structured in ways that promote development choices adding up to what Fernando Cardoso and Enzo Faletto and others have termed dependent development—characterized by openness to and alliance with foreign capital; import of organizational and production technologies; monetary, fiscal, and trade policies extending the domestic reach of international market forces; and, despite considerable variation, a general "dissociation" of the "entrepreneurial-repressive state . . . from the nation."[10] As all sophisticated versions of dependency theory make clear, development outcomes arise from a complex interplay of domestic and international forces. This book attempts to define the role of economic aid in structuring options open to Third World countries and in shaping the development process in the world economy as a whole. Quite apart from the role of other instrumentalities—military aid and intervention, covert operations, diplomatic and economic sanctions and rewards—the rules of access to development aid have themselves made alternative development strategies—socialist, statist, autarkic, redistributionist—costly to pursue. The worldwide internationalization of capital and "interdependence" of economies, which are often taken for granted today, were laboriously created against what many observers in the early postwar period saw as almost overwhelming odds, and aid played a major role in this process.

Conceptual Underpinnings

How are we to conceptualize aid? "Foreign aid," former Under-Secretary of State George Ball once observed, "is a deceptive phrase that comprehends programs and policies dissimilar in motive and effect."[11] Efforts to classify forms of aid in terms of the motivations behind them seem to produce an endless set of categories. One observer concludes that "it is impossible to discern the slightest rhyme or reason to the way in which funds have been distributed among countries."[12]

The world systems perspective, with its eclectic origins in Marxism, dependency theory, and French historiography, offers a useful starting point.[13] It suggests a structural approach to aid, seeing it at once as an important component of the world economy and as a measure of a country's location within it. It has been suggested that receipt of foreign aid is what defines the Third World.[14] But one can argue further that varying access to different types of concessional financing both reflects and produces specific locations in the world economy. When aid access is disaggregated in this way, the "rhyme and reason" behind aid become considerably clearer.

A world systems perspective directs our attention to aid's role in the larger structures within which national decision making takes place. Immanuel Wallerstein has observed that "political structures do not contain 'economies'; quite the contrary: the 'world economy' contains political structures, or states."[15] Andre Gunder Frank argues that development is "often misperceived as taking place in particular countries, when it has really been one of the processes of the world system itself."[16] Aid, as a central component of the world economy, helps set the parameters of development choices and processes.

For some critics, Wallerstein's and Frank's statements typify a tendency toward economic reductionism and the devaluation of political variables. Some have countered with the autonomy of interstate relations, others with the centrality of class relations at the national level.[17] Most social scientists within the world systems tradition have moved to incorporate these factors in a more systematic way, and recent world systems research has increasingly integrated national and intranational factors, even if the result has been to decrease the determinacy of the basic theory. But world systems work has been less successful in dealing with levels of analysis between the state and the international system as a whole, a weakness shared with a good deal of political science and political sociology.

In grappling with how to conceptualize aid and its relationship both to the world economy and to national decision making, I have used the work of "international regime" theorists. The conceptual vocabulary and research agenda of regime analysis were originally developed by political scientists dissatisfied with the "realist" tradition of political analysis. Robert Keohane and Joseph Nye provided a major formulation of the perspective in a pioneering book in 1977, in which they took the realist tradition to task for its narrowly military conception of national interests and capabilities and for its inadequate understanding of economic interdependence and forms of international exchange.[18] Regime analysis has been particularly instrumental in eliciting renewed attention to forms of international organization. This perspective has attracted scholars with diverse interests and theoretical backgrounds, all seeking to disaggregate and dislodge the state as the sole actor in international relations and to identify ways in which international relations may be regulated in the absence of an overarching authority. Using the journal *International Organization* as their semiofficial mouthpiece, these scholars have defined a research agenda that offers promising possibilities for exploring the intersection of domestic, national, and global forces.[19]

Regime analysis helps us further "unpack" the relationship between aid and development. A regime approach to aid allocation avoids the mechanistic search for statistical correlations between amounts of aid and either donor goals or recipient needs or outcomes (characteristic of many studies of aid) because it conceives of regimes as "changing the context within which states make decisions."[20] To specify an aid regime is not to identify a set of independent variables that statistically predict certain outcomes, but is rather to describe a set of "injunctions" that affect the calculations and decisions of both donors and recipients. Occasional violations of regime injunctions do not disprove the existence of the regime; instead, they draw attention to other factors (including other regimes) that may impinge on state and institutional decision making.[21]

A regime approach helps us see if there is a logic of aid provision that binds the activities of diverse donors. By drawing our attention to internationally shared and sometimes negotiated principles, norms, rules, and procedures of aid access, it directs attention to the mix, or composition, of external financing, as opposed simply to its aggregate amount. As we shall see, regime norms go much further in regulating access to different types of aid—defined in terms of source, concessionality, conditionality, and function—than in determining levels of aggregate aid. The structuring of access to different types of aid via regime norms affects the context of development choices, even if the impact on economic growth rates is indeterminate. A regime approach thereby helps identify the mechanisms by which development options are structured within the world system and development choices at the national level are affected.

Finally, a regime approach provides a basis for analyzing the changing role of aid. Viewing the aid regime as a historically evolving set of international principles, norms, rules, and procedures helps us examine changes in the aid regime's structure and impact at different times.

To date, both the world systems perspective and regime analysis offer more of a conceptual vocabulary and a set of research questions than an elaborated theory. The basic insights of the world systems perspective are that the world economy is a system and that no part can be understood independently from the whole. Regime analysis recognizes the practical impossibility of treating the whole system and breaks it down into analytically more manageable categories of regimes. The danger of this approach, however, is reification: treating regimes as separate and autonomous entities with a life of their own. Overly narrow definitions of regimes may obstruct recognition of broad interconnections—for example, when "balance of payments" or "export promotion" financing are too sharply differentiated from "development" aid. In what follows, I try to combine the holism of the world systems perspective with the analytic specificity of regime analysis.

Outline of This Book

Aid is important precisely because it is so closely related to other capital flows. This relationship makes aid a "messy" phenomenon to identify and study, however. The remainder of this Introduction specifies the boundaries of this study: the definition of foreign aid, the range of institutions considered, the relevance of other forms of external financing, and the set of countries covered. Readers unconcerned with these relatively technical details may choose to simply survey the outline of the study presented in this section and then move ahead to the next chapter to get on with the "story."

This volume has two parts. Part One explores the origins, development, and basic operating principles of the aid regime. A brief introduction explores the roads not taken, placing the origins of the aid regime within a wider set of postwar political choices by the United States, at the time the dominant actor in the world economy. The following chapter offers a reinterpretation of the European Recovery Program (popularly known as the Marshall Plan) that sees the plan as limited neither to Europe nor to recovery. Rather, it is argued, the Marshall Plan is more accurately seen as a largely successful effort to create a new worldwide order of trade and investment relationships and to forestall an alternative order based on "national capitalisms." Both the international system within which the aid regime developed and the basic operating principles of that regime are rooted in the Marshall Plan period. Chapter 2 sketches the changing structure of external financing for Third World countries and how this has affected their position as aid recipients. It documents the proliferation of aid donors and the decline of recipient dependency on single donors. The chapter concludes with the question of whether an aid regime can be said to exist in a context of multiple donors, little formal coordination, and low donor dependency. Chapter 3 answers this question affirmatively, demonstrating that an aid regime does exist and identifying its basic structures. The final chapter in Part One looks at the sectoral allocation of aid that follows from regime norms and examines in particular the management of industrial investment as a case study of regime influence. A fundamental theme in this and other chapters is the close connection between aid (concessional) and nonaid (nonconcessional) resources.

Part Two explores the crisis of the aid regime, which took shape in the mid 1970s and became acute in the early 1980s. A brief introduction links this crisis to a broader crisis of dependent development. Chapter 5 then analyzes the response of the major aid institutions to the increasingly evident inequalities engendered by regime-sponsored development. Particular attention is devoted to the World Bank's basic needs approach: its elaboration and partial (though very limited) implementation in the late 1970s and the retreat from it in the early 1980s. The fate of the basic needs approach is a lesson in the limits of regime change. Chapter 6 analyzes the relationship between aid and the buildup of debt during the 1970s, arguing that the aid regime was in part responsible for the buildup of debt—both because most aid itself created debt and because regime constraints on development choices were major factors in providing Third World countries an incentive to turn to the less conditional financing available from commercial lenders. This was particularly the case for those countries pursuing policies the chapter identifies as "state capitalist." Changes in the world economy by the early 1980s threw both state capitalism and the aid regime into crisis.

The final chapter in Part Two analyzes how the aid regime has been restructured in the wake of the Third World debt crisis. Even countries that have not had to reschedule their debt have been profoundly affected by the changes resulting from the crisis. While the major creditor countries and institutions successfully warded off calls for systemic change and insisted on a "case-by-case" approach to debt problems, new norms evolved in the debt restructuring negotiations, and resources and access to them have been restructured within the aid regime itself. Overall, these changes can be seen as reconsolidating the disciplinary functions of the aid regime, which had been undermined in the 1970s by the ability of many Third World countries to obtain alternative and less conditional financing at low real cost.

The Epilogue, "Regime Conditionality and Development Choices in the 1980s," notes the premises on which regime reconsolidation has been based and identifies several areas of contradiction and potential change. It suggests that some of the responses to the debt crisis could, under certain circumstances, contribute to even deeper and more intractable crises in the future.

Boundaries and Definitions

Defining Aid

"Development assistance," a well-known aid economist has written, "is a name covering many different relations between suppliers and recipients."[22] Foreign aid is a label, and a great deal of political ingenuity has gone into determining what it does and does not apply to.

Foreign aid is commonly divided between military aid and economic aid, the latter almost always synonymous with development aid. In the United States, Congress has authorized and appropriated funds for the two types of aid sometimes in separate and sometimes in single pieces of legislation. The Development Assistance Committee excludes all grants, loans, and credits for military purposes from its definition of development assistance.

This book focuses almost exclusively on economic, or development, aid. In reality, however, the distinction between economic and military aid is not at all straightforward. On the one hand, a donor's decision to call aid "economic" or "military" is often politically shaped and bears little relationship to either the donor's real motivation or the aid's real impact. In the United States, for example, well over half of economic aid (excluding food aid) is channeled through the Economic Support Fund (ESF), which is formally subordinated to the pursuit of U.S. military and strategic objectives.[23] The ESF is explicitly released by law from the developmental requirements that Congress has applied to other forms of economic aid. On the other hand, military aid can obviously have profound significance for the nature of development (for example, by supporting the suppression of insurgents who call for a different kind of development, by altering the intraelite balance of power, and by sometimes enabling the military to become a major force in the economy itself).

The problem of distinguishing economic from military aid is compounded by the issue of fungibility. Economic aid may allow a government to divert resources to military purposes. Military aid may have the opposite effect. Given a compliant aid recipient, a donor's decision about whether to label its aid economic or military may have less to do with its intended impact than with domestic political and other policy considerations. Joseph Jones's account of the decision to provide "military" aid to Turkey under the Truman Doctrine in 1947 makes it clear that the fungibility of aid was recognized and played upon by policymakers from the very beginning of the postwar aid regime.[24]

Limiting itself to official economic aid, this book says little about a great deal of "aid" that has relevance for the nature of development choices in the Third World, particularly if we take into account the threat or reality of covert aid to opposition forces (for example, CIA support for the Contra armies along the borders of Nicaragua). Nicaragua has estimated that U.S.-financed sabotage and hostile actions cost Nicaragua $550 million between 1981 and the fall of 1984—to say nothing of the cost of diverting resources to defense to protect its revolution—raising the issue of whether one should speak of "negative" aid.[25] The Sandinista government's ability to survive is likely itself to affect political calculations and development strategies elsewhere. However, although further research on military and covert aid is definitely needed, its social and political thrust tends to be relatively obvious—either the support of friendly regimes beset by popular insurgency or the overthrow of regimes deemed a threat to the donor's interests.[26] The social and political significance of routine economic aid, however, is less obvious and has been analyzed less.

Limiting our focus to economic aid, how do we determine what activities should be so labeled? Two common criteria are that aid comes from the official sector and that it is available on concessional terms. A basic relationship exists between these two criteria. In a capitalist world economy, the rationale for states intervening in the international flow of goods and services is that market-determined allocation is judged to be in some way insufficient. Hence, governments intervene to provide goods and services the market is not providing—or will provide only at a cost judged too high for the achievement of donor-defined goals. Virtually all government aid is therefore concessional, in the sense of providing for the transfer of goods or resources either directly (on a bilateral basis) or indirectly (through multilateral institutions such as the World Bank), on terms more generous than the market's. By and large, the concessional element of aid involves a combination of longer grace periods, longer maturities, lower interest rates, and, very occasionally, repayment in incontrovertible currency.[27]

Although donors have no incentive to provide aid if they are content with the market's allocation of goods and services, and recipients have no interest in accepting aid that does not carry terms better than those available on the market, there are some ambiguities in foreign aid's concessional status. For one thing, the degree of concessionality varies greatly—from grants, which do not have to be repaid at all, to loans of various terms. The Development Assistance Committee defines "official development assistance" (ODA) as carrying a grant element of at least 25 percent—a definition that excludes most lending from the World Bank and the regional development banks, as well as a significant proportion of bilateral flows.[28] The DAC distinguishes between ODA and "other official flows" (OOF), which carry a grant element less than 25 percent. According to the DAC's calculations, ODA constituted about two-thirds and OOF about one-third of gross official disbursements worldwide in 1983.[29] Many studies of aid look only at ODA, on the grounds that these other flows are not "really aid." To do this, however, one runs the risk of overemphasizing the importance of the terms of financial flows to the detriment of understanding the overall significance of these flows. It is important to explore why different types of official financing come with different terms and what significance this fact has for Third World development options. Hence, this book is not limited to ODA, but examines the entire range of official flows.

The concessional quality of foreign aid must be interpreted cautiously for several other reasons as well. The expected rate of return on investment is a socially conditioned phenomenon—something that has led business-oriented observers for years to worry that low-interest official loans will "create misunderstanding in the borrowing country about the rate of return on private loans or investments that is appropriate and commensurate with the risk."[30] Between the capital markets of various donors (for example, the United States and Japan), there may be different expectations about rates of return, so that a hard loan from Japan might be a soft loan from the United States.

In addition, the difference between the terms of aid and those of the market does not necessarily constitute the cost to the donor. The most extreme example is the U.S. food aid program, which accounted for 31 percent of U.S. aid to less developed countries between 1953 and 1970 and 24 percent between 1971 and 1981.[31] This program has probably cost the United States nothing at all because the cost of price support and storage in the absence of the food aid program would have amounted to about as much as "giving" it away.[32]

Finally, there are ambiguities in the calculation of the grant element of aid. Most important from the point of view of aid recipients, however, is that the grant element takes no account of the effect of "tying" aid. The bulk of bilateral aid is tied: it must be spent on commodities or services from the donor country. In addition, some donors have sought to use aid programs specifically to promote the export of their least competitive products. Economists have calculated that the tying of aid lowers its value by about 25 percent, effectively raising the real interest rate. Clearly, if aid tying were considered in calculating aid's grant element, substantially fewer official flows would qualify as ODA.

When other benefits to the donor are taken into account, the imagery of gift giving embedded in most discussions of aid becomes questionable. Donors may receive more than they give, and recipients may repay more than they receive. Nonetheless, the donor-recipient terminology reflects a basic asymmetry of power and status that lies at the core of the aid process, and I shall use it and other common aid terms in this sense. Beyond this asymmetry of power and status, however, the vocabulary should not be construed as implying anything about either motivation or consequence.

In addition to official source and concessionality, motivation is part of the Development Assistance Committee's definition of ODA. ODA must have the "promotion of economic development and welfare as main objectives."[33] The United States reports virtually all its ESF allocations as ODA to the Development Assistance Committee, and most other donors likewise classify all their nonmilitary aid as meeting the motivational requirement. By and large, the domestic unpopularity of foreign aid has led governments to use a very restrictive definition of what is foreign aid at home and a very expansive one abroad. The U.S. executive branch has been particularly ingenious in proliferating aid channels that get around congressional stinginess.

In the House Appropriations Subcommittee that handles foreign aid, Representative Otto Passman for many years made a profession of searching out the various "spigots" by which aid in one form or another is disbursed. In 1964, Passman complained: "There are sixteen spigots by which these countries can, and do, draw off our resources, our wealth through foreign aid. . . . This is a way for the spenders to do some of the things that Congress said last year would no longer be permitted through our foreign aid program."[34] In 1970, he complained about twenty-seven spigots.[35] Narrow definitions of foreign aid have allowed the executive branch to announce with great fanfare the ending of aid to such countries as Taiwan and Iran while a variety of other "spigots" remain open. A study that wishes to comprehend the role of aid in the overall world system must encompass the whole range of such spigots and their interrelationships.

To define economic aid in this broad way is to assume a stance more akin to the public's view, which tends to lump together all official transfers as "aid," than to the view of much of the literature in the field. Although including official loans from institutions like the World Bank, which fail to meet the ODA standard, is not particularly controversial, a rigid line is often drawn between "development" aid and "balance of payments" assistance from the IMF. IMF lending is not generally considered aid because of its short duration, its low grant element, and its stated goals of balance of payments/stabilization financing. Furthermore, access to IMF resources is regulated in somewhat different ways than access to most other official financing. These differences are easily overstated, however. IMF loans carry only slightly harder terms than much non-ODA official financing. IMF lending goals have become increasingly indistinguishable from much aid financing, as the IMF has come to take "developmental" considerations more into account and other aid institutions have moved into balance of payments financing. Furthermore, IMF lending is intricately tied to financing from other sources in a variety of ways, most notably through the gate-keeping function of its formal agreements. Accordingly, the IMF will be treated as an integral, if unique, part of the aid regime.

Aid and Other Forms of External Financing

Aid has always been closely related to private, nonconcessional external financing. From the beginnings of the U.S. aid programs, aid resources have been used not only to encourage but also to underwrite private flows (for example, through investment and loan guarantees and other subsidized services). Formal linkages between official and private flows expanded considerably during the 1970s under "cofinancing" arrangements, to be discussed in detail in later chapters. In September 1983, the World Bank went a step further and began to participate directly in commercial loan syndications. In the first such loan, to Thailand, the World Bank took a 25 percent share and assumed the later maturities of a sixteen-and-a-half-year loan.[36] The growth of this type of cofinancing has made the concessional/nonconcessional and official/private distinctions increasingly ambiguous.

Such formal linkages barely begin to define the relationship between aid and private capital flows, however. One cannot analyze the aid regime without constant reference to private capital; subsequent chapters will explore this relationship in detail. Just as an understanding of one form of aid requires an understanding of its relationship to other forms of aid, so an understanding of the aid regime as a whole requires an analysis of aid's relationship to other forms of external financing.

Countries

By "Third World" or "South" in this book, I refer to the countries of Latin America, Asia (excluding Israel and Japan), and Africa (excluding South Africa). Although the internal and external conditions of these countries vary greatly, they nonetheless share a sufficient number of unique and fundamental characteristics to justify use of the term "Third World." One meaning of "Third World" is entanglement in the aid regime.[37] It is clearly beyond the capacity of a single book to explore all the ramifications of this entanglement for individual societies, each with its own institutional structures and class alignments. Nonetheless, specifying the structure and functioning of the aid regime should focus attention on a central way in which location within the capitalist world economy shapes the options available to individual societies and groups within them.

Dependency and world systems theory have imparted a healthy skepticism toward such labels as "developing societies" and "less developed countries" (LDCs). We cannot assume that all Third World societies are in fact developing, and the suggestion that these societies simply have less of something (development) than the industrialized societies has been definitively refuted by dependency theorists. This book uses these labels primarily when referring to data identified as such (which generally include several southern European and other societies that fall outside the scope of this book: primarily Portugal, Yugoslavia, and Israel). It has not always been possible to eliminate these cases, which can skew the statistics. Third World countries will also on occasion be referred to as underdeveloped societies, without implying stagnation or ignoring the different growth experience of individual societies.

The Development and Functioning of the Aid Regime

Introduction to Part One: Alternatives to Aid

In tracing the origins and development of the aid regime, one must not take for granted either the scale of aid or its particular institutional forms. The aid regime evolved during a period of undisputed U.S. hegemony. The U.S. Agency for International Development (along with its predecessor institutions) was the largest source of aid until 1970, when it was overtaken by the World Bank, itself strongly influenced by the United States. The early postwar aid programs of a number of European countries were effectively underwritten by the United States. Yet even within the context of U.S. hegemony, there were always politically articulated alternatives to both the scale and particular institutional structure of aid. Along with aid, these alternatives presupposed a common set of goals whose primacy was not seriously questioned in the United States: the creation of an open, multilateral world economy characterized by the dominance of market forces and the maximum freedom of private capital to trade and invest.

Some of these alternatives were put forward relatively fleetingly; others remain a source of contention today. I shall not attempt here to assess their viability or the reasons for their failure. However, we must recognize that alternatives did exist and that the development of the aid regime reflected the failure of these alternatives. The rejection or failure of these alternatives made the development of the aid regime inevitable. Therefore, before turning to the origins of the aid regime in the Marshall Plan, I shall explore five alternatives: (1) institutional multilateralism; (2) military containment; (3) acceptance of nationalist, including socialist, revolutions; (4) trade liberalization; and (5) market-induced "adjustment."

Institutional Multilateralism

War was still raging in Europe and the Far East when representatives of forty-four countries met at Bretton Woods in 1944 to establish the institutional basis for a postwar multilateral world economy. What came to be known as the "Bretton Woods system" had at its center two new organizations: the International Bank for Reconstruction and Development (IBRD) and the International Monetary Fund (IMF). The IBRD, or World Bank, was conceived very much as the junior partner, its founders expecting that it would primarily guarantee loans by private banks and investors, not make loans itself. Together with the ill-fated International Trade Organization, these two bodies were expected to provide the necessary institutional framework for the reconstruction of classical multilateralism.[1] As late as May 1947, U.S. policymakers expected the IBRD and the IMF to provide resources for what became the Marshall Plan.[2] In the middle of 1947, however, the United States abandoned hope of relying on these relatively limited international institutions. As one account puts it:

> American planners were confident that they had the key. Unfortunately, neither they nor the political leaders who approved their program for waging—and winning—the peace realized, until it was too late, that the

tasks of clearing away the debris of war and of reviving world trade over-reached the capacity of the instruments America had constructed for these purposes.[3]

The U.S. decision to abandon institutional multilateralism and to create the Economic Cooperation Administration left the fledgling international institutions with only a minor role during the years of the Marshall Plan. Having provided $497 million in reconstruction loans in 1947, the World Bank provided only $202 million between 1948 and 1952.[4] IMF lending likewise declined sharply, from $606 million in 1948 to $119.4 million in 1949, $52.8 million in 1950, and $28 million in 1951.[5] The shift to bilateral mechanisms of aid was decisive, and despite a resurgence of multilateral institutions in the 1970s, bilateral aid remains over twice multilateral aid.

Military Containment

John Lewis Gaddis, in his interpretation of U.S. foreign policy from the 1940s to the 1980s in terms of shifting strategies of containment, defines containment

> as a series of attempts to deal with the consequences of that World War II Faustian bargain: the idea has been to prevent the Soviet Union from using the power and position it won as a result of that conflict to shape the postwar international order, a prospect that has seemed, in the West, no less dangerous than what Germany or Japan might have done had they had the chance.[6]

Whether containment stemmed predominantly from "economic" or "political" motivations need not detain us here; anticommunism and commitment to a multilateral vision of a capitalist world economy were in any case two aspects of a common worldview. The issue here is containment's relevance for the aid regime. In its purest and most simplistic form, containment meant the geographical quarantine (disease metaphors were commonly used) of the Soviet Union and other communist countries. The logic of this approach emphasized military aid to countries bordering communist countries, although it immediately became apparent that maintaining substantial military forces would require in many countries "economic" assistance compensating for domestic resources transferred to military purposes.[7] If this aid, known as defense support, is classified with military aid, military aid constituted fully 95 percent of total U.S. aid in 1954 and was still slightly over half of all aid as late as 1960.[8] Border countries received 63 percent of U.S. military assistance and 54 percent of "official development assistance" between 1953 and 1961. But by the end of the period, the logic of geographical containment through military aid had broken down, as military aid had turned out to require extensive supporting economic aid and geographical containment had become ideological containment. By 1961, the balance between aid with broadly military purposes and aid with ostensibly developmental purposes was on the verge of shifting in favor of the latter, and U.S. aid programs existed in ninety-one countries.[9] As with institutional multilateralism, given U.S. goals, military containment proved to be an insufficient alternative to the development of an aid regime.

Acceptance of Nationalist Revolutions

U.S. foreign policy toward the Third World has been so defined by opposition to nationalist and socialist revolutions that it is difficult to conceive of an alternative, especially in the tense cold war context within which the aid regime evolved. Yet we must remember that even George Kennan, so identified with containment, sought to encourage fragmentation within the communist world and stated that, while he was unsure whether Titoism would spread in Europe, he was "almost certain that it is going to spread in Asia."[10] There were always voices in the United States and Europe urging accommodation, rather than opposition, to revolutionary forces in the Third World.[11]

Ideological anticommunism played a role in discrediting these views, but accommodation to nationalist revolutions would have necessitated considerable adjustment of the goals of multilateralism as well. Although not all these revolutions were socialist or communist, and few if any were orchestrated by the Soviet Union or China, most would have given rise to domestic social transformation and a fairly high degree of statism in economic affairs.

As we shall see in the case of the Marshall Plan, opposition to statism in its various economic forms also extended to developed capitalist societies. The Marshall Plan, as well as subsequent aid programs, was as much directed against "national capitalism" as against socialism or communism. The evolution of aid—on the scale of the Marshall Plan and in its particular institutional forms—reflected the unwillingness of U.S. policymakers to accept passively both national capitalist experiments in Europe and nationalist revolution in the Third World.

Trade Liberalization

Probably the most politically viable alternative to aid would have been substantial trade liberalization by the United States and the other industrialized countries.[12] Although the intensity of the effort has varied, the U.S. executive branch has consistently sought to liberalize international trade by reducing tariffs and other restrictions. The executive branch has time and again told Congress that failure to liberalize trade necessitates high levels of aid because trade restrictions prevent underdeveloped countries from earning the dollars they need to finance development and defense. When the World Bank established its soft-loan affiliate in the late 1950s, its president, Eugene Black, made clear his conviction that this move—a distasteful one to him—had been made necessary by the failure of the industrialized countries to lower tariffs.[13] He argued that reductions of trade restrictions would increase the foreign exchange earnings of underdeveloped countries, thereby allowing them to pay for their needed imports; strengthen their capacity to serve foreign debt,

thereby making commercial loans more available; and increase foreign investors' readiness to lend and invest in underdeveloped countries.[14] Proponents of trade liberalization have pointed out how relatively minor shifts in trade could have much more significant consequences than major increases in aid. The World Bank has estimated that the elimination of trade barriers to manufactured goods alone by the advanced capitalist countries would raise LDC export earnings by $35 billion, a sum larger than all the ODA the LDCs are currently receiving.[15] Although the underdeveloped countries themselves have had less faith in trade liberalization as a panacea, they nonetheless have concentrated their proposals for a new international economic order on changes in the structure of international trade and investment more than on increases in aid.

Trade liberalization to the extent envisioned by postwar U.S. policymakers and sought by the World Bank has been blocked by industrial interests benefiting from protectionism in the advanced capitalist countries and, especially in Japan, by state-defined industrial policies. In the United States, for all the congressional attempts to influence aid programs, the role of Congress in blocking trade liberalization has probably been most important in affecting the scale of U.S. aid.[16] Since the early 1960s, trade restrictions have been part of aid programs themselves in the form of aid "tying"—the requirement that aid funds be spent on products from the donor country. Despite a modest reduction of tying in recent years, the majority of bilateral aid from the advanced capitalist countries remains tied to donor exports.

Although positions in the aid versus trade debate have often been overstated—trade liberalization could never have replaced aid entirely, given the diversity of goals sought by donors through the use of aid—the decision to opt for relatively more aid rather than relatively more trade liberalization has nonetheless carried with it significant implications for Third World development options. Dollars earned through foreign trade carry no conditions apart from financing the domestic production structure necessary to produce them. Aid dollars are always conditional, even if the level and effectiveness of that conditionality vary greatly.

Market-Induced Adjustment

In 1982, the Harvard Center for European Studies organized a symposium of academics and Marshall Plan participants to commemorate the thirty-fifth anniversary of Secretary of State George C. Marshall's call for a European recovery program in his commencement address at Harvard University. In the course of the proceedings, Harold van B. Cleveland, a U.S. State Department official between 1946 and 1948 and then a deputy director of the European Program Division of the Economic Cooperation Administration, speculated on what would have happened in Europe in the absence of the Marshall Plan. Beginning with Great Britain, Cleveland postulated the fall of the Labour government in the absence of aid and its replacement by a hard-line Conservative one that would have done "what they might well have had to do in those circumstances"—radical devaluation backed up by a restrictive monetary policy and substantial budget cuts—"what we would call a genuine stabilization program—the sort of thing the IMF has forced many countries to do at various times." Such developments would have pushed France toward a similar stabilization program, including the "general dismantling of the internal controls." Germany would have followed a similar scenario, with currency reform playing a key role. In each case, Cleveland suggested, low standards of living, high unemployment, equilibrium exchange rates, and moves toward convertibility would have resulted in a recovery based on the private sector. Capital investment financed by the Marshall Plan could have been financed by "a somewhat quicker internal recovery" brought about by market-induced adjustment.[17]

Cleveland's scenario elicited a chorus of protest from conference participants, who insisted that the political consequences of such a policy would have produced, in Lord Eric Roll's words, "the most awful political calamities."[18] Europe's social and political framework, it was argued, would not have survived, and Europe would have been delivered to Stalin. The consensus was that "the political milieu of Western Europe in 1947 did not allow an IMF-type stabilization program."[19]

The debate links the Marshall Plan to the debt crisis three decades later. The difference is that, in the 1980s, it has been assumed that the "political milieu" of the debtor countries can withstand the effects of the kind of market-induced adjustment strategies deemed too severe for Europe in the 1940s. Further, it is assumed that the crisis calls for a "case-by-case" approach rather than systemic change.[20] In response to questions about the harshness of IMF conditions, IMF Managing Director Jacques de Larosière has tartly replied on numerous occasions that debtor countries "have no alternative but to adjust."[21] But the existence or absence of alternatives is a matter of the political will and the capabilities of both donors and recipients, of creditors and debtors.

1

The Marshall Plan and the Origins of the Aid Regime

The Marshall Plan has exercised a tenacious grip on the consciousness of U.S. policymakers. It has come to symbolize boldness and success, and virtually whenever new directions in U.S. foreign aid programs have been proposed, the theme of "a new Marshall Plan" has been pressed into service. Following on the heels of U.S. military victory in World War II, the success of the Marshall Plan contributed mightily to the belief, exemplified by Joseph Jones, that the limits of U.S. foreign policy were "on a distant and receding horizon."

Officially known as the European Recovery Program (ERP), the Marshall Plan dispensed over $13 billion between 1948 and 1952 to Western European countries constituted as the Organization for European Economic Cooperation (OEEC). Over 90 percent of this aid was in the form of grants. The program was administered by a relatively independent agency, the European Cooperation Administration (ECA). It was formally concluded ahead of schedule at the beginning of 1952, when it was merged into the worldwide Mutual Security Program (MSP).

The Marshall Plan has yet to receive the detailed historical analysis it deserves; historical scholarship to date has focused disproportionately on the question of its origins.[1] A full analysis is beyond the scope of this chapter, which is concerned primarily with the Marshall Plan insofar as it provided a paradigm of aid provision and insofar as it initiated large-scale economic assistance for the Third World. Most analyses of the Marshall Plan have focused on its unique success and on favorable circumstances in Europe that contributed to that success. The following quotations from works of two political scientists reflect the prevailing view:

> What is more, virtually all the goals [of the Marshall Plan] were achieved; and they were achieved *within* the projected four-year time span and at a cost of about $4 billion *below* the $17 billion appropriated by Congress. The Marshall Plan remains the most successful program in the history of foreign aid.[2]

> After World War II the European countries had the necessary social structure and economic and institutional infrastructures needed to sustain economic and social progress. *All that was missing was capital*; and this was provided in the Marshall Aid Plan, with the result that Western Europe was able to achieve considerable economic and social progress quite rapidly. [emphasis added][3]

These statements are misleading. As Gabriel and Joyce Kolko have shown, very few ECA economic goals had been achieved by the end of 1951; indeed, the Marshall Plan was in a deep crisis that was resolved only through rearmament and the expanded aid of the Mutual Security Agency, the ECA's successor.[4] But even more important, despite its name, the European Recovery Program was not simply about either Europe or recovery; it was much more ambitious than that. In reality, the Marshall Plan's uniqueness was that it addressed the breakdown of the prewar economic order with a vision—backed up by a wide range of programs around the world—of a reconstructed

set of economic relations binding Europe, North Amei
Third World. The boldness—and real success—of the M
lay in its contribution to the construction of a new i
order, not in the quantity of capital and raw materials
Western European industries.

The international order constructed during the Marshall Plan period had profound implications for the Third World. The Marshall
Plan linked both European reconstruction and the U.S. campaign for
multilateralism to a particular model of development in the underdeveloped world. Despite the intentions of its progenitors, who expected large-scale foreign aid to be a temporary departure from previous international norms about capital flows, it constructed an
edifice of goals and means that secured a permanent place for concessional external financing within the postwar world system. Thirty-
five years later one can still trace the basic elements of the aid regime
to the complex origins and history of the Marshall Plan.

Breakdown of the Old Economic Order

Five sets of changes in the world economy set the stage for the
Marshall Plan. Together these changes created the dollar shortage
that was the basis of the worldwide economic crisis in the postwar
period. First, there was the breakdown of trade between Eastern and
Western Europe. As the "first Third World," Eastern European countries had maintained a semicolonial relationship with Western Europe, exchanging food and raw materials for manufactured goods.[5]
In 1948, however, Western European exports to Eastern Europe
were less than half of the prewar level, and imports from Eastern Europe were only one-third.[6] Instead of recovering, this trade declined
over the next five years.[7] This decline meant that European countries
had to rely on dollar imports from the United States to fulfill needs
formerly met by trade with Eastern Europe.[8] A U.S. State Department memorandum in 1950 noted that "a substantial amount of the
contemplated hard-core assistance requirements is attributable in

part to the inability of various countries . . . to re-establish normal economic trading relations with areas under Soviet domination."[9] The Organization for European Economic Cooperation (OEEC) estimated that the decline of East-West trade raised the level of Western Europe's dollar imports by "several billion dollars."[10]

Second, there was the loss—or threatened loss—of important colonial sources of dollars. France's major colonial dollar earner, Vietnam, was in rebellion. So was the Netherlands' major dollar earner, Indonesia. Guerrilla insurgency was increasing in Britain's most profitable colony, Malaya, although the rebellion never cut off Malaya's dollar exports. In addition to the loss of colonial dollar earnings, the European powers bore the substantial costs of fighting the liberation movements. France had 110,000 troops in Indochina, and the Netherlands had 130,000 in Indonesia.[11] Great Britain had 1.4 million troops around the world.[12] Adding to this, South Africa took its gold sales out of the sterling area dollar pool, eliminating another important source of dollars for Great Britain.

Third, there was Europe's loss of earnings on foreign investments, particularly in Latin America, brought about by the liquidation of overseas investments to finance the war effort. Continued sale of these investments was a condition of lend-lease aid during the war. For both France and Britain, overseas investment earnings and other associated "invisible" payments had long helped offset trade deficits. Net earnings on foreign investment alone had paid for 20 percent of Western Europe's imports in 1938—$3 billion at postwar prices.[13] In addition, Britain had run up $13.7 billion in debts, known as sterling balances, to other sterling area countries, particularly India. These countries now clamored for the right to use the balances to finance their development plans—including buying dollar goods.

Fourth, many of the European countries and their overseas territories were hit with declining terms of trade. According to one ECA analysis of the sterling area's two most important dollar exports, gold and rubber: "Had the prices of these two commodities gone up as the others did, the same exports to the United States during the five years following the war would have earned an additional

$3.5 billion for the sterling area."[14] Total Marshall Plan aid to Great Britain came to $2.7 billion. Without such declining terms of trade, some countries would not have had a dollar deficit at all.

Finally, the European countries found themselves dependent on the U.S. economy in a way they never had been before. This left them susceptible to small fluctuations in the U.S. economy at the same time that no new mechanisms had yet evolved to provide the kind of international liquidity that sterling had once provided. U.S. imports from Western European countries came to only 0.33 percent of GNP.[15] Yet the UN calculated that a 4 percent fall in employment in the United States would cost the rest of the world $10 billion in dollar earnings.[16] British Chancellor Hugh Dalton complained in 1947: "The Americans have half the total income of the world, but won't either spend it in buying other people's goods or lending it or giving it away on a sufficient scale. The Fund and the Bank still do nothing. How soon will this dollar shortage bring a general crisis?"[17]

For Great Britain, which had become dependent on U.S. lend-lease aid to continue fighting the war, this dependency carried a further implication that has resonance with the concerns of Third World nations today. Britain's need for aid after the war was partly rooted in U.S. aid policies during the war. It was official U.S. government policy to administer lend-lease in such a way that the United Kingdom's gold and dollar balances would not fall below $600 million or rise above $1 billion. This situation was easily secured by altering what the British were expected to pay for in dollars and what would be included in lend-lease. The U.S. reasoning behind this policy was that reserves less than $600 million would force Britain to resort to the kind of economic controls the United States was dedicated to preventing, whereas reserves over $1 billion would leave Britain too independent of postwar U.S. influence.[18]

The challenge before Western European countries was to respond to their radically altered positions in the world economy. As Alan Milward puts it, "The international framework in which western European capitalism had operated could no longer sustain it and . . . what had been devised at Bretton Woods was no substitute."[19] Had international conditions been different, the physical effects of the war and of the winter of 1947 might have elicited different European responses, and the United States might not have felt the need to intervene with the most massive peacetime aid program in its history.

Origins of the Marshall Plan

These international consequences of World War II were only dimly perceived in the United States before the end of the war. Although the strategic brilliance of the Marshall Plan was that it responded to the breakdown of the old economic order in Europe, the original impetus and rationale for it came from the United States, not from Europe. The case for large-scale grant assistance was made long before the particular consequences of the war were known and also long before the beginnings of the cold war. It was made in terms of a theory of World War II's causes and of perceptions of the U.S. economy's structural needs.

From the onset of the war, U.S. policymakers linked the war to a need for a new international order afterwards. Under the leadership of Secretary of State Cordell Hull, the State Department developed a frankly economic interpretation of the causes of the war, focusing on the breakdown of the world economy under the dual pressures of the fractious legacy of World War I and the depression and on the ensuing economic warfare, which led to increasing controls on international trade and capital movements. This analysis became the basis of U.S. economic policy and was stated as early as 1940 by President Roosevelt. The emergence of a multilateral world economy—based on the unobstructed movement of capital and labor—became a major wartime goal.[20]

Americans believed that their prosperity was due to rearmament and war and feared a postwar depression. A 1941 survey of the American Economic Association found 80 percent of its members predicting a postwar depression.[21] A January 1945 public opinion survey found 68 percent viewing unemployment as the single most important postwar issue.[22] A major effort to deal with these concerns was mounted during the war. In addition to the departments of State, Commerce, and Treasury, special bureaus and committees, such as the Office of Foreign Relief and Rehabilitation, the Foreign Economic Administration, and the Senate Special Committee on Post-War Economic Policy and Planning, were established during this period. Private corporate policy organizations, including the National Planning Association, the Brookings Institution, the Committee for Economic Development, the Twentieth Century Fund, and the National Association of Manufacturers, concerned themselves with the issue as well. As Warren Hickman points out, a consensus on the nature of the problem emerged as early as 1943 and could be seen in three Commerce Department reports issued that year: "The United States in the World Economy," "Markets After the War," and "Foreign Trade After the War." "By 1943, the government had become convinced that the greatest obstacle to the success of a postwar multilateral system and increased American exports was the 'dollar shortage,' and this theory by then had penetrated to the level of the domestic politician."[23] During the rest of the war and the immediate postwar period, U.S. government officials reiterated the theme of finding a way to maintain a high level of U.S. exports as the key to avoiding a postwar depression. Assistant Secretary of State Dean Acheson's famous congressional testimony, where he posed the terror of property and income redistribution against the more comfortable alternative of exporting surplus production, rested on thinking that predated the war but had been greatly developed during it.[24]

Some observers dispute the importance of these concerns by pointing to the problem of the inflation that occurred immediately after the war, caused by pent-up consumer demand.[25] Proponents of the export-dependency argument always recognized, however, that the necessity of overseas markets would not impress itself immediately upon demobilization, but only after backed-up consumer demand had been satisfied. This position was explicitly put forth both by government officials and in corporate-sponsored studies.[26] Whether or not this position was correct, what mattered was that U.S. policy-makers believed it.

Given the recognition of a postwar dollar shortage combined with a commitment to maintaining a high level of exports, how were these exports to be financed? David Eakins has traced the gradual process by which government officials and corporate leaders came to recognize that the proposed institutional framework of the World Bank, International Monetary Fund, and Export-Import Bank would be inadequate and that "an outright gift, plainly labeled as such," might be necessary.[27] This latter idea emerged in a 1947 Twentieth Century Fund study that brought together the views of a variety of government, business, and labor spokesmen. The case for the Marshall Plan was first made in economic terms, before the emergence of the cold war fears that were to secure the plan's passage through Congress.

Domestic economic justifications of aid remained dominant in the business press as late as mid 1948. Shortly after Secretary of State Marshall's speech at Harvard, in which he outlined what was to become the Marshall Plan, *U.S. News* commented: "The real idea behind the program, thus, is that the United States, to prevent a depression at home, must put up the dollars that it will take to prevent a collapse abroad."[28] In February 1948, *U.S. News and World Report* carefully listed the advantages and disadvantages of domestic versus foreign "pump priming," concluding that the latter was superior:

> Some advantages over domestic pump priming are seen in the world program that is about to begin. Effects of spending will not be so visible inside the United States. American taxpayers will not have WPA leaf-raking projects before their eyes. They won't see courthouses being built, sidewalks laid or murals painted with federal money. The result is that there may be less criticism.
>
> The foreign aid program also may promise an easier way of keeping U.S. business active and of getting rid of surpluses. Most industrial orders will be for heavy goods—machinery, trucks, tractors, electrical equipment—a sector of industry that the New Deal never could revive until the war. Foreign outlets for surplus grains and fruit and cotton may prove more effective than relief stamp programs at home.[29]

Recognition of the importance of subsidizing exports to stave off a postwar depression was not limited to the United States, which made for an unpleasant constraint that American leaders had to face. As early as January 1945, when Soviet Foreign Minister Molotov requested U.S. credits, he did so in terms of helping the United States capitalist economy avoid a postwar depression, much to the irritation of Ambassador Harriman. In September 1947, the French Institute of Public Opinion reported a poll in which 47 percent saw the proposed Marshall Plan as a way of assuring markets for American exports and another 17 percent saw it as a way of meddling in European affairs.[30] Even more ominous were reports that European leaders were balking at reforms this country wanted, figuring that aid would be forthcoming anyway because it was necessary if the United States was to avoid a depression.[31]

It is against this background of Harriman's experience with Molotov and concern about European attitudes that the Harriman committee's explicit rejection of such motivation must be understood. Charged with examining American capacity to undertake the Marshall Plan, the committee reported that it "regards as nonsense the idea which prevails to a considerable degree in this country and abroad, that we need to export our goods and services as free gifts, to insure our own prosperity."[32] Particularly in light of their other aims, U.S. leaders sought to minimize perceptions of their dependency on aid, for such perceptions could seriously constrict the U.S. bargaining position. Marshall's insistence that the European nations come to the United States with a request, rather than vice versa, was another attempt to shift the burden of dependency.

Important as U.S. concern over exports was, it does not explain the particular form the Marshall Plan took or its timing. A common assumption is that the Marshall Plan was aimed at the European Left. The simple announcement of forthcoming aid was enough to embolden the conservatives in the coalition governments of France and Italy to force the Communist party ministers out. The timing of the congressional passage of the authorization act was closely linked to the Italian elections, in which Marshall Plan propaganda was one part of a wide-ranging U.S. effort to prevent the Italian Communist party from winning.[33] Yet while State Department spokesmen and ECA figures like Hoffman later credited the Marshall Plan with preventing the victory of the Left in Europe—an assessment many historians have accepted—there is reason to believe that the European Left had already been defeated as a result of its own internal weaknesses, the great-power conservatism of Soviet foreign policy, and the policies of American and British occupation forces.[34] More recent historical scholarship has clarified that the major target of the Marshall Plan was not socialism but capitalism—or rather the national brand of capitalism that U.S. leaders saw emerging in Europe. As the Kolkos have put it, it was not the *continuity* of European capitalism that was at issue, but its *form*.[35] The Marshall Plan was necessary to resuscitate "America's flagging campaign for multilateralism."[36]

Fred Block has argued that "national capitalism," based on extensive state intervention and planning to ensure full employment, was the dominant trend in Western Europe at the end of the war:

> Although little was actually done before World War II to implement national capitalism, there is good reason to believe that after the war, there might have been substantial experiments with national capitalism among the developed capitalist countries. In fact, in the immediate postwar years, most of the countries of Western Europe resorted to the whole range of control devices associated with national capitalism—exchange controls, capital controls, bilateral and state trading arrangements. The reason these controls were not elaborated into full-scale experiments with national capitalism was that it became a central aim of United States foreign policy to prevent the emergence of national capitalist experiments and to gain widespread cooperation in the restoration of an open world economy.[37]

In the struggle to mobilize the U.S. public in support of massive aid programs, U.S. leaders again and again stressed the danger European economic policies represented. In his speech at Baylor University in March 1947, President Truman publicly sounded the tocsin about the danger of European reconstruction policies, attacking government intervention in trade, even if the actual activities (and profits) were left in private hands. He urged that "the whole world should adopt the American system" and, pointing to the dangers of autarkic capitalism, warned: "Unless we act, and act decisively, it will be the pattern for the next century."[38] Marshall warned in January 1948: "There is no doubt that if the countries of Europe should be forced to meet their present problems without further assistance from this country, the result could only be a radical increase in the restrictions and controls in force throughout that area affecting international trade and investment." He added that "it is idle to think that a Europe left to its own efforts in these serious problems of recovery would remain open to American business in the same way that we have known it in the past."[39] The Harriman committee even predicted that the United States would almost inevitably have to follow suit if Europe turned toward trade by government monopoly.[40] ECA documents, although circumspect, are equally clear on this issue. For example, a country study of France states:

> Furthermore, there appears to be a tendency of national economic planning in Europe today to move toward a reduced dependence on foreign trade generally, to move away from the objective of a more internationally specialized structure of national production and toward what is euphemistically called a "balanced" (i.e., more self-sufficient) economy.
>
> This trend, particularly in Europe, appears not to be a passing phase associated with the difficulties of a reconstruction period, but a fundamental trend, with roots extending back for more than a generation. To reverse it will require an equally fundamental solution. This is one of the great challenges which the European Recovery Program has presented to the participating countries and to the OEEC.[41]

The commitment to fighting this "fundamental trend" took many forms. It shaped many wartime policies. It guided occupation authorities. It led to the long and often bitter bargaining with the British over the British loan in 1945. It was at the basis of U.S. leaders' vision of the new international institutions they sought: the United Nations, the World Bank, the International Monetary Fund, the International Trade Organization. And it accounts for the unique focus of the Marshall Plan on building and consolidating a new international economic order. Through the Marshall Plan, the United States sought an antidote to national capitalism through new sets of international arrangements. These were to have profound implications for the underdeveloped world.

The Third World to the Rescue

From the very beginning, the struggle against national capitalism in Europe led U.S. policymakers to look to Africa and Asia to close the dollar gap. U.S. imports from Europe constituted only 0.33 percent of U.S. gross national product. Politically untouchable tariff walls made increasing most European imports impossible. U.S. investors, despite the existence of convertibility guarantees, expressed little interest in investing in Western Europe—an alternative source of dollars that Congress and the ECA had originally counted on.[42] Total U.S. direct investment in OEEC countries between 1947 and 1951 came to $279 million—only 8 percent of total U.S. foreign investment during this period.[43] U.S. policymakers looked instead to the overseas territories of European countries to bail out their colonial masters. As John Orchard, a special representative and consultant for the ECA concluded: "Indeed, the overseas territories hold more promise of contributions to the closing of the dollar gap than the countries of metropolitan Europe."[44]

The overseas territories were expected to contribute to the success of the Marshall Plan in two major ways. First, they would provide the market for European goods that had formerly existed in Eastern Europe and that the United States was not able to provide. As William Mallalieu writes:

> The United States had anticipated that the restoration of Europe would help to bring about economic viability in the rest of the world. It was soon evident, however, that the converse was equally important. The complete success of European plans required progress in the less developed areas of the world. Only increased purchasing power in the underdeveloped countries of Asia, Africa, and Latin America could provide adequate markets for European industry.[45]

Second, the overseas territories were expected to be dollar earners through their raw materials exports to the United States. U.S. demand for these raw materials was expected to draw U.S. private investment in these territories, constituting, in the words of ECA Special Representative Averell Harriman, "one of the most promising ways to assist in reaching a balance of payments."[46]

These two roles of the overseas territories were linked in a triangular trade model, in which dollars would flow into European hands indirectly through their colonies. As one economist put it: "Such a pattern of trade, to be self-sustaining, would mean a surplus of (European) exports to the nondollar world, a surplus of exports by the latter to this country, and a European surplus of imports from us, to be financed in this manner."[47] As we shall see, this description does not accurately portray the way the colonial powers actually acquired the dollars their colonies earned. But the basic idea of the triangular trade was reiterated again and again throughout the Marshall Plan.[48] The model was politically attractive because it allowed for the continuation or even the increase of European trade deficits with the United States, as long as the overseas territories ran up trade surpluses with the United States. Thus, toward the end of the Marshall Plan, when the trade deficit of participating European countries doubled during the first quarter of 1951, the ECA was able to note happily:

> The rise in Western Europe's trade deficit did not result in a drain on its hard currency reserves. On the contrary, the large United States payments deficits with the overseas territories and with the sterling area (other than the United Kingdom) resulted in additional increases in gold and dollar holdings.[49]

A State Department document submitted to the Committee on Foreign Affairs in December 1947 estimated that the overseas territories would run a trade surplus with the United States of about $2.2 billion between 1948 and 1952. As a percentage of estimated trade deficits of the metropoles, these surpluses of the overseas territories came to 51.5 percent for the U.K., 57.7 percent for the Netherlands, 39.5 percent for Portugal, and 7.5 percent for Belgium.

French overseas territories would increase the metropolitan deficit by 6.9 percent.[50] ECA's *Sixth Report to Congress* estimated that by 1952–53, the overseas territories would account for $645 million annually in dollar-earning or dollar-saving exports (and $1.5 billion if Indonesia, then in the midst of revolutionary war, were included).[51] Even the French territories, the ECA hoped, would make an "important" contribution by the end of the Marshall Plan.[52] The OEEC projected a net dollar contribution of the French overseas territories of $167 million by 1952–53, plus dollar-saving exports.[53]

The raw material exports of the overseas territories were seen as critical to both the success of the Marshall Plan in Europe and to U.S. prosperity. An important selling point of the plan in the United States was that it would provide access to raw materials and primary products in the underdeveloped world. This goal was to be achieved in three main ways. First, various mechanisms for U.S. stockpiling of raw materials were built into the operating structure of the ERP. For example, the United States could use up to 5 percent of the counterpart funds its aid generated to purchase "strategic" materials. Second, the aid treaties that were negotiated with each metropolitan country guaranteed potential U.S. investors access "to the development of raw materials within participating countries on terms of treatment equivalent to those afforded to the nationals of the participating country concerned."[54] Third, a special fund was established for investments in increased production of strategic materials.

ECA documents emphasized from the start the importance of overseas territory sources for strategic materials, as well as the agency's dissatisfaction with the relatively slow beginning of the purchasing program. A 1949 report on recovery progress, in reviewing sources of thirty-nine strategic materials, located thirty-two of them in the overseas territories of ERP countries.[55] Attention to this issue increased dramatically after the outbreak of the Korean War, when the shift to rearmament led to sudden shortages of raw materials on the world market and to sharply rising prices. These rising prices both worsened European trade balances—U.K. import prices in June 1951 were 43 percent higher than the previous year, but its export prices increased only 19 percent—and threatened to wipe out the trade advantages the United States had reaped from the devaluations of 1949.[56]

In 1951 congressional hearings on the foreign aid program, Nelson Rockefeller testified that 73 percent of U.S. strategic materials imports came from the underdeveloped areas.[57] Focusing specifically on the dependent overseas territories, an MSA document the following year reported that these territories accounted for 97 percent of U.S. columbium ore imports, 82 percent of bauxite imports, 81 percent of palm oil imports, 68 percent of cobalt imports, 52 percent of industrial diamond imports, 51 percent of imported tin, 48 percent of rubber, and 23 percent of manganese ore.[58] In an article titled "Widening Boundaries of National Interest," Rockefeller concluded: "Clearly, the success of the industrial mobilization plans of the North Atlantic Treaty countries is contingent upon the continued and increasing supply from underdeveloped areas of such strategic materials as bauxite, chrome, copper, lead, manganese, tin, uranium, and zinc," and he called for a 50 percent increase in raw materials exports from the underdeveloped areas.[59] The Rockefeller report, commissioned by Truman from the International Development Advisory Board, called for a $2 billion investment in overseas raw materials production in the next few years.[60]

Coincidentally, the three colonies with the greatest raw materials exports—Malaya, Netherlands East Indies, and Indochina—were all areas where significant anticolonial insurgency had taken place right after the war. The military efforts of Britain, the Netherlands, and France to repress these movements provided an additional link between the overseas territories and the European Recovery Plan. Resolution of colonial wars came to be seen as necessary for fulfilling U.S. political and military aims in Europe. Secretary of State Marshall reported in 1949: "When we reached the problem of increasing the security of Europe, I found all the French troops of any quality were all out in Indochina, and I found the Dutch troops of any quality were out in Indonesia, and the one place they were not was in Western Europe."[61] The Kolkos comment: "In this sense, the key to military security in Europe ultimately became to some critical degree the triumph over the Left in Asia."[62] With the shift to rearmament, this link between European security and the suppression of revolution in Asia was increasingly emphasized. As the U.S. secretary of defense testified in the foreign aid hearings in 1951: "The sooner Indochina can be stabilized, the sooner those French divisions, which are the backbone of European land defense, can be brought to full effectiveness by the return of sorely needed professional officers, noncommissioned officers, and technicians."[63]

The Limits of Largesse

Richard Freeland has shown how the tactics used by the Truman administration to secure congressional passage of the Truman Doctrine's aid package for Greece and Turkey and of the Marshall Plan were major factors in creating the anticommunist consensus that has defined and bedeviled U.S. politics for over thirty years.[64] In the pursuit of short-run considerations, liberal Democrats unleashed a political dynamic that made them vulnerable to attacks from the Right. In the same way, linking Europe's fate to its dependencies, particularly those in Asia, had double-edged potentialities. Right from the beginning, "Asia firsters" in Congress tried to turn the triangular trade argument against the Truman administration's European orientation. In the hearings in 1947 on the interim emergency aid bill, Congressman Walter Judd repeatedly sought to show how the argument implied a need for greater military intervention in Asia, particularly in the civil war in China. Arguing that "we have got to win in Asia, too, or we will ultimately lose in Europe," Judd raised the issue of the triangular trade directly: "It would make it difficult, if not impossible, for certain European countries, especially England, France, and Holland, to restore the prewar pattern of trade with Asia, thereby endangering the success of the Marshall Plan in Europe."[65] Although this line of criticism continued to reappear and was eventually picked up and amplified by Senator Joseph McCarthy, the differences between "Asia firsters" and "Europe firsters" were relatively minor. As we shall see, administration leaders were prepared to use the Marshall Plan to combat revolution in Asia wherever they saw a potential for success. But after repeated missions to China and agonizing reevaluations, the Truman administration concluded that further major efforts in China would be wasted. As Secretary of State Dean Acheson's covering letter to the State Department White Paper on the Chinese Revolution in 1949 stated: "It was the product of internal Chinese forces, forces which this country tried to influence but could not."[66]

The linking of European recovery to progress in the underdeveloped world carried another set of potential political liabilities as well: that the leaders of independent Third World nations, particularly in Latin America, would expect the same kind of largesse extended to the much wealthier countries of Europe. In fact, speculation emerged almost immediately that "Marshall Plans" for the poorer parts of the world would soon follow.

It is striking how quickly and how explicitly American leaders moved to dash these hopes. As early as December 2, 1947, Under-Secretary of State Will Clayton wrote a memorandum urging the American representatives at the upcoming Bogotá Conference to point out to the Latin Americans that "the Marshall Plan is wholly inapplicable to the Latin American situation and that we cannot consider extending it to that area." Needy governments were to be directed to the World Bank or the Export-Import Bank.[67] U.S. diplomats lectured the Latin Americans on how their interests would be served by the Marshall Plan's emphasis on Europe, although internal State Department correspondence suggests some doubt about this.[68] When Truman's Point Four speech again raised hopes about large-scale U.S. aid, Acheson, Assistant Secretary Thorp, and other State Department officials quickly moved to dampen them.[69] The U.S. cochairman of a joint U.S.-Brazilian technical commission reported:

> Some people seemed to have the misconception that the United States would soon be forced by the world situation to adopt a "Marshall Plan" for South America. . . . If, at first, these attitudes influenced any of the

Brazilian members of the Central Commission or Subcommissions with whom we came in regular contact, they were soon dispelled.[70]

Ambassador-at-Large Phillip Jessup was dispatched to Asia in early 1950 to dispel comparable illusions there.[71] Congressmen traveling in the Near and Far East engaged in similar efforts.[72]

This explicit advertising of American misanthropy had an explicit purpose: to render reliance on foreign investment the only possible development strategy for the underdeveloped nations. Acheson made very clear the refusal of the American government to step in where private enterprise was ready to do the job, asserting that it would be American policy "not to extend loans of public funds for projects for which private capital is available."[73] Acheson's statement reflected considerable concern in the business community over competition from government aid programs. For example, a *Fortune* editorial, after criticizing a United Nations soft-loan proposal, went on to observe:

> Word has been spreading throughout the underdeveloped world that private capital, while still as international by nature as in John Bright's day, responds best to kindness and cannot be coerced. This happy trend faces one danger: the U.S. could stop it in its tracks by dangling the rosy alternative of "little Marshall plans" or loans to backward governments.[74]

Despite business fears, those areas capable of attracting private investment were rigorously excluded from substantial foreign aid during this period. Latin America's ability to attract a disproportionate share of U.S. private investment was the root cause of its inability to pry aid out of the U.S. government. The data in Table 1 show that Latin America accounted for 55.2 percent of total net U.S. direct investment in 1946 and 1947 and 50.6 percent between 1948 and 1951. Its share of U.S. economic aid between 1948 and 1952 was about 0.8 percent.

The Marshall Plan had been in operation less than one year when Truman included his celebrated "Point Four" in his inaugural speech, proposing an ambitious program of technical assistance to promote development in the underdeveloped world. Louis Halle's personal account makes it clear that "Point Four" was basically a public rela-

TABLE 1   Net U.S. Direct Investment Abroad, by Area,
1946–51 ($ millions)

	1946	1947	1948	1949	1950	1951
All areas	183	724	684	786	702	603
OEEC countries	18	48	48	31	75	77
OEEC dependencies	6	53	69	28	9	5
Canada	38	13	77	119	265	271
Latin America	59	442	321	429	191	187
Middle East	21	91	123	113	117	−15
Other	41	77	46	66	45	78

SOURCE: *Balance of Payments of the United States, 1949–51*, supplement to the *Survey of Current Business* (Washington, D.C.: U.S. Department of Commerce, 1952).

tions gimmick, added to Truman's speech at the last minute to provide something new in an essentially routine presentation.[75] The program did not get under way until twenty-one months later. To some extent, it departed from Acheson's early policy of almost total aid neglect for Latin America in that the great majority of its projects were in Latin American countries.[76] But overall, Point Four reiterated the message contained in the American repudiation of new "Marshall Plans." Because a major purpose of the technical assistance it offered was to pave the way for private capital, it provided an official platform for American spokesmen to emphasize the crucial function of private investment. (In fact, Congress added "the improvement of investment climates" as a second basic objective of the program.) The program's paltry disbursements reminded the Latin American nations that U.S. aid was not going to solve their problems. In its first year, only $26.9 million was spent worldwide, and even by 1953, only $156 million.[77]

The Third World Contribution to Multilateralism

The Marshall Plan embodied a theory of how the underdeveloped areas could contribute to European recovery and to the development of a multilateral world economy. The underdeveloped areas did play an important role in the Marshall Plan, but expectations about their contribution to multilateralism and European recovery were only partially realized.

Success in Europe was predicated, in the eyes of the ECA, on the restoration of the triangular trade pattern. Hence, Marshall Plan aid was extended to projects in the European overseas territories in Africa and Asia. An ECA country study of the Netherlands, noting that the economic recovery of Indonesia would "represent a major contribution to a viable Europe," suggested that a "program of economic aid to Indonesia whenever it could be appropriately extended might therefore make a direct contribution to Europe at least as large, dollar for dollar, as any other proposed use of ECA funds."[78] The logic of this position led the Marshall Plan into deep involvement in large parts of the Third World.

There were potential dangers from the U.S. point of view in legitimating the European countries' reliance on their colonies. This policy, as well as that of promoting economic integration in Western Europe, increased the risks both of discrimination against the dollar and of regional blocs. It is in this context that the insistent pressure for devaluation of European currencies brought to bear by the United States in 1948–49 must be understood. As ECA Administrator Paul Hoffman wrote the acting U.S. special representative to the OEEC in Paris, removal of intra-European trade barriers without devaluation of European currencies would likely lead to further insulation from the United States: "The U.S. could not agree to the removal of intra-European trade and payments barriers if participating countries felt that such removals made it necessary or desirable for them to increase existing barriers between dollar and nondollar areas."[79] And as an ECA report to the Congress stated, the purpose of devaluation in 1949 was not, in the traditional manner, to raise European exports— increased exports would constitute too much of a strain on the already overburdened British economy in particular—but rather "to divert exports to the hard currency areas" and to facilitate the re-emergence of multilateral trading channels.[80]

For the first two years of the Marshall Plan, the U.S. trade surplus continued with all parts of the world, including the overseas territories. Despite the wartime devastation of some of the principal colonial exporting areas, exports from the overseas territories to the United States were substantial in comparison with exports from the metropolitan areas, as shown in Table 2. The colonies of the United Kingdom, Netherlands, and Portugal exported more to the United States than did their metropoles. Table 3 shows that by 1950, all the colonial empires except France's had a trade surplus with the United States and that only the French colonial deficits made the overall balances negative in 1947 and 1949.

As Table 4 shows, in 1950, the United States ran its first postwar deficits with Africa, Asia and Oceania, and Latin America. In the third quarter of the year, the United States even had a brief overall trade deficit, although a surplus reappeared in the final quarter. The emergence of these deficits reflected three major factors: a U.S. business recovery, which raised imports; the devaluations of European currencies, which redirected exports to the United States and lowered imports from this country; and the outbreak of the Korean War, which expanded the demand for raw materials and drove up primary product prices. The ECA welcomed these developments:

> This change in the pattern of United States trade is a development of great importance to the participating countries. It makes possible the successful realization of that part of their program which required greater dollar earnings from exports to their countries to finance the deficit incurred in trade with the United States. For a considerable time, it appeared that this objective would not be obtained. In the first half of the year, however, the United States began to develop a trade deficit with every principal trading area except Canada and [Western Europe, the Philippines, and Japan].[81]

The OEEC likewise commented: "For the first time since the war, there existed clear opportunities for Western Europe to earn dollars multilaterally to a significant extent by earning surpluses on countries gaining dollars from the United States."[82] The ECA saw proof that the triangular trade system was working in the fact that the doubling of the Western European trade deficit in early 1951 was more than offset by U.S. deficits with the overseas territories and the independent sterling area. It estimated the U.S. trade deficit with

TABLE 2 Exports of Overseas Territories to the United States as Percentage of All OEEC Exports and Metropolitan Country Exports to the United States, 1947–50

Year	All OEEC	Belgium	France	Netherlands	Portugal	United Kingdom
1947	80.3%	55.1%	51.3%	318.1%	72.2%	194.7%
1948	65.6	31.4	39.3	311.1	64.5	149.0
1949	67.7	38.0	33.3	210.2	127.3	163.2
1950	64.5	32.8	28.2	202.9	105.9	159.9

SOURCE: Calculated from data in Economic Cooperation Administration, Division of Statistics and Reports, *Recovery Guides: A Record of Progress in the ERP Countries #22* (Washington, D.C., October 1951), pp. 112–115.

TABLE 3 Balance of Trade of Overseas Territories with the United States, by Metropolitan Country, 1947–50

Year	Belgium	France	Netherlands	Portugal	United Kingdom	Total
1947	−18.0	−163.2	+9.6	−18.0	+58.8	−130.8
1948	−16.8	−104.4	+45.6	−18.0	+114.0	+20.4
1949	−8.4	−121.2	+32.4	−12.0	+72.0	−37.1
1950	+4.8	−54.0	+93.6	+0.2	+334.8	+379.4

SOURCE: Economic Cooperation Administration, Division of Statistics and Reports, *Recovery Guides: A Record of Progress in the ERP Countries #22* (Washington, D.C., October 1951), pp. 112–115.

TABLE 4   United States Balance of Trade with Africa, Asia and Oceania, and Latin America, 1947–52 ($ millions)

	Africa			Asia and Oceania			Latin America		
	Exports	Imports	Balance	Exports	Imports	Balance	Exports	Imports	Balance
1947	822.0	327.6	458.4	2649.6	1210.8	1438.8	4068.0	2269.2	1798.8
1948	784.8	393.6	391.2	2282.4	1509.6	772.8	3362.4	2505.6	856.8
1949	621.6	337.2	284.4	2450.4	1364.4	1086.0	2902.8	2442.0	460.8
1950	362.4	493.2	−130.8	1689.6	1908.0	−218.4	2812.8	3102.0	−289.2
1951	580.8	589.2	−8.4	2485.2	2509.2	−24.0	3771.6	3547.2	−224.4
1952	568.8	607.2	−38.4	2338.8	2056.8	282.0	3534.0	3634.8	−100.8

SOURCE: Calculated from data in *Business Statistics*, 1955 biennial edition, supplement to the *Survey of Current Business* (Washington, D.C.: U.S. Department of Commerce, 1955), pp. 104, 108.

Latin America, the overseas territories, and the rest of the sterling area to be $465 million in the first quarter of 1951.[83]

Despite the optimism of the ECA and OEEC in 1950 and early 1951, there was considerable shrinkage in the U.S. deficits with the underdeveloped areas in 1951 and 1952, with a surplus with Latin America reemerging in 1951 and with Asia and Oceania in 1952. In addition, OEEC countries continued to run a deficit with the "dollar countries" of Latin America and the Philippines, amounting to $250 million in 1951.[84] The failure of the triangular trade to reach projected proportions was one reason for the continuing dollar imbalance that existed at the end of the Marshall Plan.

The aggregate figures hide the contribution of specific overseas territories for particular European countries, a contribution that in some cases was substantial and critical. For the French, the anti-colonial rebellion in Indochina and the reliance of some colonies on imported food destroyed any hopes to be gaining foreign exchange benefits from the colonies by 1952. The franc area, excluding France, ran a deficit with the dollar area of $108 million in 1950 and $127 million in 1951.[85] Indonesia gained its formal independence from the Netherlands in 1949, although the Netherlands continued to benefit from its other colonial possessions. Portugal and Belgium registered some gains, but the United Kingdom received by far the greatest dollar benefits from its colonies. Between 1950 and 1952, the dollar surpluses of British colonies amounted to over $1.1 billion, which more than equaled the trade deficit of the U.K. itself with the United States for the Marshall Plan period.[86]

The Appropriation of Colonial Dollars

The role that the ECA envisioned for the underdeveloped areas—particularly the overseas territories—reinforced and provided new sanctions for the type of export-oriented development that had always been the basis of European colonial policy. The difference was that the overseas territories were to be opened more to U.S. investment and their exports directed more to the United States and other "hard currency" areas. The Overseas Territories Committee of the OEEC, citing the dependence of the colonies on Europe, asserted in 1948:

> It is, therefore, as much in the interests of the peoples of the Overseas Territories as those of the people of Europe that the economies of the participating European countries should, within the shortest possible time, be reconstructed and set once again upon secure foundations. Thus, it is reasonable to expect that, in return for the benefits which they will derive from the European Reconstruction Programme, the Overseas Territories should contribute to the extent that their economic and social structure permits, to the success of that programme.[87]

Concluding that the interests of Europe and its colonies were "complementary and not conflicting," the committee recommended that "the Overseas Territories should give priority in framing their development programmes to those projects that are likely to yield a maximum return in terms of productivity and of hard currency earnings and savings during the period of special difficulty in Europe."[88] The committee looked forward to substantial increases in dollar-earning raw material exports, with rubber increasing by 238 percent, coal by 919 percent, bauxite by 195 percent, and so forth.[89]

Between 1948 and 1952, the European countries did succeed in substituting colonial for dollar sources of supply. This substitution lowered their trade deficits with the United States but posed a problem for the triangular trade model that guided ECA thinking. The ECA had assumed that the metropoles would acquire the dollars earned by their overseas territories and other underdeveloped countries through trade surpluses: "The West European countries will have to develop a trade surplus with such regions so that their accounts can be balanced through triangular trade relationships."[90] In fact, however, reliance on colonial sources of supply to substitute for U.S. imports meant that the metropoles generally ran a deficit with their colonies. The United Kingdom, for example, exported $3.6 million worth of goods to its overseas territories between 1948 and 1952 but imported $3.7 billion,[91] requiring colonial dollars to be appropriated by means other than trade. For Britain, two mechanisms were primary: dollar pooling and marketing boards.

Dollar pooling—the placing of all dollar earnings in a central ac-, count in London—was a traditional characteristic of the sterling area. Dollar pooling meant that gold and dollar resources of sterling area countries and territories "ultimately flowed to the United Kingdom and thus became available to cover its deficit with the United States."[92] During the war, the U.K. had been able to block withdrawals from the dollar pool with formal restrictions and to use the dollar pool to finance its war effort. Setting a timetable for releasing the blocked balances remained a difficult policy issue for a number of years. After the war, however, it was politically difficult for the U.K. to prevent the independent sterling areas from using their current dollar balances. Ireland, Australia, New Zealand, India, Pakistan, Burma, and Iraq all became substantial net dollar users, although their net withdrawals were offset by net contributions of South Africa and Ceylon, resulting in a small surplus of $46 million between 1948 and 1952. The overseas territories, in contrast, made a net contribution of about $1.8 billion to the dollar pool during this period. Malaya was by far the major dollar earner, accounting for almost $1.2 billion, and West Africa emerged as a major dollar-earning area after the war as well, accounting for almost $500 million.[93]

Marketing boards also ensured that the colonies did not spend too many of their dollars on imports. By paying peasant producers local currency at prices far below the world market level, marketing boards played a major role in seeing that these dollars ended up in London. Colonial marketing boards with monopolies on the purchasing and exporting of various crops were expanded rapidly after World War II, particularly in Africa, where the proportion of total exports controlled by marketing boards varied from 66 percent to 100 percent. For the five crop years between 1947 and 1952, for example, the average price paid to the Gold Coast's cocoa producers was only 56 percent of the export price. The difference was largely invested in long-term, low-yielding British securities in London.[94]

West African marketing board reserves in London totaled £150 million in September 1950, and according to Mallalieu: "In 1951–52 the colonial marketing boards, by depositing in London the dollars obtained by sale of rubber, tin, and cocoa, probably prevented the collapse of sterling exchange."[95] Susan Strange argues that marketing board deposits were crucial in allowing Britain to pay off its blocked sterling balances to independent sterling area members: "Certainly, Britain would have been quite unable to repay the war debts to India if British Africa had achieved its independence ten years earlier than it actually did."[96]

Other European colonial powers used these and similar mechanisms to appropriate colonial dollar earnings. For France and Portugal, which maintained the fiction of unified empire, the mode of appropriation (for example, through taxation) was sometimes more direct. Overall, the 1947 U.S. State Department prediction of a $2.2 billion gain from the colonies proved impressively accurate.

Marshall Plan Aid in the Third World

Measuring the significance of the Marshall Plan for the overseas territories is not an easy task. Not all aid directed toward the overseas territories was labeled as such. For example, the ECA repeatedly stated that circumstances in Indochina made Marshall Plan aid there impossible. However, a classified State Department policy statement in September 1948 revealed: "With respect to the important question of whether ECA assistance should be extended to the area, we have informed the French that because reconstruction and development of Indochina is impossible under the present conditions of warfare that pertain there, no direct ECA financing for Indochina will be forthcoming at present *although French requirements will be readjusted accordingly*." (emphasis added)[97] Given the fungible nature of aid, it can be argued that all colonial expenditures were indirectly financed by the Marshall Plan. This position has been suggested by one World Bank economist in the case of Africa:

> In general economic terms, one could just as well argue that the aid given to African countries by Britain and France during this period was a mar-

ginal use of resources, and that if the Marshall Plan had not been received in the first place, there would have been no aid to Africa. On this basis, one could label all the French, British and Portuguese aid to Africa during this period as indirect American aid.[98]

The ECA noted at the time that "the availability of ECA funds for their own dollar import needs helped (European) countries to provide from their reserves the dollars needed by their overseas territories."[99]

With these considerations in mind, we may examine Table 5, recognizing that it greatly underrepresents the purely economic significance of the Marshall Plan for the overseas territories. Aid was avail-

TABLE 5   Marshall Plan Aid to Overseas Territories as of June 30, 1951

Type of Aid	Amount ($ millions)
Dollar aid to metropoles for overseas territories	
France	286.8
Netherlands	101.5[a]
United Kingdom	98.0[b]
Belgium	15.0[b]
Portugal	0.7
Overseas development fund	63.8
Strategic materials development	
Dollars	24.5
Counterpart	22.5
Counterpart from European aid	140.3
Technical assistance for overseas territories	0.9
Total	754.0

SOURCE: Economic Cooperation Administration, *Eighth Report to Congress* (March 31, 1950), p. 54, and *Thirteenth Report to Congress* (June 30, 1951), pp. 46–49.

[a]Aid for Indonesia only.

[b]Quarter of March 30–June 30, 1951, only. With the exception of Portugal, no country appears to have received any significant quantity of this type of aid prior to this quarter.

able in several forms. Particularly in the cases of France and the Netherlands (until Indonesia gained its independence), substantial dollar aid to the metropoles was officially earmarked for their colonies. For France and the Netherlands, this came to $388.3 million; unfortunately, the ECA provided no comparable cumulative figures for the other European metropoles. Counterpart generated by dollar aid for the metropole could be released specifically for colonial expenditures; this came to $140.3 million, almost all in the form of French francs. The ECA Special Reserve Fund, later renamed the Overseas Development Fund, made $63.8 million of investments, mostly in Africa. These included $32.1 million in French Africa, $17.3 million in the Belgian Congo, $11.5 million in British Africa, and $663,000 in Portuguese Africa.[100] Another $47 million was invested directly in the production of strategic materials. If we assume that the dollar forms of aid generated counterpart that was spent in the overseas territories, the overall total would surpass $1 billion.

The Marshall Plan's relationship to colonialism in Asia, where the postwar reimposition of colonial authority was resisted by significant popular movements, was more varied and complex than it was in Africa. Within their staunchly anticommunist and counterrevolutionary framework, U.S. policymakers were flexible in their responses, depending on their assessment of the nature of the popular forces and the options open to the colonial powers. One extreme is represented by British Malaya, where British counterinsurgency efforts seem to have enjoyed full U.S. support. In 1950, the ECA announced a road-building project, partly for purposes of "internal security," costing $410,000.[101] In early 1952, the MSA shipped close to $500,000 worth of earth-moving equipment to support the British effort to deny the rebels their rural bases of support.[102] Subsequently, a National Planning Association report concluded: "The United Kingdom effort to suppress guerrilla warfare in Malaya would seem to have been indirectly financed out of aid that ostensibly was going to Europe."[103]

Indochina represents an intermediate case. State Department documents in 1948–49 reflect considerable U.S. frustration with

French intransigence toward nationalists of all political stripes. However, recognizing the popularity of Ho Chi Minh and his forces, U.S. policymakers were forced to admit that they could offer no alternative course of action.[104] During this period, they sought to maintain some pressure on the French by refusing to fund projects directly for Indochina, but at the same time, they took account of the dollar cost of France's war in calculating French aid requirements. The Griffin Mission, sent to Indochina and elsewhere in Southeast Asia in early 1950 to expand the U.S. aid presence, noted:

> In the last analysis, of course, the French financial contribution to the area has been made possible by ECA aid to France, and the balance-of-payments deficit of the area has been taken into account in calculating France's need for ECA aid. The United States is therefore already indirectly aiding Indochina.[105]

The Griffin Mission proceeded to endorse France's "Bao Dai solution" but to insist that future ECA aid be negotiated directly with the Bao Dai government, so as to increase his legitimacy in the eyes of Vietnamese nationalists. Within a year, thirty-one ECA personnel were in Indochina, and $21.8 million of U.S. economic aid had been allocated.[106]

Indonesia represents the other extreme, where the United States was prepared to use Marshall Plan aid to pressure the Netherlands to relinquish control. After originally giving cautious support to Dutch efforts to regain control of Indonesia and authorizing over $100 million of aid to the Netherlands for use in Indonesia, U.S. policymakers grew increasingly impatient with the Dutch refusal to come to terms with the nationalists, in control of the Indonesian Republic, whom the United States came to recognize as anticommunist and programmatically conservative. In a revealing survey of counterinsurgency efforts elsewhere in Southeast Asia, Acting Secretary of State Robert Lovett in late 1948 argued that French intransigence in Indochina had succeeded only in suppressing all sectors of the nationalist movement except the communists, leaving the French "with the choice of reconstructing and defending a genuine nationalist movement of leaders of generally uncertain capacities and popular following or of facing the alternatives of continuing a hopeless war or abandoning Indochina altogether to the Communists."[107] The State Department desperately sought to convince the Dutch that the way to prevent revolution in Indonesia was to come to terms with anti-communist nationalists. As Lovett described a meeting with the Dutch ambassador:

> I pointed out that Mr. Cochran as well as the Department were deter-mined that the growing Communist strength in Indonesia be contained and, if possible, eliminated; that we felt the Communist threat in Indonesia was grave and immediate; that in our opinion, the Communist threat could be met within the Republic only by Hatta since the intrusion of the Dutch in the Republic would, we believed, immediately polarize nation-alism and communism in a united front against Netherlands' aggression.[108]

He urged Dutch acceptance of a U.S. plan to strengthen "Mr. Hatta and his government sufficiently to enable him successfully to liqui-date Communists within the Republic."[109] After the fledgling re-public violently suppressed a military revolt in Madiun that drew communist backing, the United States secretly informed the Dutch that any military action against the republic would result in the cessa-tion of U.S. aid. When the Dutch proceeded to take such action in December, all U.S. aid earmarked for Indonesia was suspended. In 1950, ECA aid was resumed to the now independent Republic of Indonesia.

Between 1948 and 1952, the ECA gradually became involved in aid programs to other underdeveloped areas besides the overseas ter-ritories. The original Marshall Plan legislation included an autho-rization of $463 million for China, which was to be administered by the ECA. In January 1949, Truman transferred the administration of economic aid in South Korea from the army to the ECA. In the fol-lowing year, after the Chinese Revolution ended ECA activities on the mainland, Congress authorized the use of the leftover Chinese funds in the neighboring areas of Southeast Asia; this became the basis of programs in Taiwan, Indochina, Thailand, Indonesia, and

Burma. A substantial aid program was initiated by the ECA in the Philippines in 1951, and the ECA financed a large shipment of grain to India in the same year. Data on most forms of U.S. foreign aid to the independent countries in the Third World between 1948 and 1952 are presented in Table 6. Outside of East Asia, most economic aid was administered by the Technical Cooperation Administration, formed in 1951.

During this period, the great bulk of aid to the Third World was administered by the ECA and represented an attempt to intervene in civil and revolutionary struggles in Asia. Sixty-four percent of the total went to Taiwan, Korea, and the Philippines, and a $248.7 million loan to India made to avert famine was credited with "preventing the establishment of a new Communist bridgehead in Asia." [110]

The Marshall Plan and Rearmament

For U.S. policymakers, the European dollar gap posed the central threat to the achievement of multilateralism and constituted the main way of measuring the effectiveness of Marshall Plan aid. Yet within a year of its initiation, both Americans and Europeans realized that the four-year plan was not going to be sufficient to eliminate the dollar gap and to restore a multilateral world economy. In the fall of 1949, the OEEC directors concluded that the problem of the dollar gap could not be solved. [111] Along with other economists, John Kenneth Galbraith warned that not only could the Marshall Plan not meet its goals by 1952, but that European countries were already taking steps in anticipation of the aid cutoff to protect themselves in ways contrary to American purposes. [112] The business press in both Europe and the United States also recognized that success was impossible by 1952 and speculated about ways the Truman administration might try to drum up support for continued aid through war scares. [113] The Point Four legislation, however, had only squeezed through Congress by one vote, and the outlooks of many policymakers were gloomy. [114]

This pessimism about the Marshall Plan meeting its own goals

TABLE 6   U.S. Foreign Aid to Underdeveloped Countries
(Excluding Overseas Territories), 1948–52 ($ millions)

Region/Country	Economic Aid	Military Aid	Total
Near East and South Asia			
Afghanistan	16.9	—	16.9
India	248.7	—	248.7
Iran	16.5	16.7	33.2
Iraq	0.5	—	0.5
Jordan	5.2	—	5.2
Lebanon	1.8	—	1.8
Nepal	0.2	—	0.2
Pakistan	11.1	—	11.1
Saudi Arabia	5.2	—	5.2
Syria	0.4	—	0.4
Turkey	225.1	235.9	461.0
Regional	2.7	—	2.7
Total	534.3	252.6	786.9
East Asia			
Burma	10.2	—	10.2
Indochina	47.1	245.1	292.2
Indonesia	207.4	3.9	211.3
South Korea	485.6	11.7	497.3
Philippines	587.7	78.7	666.4
Ryukyu Islands	124.5	—	124.5
Taiwan/China	467.8	47.9	515.7
Thailand	17.1	16.4	33.5
Regional	0.7	1.9	2.6
Total	1948.1	405.6	2353.7
Africa			
Egypt	1.5	—	1.5
Ethiopia	1.3	—	1.3
Liberia	12.6	—	12.6
Libya	1.8	—	1.8
Morocco	0.3	—	0.3
Tunisia	0.2	—	0.2
Total	17.7	—	17.7

SOURCE: Agency for International Development, *U.S. Overseas Loans and Grants and Assistance from International Organizations, Obligations and Loan Authorizations, July 1, 1945–June 30, 1970* (Washington, D.C., May 14, 1971).

NOTE: Excluding European LDCs and Israel. Figures include Export-Import Bank loans.

Continued on next page

TABLE 6—*continued*

Region/Country	Economic Aid	Military Aid	Total
Latin America			
Argentina	101.5	—	101.5
Bolivia	19.2	—	19.2
Brazil	109.4	—	109.4
Chile	64.4	—	64.4
Colombia	11.9	—	11.9
Costa Rica	3.4	—	3.4
Cuba	12.2	—	12.2
Dominican Republic	0.3	—	0.3
Ecuador	11.6	0.1	11.7
El Salvador	1.2	—	1.2
Guatemala	6.4	—	6.4
Haiti	16.3	—	16.3
Honduras	1.3	—	1.3
Mexico	178.7	—	178.7
Nicaragua	2.9	—	2.9
Panama	6.4	—	6.4
Paraguay	3.2	—	3.2
Peru	24.8	0.1	24.9
Uruguay	3.4	—	3.4
Venezuela	10.5	—	10.5
Regional	1.8	—	1.8
Total	590.8	0.2	591.0

was justified. In 1951 the dollar gap was the worst since 1948.[115] Most of the progress the Economic Cooperation Administration praised so lavishly had been achieved by continuing discrimination against dollar imports. Even worse, the ECA feared that the inflationary impact of the Korean War would lead to "a retreat to autarkical policies."[116] Price stability, currency convertibility, elimination of dollar import discrimination and other controls, and regional economic integration remained a long way off at the end of the Marshall Plan period. The United States had succeeded in putting these goals on the European political agenda, but their fulfillment was by no means assured as of 1952.

In terms of the concrete economic objectives that motivated it, the Marshall Plan was, in the Kolkos' stark words, "a failure."[117] It came to be popularly defined as a success partly through a redefinition of goals. The multilateral goals of the State Department and the ECA gave way to retrospective political and military goals. At the end of the Marshall Plan, conservative social forces had retained and greatly strengthened their political control in all the Western European countries. European resistance to rearmament had been overcome, and Europe was now militarily organized under U.S. hegemony against the Soviet Union. The historic economic linkages between Western and Eastern Europe had been broken. In the popular mind, the Marshall Plan had prevented Europe from "going communist."

What really saved the reputation of the Marshall Plan, however, was the continuation of massive aid to Europe *after* the official close of the plan. The common claim that the Marshall Plan completed its task ahead of time and with less money than expected totally ignores the fact that American aid to Europe simply took on a new name in 1952. The bulk of American aid to Europe came *after* the end of the Marshall Plan, under the auspices of the ECA's successor, the Mutual Security Agency. Total official economic and military grants and loans to European countries during the Marshall Plan years came to $16.4 billion. Under the Mutual Security Agency, $18.9 billion more was provided.[118]

This continuing high level of aid is traditionally deemed due to the crisis in military power brought on by the Korean War and the subsequent intensification of the cold war. As early as November 1950, a presidential committee claimed that, except for the Korean War and the new requisites of the cold war, aid to Europe could have been discontinued in 1952.[119] The claim, however, was disingenuous. Truman had created the committee—before the outbreak of the Korean War—because his administration recognized the fact that the Marshall Plan was not going to solve the problem of the European dollar gap. Acheson's memorandum to Truman on February 16, 1950, in which he proposed the formation of the committee, posed the problem bluntly:

It is the understanding of Congress and the people that the European Recovery Program will be brought to a close in 1952. It is expected that unless vigorous steps are taken, the reduction and eventual termination of extraordinary foreign assistance in accordance with present plans will create economic problems at home and abroad of increasing severity. If this is allowed to happen, United States exports, including the key commodities on which our most efficient agricultural and manufacturing industries are heavily dependent, will be sharply reduced, with serious repercussions on our domestic economy. European countries, and friendly areas in the Far East and elsewhere, will be unable to obtain basic necessities which we now supply, to an extent that will threaten their political stability. . . . This is the problem of the "dollar gap" in world trade.[120]

Noting that "existing plans are inadequate to meet the needs of the present situation," Acheson called for Truman himself to lead a campaign to close the dollar gap.[121] Yet as Acheson recognized, the only conceivable short-run economic solution—a vast increase in U.S. imports—was politically impossible.

In this context of deep pessimism about an economic solution to the dollar gap by 1952, rearmament emerged as the only practical solution to a political-economic dilemma.[122] Adoption of a critical National Security Council document (NSC-68) committed the Truman administration to a massive military buildup months before the Korean War broke out. State Department documents show that U.S. policymakers saw rearmament as solving the problems that economic aid could not solve. One document, for example, justified a military approach by observing that Congress was more favorably disposed to military aid than to aid for economic recovery. It added: "The distinction between aid in support of foreign military effort abroad and aid for economic recovery is largely artificial."[123]

Rearmament solved a variety of problems. It greatly mitigated the problem of congressional resistance to a continuing aid program. It allowed the United States to continue financing the dollar gap of European countries through the 1950s, thereby making possible the kind of regional economic organization of Europe that the United States deemed most desirable. At the same time, rearmament eliminated one of the dangers inherent in the ECA plan for economic integration—that it contained no safeguard to prevent an economically unified Europe from evolving separately from the U.S. economy—by assuring a continual flow of dollars into Europe as well as by tying Europe to American military hardware.[124] Finally, rearmament, as military Keynesianism, gave the same kind of boost to the sluggish European economies as it did to the U.S. economy, thus stepping up the rate of economic growth. Ultimate attainment of the multilateral goals of the Marshall Plan—as well as the attainment of relatively full employment at home—was dependent on the shift to rearmament in Europe, itself partly justified on the basis of developments in the underdeveloped world.

Conclusion

It is easy today to dismiss as naive Hoffman's statement that "we have learned in Europe what to do in Asia," for the problems of Third World underdevelopment have proven to be far more intractable than Western policymakers and aid officials first realized. Yet the basic theme that emerges from the analysis of the origins, theory, and functioning of the Marshall Plan in this chapter is that there is no radical discontinuity between the Marshall Plan and the later aid programs focused more exclusively on the Third World. The Marshall Plan not only shaped the international context within which the aid regime subsequently evolved, but it also created a body of operating principles and procedures that remain an integral part of the aid regime. It also initiated large-scale economic aid programs in the underdeveloped world.

The continuity between the Marshall Plan and subsequent aid programs can be viewed in various ways. As we have seen, the European Recovery Program went beyond Europe and recovery; it envisioned a reconstructed international order in which the underdeveloped areas, as recipients of U.S. aid and foreign investment and as vastly increased exporters of raw materials to U.S. industry, would play a critical role in relieving the dollar shortage in Europe, which was seen both as the cause of national capitalisms and as the obstacle to recovery and multilateralism. From its beginning, aid has been as much about the nature as about the pace of economic growth. Although aid's use to block socialism has been well understood, its role in limiting national capitalism extends well beyond the Marshall Plan period. Indeed, one can argue that statism and national capitalism have been the real threats economic aid has been used to counter in most underdeveloped societies, rather than the more visible and publicized challenges from the socialist or communist left.

As in the subsequent development of the aid regime, Marshall Plan aid evolved from a mix of domestically derived motivations and goals, often reflecting specific interest groups, and from the need to respond to problems of the world system as a whole. Although domestic and international factors have always interacted, the mesh between them—in terms of consistency and efficacy—has been variable. The Marshall Plan originated out of a successful meshing of U.S. policymakers' concerns about the structural needs of the U.S. economy with their recognition that only a reconstructed international order could address the problem of the dollar gap and of consequent tendencies toward national capitalism. Yet even then, passage of the enabling legislation in the U.S. Congress had to be based heavily on cold war scare tactics. The aid regime that evolved has always been compromised by "exogenous" factors, and the Marshall Plan itself was no exception to this.

Under the Marshall Plan and Point Four, the United States established aid programs in most of the overseas territories of the European colonial powers and in forty independent Third World countries. Over one-fifth of U.S. aid between 1948 and 1952 went directly to the underdeveloped areas. In both Europe and the underdeveloped world, specific procedures and techniques were devised that subsequently became diffused in the aid regime. The use of counterpart funds, called "the indispensable idea" by Paul Hoffman, became, as we shall see, a widely emulated method of expanding the leverage of aid.[125] The withholding of aid from Latin America, although superseded by expanded definitions of aid's role in the 1960s, reflected a norm of "strategic withholding" of aid where private capital was available that remains at the center of the aid regime. Finally, the choice of aid over other alternatives set the stage for the institutionalization of aid within the world economy after the formal close of the Marshall Plan era.

2

The Changing Structure of External Financing and Aid Dependency

Economic assistance to the Third World during the Marshall Plan period essentially involved a single country and a single agency: the United States and its Economic Cooperation Administration. The supplementary aid flows from European countries during this time were, as we have seen, largely underwritten by the United States. And U.S. control of the World Bank and the International Monetary Fund ensured their insignificance during this period.

By the 1980s, however, the aid picture had become enormously more complex. Separate aid programs were now administered by all sixteen countries of the Development Assistance Committee, by at least eight communist and ten OPEC countries, by approximately twenty multilateral organizations in addition to various components of the United Nations system, by hundreds of private organizations, and through assorted other arrangements.[1] Aid programs had even been initiated by several Third World countries.[2]

This chapter provides a descriptive overview of the proliferation of actors in the aid regime. It traces first the entry of new donors, showing how each decade since the 1940s was marked by different kinds of institutional innovations.[3] It then examines aggregate shifts in the composition of external financing for Third World countries over time, focusing on both shifts in the balance between aid and other forms of external financing and in the roles of different aid donors. Finally, it examines the way these changes have affected the degree of dependency of Third World countries on single donors.

The chapter focuses on the years from 1956, the first year for which relatively complete aid data are available, to 1980, by which time a crisis of debt was rapidly spreading throughout the Third World. Developments in the aid regime since 1980 are analyzed in later chapters. The question of whether the behavior of the actors described in this chapter testifies to the existence of an international regime is dealt with at length in the next chapter.

Stages of Institutional Development of the Aid Regime

The institutional complexity of the contemporary aid regime has evolved gradually through a process that may be divided into four stages, roughly corresponding to decades. The 1950s were a period of the dominance and diversification of bilateral aid programs of the advanced capitalist countries—a state of affairs assured, ironically, by the advent of small Soviet and Chinese aid programs in the middle of the decade. The 1960s were marked by the emergence of new forms of multilateralism, largely either under the auspices of, or modeled after, the World Bank. The 1970s witnessed the sudden emergence of Middle Eastern oil-producing countries as major aid donors, as well as an expansion of World Bank lending and other activities that consolidated its position as the leading aid institution. In the mid to late 1970s, the expansion of nonconcessional private bank lending in lieu of official financing came to constitute a fundamental challenge to the functioning of the aid regime, a challenge culminating in the debt crisis. This crisis in turn has given rise in the 1980s to a variety of regime changes that are explored in later chapters.

1950s: Western Bilateralism

External financing for the Third World during the 1950s had two primary characteristics. First, private sources of financing (mostly private investment) constituted a uniquely large proportion of total financing during the early and middle parts of the decade. Foreign private investment just about equaled official financing in 1957, although its share of total financing declined quite steadily thereafter. Second, official financing was heavily dominated by the advanced capitalist countries; bilateral aid from those countries that later constituted the Development Assistance Committee (DAC) amounted to 87.9 percent of total official financing between 1956 and 1960. Of this, the U.S. portion was 67.6 percent in 1956 and 60.5 percent in 1960.

In 1954, the USSR made its first commitment of economic aid to a noncommunist underdeveloped country (Afghanistan); China's first similar commitments were made in 1956. By 1960, however, China had made commitments to only seven such countries, and the Soviet Union to thirteen.[4] Actual disbursements during this period by the USSR, China, and Eastern European countries came to only about 4 percent of official financing and 2.4 percent of all external financing, official and private. Thus, despite the alarm sounded in the United States about the "Sino-Soviet economic offensive," communist aid constituted only a very minor source of external financing in the 1950s.[5]

Soviet leaders and some scholars contend that the relatively small Soviet aid program at this time can be credited with much of the expansion of aid by the capitalist countries. Premier Khrushchev, for example, once suggested that aid from capitalist countries "should also be viewed as a particular kind of Soviet aid" because it would not have been extended without the challenge posed by the USSR.[6] Although it is impossible to quantify precisely the effects of Soviet aid on Western aid, it seems clear that the advent of Soviet aid raised the level of Western aid, increased the ability of nonaligned countries to press for aid from the West, and forced Western countries to soften the terms of some of their aid.[7]

The specter of communist aid led the United States to press the OEEC countries (reconstituted in 1961 as the Organization for Economic Cooperation and Development [OECD], with an expanded membership including Canada and Japan) to initiate or expand their own aid programs. A good deal of such "aid" in the late 1950s went to the donors' colonial empires. By the end of the decade, however, most of the advanced capitalist countries were operating full-scale aid programs, and the rest (for example, the Scandinavian countries) followed suit in the early 1960s. Nonetheless, the United States in 1960 still accounted for over three-fifths of bilateral aid from the advanced capitalist countries.

The relationship between economic and military aid was particularly close in the 1950s. Cold war concerns had a life of their own, but it is misleading to draw too sharp a contrast between this aid, so heavily justified on the basis of cold war rationales, and later aid justified more purely on "developmental" grounds. Aid during the 1950s shaped the nature of development as much as subsequent aid did; indeed, it consolidated the world system that defined the basic mix of opportunity and constraint facing Third World countries in the "development decades" of the 1960s and 1970s.[8]

The link between cold war and developmental goals during this period was particularly evident in the search for visible showcases of Western benevolence. When the Griffin Mission was sent out in 1950 to establish a U.S. aid presence in Southeast Asia, it was charged "to find justified projects . . . that will have immediate political significance" and that would affect "considerable numbers of people and [have] a desirable political effect, strengthening existing governments and indicating sincere American interest in the welfare of the peoples of Southeast Asia."[9] Soviet aid programs during this period evinced a similar showcase mentality, even if the Soviet stake in propping up existing governments was smaller.[10]

William Lederer and Eugene Burdick's novel *The Ugly American* provides a revealing look at the assumptions behind U.S. aid programs during this period.[11] Although written as a critique of alleged incompetence on the part of U.S. officials abroad, the book shares the prevailing notion that showcase projects can win the struggle for the hearts and minds of Third World peoples. The authors' fictionalized success stories substitutes Hardy Boys' antics for the official Ugly American: a Catholic priest puts out a phony communist newspaper to discredit communism; an American colonel affects poverty and wins over the locals through his aw-shucks attitude; he also exploits the local tradition of palmistry to affect the military policy of an Asian state. Despite the novel's acid view of U.S. officialdom, it reflects prevailing assumptions about the utility of foreign aid for furthering cold war goals, the effectiveness of gimmickry, and the close relationship between "military" and "developmental" goals.

1960s: New Forms of Multilateralism

Bilateral aid for the advanced capitalist countries constituting the DAC remained the largest single form of external financing through the 1960s, but its share of the total declined from 54.2 percent in 1960 to 37.9 percent in 1970. The most rapidly growing sources of aid during this decade were the multilateral organizations; their rate of growth was almost seven times that of DAC bilateral aid. This growth was partly a result of the creation of new multilateral institutions. At the beginning of the decade, the IBRD with its affiliate, the International Finance Corporation (IFC), and the United Nations provided almost all multilateral aid. New multilateral institutions accounted for 40 percent of multilateral aid in 1970, however, and 50 percent by 1980.

The institutions emerged largely in response to Third World pressures, but at the same time, they represented a defeat of the effort of Third World countries to establish a UN institution providing capital assistance over which they would exercise control.[12] Instead of a Special United Nations Fund for Economic Development (SUNFED), the underdeveloped countries got a soft-loan window at the World Bank (the International Development Association) and a series of regional development banks closely modeled on the World Bank itself: the Inter-American Development Bank (IDB) in 1959, the Central American Bank for Economic Integration (CABEI) in 1961, the African Development Bank (AfDB) in 1964, the Asian Development Bank (ADB) in 1966, the East African Development Bank (EADB) in 1967, and the Caribbean Development Bank (CDB) in 1970.[13] By far the most significant in terms of overall lending has been the International Development Association (IDA).

The IDA was not really a new institution at all, but rather a "legal fiction" that enabled the IBRD to make soft loans as well as hard ones.[14] In essence, the IDA was designed to meet the contradictions of the IBRD's success. The IBRD had been so successful at raising money on private capital markets and loaning it to underdeveloped countries that it was in danger of putting itself out of business, due to its major borrowers' growing incapacity to service their accumulating IBRD debt. The Bank's lesser borrowers were not considered sufficiently creditworthy to borrow more at IBRD rates. The IDA provided a means to expand overall World Bank operations, help LDCs repay their debts and continue borrowing, and build up a constituency among the poorer Third World countries to bolster the Bank's claim on resources from the advanced capitalist countries. As one analysis has noted: "Although LDC governments would have preferred a low-interest loan agency under their control, they went along with IDA and, indeed, championed it because strategically they recognized that it was their only hope of funds on these terms."[15]

The basic IBRD/IDA model was taken over by most of the regional development banks. As one analysis of their constitutional instruments notes, "many of the institutional provisions and some of the provisions relating to operations were copies *verbatim* from the IBRD Agreement."[16] At the core is a *bank*, raising money on international capital markets, generally through the sale of long-term bonds, and lending this money at rates of interest allowing the bank both to pay its own expenses and to pay a rate of interest on its bonds sufficiently high to attract private investors. These bonds are backed by subscriptions in gold or convertible currencies by member countries, most of which is "callable" rather than actually paid in. Because of this official backing, the MDBs have been able to raise money on capital markets more cheaply than most borrowers, and this in turn has enabled them to lend at rates about three-quarters of normal market rates. Membership in these institutions is open to both donor and recipient countries, but voting is weighted according to financial contribution. The arrangements vary; the voting strength of donor countries is generally less than their share of subscriptions but sufficient to maintain control or at least substantial influence. In the IDA, "Part I Members," consisting of the advanced capitalist countries and Kuwait, accounted for 95.8 percent of subscriptions in 1981 and 65.5 percent of the votes.[17] In the Asian Development Bank, the industrialized countries control 56 percent of the vote, in the Inter-American Development Bank, 46.5 percent.[18] However, votes alone count for little, as the African Development Bank discovered. Between its formation in 1964 and 1979, the AfDB allowed only African countries to be members, but it was unable to attract significant capital from the advanced capitalist countries and therefore had little to lend. Only after it gave significant voting rights to donor countries did this situation change.

The regional banks have also established IDA-type affiliates, generally called special funds. Like the IDA, these funds raise their money from subscriptions (grants) by governments and loan it at soft terms. Donor governments have commonly exercised greater control over these affiliates than over the core banks.

A rather different multilateral approach to aid evolved during this period from negotiations between the European Economic Community (EEC) and an expanding group of "associated" Third World countries, mostly African ex-colonies. The Yaoundé Conventions of 1963 and 1969, followed by the Lomé Conventions of 1975 and 1979, covered both trade and aid relationships.[19] Although the second Lomé Convention in particular resulted in some interesting institutional innovations (to be discussed later), most EEC aid has been channeled through the European Development Fund (EDF), controlled by EEC donors. France has provided a disproportionate share of the contributions to the EDF, and it is widely perceived as a basically French institution, concentrating its Third World investments in French-speaking countries.[20] A third Lomé Convention was signed in December 1984, providing for about $6 billion in financial transfers between 1985 and 1990.

The decade of the 1960s also saw the reorganization of bilateral programs, reflecting both the increase in their number and a redefinition of the relationship between military and economic aid. A gradual shift to a more "economic" emphasis was evident in the periodic name changes of the U.S. aid agency: from the Mutual Security Agency to the Foreign Operations Administration to the International Cooperation Administration to, finally, the Agency for International Development in 1961.[21] Around the same time, in several European countries, aid programs scattered within various ministries were centralized in newly created aid agencies.[22] However, French aid has remained highly decentralized, and the ministerial status of aid agencies elsewhere, such as in Britain, has varied with the attitude of the party in power.

While the 1960s witnessed the establishment of relatively independent aid agencies within the majority of DAC governments and the evolution of a semiofficial development community outside (sometimes taking the form of a "development lobby"), the relationship between development aid and military aid was reconceptualized rather than severed. Long-term development aid came to be seen, particularly in the United States, as insurance against revolution in the long run and as an important component of counterinsurgency programs in the short run. Vietnam was the top recipient of U.S. "economic" aid during this period, and a significant proportion of

U.S. aid elsewhere was explicitly targeted for police and counter-insurgency operations.[23] Although for reasons of creditworthiness and political credibility the multilateral institutions have tended to avoid "hot spots" such as Indochina during the 1960s, a prime motivation behind the expansion of multilateral aid has been aptly characterized, in the case of the World Bank, as "defensive modernization," the belief that the alternative to aid-supported development is revolution inimical to Western donor interests.[24]

Multilateral institutions more than doubled their share of total flows between 1960 and 1970, but official financing during the 1960s was still dominated by the bilateral programs of the advanced capitalist countries. Between 1960 and 1970, multilateral aid was equivalent to only 15 percent of DAC bilateral aid. In 1970, however, World Bank loan commitments surpassed grants and loans from USAID, hitherto the world's largest aid institution.

1970s: OPEC Bilateralism and the World Bank Offensive

Certainly the most unexpected institutional development during the 1970s was the explosion of aid flows from the major oil-producing countries of the Middle East, members of the Organization of Petroleum-Exporting Countries (OPEC). There were several small bilateral OPEC aid programs extending back into the early 1960s, but the big expansion occurred in the wake of the oil price rise of 1973, which placed enormous dollar reserves in the hands of OPEC members. By far the greatest proportion of these reserves was placed on deposit with commercial banks in the advanced capitalist countries, but some was lent out directly to Third World countries at concessional rates. Whereas in 1972 OPEC aid amounted to only 5 percent of official financing, in 1975 and 1976, OPEC aid was greater than all non-OPEC multilateral aid combined and accounted for about 25 percent of official financing. Although OPEC countries established a number of multilateral institutions at this time (the Arab Fund for Economic and Social Development in 1973, the Arab Bank for Economic Development in Africa in 1973, the Islamic Development Bank in 1975, and the OPEC Fund for International Development in 1976 [then named the Special Fund]), the vast bulk of OPEC aid remained bilateral. In fact, in its decentralization and close alignment with overtly political goals, OPEC aid has resembled the French model more than those where aid is channeled through a centralized and relatively autonomous aid agency. Only a rather small proportion (around 20 percent) of OPEC bilateral aid gets channeled through the official development agencies of the OPEC countries: the Abu Dhabi Fund, the Kuwait Fund, the Saudi Fund, the Iraq Fund for External Development, and the Libyan Arab Foreign Bank. Most OPEC aid moves through other, more directly political, channels, usually the Ministry of Finance.[25]

As a proportion of GNP, OPEC aid peaked in 1976, with its ODA constituting 2.29 percent of OPEC GNP. DAC members' ODA in that year came to 0.33 percent of GNP.[26] OPEC aid has remained significant, although by 1980, its share of total external financing was only a little more than half its 1975–76 level. OPEC ODA in 1980 had declined to 1.35 percent of GNP, although it remained over three times the DAC figure of 0.37 percent.[27]

Marshall Plan aid was overwhelmingly in the form of grants, but aid to Third World countries in the later 1950s and the 1960s was increasingly extended on a loan basis. By the mid 1960s, UN studies were showing that if aid continued at 1965 levels and terms, net lending would become negative in 1970, beginning thereafter even to offset the flow of grants.[28] In fact, the IBRD in 1970 received more in debt service on past loans than it disbursed in new loans— although if only less developed countries are considered, there was a small positive flow.[29] The particularly rapid expansion of the institutions of the World Bank during the 1970s must be understood in this context. World Bank Group lending grew sevenfold between 1970 and 1980. Equally important, the Bank moved aggressively during the decade to establish a preeminent position in terms of policy, research, aid coordination, education, and other activities. Although it remained a centralized institution, with most of its staff in Washington, D.C., by the early 1980s it nonetheless had established a network of country and regional offices in effect replacing USAID field missions, which had been pared back in the 1970s.

The expansion of World Bank lending in the 1970s was supplemented by the creation of several new types of lending by the Bank's sister institution, the IMF. Special oil facilities for countries most seriously affected by oil price increases were established in 1974 and 1975, and between 1976 and 1981, the IMF made $3.7 billion in long-term loans from a trust fund created by the sale of some of the IMF's gold.[30] These new types of lending carried only moderate levels of conditionality and contributed to a decrease in high-conditionality lending by the IMF during this period. At the same time, the institutional bases of expanded high-conditionality lending by the IMF were also created during this period—in the Extended Fund Facility (established in 1974), in the Supplementary Financing Facility (between 1979 and 1982), and subsequently in the Enlarged Access Policy (established in 1981). These new types of lending allowed the IMF to increase the level and duration of its high-conditionality lending. Although they were only moderately used at first, they positioned the IMF to play a central financing role when the debt crisis broke out at the end of the decade.

Late 1970s: The New Role of Private Financing

The most striking innovations in external financing in the mid to late 1970s occurred not in the aid regime but in the practices of private commercial banks. The late 1970s showed a partial return to the situation of the mid 1950s, when private flows were about equal to official flows. The composition of these private flows was dramatically different, however. Whereas in the 1950s they consisted almost entirely of direct private investment, in the later 1970s lending by private commercial banks far surpassed flows of direct private investment.

The extraordinary expansion of commercial bank lending during the 1970s did not represent any sudden improvement in the inherent creditworthiness of Third World countries, with the possible exception of the oil-producing countries. Changes on the supply side had more to do with developments in the rest of the world economy.[31] Large-scale commercial bank lending to Third World countries was made possible by the development of the Eurodollar market, generated initially by recurrent U.S. balance of payments deficits. The Euromarket (a term that commonly includes all offshore financial markets, including those in the Third World) expanded rapidly due to two types of flows during the 1970s. The most commonly recognized of these was the enormous petrodollar surpluses generated by the 1973–74 oil price rises. OPEC countries placed $22 billion on Eurocurrency deposit in 1974 alone.[32] Euromarket expansion was also based on flows from within the industrialized countries, attracted by the lack of regulation and high profitability of Euromarket operations. In fact, it happened that the U.S. capital controls program ended in January 1974, just after the 1973 oil price rises. By the end of the decade, flows from within the advanced capitalist countries were considerably more important than OPEC flows. (In 1982, in the face of declining oil prices, the OPEC countries as a whole became capital importers.) An enormous stock of capital accumulated in the Euromarket, resulting, in the words of Benjamin Cohen, in an unprecedented "privatization of liquidity creation."[33]

Partly stimulated by tax loopholes, along with local currency loans and investment guarantees from the U.S. aid program, U.S. banks had expanded their foreign operations in the Third World rapidly from the mid 1960s. As an OECD study observes:

> It is commonly believed that the growth of bank lending to developing countries was a phenomenon associated essentially with "recycling" of oil surpluses following the first and second oil shocks. This is a mistaken interpretation of recent financial history. In fact, the major part of the expansion of the role of the banks in the financing of developing countries took place in the late 1960s and early 1970s, *before* the first oil shock.[34]

Between 1965 and 1976, the number of U.S. banks with foreign branches rose from 13 to 125 and the number of foreign branches from 211 to 731.[35] A study of thirteen large U.S. bank holding companies revealed that 95 percent of their increased earnings between 1970 and 1976 came from international operations.[36] European offshore banking also expanded rapidly during this period, especially from the early 1970s onward. Faced with low growth and stagflationary conditions in the advanced capitalist countries in much of the 1970s, the Euromarket banks looked increasingly to the Third World as "the only way to expand business in the face of slackening domestic credit demand and increased competition among banks."[37] Further, making a few mega-sized loans to governments was far more profitable than making many small loans to domestic private companies; huge "economies of scale" were "inherent in lending millions of dollars to a single dictator or minister at a stroke instead of plodding along placing a hundred thousand here and a hundred thousand there to put up shopping centers or industrial parks."[38] In addition, the process was considerably more fun; as John Makin comments:

> Once you have been met and guided through customs by a solicitous driver who then whisks you through traffic in an air-conditioned limousine to your luxurious hotel and thence to an elegant dinner with the truly charming people who head the finance ministries of developing countries, it is a real come-down to grab a cab and check yourself into one of the inevitably tacky hostelries that pass for the "best" in towns where so many American companies see fit to locate themselves. Dinner conversation in places like that, if someone meets you for dinner at all, is less than exotic.[39]

What was most critical in the newfound readiness of bankers to lend to Third World countries, however, was an array of technical innovations that reduced risks for the banks. The three most important were syndication, cross-default clauses, and floating interest rates. Syndication spreads the risk on large-scale loans by involving a number of banks, under the leadership of a "lead" bank that handles the actual negotiations and arrangements and customarily adds a percentage surcharge as its fee. Syndication allows banks to diversify their loan portfolios; from the debtor's perspective, it means that default on a loan will involve conflict with a whole range of banks. Cross-default clauses extend both these functions of syndication by specifying that a default by a borrower to any single lender will be taken as a default against all lenders. This effectively prevents a borrower from playing off lenders by defaulting against some creditors and paying others in return for special consideration.

Syndication and cross-default clauses deal with the political risk of default, but floating interest rates deal with the more purely financial risk created by inflation. The Eurobanks in the mid 1970s greatly expanded the use of floating interest rates, generally specified as the London Interbank Offering Rate (LIBOR, the rate the banks charge each other for the use of money), recalculated every six months, plus a percentage "spread" to cover the banks' costs, risks, and profit. Because, as bankers were fond of saying, sovereign borrowers do not go bankrupt, floating interest rates appeared to shift the financial risks of interest rate instability entirely to the debtor.

These changes on the supply side of private external finance radically altered the external financing options—and consequently the development strategy options—of many Third World countries during the late 1970s and early 1980s. Chapter 6 explores the reasons why Third World countries availed themselves of this opportunity and some of the consequences. In 1977, commercial bank lending surpassed for the first time the flow of direct investment, and by the following year, it was more than twice the latter. From the mid 1970s, U.S. banks as a whole have made more profits on their overseas than on their domestic operations, and for some (for example, Citicorp), foreign profits have accounted for as much as 80 percent of total profits.[40]

Although the expansion of international bank lending took place outside the aid regime itself, it rested in part on developments within the aid regime and in turn had an important effect on the regime. The "debt crisis" and subsequent developments have reflected the interaction of the aid regime and the "privatization of liquidity creation."

Aggregate Shifts in External Financing: An Overview

The institutional evolution of the aid regime detailed in the previous section has resulted in considerable changes in the composition—in terms of sources—of external financing over time. Table 7 allows us to examine these changes beginning with 1956, the first year for which there are reliable data, and then for five-year intervals between 1960 and 1980. The data distinguish between flows from official sources (governments and multilateral institutions) and from private sources (private investment, bank lending and portfolio investment, and private export credits). From 1965, flows from private voluntary agencies are also included, although they will not receive further attention in this book. Table 8 provides a percentage breakdown of the components of official and private flows separately.

Let us start with the overall balance between official and private flows. From 1956 through 1976, official flows were consistently larger than private flows. In the mid 1950s, official flows were only slightly more than half of total flows, but this rose to about two-thirds in the early 1960s. From the late 1960s through the mid 1970s, official flows were generally between 55 percent and 60 percent of total flows. However, with the rise of Euromarket lending in the later 1970s, private flows surpassed official flows from 1977 through 1979 and were almost equal to the latter in 1980. Within private flows, the most striking change was the decline in the share of external financing accounted for by private foreign investment: from over two-fifths of all flows in 1956 to only about one-tenth in 1980. Within the category of private flows, private investment's share fell from close to 86 percent to 23 percent. After a period in the late 1960s and early 1970s when private export credits (mostly suppliers' credits) were the largest category, commercial bank lending emerged as the largest category of private flows in the later 1970s.

Within the category of official financing, bilateral aid from the advanced capitalist countries declined in relative terms, although it remained the largest type of official aid in 1980. The nadir of the DAC share of total flows occurred when the share of bank lending was the

1956, 1960, 1965, 1970, 1975, 1980 ($ millions and percentage)

Source of Flow	1956 $ m.	%	1960 $ m.	%	1965 $ m.	%	1970 $ m.	%	1975 $ m.	%	1980 $ m.	%
Governments of advanced capitalist countries[a]	2,900	47.5	4,236.4	54.2	5,773.1	51.8	6,587.4	37.9	12,760.1	26.7	23,027.1	27.0
International organizations[b]	272.5	4.5	386	4.9	892	8.0	1,784	10.3	6,025	13.0	12,166	14.3
Governments of communist countries[c]	27.5	0.5	368.5	7.0	312.9	4.2	1,176	6.8	1,072	2.2	1,887	2.2
Governments of OPEC countries and OPEC multilateral organizations	n/a		n/a		n/a		443.5	2.5	6,659.3	14.0	6,519.7	7.7
Total official	3,199.7	52.5	4,990.9	66.1	6,978.0	64.0	9,990.9	57.5	26,697.4	55.9	43,599.8	51.2
Private direct investment	2,500[d]	41.0	1,847.9	23.6	2,207.4	19.8	3,557.2	20.4	10,199.9	21.4	8,896.2	10.4
Bank lending and portfolio investment			408.2	5.2	836.0	7.5	777.0	4.5	5,416.8	11.4	17,702.3	20.8
Private export credits	400	6.6	390.9	5.0	740.7	6.6	2,210.9	12.7	4,067.3	8.5	12,567.7	14.8
Total private	2,900	47.5	2,647.0	33.9	3,784.1	34.0	6,545.1	37.6	19,684.0	41.3	39,166.2	46.0
Private voluntary agencies	n/a		n/a		227	2.0	854.6	4.9	1,341.8	2.8	2,370.9	2.8
Total	6,099.7	100.0	7,637.9	100.0	10,989.1	100.0	17,390.6	100.0	47,722.2	100.0	85,136.9	100.0
Memorandum: IMF[e]	38.8		112.7		422.4		358.3		2,684.1		3,453.1	
Number of standby agreements	4		15		27		31		20		34	

SOURCE: Wherever possible, data have been taken from Organization for Economic Cooperation and Development, *Development Co-operation: Efforts and Policies of the Members of the Development Assistance Committee*, 1981 and earlier reviews. Data for communist countries and international organizations before 1970 were collected from a variety of UN and other sources.

[a] Members of the Development Assistance Committee, OECD.
[b] Not including OPEC institutions.
[c] Figures before 1970 exclude "communist" LDC recipients; figures from 1970 onward include them.
[d] Includes a small amount of bank lending/portfolio investment.
[e] Refers to gross purchases of currencies and special drawing rights. Figures from 1980 include also profits of IMF gold sales distributed to LDCs, but not trust fund loans, which are included in the figure for international institutions.

TABLE 8   Percentage Breakdown of Total Official Flows and
           Total Private Commercial Flows, by Source,
           1956, 1960, 1965, 1970, 1975, 1980

Source of flow	1956	1960	1965	1970	1975	1980
Governments of advanced capitalist countries[a]	91%	85%	83%	66%	48%	53%
International organizations[b]	9	8	13	18	23	28
Governments of communist countries[c]	1	7	4	12	4	4
Governments of OPEC countries and OPEC multilateral organizations	—	—	—	4	25	15
Total official	100%	100%	100%	100%	100%	100%
Private direct investment	86%[d]	70%	58%	54%	52%	23%
Bank lending and portfolio investment	—	15	22	12	28	45
Private export credits	14	15	20	34	20	32
Total private	100%	100%	100%	100%	100%	100%

SOURCE: Wherever possible, data have been taken from Organization for Economic Cooperation and Development, *Development Co-operation: Efforts and Policies of the Members of the Development Assistance Committee*, 1981 and earlier reviews. Data for communist countries and international organizations before 1970 were collected from a variety of UN and other sources.

[a]Members of the Development Assistance Committee, OECD.
[b]Not including OPEC institutions.
[c]Figures before 1970 exclude "communist" LDC recipients; figures from 1970 onward include them.
[d]Includes a small amount of bank lending/portfolio investment.

highest; it fell to between 22.4 percent and 23.7 percent between 1977 and 1979.

Tables 7 and 8 also document the steady increase in the importance of flows from multilateral organizations (excluding OPEC multilateral organizations, which are combined with OPEC bilateral aid). In 1980, these institutions accounted for 28 percent of official flows and slightly more than 14 percent of all flows. Combined aid from multilateral institutions lost its second-place status to OPEC aid in 1975–76, but by 1980, its share of total official flows was almost twice OPEC's. OPEC aid is highly concentrated among a few donors.

Tables 7 and 8 show that aid from communist countries has never constituted a significant proportion of total flows. Apart from a few strategically placed countries, communist aid has never constituted a real alternative to aid from other sources. While aid to Cuba has remained high, no other Third World country not bordering on a donor communist country has found it possible to meet the bulk of its external financing needs through communist aid.[41] The share of aid from communist countries declined significantly in the 1970s. In fact, the decline is greater than the figures in Table 7 suggest because the data before 1970 do not include aid to "communist" LDCs.

Substantial changes occurred between the late 1950s and 1980 not only in the balance between the general categories of external financing but also among the individual donors and sources within these categories. The following are the most salient of these changes:

1. The decline of importance of U.S. bilateral aid. (Although the United States remained the largest bilateral donor, U.S. aid constituted only 23.8 percent of bilateral aid from DAC countries and 12.6 percent of all official aid in 1980.)

2. The rise to dominance of the World Bank among the multilateral institutions. (The share of total multilateral aid of the World Bank institutions has declined from the mid 1960s, but World Bank Group aid in 1980 was more than double its closest multilateral competitor. The Inter-American Development Bank was the only other MDB whose loans surpassed those of the World Bank in some countries—a small majority—in its region.)

3. The instability of flows from communist and OPEC donors. (These flows fluctuated more from year to year than other official flows, and there tended to be more fluctuation in the ranking of donors.)

4. A shift from the early 1970s in the sources of private financing from the United States to Europe, although the United States remained by far the single largest source.

The Decline of Donor Dependency

In the 1950s and 1960s, a division of labor among the major aid donors made most underdeveloped countries dependent on a single country for the bulk of their foreign aid. The major European countries concentrated on their ex-colonies. France allocated 92 percent of its aid to franc area countries between 1960 and 1966 and Great Britain, 90 percent to sterling area countries. Ninety percent of bilateral foreign aid to sub-Saharan countries in the franc area, and 69 percent to North African franc area countries, came from France during this period. British Commonwealth countries apart from India and Pakistan received 67 percent of their bilateral aid during this period from Great Britain. Latin American countries during these years received 89 percent of their aid from the United States, even though they accounted for only 15 percent of U.S. aid worldwide.[42]

As a result of this division of labor among the aid donors, 86 percent of ninety-two underdeveloped countries surveyed by the OECD relied on a single DAC country for 50 percent or more of their bilateral DAC aid in 1967. In fact, 62 percent received over 70 percent from a single donor.[43] This high donor dependency characterized all the regions of the Third World, as shown by Table 9.

Donors' tendencies to concentrate their aid on a few countries with some form of special relationship has continued. In 1980, the top ten aid recipients of the United Kingdom, accounting for 61 percent of Britain's total aid, were all ex-colonies.[44] Of French ODA, 41.6 percent went to the nonsovereign overseas departments and territories (DOM-TOM), with the majority of the remainder going to ex-colonies in Africa.[45] Belgium allocated 53 percent of its ODA in 1980 to its ex-colonies.[46] By and large, the new bilateral donors have

TABLE 9   Changes in Single Donor Dependency: Countries Receiving 50 Percent or More of Their DAC Bilateral ODA from a Single DAC Country, by Region, 1967 and 1980

	1967			1980		
	Number of Countries	%	N	Number of Countries	%	N
Africa	34	81	42	13	32	41
Near East/South Asia	15	88	17	7	47	15
East Asia/Oceania	9	82	11	6	50	12
Latin America	21	95	22	12	57	21
Total	79	86	92	38	43	89

SOURCE: Organization for Economic Cooperation and Development, *Geographical Distribution of Financial Flows to Less Developed Countries, 1966–1967* (Paris: OECD, 1969), and *Geographical Distribution of Financial Flows to Developing Countries, 1977/1980* (Paris: OECD, 1981).

similarly concentrated their aid; 80.1 percent of OPEC bilateral ODA went to Arab countries in 1980.[47]

In spite of continuing patterns of donor concentration, the institutional differentiation of the aid regime has resulted in a substantial decline in recipient dependency on single donors. In terms of DAC bilateral aid receipts, as Table 9 indicates, the proportion of countries receiving 50 percent or more from a single donor dropped to 43 percent in 1980—half that of 1967. In fact, the decline in single donor dependency was substantially greater than is indicated by these figures. In 1967, DAC bilateral aid accounted for 82 percent of all official flows and 51 percent of all flows, official and private. By 1980, however, DAC bilateral aid constituted only 53 percent of total official flows and 27 percent of all flows.

Table 10 allows us to examine regional variations in the reliance of Third World countries on the following categories of external financing: (1) DAC bilateral flows (both ODA and OOF), (2) OPEC bilateral flows, (3) flows from the Soviet Union and Eastern Europe (CMEA), (4) multilateral agency flows, and (5) private sector flows. Of these categories of external financing, aggregate DAC bilateral aid is the largest for less than half the ninety-one countries covered, and close to two-thirds of these are located in sub-Saharan Africa. Relatively few countries rely on either aggregate OPEC aid or CMEA countries for the largest share of their external financing, but multilateral institutions and the private sector each account for the largest share in eighteen countries.

The donor categories in Table 10 lump together rather diverse countries and agencies. Table 11 breaks down the data on aid receipts further, identifying the largest single donor in terms of (1) individual DAC countries, (2) individual multilateral agencies, (3) aggregate CMEA assistance, and (4) aggregate OPEC bilateral assistance. Although aggregating CMEA assistance makes some sense, based on the close alignment of the aid and general foreign policies of the Soviet Union and the Eastern European countries, the aggregation of OPEC bilateral data in DAC sources is more unfortunate because

TABLE 10   Largest Source of External Financing, by Region, 1978–80 (number of countries)

Largest Source	Africa	Near East/ South Asia	East Asia/ Oceania	Latin America	Total
DAC bilateral[a]	28	4	7	4	43
OPEC bilateral[a]	3	4	0	0	7
USSR and Eastern Europe[a]	0	1	2	1	4
Multilateral[a]	5	2	2	9	18
Private sector[b]	5	2	3	8	18
Total	41	13	14	22	90

SOURCE: Organization for Economic Cooperation and Development, *Geographical Distribution of Financial Flows to Developing Countries, 1977/1980* (Paris: OECD, 1981).

[a]Includes both ODA and other official flows.
[b]Includes private investment, private bank lending and portfolio investment, and private export credits.

TABLE 11   Largest Individual Donor of Official External Financing, by Region, 1978–80 (number of countries)

Largest Donor	Africa	Near East/ South Asia	East Asia/ Oceania	Latin America	Total
DAC countries					
United States	2	2	3	6	13
France	13	0	0	0	13
Japan	0	3	6	1	10
United Kingdom	7	0	0	0	7
Belgium	3	0	0	0	3
Germany	1	0	0	2	3
Sweden	3	0	0	0	3
Australia	0	0	2	0	2
Canada	0	0	0	1	1
Multilateral agencies					
IBRD/IDA	3	1	0	5	9
IDB	0	0	0	8	8
EEC	2	0	0	0	2
IMF trust fund	1	0	0	0	1
USSR and Eastern Europe	0	2	3	1	6
OPEC bilateral	5	5	0	0	10

SOURCE: Organization for Economic Cooperation and Development, *Geographical Distribution of Financial Flows to Developing Countries, 1977/1980* (Paris: OECD, 1981).

considerable differences exist among OPEC donors on a number of aid-related issues.

Table 11 shows that aid sources have been remarkably diversified since the period of high donor dependency in the 1950s and 1960s. France alone has come close to maintaining its ties of aid dependency basically intact. Only thirteen countries worldwide between 1978 and 1980 drew the largest share of their aid from the United States (the same number from France). In Africa, Sweden and Belgium were the largest donors for more countries than the United States. Japan took first place in much of East Asia, while the multilateral agencies made a particularly strong showing in Latin America. For ten countries in the Middle East and North Africa (including Mauritania and Sudan), OPEC bilateral and multilateral aid constituted the largest source.

Leading donors do not always provide a large proportion of total external financing, however. Analysis of OECD data on aid flows reveals that only nineteen countries in 1978–80 received 50 percent or more of their net official financial inflows from a single source (as categorized in Table 11). Because four of these relied much more heavily on private capital markets than on official flows, only fifteen countries can be said to exhibit high donor dependency defined this way. Of these fifteen countries, the dominant donor in six cases was a DAC country: the United States two, France two, Japan one, and Australia one. (The two countries meeting this definition of high donor dependency on the United States were Taiwan and Trinidad and Tobago.) Five countries received half or more of their official aid from OPEC countries and institutions and four from CMEA countries combined. Together these "high-dependency" recipients accounted for 16.7 percent of the countries surveyed.

Conclusion

The structure of external financing for "development" and other broadly economic purposes in Third World countries changed radically over the years between 1956 and 1980. Many forms and sources of external financing now exist, although they are not equally available to all underdeveloped countries.

The issue that will preoccupy us in the next two chapters is how to interpret these changes. During the Marshall Plan and Mutual Security periods, overwhelming U.S. predominance and lack of alternatives gave the United States tremendous leverage both in shaping a new international order and in blocking forms of development to which it was opposed. By the early 1980s, however, single donor dependency was no longer an effective means of control in most cases.

The vast majority of Third World countries had significantly diversified their sources of supply. The decline of single donor dependency was very likely one of the structural bases for the movement for a new international economic order among the underdeveloped countries.

In addition, a major component of the economic assistance of the advanced capitalist countries constitutes export promotion, which decreases their ability to achieve compliance in specific spheres. Various other aspects of the current aid system militate against old-fashioned horse-trading as well: the relatively public nature of aid negotiations in consortia and consulting groups of a variety of donors, increased competence of individual specialized ministries and agencies within governments of underdeveloped countries in negotiating aid agreements, and the need for multilateral agencies to cloak their political concerns in technical imperatives. It is reasonable to assume that the aid negotiation process by the late 1970s was generally characterized by greater dignity and less overtly acknowledged inequality than in the past.

But the more fundamental question of the effect of the system as a whole remains open, especially its impact on the general shape of world development and of development choices within nations. The literature on this subject tends toward two polar positions. At one pole, it is argued that governments are so anxious to promote their exports through aid financing and that aid agencies are so anxious to give away money within their budgetary cycle, so as to justify claims on greater resources in the future, that underdeveloped countries can pretty much pick and choose and largely dictate terms. This perspective emphasizes the opportunities underdeveloped countries have for playing donors off against each other and using aid for their own particular purposes. At the other pole, single donor dependency is seen as being replaced by a kind of "united front" among the major donors, generally with the World Bank and the IMF playing a leading role in organizing and coordinating donor solidarity. This view emphasizes the constraints the aid system places on underdeveloped countries and the way that recourse to aid necessarily means acquiescence to externally dictated forms of development.

There is some truth to each of these positions, but truth does not lie precisely in the middle. The next chapter draws on the concept of international regimes as a useful way of identifying and analyzing the coexistence of both competition and conflict on the one hand and a systemic logic on the other. Both constrain underdeveloped countries but offer, under certain circumstances, some room for maneuver.

3

The Structure of the Aid Regime

We have seen how external financing for underdeveloped countries has become highly differentiated. The types of important flows have grown in number, the number of bilateral donors has increased substantially, and multilateral institutions have proliferated. Although individual countries have not had equal access to all these new types and sources of flows, almost all countries have nonetheless succeeded in diversifying their sources of external financing. The implications of these changes remain unexplored, however. What is the experience of the underdeveloped countries with this differentiated structure of external financing? Is there a logic to the system as a whole? To what extent does the structure of external financing determine the patterns of societal development and change in the Third World?

No formal mechanism of systemwide coordination exists. The United Nations has virtually no influence over bilateral aid programs and practically none over the multilateral institutions officially affiliated with it, such as the International Monetary Fund and the World Bank. The multilateral banks consult regularly but guard their decision-making autonomy jealously. The advanced capitalist countries have banded together in the Development Assistance Committee, but they have been careful to give it no power over themselves. The Arab League has proved incapable of coordinating aid by the Arab OPEC members. Compared to trade, for example, aid is a strikingly "unmanaged" component of the world economy: there are practically no formal mechanisms of multilateral control.[1]

As noted in the Introduction, this study draws on the work of political scientists and others who are interested in how international relations may be regulated even in the absence of formal mechanisms of management and authority. These scholars have evolved a form of analysis centered on the concept of *international regimes*, variously referred to as "governing arrangements that affect relationships of interdependence,"[2] as "regulatory frameworks," and as "mediating institutions."[3] The field is still young, characterized by "proliferating taxonomies" and by lack of agreement on exactly what the regime concept refers to.[4]

A full exploration of the evolving concept of international regimes is beyond the scope of this book. However, the next two sections take up several theoretical problems involving the definition of the concept and its applicability to concessional external financing. Regime analysis offers conceptual tools for analyzing international relations that fall between anarchy and domination and that contain elements of both cooperation and conflict, coordination and competition. It allows us to address a weakness in some world systems formulations—the ways interstate relations intersect with the world economy. In terms of aid, regime analysis helps identify modes of regulation of access to aid that prevail without formal interstate management.

Defining Regimes

Stephen Krasner has offered the following definition of international regimes:

Regimes can be defined as sets of implicit or explicit principles, norms, rules, and decision-making procedures around which actors' expectations converge in a given area of international relations. Principles are beliefs of fact, causation, and rectitude. Norms are standards of behavior defined in terms of rights and obligations. Rules are specific prescriptions or proscriptions for action. Decision-making procedures are prevailing practices for making and implementing collective choice.[5]

Different regime theorists, however, have emphasized different aspects of this definition. For Donald Puchala and Raymond Hopkins, international regime is a subjective concept, referring to "attitudinal phenomena" that are assumed to exist wherever "there is discernibly patterned behavior."[6] They insist that regimes be defined independently of behavior, as a set of subjective variables explaining behavior. They see regime analysis as "alerting students of international affairs to subjective and moral factors" and see regimes as ranging from purely ideological "facades" rationalizing the exercise of power to situations "where regimes are determinative" of behavior.[7] In other words, regimes have no necessary relationship to behavior; they are one among many possible independent variables.

Oran Young defines regimes in terms of the behavior of actors and explicitly rejects norms as defining characteristics. Regimes are "recognized patterns of behavior or practice around which expectations converge."[8] An approach of this sort tends to treat regimes primarily as something to be explained—regimes are the dependent variable.

Most regime analysts seem to be groping for a middle ground. In the extreme case, to identify the concept of international regime simply with outcomes would be an exercise in renaming. At the same time, most analysts have in mind something more than attitudes. Krasner has invoked the metaphor of tectonic plates to suggest a more complex relationship between regimes and other determinants of outcomes. Regimes represent one "plate"; other relevant determinants of outcomes, such as the distribution of power among states, represent other plates.

Pressures between the plates vary over time. When regimes are first created there is little pressure. Over time pressure develops at the interface of the plates as they move at different rates. These pressures may be relieved by imperceptible incremental movements, but often the pressures build. The higher the level of incongruity, the more dramatic the ultimate earthquake that finally realigns the plates.[9]

Thus, a regime's ability to cause events varies over time and between issue areas.

Rather than make a priori assumptions about whether the subjective or behavioral components of regimes carry greater causal weight, it is more useful to view Krasner's four categories of principles, norms, rules, and procedures as different levels of analysis. The defining characteristics of a regime should display form on each level. Each core principle of an international regime should be further specified in terms first of general norms, then specific rules, and finally concrete procedures.

Around the borders of a regime, in contrast, one will find principles and norms that are articulated but not actualized through rules and procedures, and rules and procedures that are at best weakly grounded in principles and norms. An example of a nonactualized norm would be the internationally adopted target of 0.7 percent of GNP for official development assistance (ODA) by the advanced countries. Despite lip service given this norm, about half the DAC countries are moving away rather than toward it. Only four DAC countries fulfilled the norm in 1983. The norm nonetheless provides both a basis for Third World claims for more aid and a pressure point in the politics of "burden sharing" among donors. An example of a nonlegitimated procedure is the "tying" of aid, whereby the aid of bilateral donors is restricted to the purchase of products from the donor country. This procedure, although widespread and very costly to underdeveloped countries, finds little defense at the level of principle and norm. Indeed, the major donor countries have been willing to pass resolutions condemning the practice of tying while doing little about it for domestic economic and political reasons. Nonactualized norms and principles and nonlegitimated rules and procedures such as these should be part of regime analysis, but they should not be seen as defining the regime itself. Instead, they represent the interaction of the regime with other causal factors. They draw attention to areas of conflict and competition both among donors and between donors and recipients.

The Regime Concept and Economic Assistance

Several regime analysts have referred in passing to a development assistance regime, but to my knowledge no attempt to analyze such a regime as a whole has been undertaken. Benjamin Cohen and Charles Lipson have identified respectively a "balance of payments financing regime" and a "debt regime," both of which overlap considerably with what I have defined as the aid regime.[10] But rather surprisingly, a regime analysis of economic assistance on a worldwide basis has not hitherto been made.

The lack of work in this area may reflect skepticism about whether an aid regime actually exists. John Ruggie has coined the phrase "quasi regime" to apply to international development assistance, arguing that its norms represent aspirations rather than commitments, that the components of the would-be regime are largely unrelated, and that compliance mechanisms are few and weak. Ruggie appears to see the failure of the major donors to achieve the 0.7 percent ODA goal as evidence of the weakness of the regime.[11] The quantity of concessional finance may be less significant for the nature of development than its structure, however. I shall argue that the close relationship of components of the aid regime comes into focus when one considers the nature of development promoted by the regime.

Three unique features of economic assistance raise questions about the applicability of the regime concept: bilateralism, power asymmetry, and the diverse purposes of aid.

Bilateralism.   The regime concept assumes a world characterized by "complex interdependence." Most applications of the regime concept have focused on areas of multilateral negotiation: trade and monetary relations, law of the sea, nuclear nonproliferation, and so forth.[12] Most aid, however, flows through bilateral channels; it is a matter negotiated by two states alone. Even multilateral aid is negotiated in a basically "bilateral" way; as John White notes: "Far from providing a multilateral framework within which the transfer of resources may be governed by common criteria, which was the model the dim outline of which seemed to be emerging in the 1950s in the OEEC, [the multilateral agency] constitutes yet one more independent entity with which the recipients of aid have to negotiate."[13] Given the diversity that characterizes these bilateral relationships, is it meaningful to speak of a worldwide economic assistance regime at all? Or at best can we speak of regimes associated with individual donors?

There is no theoretical answer to these questions; they must be studied empirically. But the demonstrated existence of an international regime that governs access to most forms of external financing would have important theoretical implications for our understanding of the world system and the trajectories of development in the Third World.

Power Asymmetry. Regime analysts recognize imbalances of power between actors in any given regime, but their frequent emphasis on interdependence, reciprocity, and the normative characteristics of regimes tends to assume more equal forms of bargaining than those that characterize aid.[14] The fact is that underdeveloped countries have few means to force donors to provide aid; their main option in cases of disagreement is to choose not to receive aid at all. More fundamentally, they have virtually no means of challenging the distribution or nature of aid overall; bilateral aid negotiations simply do not provide a basis for raising this issue in a meaningful way. Although Third World countries have been able to band together to negotiate over trade and other issues, there have been almost no forums to negotiate collectively over issues of aid. To the extent that they have been able to raise issues of aid in settings such as UNCTAD and the Lomé negotiations with the EEC, they have been limited to bargaining over quantitative targets for aid.

Oran Young has distinguished between regimes that are spontaneous, negotiated, and imposed.[15] Within the latter category, he distinguishes between situations of overt hegemony and situations in which the dominant actors are able to promote institutional arrangements favorable to themselves through various forms of leadership and the manipulation of incentives. From the point of view of aid recipients, the aid regime is largely this kind of de facto imposed regime. To the extent that underdeveloped countries have significant aid options, the reason is less likely to be their power to affect the regime than the existence of differences among donors. Between donors, the aid regime is a combination of spontaneous and negotiated orders. Donor desires to share the "burden" of aid and to prevent mutually harmful competition in export financing have resulted in negotiated regime norms; common interests and shared ideology have resulted in the "spontaneous" alignment of other regime norms.

Diverse Purposes of Aid. What by international convention is called economic assistance is actually an arbitrary congerie of intergovernmental transfers. Given the vast range of objectives served by different forms of economic assistance, it might seem doubtful that a single regime could be identified. Perhaps there are as many regimes as there are types of aid or no predictive regimes at all.

Whether the regime concept applies to multipurpose foreign aid depends partly on what we expect the concept to do. If we conceptualize the regime as a dominant independent variable from which we can deduce actual outcomes (for example, the actual allocation of aid), then the utility of the concept appears doubtful. As numerous studies of aid allocation make clear, no single set of variables can explain why individual countries get the amount of aid that they do.[16] If we return to Krasner's tectonic plate analogy and use the regime concept to specify a framework of assumptions about how access to economic assistance is governed in normal circumstances, however, we can better identify the standard operating presumptions underlying aid allocation and the conditions for departures from these assumptions. Although almost all aid allocation studies have focused on country allocations (usually defined as the amount of aid per capita), our primary focus will be on the balance between different types of external financing in the total package of any given country and on the balance between the function or sectoral uses of that financing. As we shall see, regime norms govern these latter areas considerably more than overall country aid allocations.

What the Aid Regime Regulates

When the regime concept is applied to foreign aid, it means that there exist among donors widely shared notions about the conditions that should govern access to concessional external financing and about the general type of development such access should promote. The aid regime conceptualized this way stands separate from the variety of other motivations of individual donors—export promotion, military security or hegemony, overthrow of particular governments, suppression of specific insurgencies, and so on. If these motivations overwhelm the allocation of aid, the regime concept will have little usefulness—it will be reduced to the "empty facade" Hopkins and Puchala define as one of their limiting cases.[17] In fact, however, we can identify a set of operating presumptions widely shared among aid donors that is reflected in the basic operating procedures of almost all major aid agencies. The near-universality of some of these assumptions has hidden them from view; they are easily taken for granted. Their implications for the process of world development, however, are profound.

The aid regime, therefore, consists of a set of operating presumptions, some implicit in the outlook of those who make decisions, others explicitly institutionalized in constitutions and other agreements, that regulate access to concessional forms of external financing. More specifically, these components are regulated by the aid regime:

1. *The framework for negotiating concessional financial transfers for ostensibly developmental purposes.* Before taking this framework for granted simply as "the way things are," one should remember that the Third World has sought for over thirty years to create an alter-

native. The fundamental characteristic of this framework is its pervasive *bilateralism*. Aid negotiations are separated from multilateral structures dealing with other international economic issues, and aid is negotiated between single donors and single recipients.

2. *The identification of situations for which concessional flows are deemed appropriate.* The central principle here is that concessional capital should not be allowed to compete with private capital. Donors should engage in *strategic nonlending* where the refusal to lend will result in private capital doing the job. This norm shapes the country allocation of aid only weakly but has powerful effects on the allocation of aid between different uses. Aid has been readily allocated for physical and social infrastructure but generally withheld from directly productive enterprises.

3. *Relations between donor institutions.* The basic premise is that the degree to which financial resources depart from market terms should be proportional to the market's inability to fulfill a given need. Because different types of aid flows carry different terms, the result is a kind of *institutionalized noncompetition* among aid agencies. The aid regime provides grounds for determining which aid source is the most appropriate for any given request, and it provides a rationale for avoiding interagency competition.

4. *The relationship between aid and broader development policies.* The operating presumptions discussed so far are articulated explicitly, but those governing the relationship between aid and broader development policies are often shrouded in ideological pronouncements about "partnership" and "international cooperation." There is some disagreement among donors about circumstances that justify conditioning aid on broader development policies and about the precise content of policies to be advocated. Nonetheless, we can identify a set of operating presumptions that provides a general basis for linking aid and consideration of the recipient's development policies and also provides specific means for disciplining the recipient. In the sanitized but revealing jargon of the development agencies, this phenomenon is known as *conditionality*.

5. *The relationship between aid and debt.* The entire system of external financing for the Third World rests on the accumulation and

servicing of debt. Hence, norms relating to repayment of debt occupy a special status in the aid regime. These norms specify the expected behavior of debtor countries and govern the response of aid donors to debt-servicing crises. They define the ultimate conditions of aid access, for a country violating these norms will find itself cut off from almost all forms of external financing.

Each of these five regime components includes principles, norms, rules, and procedures. An abbreviated summary is provided in Table 12, and each level is analyzed in more detail in the next section. There is, of course, less than total agreement among donors about the specifics of the regime, even if most agree on the basic principles. In addition, donors have changed their views over time about exactly how the basic principles should be put into practice. However, these changes represent what regime analysts call "norm-governed" change; the basic principles remain essentially unchanged.[18] Furthermore, although I believe these five regime aspects depict the core of the aid regime, they should be considered along with norms and principles that donors articulate but generally fail to implement and with rules and procedures that donors follow but do not articulate at the level of principle and norm. As noted before, these represent points of intersection with nonregime causal factors and points of contention among various donors. Some will be touched on in this chapter. Finally, although this is essentially a donor-imposed regime, the specific rules and procedures are in part a response to the pressures brought to bear by the Third World countries over the years. The regime does represent a compromise, even if it is one heavily weighted in favor of the donors.

Regime Boundaries

Before undertaking a detailed analysis of the components of the aid regime, we must more clearly specify its boundaries. How inclusive is the regime? Which sets of aid relationships are shaped by regime norms? Which are not?

TABLE 12   Summary of the International Regime of Economic Assistance

Subissue Area	Principles	Norms	Rules	Procedures
Negotiating framework	No LDC rights to aid. Aid granted at donor discretion. Aid is a matter between a single recipient and either single or multiple donors.	Decision to grant aid based on analysis of specific circumstances of recipient. Donor must have access to relevant information. Donor's interest extends through life of project.	LDC must make formal application through institutionally specified channels. Negotiations, but no appeal.	Donors establish procedures for application, appraisal, and implementation.
Identification of appropriate uses for aid	Public capital should not compete with private capital, either domestic or foreign.	Donors should be prepared to engage in strategic nonlending to encourage reliance on private capital.	LDC to provide evidence that private capital unavailable. Donor is prepared to check.	Formal mechanisms of liaison between aid agencies and private sector institutions. Lending guidelines—regional, country, and sectoral withholding.
Relations among donors	Degree to which aid departs from market terms proportional to inability of market to fulfill need.	Alternative potential donors to defer to donor prepared to provide aid at terms most approximating market's. Institutionalized noncompetition between donors.	LDC to check availability of less-concessional aid before applying for more-concessional aid. Donor is prepared to check.	Formal and informal liaison between donors. Cofinancing. Formal eligibility and graduation criteria.

Relation between aid and development policy	General interest of donor in recipient's policies is legitimate.	Degree of conditionality variable with type of aid.	Link between aid and policy to be justified on ostensibly technical and economic grounds. Conditionality preferably imposed by multilateral institutions.	Treaties, grant and loan agreements, and special agreements, such as standby agreements, apply conditionality at different levels.
Relations between aid and debt	Continued access to aid depends on fulfillment of debt obligations by recipient, to *both* official and private creditors. All adjustments require agreement of creditors.	In crises, MDBs and private creditors have first claim. Debt relief contingent on acceptance of external discipline.	Debt relief only at points of crisis. All creditors of given type must be involved. Aid contingent on debtor behavior.	Separate "clubs" of official and private creditors. Agreement with IMF commonly a prerequisite for further aid.

The organizational core of the aid regime consists of the World
Bank and USAID. As Guy Gran puts it:

> The World Bank is commonly viewed as the principal teacher of eco-
> nomic development in the world today. The U.S. bilateral agency, AID,
> directly backed by the power of the United States, produces the second
> most powerful lesson in global development education. Separately and
> together they largely determine the ideology and operational model of a
> host of UN and regional agencies. By subcontracting they mold or con-
> trol dozens of private groups and consulting firms.[19]

But shared norms about aid access go beyond these institutions to
include most bilateral, and practically all multilateral, institutions.
The existence of these shared norms testifies partly to shared ideology, partly to constraints built into the world economy, and partly
to negotiated agreement among donors and recipients.

First, there are the other advanced capitalist countries in the Development Assistance Committee. Although the DAC has not played
the active role some of its supporters hoped it would, shared membership in the DAC does represent a recognition of common interests
and common norms about aid allocation. Even the Swedish aid program, arguably the most unorthodox among the DAC programs, is
based on many shared norms and promotes at least in part similar
outcomes (for example, through the Small Industries Development
Organisation, which promotes joint ventures with Swedish private
companies).

Second, there are the other multilateral development banks
(MDBs). As we have seen, practically all of these have been closely
modeled on the World Bank and are similarly constrained by their
joint dependence on international capital markets and on subscriptions by donor governments. The African Development Bank was
the only regional bank to be structured originally in a genuinely alternative way, but a combination of suspicion in international capital
markets, disinterest of donor governments, and wrangling among
African countries themselves resulted in the failure of the bank to
play the innovative role hoped for by its founders and some observers. "The bank and its African member states have had to pay a high
price for their desire to do things in their own way, including, per-

haps, frustration of the desire itself."[20] A chastened and restructured African Development Bank has increased its rate of growth in recent years, but at the cost of its difference from the other MDBs.

Behind bilateral DAC donors and multilateral development banks, OPEC countries have been the third major source of aid since the mid 1970s. Their inclusion in the aid regime is more problematic, partly because relatively little is known about the substantial proportion of this aid, which is funneled through ministries of finance. Based on specific regional political-military interests, this aid probably is less constraining in its implications for development choices than aid allocated on the basis of regime norms; it is, however, available to only a few Middle Eastern countries. In contrast, project aid made available through OPEC bilateral and multilateral aid institutions is practically indistinguishable in its allocation process and sectoral content from DAC and MDB aid. A significant proportion is cofinanced with the World Bank and other MDBs, and OPEC donors have shown themselves ready to avail themselves of the same disciplinary mechanisms (for example, IMF standby agreements) in dealing with troubled aid recipients.[21] This type of OPEC aid appears to conform with regime norms.

Communist aid donors clearly do not subscribe to at least some of the regime norms outlined in this chapter. But as we have seen, communist aid has been very limited and for most Third World countries has not constituted a significant alternative to regime-governed aid flows.

There is, finally, the issue of financing from the International Monetary Fund. This financing is often not classified as aid because of its relatively hard terms (near-market interest rates and only medium-term maturities) and because of its stated purpose of temporary balance of payments financing, rather than long-term development. As noted earlier, Benjamin Cohen has identified a "balance of payments regime," with the IMF the main actor, separate from the "development assistance regime." He concludes, however:

> In fact, we are witnessing a partial convergence of the roles of the Fund and the Bank—that is, a partial overlapping of the regimes governing access to payments financing and development assistance. Here, in

the blurring of the jurisdictional boundary between these two regimes, is perhaps the most significant impact of the 1970s. In the 1980s it will be increasingly difficult to maintain a clear distinction between these two forms of lending.[22]

In my view, the distinction is no longer tenable. The claim that IMF financing, unlike aid, is not sufficiently concessional does not hold up if the aid regime is conceptualized, as it is here, as encompassing the whole range of official financial instruments; IMF terms are no worse than some export credits. Furthermore, because most borrowers come to the IMF only as a lender of last resort, when their access to alternative financing has been exhausted, IMF lending can be seen as highly concessional in comparison to the virtually usurious rates that would be necessary to pry further financing out of international capital markets. Beyond this, the distinction between balance of payments and development financing has been virtually wiped out by the World Bank's move into structural adjustment lending and the IMF's readiness to finance relatively long term (three-year) adjustment programs. Indeed, it is common today for the same set of policies and programs to be financed jointly by the IMF and the World Bank. Other aid is often also made contingent on agreement with the IMF. Thus, although the IMF is far from just another aid agency, its activities must be included in an analysis of the aid regime.

The next sections analyze the components of the aid regime in more detail. Although I attempt to separate out the different levels of principles, norms, rules, and procedures, these analytic distinctions overlap in practice. Nonetheless, they help us understand the coherence of the whole.

The Negotiating Framework: Bilateralism

Virtually all aid flows consist of negotiated transfers between single aid donors and single aid recipients, despite thirty years of Third World efforts to create an alternative framework.[23] The negotiating framework concentrates decision-making authority in the donor, separates aid negotiations from multilateral settings dealing with other international economic issues, and isolates the recipient. It may be summarized as follows:

Principles. LDCs have no automatic rights to or claims on concessional financial assistance. Aid is something "granted" to an aid-seeking nation or other entity at the discretion of the donor. Full decision-making authority about the allocation of aid belongs to the donor.

Norms. Donor decisions about the allocation of aid thus depend on analysis of particular situations, with considerations ranging from the potential recipient's general circumstances to the specific uses to which the aid will be put. It is the aid-seeking nation's responsibility to make available information relevant for making this decision. The donor's interest in aid extends through the life of the project; thus, continued access to relevant information is expected.

Rules. The LDC must formally apply for aid through the proper institutionally specified channels. In cases of limited disagreement, negotiations between donor and recipient may take place. However, the final decision is the donor's alone, and there are no provisions for appeal.

Procedures. Roughly comparable procedures for application, appraisal, and implementation exist among all the major donors. These procedures presuppose an active donor presence at all stages of the process.

In 1954, the Randall Commission on Foreign Economic Policy, appointed by President Eisenhower, disclaimed any obligation of the United States to provide aid in no uncertain terms: "Underdeveloped areas are claiming a right to economic aid from the United States. . . . We recognize no such right." [24] Although the language of aid diplomacy has softened since then, it is a fact of life for Third World countries that aid flows remain almost entirely at the discretion of the donors. The only area in which Third World countries have had any success in establishing a principle of automatic access to external financing has been compensatory financing for shortfalls in export earnings. However, such transfers have been small and not always automatic. The STABEX compensatory financing scheme with the European Economic Community, hailed by observers as "ground breaking," covers less than half of Third World countries and only a very limited range of their exports.[25] It is also inadequately funded. In 1981, it paid out only $160 million, despite the fact that lowered international demand and adverse movement in the volume and terms of trade cost the Third World about $40 billion (not including oil exports, which declined even more).[26] Compensatory financing from the IMF has been considerably greater—fluctuating between less than $1 billion and about $4 billion in fiscal years 1981 through 1985—but IMF compensatory financing carries greater conditionality and must be repaid, at a nonconcessional rate of interest, within a relatively short time.[27] To date, Third World attempts to ensure automatic access to external financing have met with little success.

The pervasive bilateralism of the aid regime separates aid negotiations from other issue areas and from arenas in which recipients can exercise a collective voice. The major donors maintain the separation despite obvious interconnections. For example, when Third World countries seek to reform the international monetary system to promote the transfers of real resources,

> the Group of 24 [representing Third World countries] encounters the strongly held conviction in the Group of 10 [representing the advanced capitalist countries] that it is not the role of the international monetary system to facilitate transfers of real resources. That function is rather the role of development financing in its various forms, and it is best to have a one-to-one matching of policy instrument and objective. Hence, the dialogue between the Group of 24 and the Group of 10 often takes the form of skirmishes at the border between monetary arrangements proper and development financing.[28]

Similarly, donors have insisted that issues of debt relief be negotiated entirely separately from issues of financing development.[29]

Where the Third World has been able to speak with a collective voice, as in the various UN organs, there is no effective control of aid transfers. The major aid institution in which recipients have a say, the United Nations Development Program (UNDP), is basically limited to research, technical assistance, and preinvestment surveys, often for projects to be picked up by the World Bank.[30] Despite Third World hopes, the UNDP has never been allowed to become a source of development capital. In the other multilateral organizations, such as the World Bank and the regional development banks, there are no institutional means by which underdeveloped countries can act in concert as recipients. Although Third World countries may be "members" of such organizations, the experience of applying for aid from them differs little from applying to the major bilateral aid agencies. In fact, the narrower range of lending criteria of the multilateral development banks may leave recipients with less bargaining power than they have with more diversely motivated bilateral aid donors.

There are almost no departures from the bilateral negotiating framework on the recipients' side. There exist no mechanisms to enforce compliance with Third World demands voiced in the relatively powerless United Nations General Assembly and the United Nations Conference on Trade and Development (UNCTAD). The only significant case to date in which a group of Third World nations has been able to negotiate collectively with donors and to link aid with other issue areas has been the Lomé Convention, negotiated between forty-six African, Caribbean, and Pacific (ACP) states and the European Economic Community (EEC) in 1974–75 and renegotiated in 1979 and again (now with sixty-four ACP states) in 1984.[31] These negotiations were unique in the degree to which aid questions were included in a package of international economic issues and in the multilateral nature of the negotiating process. Furthermore, the agreements broke down the distinction between trade and aid (for example, with the use of aid to compensate countries automatically for export price fluctuations) through the STABEX arrangements mentioned earlier. Nonetheless, the Lomé agreements limited the departure from bilateralism: the EEC identified which countries it was willing to negotiate with; a total aid figure was agreed upon, but decisions about its use remained firmly in the hands of the EEC countries; and ACP concessions in the areas of trade and investment were so great that a U.S. government study concluded:

> The arrangement includes a variety of aid provisions, but is fundamentally an economic deal which benefits the European Community as well as the Third World countries. In particular, the program is designed to provide long-term guaranteed EC access to ACP mineral and energy resources. The Lomé arrangements also provide a framework for European investment in Third World ventures which reinforce European access to Third World natural resources and markets.[32]

Studies of the effects of Lomé I and II have found little change in trading and aid relationships.[33]

Departures from a purely bilateral framework of aid occur mainly on the donor side, further isolating the recipient and enhancing the donors' capacity to act as a cartel. These departures take two main forms. The first, and most rapidly growing, is cofinancing. Cofinancing arrangements may link two aid agencies in a single project (for example, the World Bank and the Asian Development Bank), or they may link an aid agency with private capital. In 1982, the World Bank began negotiating agreements with bilateral and other multilateral agencies to provide set sums for future cofinancing, in effect, expanding the Bank's available capital.[34]

The second, and older, form of donor aggregation consists of coordinating groups that bring together a single recipient with its multiple donors. (There are no groups bringing together a single donor with its multiple recipients.) The first such group, the Aid-India Consortium, was established in 1958; there are currently about two dozen such groups, most of them chaired by the World Bank. Those coordinating groups that include consultation, study, *and* the pledging of aid are known as consortia; those that do not officially include aid pledging are known as consultative groups.[35] The average number of donor members of these groups is about ten. Donors have demonstrated a clear preference for consultative groups over consortia, probably because institutionalizing the pledging process may allow donors to be pressured to fill the recipient's annual budgetary gap.[36] Consortia and consultative groups create a united front of donors against the recipient and influence recipient policies.[37] But although donors have found it convenient to band together in such groups, they do not give control of their individual programs to the group as a whole.

Donors have effectively resisted proposed changes in the aid regime that would compromise their decision-making authority. First, the advanced capitalist donors have consistently opposed recipient-controlled institutions. As we have seen, the IBRD-controlled IDA was devised to offset demands for a UN fund that would have been largely under Third World control. Those institutions in which aid recipients do have a large say (for example, the UNDP and the African Development Bank) have been starved of capital funds.

Second, the dominant donors have been reluctant to share control of the major multilateral institutions, particularly the World Bank and the International Monetary Fund, even as these institutions came to rely on new sources of funds. The IMF in particular has sought to utilize OPEC countries' funds without expanding their voting power proportionately. Although the OPEC share of IMF votes was increased from 5 percent to 10 percent in 1978 and 11.6 percent in 1983, this is far less than the increased significance of OPEC financing would warrant. Similarly, during the Lomé negotiations, the EEC countries successfully resisted Nigeria's attempt, as a relatively oil-rich country, to join the ranks of the donors in decision making. South Korea's recent bid to join the OECD did not succeed either.

In sum, the bilateral negotiating framework of the aid regime concentrates decision-making power in the hands of donors with relatively few constraints. Whether that power is translated into effective and consistent intervention in recipient societies depends on the aid regime's definition of a consistent program, coordination of donors' activities so that the actions of some do not undermine those of others, and establishment of mechanisms to link aid with processes of societal change. These tasks are the function of the four other core components of the aid regime.

Identification of Appropriate Uses: Strategic Nonlending

A donor's decision to provide aid generally entails approval of both the recipient country and the particular use to which the aid will be put. Most studies of aid allocation have focused exclusively on the distribution of aid, and they have failed to find a consistent rationale. The observable patterns that do exist, such as the bias in favor of small countries and against large ones, generally result from ad hoc considerations rather than from a coherent set of principles and norms.[38]

Much stronger regime norms exist for the specific uses to which aid may be put within countries. From its origins in the early postwar period, foreign aid from the United States and the multilateral institutions, and later from other DAC members, has been administered so as *not* to compete with private investment or lending. At the beginning of the U.S. aid program, Secretary of State Acheson stated the policy that virtually all aid agencies have faithfully followed: "In providing assistance for economic development, it would be contrary to our traditions to place our government's public funds in direct and wasteful competition with private funds. Therefore, it will be our policy, in general, not to extend loans of public funds for projects for which private capital is available."[39] The current head of USAID and the U.S. International Development Cooperation Administration, like virtually all his predecessors, has reiterated this basic stance: "We must be careful here to *facilitate* business involvement and not to *substitute* for private capital."[40] The basic principle has also been set forth time and again by the heads of other DAC agencies and by the major multilateral institutions. Thus foreign aid almost never represents a policy alternative to private investment or borrowing, but rather is a recourse when all else fails.

David Baldwin's observation that the World Bank "exists to drum up business for its competition, the private investors," applies to most agencies.[41] The key technique, as Baldwin pointed out years ago in a path-breaking analysis, is "strategic nonlending."[42] On the one hand, an aid institution will refuse to finance a project for which private investors or lenders can be found, thus forcing the aid-seeking government to accept the terms of the private investors or lenders or else go without external financing. On the other hand, aid organizations may withhold aid even from projects for which private investors cannot be found in order to influence government policy to foster a more satisfactory "investment climate." In both cases, the function of strategic nonlending is to maximize the role of the private sector and to open it to foreign penetration.

This policy of avoiding competition with the private sector is written into the statutes of USAID and a number of the other major bilateral aid agencies. It is similarly part of the constitutions of each part of the World Bank Group, as well as the African, Asian, Caribbean, and Inter-American Development Banks.[43] Aid agencies are prepared to approach private banks and investors on their own to ensure that the loans they are considering cannot be privately financed.[44] The fact that in most instances private capital will be foreign capital is considered irrelevant; it does not justify the use of aid as an alternative.

The way the aid regime governs the identification of appropriate situations for concessional flows can be summarized as follows:

Principles. Public capital should not compete with private capital, either domestic or foreign. Public capital should supplement and facilitate the utilization of private capital.

Norms. Donors and recipients should ensure that official capital complements private capital. Donors should be prepared to engage in strategic nonlending—the selective withholding of aid to encourage the maximum utilization of private capital.

Rules. The recipient should demonstrate that private capital is unavailable for the proposed use of aid. The donor should be prepared, if any doubt exists, to check independently with private institutions to make sure that private financing is unavailable.

Procedures. Established forms of liaison with private institutions make for de facto vetoes by the private sector. Implicit or explicit lending guidelines implement the norm of strategic nonlending, designating regions, countries, or sectors considered off limits because of the assumed availability of private capital.

Application of the norm of strategic nonlending has varied over time. There have been three major forms. The first is *regional withholding*. During most of the 1950s, the United States argued that Latin America's development needs could be met by private capital, and therefore capital assistance was almost completely denied Latin American countries. The United States even opposed proposals for a Latin American development bank modeled on the World Bank on the grounds that private capital was available and equal to the task. This strategy of regional withholding of aid broke down in the wake of Vice-President Nixon's tumultuous tour of Latin America in 1958 and, more important, the Cuban Revolution, which resulted in the expropriation of $1.4 billion in U.S. private investment. Private investment in Latin America had been considered so safe that none of the expropriated enterprises in Cuba had been insured under the U.S. government's investment insurance program.

The second is *country withholding*. Although regions are no longer excluded from aid, specific countries may be—when they are perceived as achieving a degree of creditworthiness that allows them to satisfy their external financing needs on private capital markets. This practice has been formalized in the practice of "graduation" from aid. Such graduation transforms the possibility of tapping private sources of financing into a necessity.

The third form is *sectoral withholding*. Most ballyhooed cases of graduation have in fact entailed passing from more-concessional aid flows to less-concessional aid flows. Only a handful of Third World countries have been graduated from the aid system altogether. Hence, the most important form that strategic nonlending takes today is sectoral withholding, in which donors "reserve" certain sectors for private capital and systematically withhold aid from them. Such lending as does occur in these sectors is generally tied to the expansion of private enterprise. A variant of this is intrasectoral withholding. For example, aid may be provided for government investment in the riskier and less profitable "upstream" operations of an industrial sector but withheld from the more profitable "downstream" subsectors in order to facilitate the entry of private firms.[45]

Throughout the history of the aid regime, the sectors that have been identified as potentially the most attractive for private investors and therefore denied aid most consistently have been mining and manufacturing. Aid has been used primarily to create the physical and social conditions for private investment in these sectors, to create what is generally known as infrastructure.

A 1982 U.S. Treasury Department study has classified all 1980 loans of the major multilateral development banks in terms of whether the activity financed would have been in the private sector in the United States. On this basis, only 8.2 percent of IBRD/IDA lending, 5.6 percent of Inter-American Development Bank lending, and 5.8 percent of Asian Development Bank lending were "competitive" with the private sector as it is defined in the United States. In terms of sectoral allocation, the report concluded: "The MDB sector allocation process should be based upon the economic or social priorities of the borrower government—but only to the extent that their priorities are consistent with the basic economic principles of the MDBs."[46]

A primary goal of sectoral withholding has been to prevent state ownership of the means of production. To the extent that this goal is achieved, it forces the state to be both politically and financially dependent on processes of private capital accumulation—to occupy a structural position defining it as a "capitalist state."[47]

Relations Among Donors: Institutionalized Noncompetition

Aid-seeking governments today face an array of agencies that at first seem rather bewildering. A few, particularly some of the UN agencies, have specialized functions, such as refugee assistance, that define their role in the system. What distinguishes the others—or sometimes different programs within them—is the hardness or softness of the terms they offer on their aid, in other words, the degree to which their aid departs from market terms. The different bilateral and multilateral types of aid with their various terms form a financial spectrum, as summarized in Table 13.

Closest to market terms, on the left side of Table 13, are agencies that make unguaranteed loans at near-market terms to, or equity investments in, private or joint public-private enterprises. The World Bank affiliate, the International Finance Corporation, is the dominant institution of this type. The Inter-American Development Bank has had a small equity investment program as well, which it is moving to expand; the Asian Development Bank has also begun to make equity investments. Next closest to market terms are government export credits, sometimes financed directly by government loans but more often financed indirectly through government insurance schemes. Although official export credits carry an interest rate close to that of the multilateral development banks, their overall terms are usually considerably harder, due to shorter grace periods and maturities and to aid tying. The hard-loan windows of the multilateral development banks occupy an intermediate position on the financial spectrum. Their loans do not generally qualify as ODA, but they carry softer terms than recipient countries could generally obtain on capital markets. Low-interest loans from most bilateral aid agencies and from the soft-loan windows of the regional development banks easily meet the ODA standard, as do the loans of the MDB soft-loan windows, which carry only a service charge. Finally, furthest from market terms are grants, mostly from bilateral agencies and the United Nations. Technical assistance makes up a large proportion of grant aid.

Assuming a natural desire to avoid the accumulation of debt, we might expect aid-seeking governments to approach those agencies offering grants first and then reluctantly to move across the financial spectrum to agencies offering harder terms. In fact, the opposite is

TABLE 13   The Financial Spectrum of Official Aid Institutions

	Overall Terms of Aid					
	Harder Terms · Softer Terms					
Terms of aid	Equity investments/loans to private sector	Official export credits	Medium-interest loans	Low-interest loans	No-interest loans	Grants
Typical terms	Market rates of return expected. Joint enterprises common. No government guarantee.	Tied aid; near-market interest rates. Medium maturities.	Intermediate interest rates; mostly untied. Medium- to long-term maturities. Govt. guarantee usually required.	Low interest; mostly tied. Long-term maturities, grace periods. Govt. guarantee required.	Service charge only; untied. Long-term maturities, grace periods. Govt. guarantee required.	No repayment. Amount often inflated by cost of technical assistance.
Major institutional sources	International Finance Corp. Special programs of regional MDBs.	Bilateral export-promotion agencies.	IBRD; regional MDBs.	Bilateral aid agencies; soft-loan windows of regional MDBs.	IDA; some bilateral aid agencies.	United Nations; bilateral aid agencies; European Dev. Fund.
Average interest rates, 1980		6.8% (DAC official export credits)	6.6% (MDBs)	1.9% (DAC ODA)	0.75% (IDA)	None

SOURCE: Interest rates from Organization for Economic Cooperation and Development, *Development Co-operation: Efforts and Policies of the Members of the Development Assistance Committee, 1981 Review* (Paris, 1981), p. 70.

supposed to happen. The aid agencies operate with a set of common assumptions that direct the potential recipient to go first to the *least* competitive source of aid (and this, as we have seen, only after private financing has been found unavailable) and to approach the sources with easier terms only as those with harder ones express their lack of interest. Just as the aid system as a whole comes into play only when private capital is unwilling to do the job, so aid agencies with softer terms are supposed to make their aid available only when aid agencies with harder ones have expressed their unwillingness to do so. The aid-seeking government is thus offered the form of aid that comes as close to market terms as the profitability of the proposed use of aid and the creditworthiness of the country allow.

The basic regime norm governing interdonor relations may be summed up as *institutionalized noncompetition*. Each agency offers the hardest terms deemed justifiable by a particular proposal and is prepared to defer to any agency offering still harder terms. At times, this system has been institutionalized in a formal way. When the Development Loan Fund (DLF, the forerunner of AID development loans) was established in 1957, for example, its legislative mandate insisted that it "be administered so as not to compete with private investment capital, the Export-Import bank, or the International Bank for Reconstruction or Development"—all of which, it may be noted, offered harder terms than the DLF.[48] Similarly, AID and the U.S. Export-Import Bank have an interdepartmental loan committee and a staff liaison group to "ensure that Eximbank has first refusal on any loan application to the United States Government and that A.I.D. does not extend a loan which Eximbank might be willing to finance."[49] Again, the bank's terms are considerably harder than AID's. Similar institutional arrangements are found in the programs of other DAC members. This regime component can be summarized as follows:

> *Principles.* The degree to which aid flows depart from market terms should be proportional to the inability of the market to fulfill a given need. Concessionality depends both on the recipi-

ent's general creditworthiness and on the specific uses to which aid will be put.

Norms. Alternative potential donors should defer to the donor prepared to provide aid at terms most approximating those of the market. Relations between donors should be characterized by institutionalized noncompetition.

Rules. Aid-seeking governments should check out the availability of less-concessional alternatives before applying for more-concessional ones. Donors should make sure, if there is doubt, that aid with terms more closely approximating the market's is not available.

Procedures. A variety of forms of liaison enables donors to share information about aid requests and determine the availability of alternative sources of financing. Cofinancing arrangements may allow donors to vary the degree of concessionality for different parts of large-scale integrated projects. Recipient access to the most concessional types of financing may be limited by statute. Countries reaching a certain stage of per capita income or creditworthiness may be formally "graduated" into ineligibility.

The regime norm of institutionalized noncompetition provides interdonor coordination without formal coordinating mechanisms. The coordination limits as much as possible the systemwide cost of financing concessional transfers to underdeveloped countries. Other motivations may intervene, however, to make individual donors willing to shoulder extra costs. A major such motivation is export promotion. Donors' desire to secure markets for their exporters may compromise the previously outlined regime norms and allow Third World countries to bargain for better terms than regime norms would normally allow. Most interdonor competition, however, appears within delimited ranges of the aid spectrum rather than widely across it. It thus involves parallel institutions: export banks bidding against each other, MDBs competing to be part of an attractive project, and so forth. In order to avoid mutual damage, donors have on occasion formally limited competition among themselves. For example, the advanced capitalist countries since 1978 have set minimum interest rates and maximum maturities for government-supported medium- and long-term export credits. Minimum interest rates for five- to eight-and-a-half-year credits under the agreement in 1983 were 10 percent for "relatively poor" countries and 11.35 percent for "intermediate countries." [50]

Cofinancing, involving a mix of loans with different terms, allows aid institutions to vary the overall terms of aid more than has been the case so far—particularly for institutions, like the IBRD and IDA, that have traditionally lent at the same rate to all borrowers. In fact, World Bank participation in commercial loans, which began in 1983, has been criticized by potential recipients as "graduation in disguise":

> They fear the bank could make future loans contingent on cofinancing and at the same time decrease its participation. This would provide the commercial bankers with the muscle of the World Bank in terms of conditionality and strictness of repayment schedules, but would bar the borrowers from the benefits of the World Bank loans—essentially lower costs, longer maturities, and grace periods. [51]

The first of these cofinanced loans, syndicated in Japan and made to Thailand, appears to augur a new component in the financing spectrum, with terms in between those of the multilateral development banks and the commercial banks, but providing commercial partners, in the words of the World Bank, "with more security through closer association with the World Bank." [52]

Aid and Development Policy: Conditionality

Access to aid is generally conditioned on policy measures. To the extent that policies are narrowly military or political, reflecting the interests of individual donors (for example, willingness to host military bases, readiness to vote a certain way in the United Nations, ability to offer diplomatic support for donor foreign-policy goals), these linkages between aid and policy are not of major interest here. They tend to be negotiated on an ad hoc basis, donor by donor, and do not generally reflect overall regime norms. Nor is the issue here the many subtle ways in which aid agencies may indirectly influence development policies through the role of local representatives, research and publications, training sessions, and the like. Rather, this section deals with regime norms that explicitly condition access to aid on general policies shaping the nature of the development process.

Three levels of conditionality may be distinguished. First, there are conditions that govern access to any aid from a given donor. To receive aid from any of the institutions of the World Bank Group, for example, a country must accept the obligations involved in being a member of the IMF. To receive U.S. aid, a country must generally agree to accept investments under the investment guarantee programs of the U.S. government. A few countries have balked at this level of conditionality—Mozambique refused to join the IMF until 1984, for example—but they have had to forego certain types of aid as a result.

A second level of conditionality concerns project-related policies of the recipient country. Because all sorts of government policies may have some kind of impact on an aid-financed project, there may be contention over what policies are appropriately included here. An important example of this kind of conditionality has been the World Bank's insistence that consumers of public utilities bear the full cost of the services they receive. In other words, these services are not to be subsidized by society as a whole. Although this principle has traditionally applied primarily to electricity and running water, a recent article in a joint World Bank/IMF magazine seeks to extend it:

> The World Bank has emphasized that reliance on user charges should be extended from the traditional sectors of power, water, and transport to irrigation, agricultural credit, and urban sites and services schemes. Even in such social sectors as health and education, a modest reduction in the subsidy for some services may be appropriate.[53]

This type of conditionality is often subject to long and hard bargaining with officials of the relevant ministries. If bargaining results in eventual agreement, the outcome is formalized in a legal agreement with the government. In the case of the IBRD and IDA, these loan agreements are published as United Nations treaties.

The third level of conditionality is often shrouded in secrecy and obscured by high-sounding euphemism. It involves the linkage between aid and national development policies (for example, government credit policies, protectionism, state investment policies, constraints on foreign investment, and so forth). As we have seen, the use of aid to influence broad national economic policies goes back to the Marshall Plan. A shift to project lending in the 1950s diluted the focus on policy, although during this time the IMF was evolving its distinctive set of prescriptions. In the 1960s, AID led the way in reasserting the primary importance of aid's contribution to general development policy, rather than to specific projects. In a series of papers in the mid 1960s, AID officials worked out a basic rationale:

> In the long run, aid's "influence potential" is much more important than its resource contribution. This is true for two reasons. Total aid from all sources has probably contributed roughly 20 percent of total investment in the developing countries in the past few years. The use made of the remaining 80 percent is clearly much more important in accelerating growth than is the use of aid alone. Furthermore, policies and procedures—import licensing arrangements, investment codes, marketing board pricing policies, power and transportation rate structure, tax provisions, to name only a few—affect economic development at least as powerfully as the presence or absence of adequate infrastructure or technical skills. Successful efforts to influence macro-economic and sectoral policies are likely to have a greater impact on growth than the added capital and skills financed by aid.[54]

The recent decline in AID's development lending, combined with the reorientation of the U.S. nonsecurity aid program toward technical assistance, has reduced AID's ability to exercise overall policy leverage. Other DAC countries have taken up the slack, to some extent, by imitating AID-pioneered organizational structures and techniques such as country programming. In addition, the World Bank's gradual move into nonproject lending, initiated in 1971 and reformulated as "structural adjustment" lending in 1980, reflects and betokens an increasing Bank role at this level. In words echoing the AID rationale previously quoted, the U.S. Treasury Department study of multilateral development banks mentioned earlier states:

> This philosophical orientation requires that U.S. policy seek greater emphasis upon the MDB financial role as catalysts for private flows (the "banking" function) and their advisory role as sponsors of appropriate policies—as distinct from their significance as sources of official capital transfers. We should also emphasize the broader development role of these institutions, which lies primarily in the area of encouraging the most effective economic policies, including greater LDC reliance on market forces.[55]

The main agent of conditionality, however, is the International Monetary Fund. The Treasury report also notes:

> It was observed that the collaboration of other donors and the IMF is particularly important when it comes to influencing macro-level policy. Thus, structural adjustment loans are usually approved only when the borrower has negotiated an Extended Fund Facility agreement with the IMF, a factor which is producing increasingly close Bank/Fund collaboration. Without the added weight and broader focus achieved through collaboration with other donors, the Bank's leverage over macro-level policy is limited.[56]

Any summary of regime principles, norms, rules, and procedures governing the relationship between aid and development policies must be particularly tentative. Other foreign policy objectives may compromise the relationship. There are limited but real differences in philosophy among the aid agencies. Overall, regime norms provide justification and specification of the connection rather than a precise definition of the policies to be advocated.

Principles. Donors have an interest in the broad policy context in the recipient country both because of the always present possibility of fungibility and because the development process depends more on national development policies than on marginal increments of capital or technical assistance.

Norms. The degree to which aid is properly linked to policy conditions depends on the degree to which the uses of aid are affected by those conditions. In general, conditionality may be expected to increase as one moves from project to sector to program to structural adjustment and balance of payments assistance.

Rules. The link between aid and policy is always made on ostensibly technical and economic grounds. Such a seemingly apolitical stance is generally most effectively taken by multilateral institutions, particularly the IMF and the World Bank.

Procedures. Different procedures apply conditionality at different levels. At the entry level, conditions are defined in treaties. At the project level, they take form in loan agreements. At the national policy level, the most common forms are standby agreements with the IMF and "memoranda of understanding" with the World Bank. These commit the recipient to carrying out a package of policies hammered out in prior negotiations.

The shift in the locus of conditionality from bilateral agencies to the multilateral development banks and to the International Monetary Fund has carried implications about both the level and the content of conditionality. Although the IMF's *Articles of Agreement* "give no express guidance on what policies the Fund should encourage members to follow under its policies of conditionality" and make no mention whatsoever of standby agreements, the IMF has over the years moved steadily in the direction of more stringent conditionality.[57] Through the first amendment, the dominant members have denied the Fund the right to create any new unconditional (or more accurately, low-conditional) facilities besides the existing reserve, or gold, tranche policy.[58] New facilities established in the 1960s carried moderate levels of conditionality, but the major new facilities in the 1970s—the extended and supplementary financing facilities and the enlarged access policy—have all carried high levels of conditionality. The various types of IMF lending and their degrees of conditionality are listed in Table 14. Access levels in Table 14 are those in effect before the 1983 quota increase. Subsequent changes will be discussed in Chapter 7.

The point at which increasing levels of IMF conditionality become operative depends on a country's quota. Quotas of Third World countries vary greatly—from $3.2 million for the Seychelles to $2.4 billion for India. Although borrowers must state that their need for financing is consistent with IMF purposes, the IMF cannot challenge a member's access to resources equivalent to 25 percent of its quota. This first drawing is known as the gold, or reserve, tranche. Access to the next 25 percent carries moderate conditionality, and further access carries high conditionality.

As a proportion of member country imports, IMF quotas have declined from 13 percent in 1950 to around 4 percent at the end of 1980.[59] The 1983 quotas increase of 47.5 percent will not raise this proportion above 6 percent. Furthermore, the United States was successful in pressuring the Fund to lower access to Fund resources in 1983, 1984, and 1985. Use of high-conditionality resources has been ensured by the technique of increasing the percentage of a member's quota that it can borrow against, rather than increasing quotas proportionately as the need for IMF resources has grown. As Sydney Dell points out:

> The effect of this is that, of the cumulative 600 percent of quota available to members for drawings, only 25 percent is provided at low (first-credit-tranche) conditionality; whereas if quotas had been increased six-fold, which would have been the normal way of proceeding, first-credit-tranche conditionality would have applied to the equivalent of 150 percent of current quotas.[60]

The aid regime's centralization of policy conditionality in the hands of the IMF and the World Bank carries definite implications for the content of that conditionality. Despite IMF claims to take a flexible approach and to "pay due regard to the domestic social and political objectives" and "economic priorities"[61] of its members, it is evident from both Fund statements and from case studies that IMF policy prescriptions and performance criteria vary little among individual cases.[62] The elevation of balance of payments adjustment to a level of priority accorded to no other objectives predetermines the general thrust of its prescriptions, as does the way the IMF chooses

TABLE 14   Policies and Facilities of the International Monetary Fund
(before 1983 quota increase)

Policy/Facility	Eligibility
Reserve tranche	All members. Statement of balance of payments need.
Credit tranches	All members. Approved program to solve balance of payments problems.
Compensatory financing facility (est. 1963)	All members. Support short-term program to deal with temporary and exogenously induced export shortfalls. (Cereal imports covered since 1981.)
Buffer stock facility (est. 1969)	All members. Support efforts to stabilize export prices through approved buffer stock arrangements.
Oil facility (1974)	All members with balance of payments problems due to increased oil prices.
Oil facility (1975)	UN-defined "Most Seriously Affected Nations" (MSAs) plus designated others.
Trust fund (1976–81)	Members below defined income level with approved balance of payments programs.
Extended fund facility (est. 1974)	All members. Support programs to overcome structural obstacles to balance of payments.
Supplementary financing facility (1979–82)	All members. Long-term approved program requiring greater resources than available under credit tranche and extended facility.
Enlarged access policy (est. 1981)	All members. Large long-term need relative to quota with approved long-term program.

NOTE: There also existed an oil facility subsidy account between 1975 and 1983 to subsidize interest on oil facility drawings, and there exists a supplementary financing facility subsidy account (established in 1980) to subsidize interest on drawings from the SFF. Disbursements on previous SFF commitments were still being made in fiscal year 1984. Details on postquota increase access policies are provided in Chapter 7.

Continued on next page

TABLE 14—*continued*

Resources Available	Level of Conditionality
100% of reserve tranche	Low
100% of quota in four 25% tranches	Moderate for first, high for upper tranches
100% of quota	Moderate
50% of quota	Moderate
75% of quota or amount of price increase	Moderate
125% of quota or 85% of price increase	Moderate
Loans with low interest rates	Moderate
140% of quota	High (same as upper credit tranches, but wider range of policies covered)
Up to 140% of quota	High
Up to 450% of quota over three years	High

to define and classify accounting categories.[63] As one IMF official admits:

> In fact, the determination of balance of payments surplus or deficit is far from being a fully objective exercise. It has the clearly normative aspect of providing a guide for economic policy.[64]

The same point has been made more generally with respect to project evaluation, particularly the determination of rates of return. Seemingly technical concepts of shadow pricing, opportunity costs of capital, discount rates, and so forth all reflect normative judgments and connote specific policy preferences.[65]

Aid and Debt: Creditworthiness

Norms dealing with debt occupy a special status in the aid regime because the entire system of external financing rests on the accumulation and servicing of debt. Norms in this area are not only well defined but also mark the boundaries of the regime: a country flagrantly violating these norms will find itself cut off from almost all sources of external financing.

The relationship between aid and debt is close for several reasons. First, most aid flows create debt. In 1980, of the $43.7 billion net flows from official sources, 50.5 percent were loans and 49.5 percent were grants or loans repayable in local currency. Among the loans, about half met the ODA level of concessionality, and about half did not.[66] Between 1980 and 1982, public debt to official sources grew by over $40 billion. Second, the normal functioning of the aid regime encourages debt through the withholding of aid where financing is available from private sources.

A result of the upsurge of private bank lending has been the steady shrinking of the proportion of total flows, both public and private, taking the form of grants. Table 15 shows the changing balance between grants and loans for most external flows (excluding technical assistance) between 1965 and 1983. The change is striking: a decline from a high of 36.6 percent in grants in 1965 to a low of 6.4 percent in 1979, with an erratic rise to 8.8 percent in 1983. The corollary to this has been the massive expansion of Third World debt, which is detailed in Table 16. The data are from the World Bank and do not include either debt with maturities of less than one year or non-guaranteed private sector debt, both of which are sizeable in some countries.[67] Medium- and long-term public debt of Third World countries increased from $75.1 billion in 1970 to $634.4 billion in 1983. The structure of that debt also changed in a way increasing the

TABLE 15   Grants and Loans as Percentage of Total External Resource
Flows to LDCs, 1965–83 (disbursements)

Year	Grants[a]	Loans
1965	36.6	64.4
1966	33.3	66.7
1967	27.5	72.5
1968	24.4	75.6
1969	24.2	75.8
1970	20.7	79.3
1971	18.1	81.9
1972	19.1	80.9
1973	8.5	91.5
1974	8.4	91.6
1975	8.8	91.2
1976	6.9	93.1
1977	6.6	93.4
1978	6.9	93.1
1979	6.4	93.6
1980	8.6	91.4
1981	7.9	92.1
1982	7.7	92.3
1983	8.8	91.2

SOURCE: World Bank, *Annual Reports*, 1974, p. 92; 1975, p. 97; 1981, p. 142; 1982, p. 142; 1983, p. 150; 1984, p. 162; 1985, p. 186.
[a] DAC bilateral and multilateral only. Excludes grants for technical assistance.

burden of debt servicing: the share of public debt to private creditors increased from 30.1 percent to 51.1 percent between 1970 and 1983.

In a situation of rising debt service on past aid, gross aid flows must rise faster than debt service for there to be any increase in net aid flows. But what induces governments to keep up the payments on past aid in the absence of any international sovereign authority? Charles Lipson has provided an excellent analysis of what he calls the "international organization of Third World debt," focusing particularly on the sanctions available to private creditors.[68] Although I draw on Lipson's analysis, my focus is limited to how access to continued

TABLE 16 Medium- and Long-Term External Public Debt Outstanding (Including Undisbursed), 1970–83 ($ billions)

Type of Creditor	1970	1971	1972	1973	1974	1975	1976	1977	1978	1979	1980	1981	1982	1983
Bilateral official	38.6	44.9	51.1	54.8	67.3	75.6	85.6	100.0	119.6	129.5	148.3	153.9	158.5	166.8
Multilateral	13.9	16.6	20.0	23.7	30.0	37.1	43.9	55.2	68.6	82.2	98.9	114.2	130.0	143.3
Private	22.6	27.2	32.1	40.9	58.1	75.0	93.5	120.9	159.9	197.4	218.6	253.2	281.0	324.3
Total	75.1	88.7	103.2	119.4	155.4	187.7	233.0	276.1	348.1	409.1	465.8	521.3	569.5	634.4

SOURCE: World Bank, *Annual Reports*, 1978, p. 123; 1984, pp. 152–153; 1985, p. 177.

aid is governed by regime norms relating to debt. This basic regime component may be summarized as follows:

Principles. Continued access to aid (both loans and grants) depends on the fulfillment of debt obligations, to *both* official and private creditors, by the recipient. All adjustments in debt servicing require the agreement of creditors.

Norms. In times of debt-servicing difficulties, a debtor country must demonstrate its continued *creditworthiness*, both to maintain access to aid and to reschedule debt payments. Debt service to the MDBs and the IMF has priority; default on multilateral debt would block both new aid and rescheduling. Parity is claimed between official bilateral debt and debt to private financial institutions, but in reality, the consequences of defaulting on commercial bank debt are likely to be more severe than defaulting on official bilateral debt. Debt arising from suppliers' credits has lowest priority. Borrowers seeking debt relief must exert themselves to keep up interest payments and must be prepared to submit to some form of discipline, to be monitored externally.

Rules. Creditors will meet to consider debt relief only when a crisis point has been reached, and generally they will negotiate only over that portion of the debt that is currently due. The debtor must meet with all creditors of a given type (official or private) collectively and reach an agreement with them as a group. Aid will generally be cut off in cases of debt repudiation or outright default, but as long as interest payments are kept up and good-faith negotiations are taking place, aid will generally not be withheld.

Procedures. Creditors negotiate collectively with recipients in informal but routinized meetings known as clubs. (Official creditors meet as the Paris Club, private creditors as either the London Club or the New York Club.) Official creditors will generally offer rescheduling, private creditors, a combination of refinancing and rescheduling. Both clubs commonly insist on the debtor reaching agreement on policy changes and performance measures with the IMF. Continued aid is generally made contingent on such agreement.

The measure of the effectiveness of regime norms about debt is that Cuba and North Korea constitute the only cases of outright repudiation of public debt in the Third World in the past thirty years. Even Iran after the shah and Nicaragua after Somoza formally stated that they would honor the debts of the prerevolutionary governments. There have been almost no outright defaults, either. In most circumstances, regime norms allow debtors to avoid formal default at the last minute through rescheduling and refinancing negotiations because both creditors and debtors generally have an interest in avoiding the consequences of default. The rule that creditors will agree to meet only when a crisis is at hand keeps up the pressure until the last minute, but once creditors agree to meet, it becomes a moot point whether default has actually occurred. Mexico in 1982 is a case in point.

Although the number of reschedulings has been rising in recent years, in no instance has debt been wiped off the books. Debt relief of this kind (known in aid circles as retroactive terms adjustment) has been strictly a unilateral matter, separate from the Paris and London clubs.[69] The exception that proves the rule is Indonesia after the military seizure of power in 1965. When the new pro-Western military government turned to the West for aid, Indonesia's new creditors, meeting in the Paris Club, supported the postponement of debt service on debts incurred during the Sukarno era—debts that were owed, conveniently, primarily to communist countries. In 1970, the Paris Club worked out an unprecedented and unique agreement allowing Indonesia to pay its pre-Sukarno debts on extremely generous terms that amounted to a cancellation of part of its debt. The generosity was based on a desire to cement the new relationship between Indonesia and the advanced capitalist countries and a willingness to override the sanctity of contracts in a situation where the debt was owed primarily to non–Paris Club countries. As one World Bank economist concluded:

> The Paris Club, which had previously pursued a relatively cautious and basically commercial approach, displayed a flexible and imaginative attitude in dealing with Indonesia. . . . Ironically, the very large debt owed

to the socialist bloc facilitated the liberal treatment by Western creditors who were concerned that otherwise, their newly-resumed aid programmes would in effect help to pay off Indonesia's heavy indebtedness to the socialist bloc which had discontinued lending after Sukarno's downfall. Thus, the Paris Club credits required Indonesia to supply the agreed-upon terms of all creditors, including those outside of the Paris Club. This condition was a key requirement.[70]

Apart from the circumstances associated with switching blocs, such generosity is unavailable from the aid donors.

The IMF and the multilateral banks have claimed for themselves a special creditor status: debt service to them is to have top priority, and their debt is not open to renegotiation. To date, the multilateral institutions have successfully upheld their claim; no country has repudiated or defaulted on multilateral debt, and no multilateral debt has been renegotiated. In the debt renegotiations of the 1960s and 1970s, the rescheduling of official bilateral debt sometimes enabled debtor countries to maintain debt service not only on their multilateral debt but on their debt to private creditors as well. In such cases, David Gisselquist argues, creditor governments "took a dive so that private creditors could continue to collect."[71] Citibank's Irving Friedman has said that banks lent money to the Third World on the assumption that their claims would be honored before those of other creditors.[72]

Regime norms linking aid to the servicing of debt to private collectors are sometimes formalized. The World Bank has stated that its articles of agreement give it "a direct interest in the creation and maintenance of satisfactory relations between member countries and their external creditors" and that "accordingly, the normal practice is to inform governments who are involved in such disputes that the Bank or IDA will not assist them unless and until they make appropriate efforts to reach a fair and equitable settlement."[73]

Regime norms safeguarding the position of private creditors are not unproblematic, however. For one thing, public perception of aid agencies as standing ready to bail out private investors can damage the agencies' jealously guarded image of organizational integrity and hurt them politically in terms of future replenishments and quota increases. For example, both liberals and conservatives took a stand against "bailing out the banks" through the IMF quota increase in 1983. Since 1978, the United States has had an official policy that U.S. participation in official debt renegotiation is contingent on the debtor country making "all reasonable efforts to reorganize unguaranteed private credits falling due in the period of the reorganization on terms comparable to those covering government or government-guaranteed credits."[74] In reality, however, this principle of comparable treatment has been interpreted very loosely. In the renegotiations of Turkey's debt to official and private creditors in 1978 and 1979, for example, public creditors rescheduled interest payments while private creditors continued to collect them. In addition, private creditors regularly assess front-end refinancing fees.[75] The disparity between the terms of rescheduled private and official bilateral debt increased in the debt renegotiations in 1982–84.

The ability to manipulate debt to official creditors to safeguard debt to private creditors has also been undermined by the changing structure of official debt. As Table 16 shows, bilateral official debt declined from 51.4 percent of total public debt in 1970 to 26.3 percent in 1983. Debt servicing to private creditors dwarfs debt servicing on bilateral ODA: $58.6 billion compared to $2.9 billion in 1982.[76] Even among the countries the World Bank classified as "low income," debt service to private creditors was the largest single category of debt service for almost half in 1982. Norms established in earlier years were insufficient to deal with the new structure of debt that lay at the basis of the debt crisis of the early 1980s.

In some ways, the increased role of private external financing represents the fulfillment of long-sought regime goals. Regime norms played a role in encouraging many Third World countries to turn to private capital markets in the 1970s. But as we shall see in subsequent chapters, the major aid institutions in the late 1970s began to express misgivings about the way the shift to private financing had taken place. The World Bank in particular repeatedly warned of the danger of "graduating" countries too quickly because of lack of aid resources or because of too easy access to commercial financing.[77] The donors have been compelled to uphold regime norms about debt, but these have increasingly come to threaten the achievement of other regime goals.

4

Sectoral Allocation and the Management of Industrial Investment

Aid regime norms shape the sectoral alloca-
tion of aid, which in turn has important implications for the development options of aid recipients. Regime norms furthermore provide
the framework within which allocation decisions are made within
sectoral programs. The operationalization of regime norms within
sectoral programs has gone far in shaping processes of development
in many Third World countries.

The first part of this chapter analyzes the degree to which different
aid institutions concentrate their activities in particular sectors or
specialize in particular types of aid. There is a distinct, although over-
lapping, division in labor among the aid donors. But whereas various
donors specialize in social infrastructure, or physical infrastructure,
or agriculture, virtually all donors withhold aid from industrial projects. This pattern of strategic withholding is designed to encourage
reliance on foreign private capital. The aid regime's impact on indus-

trial development is based on much more than strategic withholding, however. The aid regime uses a range of mechanisms to influence industrial development in a more active way as well. The bulk of this chapter is devoted to an analysis of these mechanisms and constitutes a case study of how aid regime norms are specified within the industrial sector.

Institutional Specialization

Sectoral and functional allocations of different aid institutions have varied significantly over time. Changes at the regime level have been less dramatic, however, because shifting priorities among one set of institutions have often been balanced by shifting priorities among others. Particularly as the U.S. and some other bilateral programs were cut back, multilateral agencies such as the World Bank expanded into new areas. This has meant increased specialization in some programs and lessened specialization in others. (The U.S. development program is now almost entirely limited to technical assistance programs in agriculture, health, and education, whereas the World Bank is prepared to fund a greater variety of projects and has moved into nonproject lending.) Nonetheless, a considerable degree of sectoral and functional specialization continues to exist, with important implications for the options of recipient countries.

Table 17 presents data on the sectoral and functional allocation of aid for those sources for which data are available. The data refer to commitments made in 1980 and therefore provide a more current reading of institutional priorities than disbursements, which may stem from commitments made a number of years earlier. The data cover the individual institutions of the World Bank Group (IBRD, IDA, IFC), the major regional development banks (IDB, AfDB, ADB), the combined bilateral aid of OPEC members, and the combined bilateral aid of the advanced capitalist countries. The IMF figure covers gross drawings by LDCs on both regular credit tranches and on special IMF facilities, plus trust fund loans and profits of IMF

TABLE 17 Sectoral/Functional Distribution of 1980 Commitments of Major Multilateral Institutions, DAC Bilateral ODA, and OPEC Bilateral ODA ($ millions and percentage)

Sector/Function	IFC	IBRD	IDA	IDB	ADB	AfDB	DAC-ODA[a]	OPEC-ODA	IMF[b]	Total
Social infrastructure	$0.0 0.0%	$674.9 8.8%	$257.0 6.7%	$351.0 15.2%	$120.6 8.4%	$36.9 6.5%	$5677.8 24.7%	$130.0 2.0%	$0.0 0.0%	$7284.0 14.3%
Physical infrastructure	$0.0 0.0%	$3630.4 47.5%	$1425.5 37.2%	$1010.0 43.7%	$713.0 49.7%	$247.1 43.3%	$4909.8 21.4%	$806.2 12.4%	$0.0 0.0%	$12,742.0 25.2%
Industry and mining	$564.9 83.0%	$393.5 5.2%	$29.0 0.8%	$174.7 7.6%	$6.2 0.4%	$52.8 9.2%	$1351.7 5.9%	$91.1 1.4%	$0.0 0.0%	$2663.9 5.3%
Agriculture	$27.2 4.0%	$1700.4 22.2%	$1758.0 45.8%	$623.0 27.0%	$467.9 32.6%	$156.5 27.4%	$2825.2 12.3%	$45.5 0.7%	$0.0 0.0%	$7603.7 15.0%
Development finance co.	$61.3 9.0%	$965.0 12.6%	$112.5 2.9%	$40.3 1.7%	$127.0 8.8%	$77.6 13.6%	—[a]	—[c]	$0.0 0.0%	$1383.7 2.7%
Other sector	$27.2 4.0%	$0.0 0.0%	$13.0 0.3%	$110.0 4.8%	$1.0 0.1%	$0.0 0.0%	$2663.5 11.6%	$292.6 4.5%	$0.0 0.0%	$3107.3 6.1%
Food aid	$0.0 0.0%	$0.0 0.0%	$0.0 0.0%	$0.0 0.0%	$0.0 0.0%	$0.0 0.0%	$1531.2 6.6%	$0.0 0.0%	$0.0 0.0%	$1531.2 3.0%
Program and other nonproject aid	$0.0 0.0%	$280.0 3.7%	$242.5 6.3%	$0.0 0.0%	$0.0 0.0%	$0.0 0.0%	$4109.3 17.5%	$5136.4 79.0%	$6007.7 100.0%	$15,685.9 28.4%
Total	$680.6 100.0%	$7644.2 100.0%	$3837.5 100.0%	$2309.0 100.0%	$1435.7 100.0%	$570.9 100.0%	$22,978.5 100.0%	$6501.8 100.0%	$6007.7 100.0%	$51,965.9 100.0%

SOURCES: Organization for Economic Cooperation and Development, *Development Co-operation: Efforts and Policies of the Members of the Development Assistance Committee, 1982 Review*, pp. 155, 228–231; International Finance Corporation, *Annual Report 1980*, p. 16; World Bank, *Annual Report 1980*, pp. 121–125; Inter-American Development Bank, *Annual Report 1980*, p. 32; Asian Development Bank, *Annual Report 1980*, pp. 36–37; African Development Bank, *Annual Report 1980*, p. 29; International Monetary Fund, *Annual Report 1982*, p. 75.

[a] DAC bilateral ODA figures do not include $1,396 million in "debt reorganization." DAC data include "construction" along with financing for development finance companies in the "industry and mining" category. The food aid figure for DAC countries does not include food aid from Belgium, Denmark, France, and Italy, which is included in the "program and other nonproject aid" category.

[b] The IMF figure includes gross purchases of currencies and special drawing rights, as well as IMF trust fund loans and profits of gold sales distributed to LDCs.

[c] Included in other sectoral categories, probably industry and mining.

gold sales distributed to developing countries. Although its sectoral or functional uses may be implicitly tied by conditionality, I have classified all IMF activities as program lending. Together these sources accounted for about 90 percent of official external financing to the Third World in 1980.[1]

Varying sectoral classification schemes used by the different aid agencies complicate comparisons, but the overall division of labor demonstrated in Table 17 provides a striking illustration of the regime norms discussed in Chapter 3, particularly strategic nonlending and institutionalized noncompetition.

By and large, the multilateral development banks (MDBs) give highest priority to physical infrastructure and agriculture. The same is true of that part of OPEC bilateral aid that is not provided as budgetary support. OPEC states and development institutions will generally finance only a small proportion of a project (5 percent in the case of the Saudi Fund for Development, for example), with the result that most of their project aid goes to cofinance projects of the non-OPEC multilateral development bank.[2] It therefore reflects the sectoral priorities of the World Bank and the regional development banks.

In contrast, the top sector for bilateral aid from the advanced capitalist countries of the Development Assistance Committee (DAC) is social infrastructure—education, health, public administration, and so forth. According to a recent study by the Congressional Budget Office, the United States now assumes that physical infrastructure projects will be handled by the multilateral banks; over 70 percent of AID's expenditures are for projects of low capital intensity.[3] The focus on social infrastructure is particularly strong for France, the second largest bilateral donor. Of French ODA, 54.6 percent was allocated for social infrastructure projects.[4]

Although institutional activities overlap in some fields, in others, few institutions get involved. Among the institutions surveyed in Table 17, food aid is available only from individual DAC countries (with the United States accounting for 68 percent), although multilateral food aid is also available through the European Economic

Community and the UN World Food Program. In 1980, food aid through these two channels came to about $733 million.[5]

There are relatively few sources of program aid, which is not tied to particular projects. It comes under a variety of names but usually functions as general budgetary or balance of payments support. Almost all program aid in 1980 came from a few individual DAC countries (with the United States accounting for over two-fifths), from a few OPEC countries, and from the IMF. Access to most bilateral program aid is very restricted, however, and is based on overtly "political" criteria. Of all OPEC bilateral aid in 1980, 80.1 percent went to Arab countries.[6] When Egypt, the largest recipient, signed a peace treaty with Israel, its bilateral OPEC aid dropped from $1.3 billion in 1977–78 to $1.9 million in 1980.[7] Almost all U.S. program aid is under the auspices of the Economic Support Fund (ESF), which accounted for 34.5 percent of U.S. aid worldwide in 1983. By law, ESF provides "balance of payments, infrastructure, and other capital and technical assistance to regions of the world in which the United States has special foreign policy and security interests."[8] In 1983, over half of ESF aid (then labeled Security Supporting Assistance) went to Egypt and Israel alone.[9]

Political limitations on access to bilateral program aid mean that for most countries, the only major sources of nonproject aid are the International Monetary Fund and, with the growth of its "structural adjustment lending," the World Bank. The sources of nonproject aid are low at precisely the time when the need for it is high—due to the vulnerability to the extreme fluctuations of the world economy since the early 1970s. The oil price shocks, declining terms of trade, food shortages, and deep recession in the advanced capitalist countries have all created serious balance of payments problems for Third World countries. The institutional specialization of the aid regime, concentrating most program lending in the IMF and the World Bank, has made it very difficult for most Third World countries to resist the conditionality of loans from these two institutions. The only major alternative—borrowing at nonconcessional rates from private capital markets—has been available to only a limited number of Third World countries and has offered, as we shall see in Chapter 6, only a temporary escape.

Table 17 helps lay to rest a very prevalent myth: that economic aid is largely used to finance ambitious industrial projects in the Third World. Reflecting a widespread view, the development commissioner of the European Economic Community asserted in 1983: "We committed some fundamental errors twenty years ago by giving priority to Third World industrialization."[10] But only 5.4 percent of the commitments listed in Table 17 were for projects in the industry and mining sectors, and even this figure, as we shall see, is probably overstated.

This low level of aid for industrial projects is an example of sectoral withholding resulting from the norm of strategic nonlending, and it has characterized foreign aid from its origins. Cumulative World Bank lending for industry constituted only 6.8 percent of its total lending between 1946 and 1982.[11] AID's predecessors lumped industry together with power, a favored sector in the 1950s, but separate data available from the mid 1960s onward show that industry and mining projects always accounted for less than 10 percent of AID project aid, itself less than half of total U.S. aid.[12] The only significant departure from this pattern has been communist aid, which has historically focused on large industrial projects. But as we saw in Chapter 2, communist aid has been too limited in size and too focused on a few countries to make much difference for the Third World as a whole. (It could be argued, however, that those deviations from the regime policy of strategic nonlending in the industrial sector that have occurred can be attributed largely to the competition of communist aid.)

Table 17 points to a sharp discontinuity between the International Finance Corporation (IFC) and all the other donors in terms of the sectoral allocation priorities. None of the other institutions allocated even a tenth of their aid for industrial and mining projects, whereas the IFC allocated fully 83 percent. The IFC is the exception that proves the rule. The IFC, it will be recalled, spans the border between the aid regime and private flows, making loans to and investments in private enterprises, without government guarantee. Although total IFC activities look small compared to its sister institutions in the World Bank Group, its industrial lending and investments in fiscal year 1980 surpassed those of the IBRD, IDA, ADB, and AfDB combined. The total costs of the projects in which IFC invested in 1980 came to $2.4 billion, surpassing all the alternative sources of industrial investment in Table 17 together.[13]

The data in Table 17 indicate that although DAC bilateral aid to industry and mining may be small as a percent of the total, it is large in absolute terms. The DAC figure is inflated, however. First, it includes the category of "construction" in addition to industry and mining. It is likely that this category includes significant amounts of aid more appropriately classified as physical infrastructure. Based on past USAID practice, we may surmise that such aid amounts to as much as half the total figure. Second, the DAC figure also includes commitments to development finance companies (DFCs) in recipient countries. Aid to DFCs is very different from direct aid for industrial projects, as I discuss later in this chapter. The World Bank Group and the regional banks list aid for DFCs as a separate category; unfortunately, the DAC does not make this distinction. Third, DAC bilateral industrial aid comes from only a few countries. Japan and Germany alone account for 62 percent; the only other country providing more than a token amount is Sweden, which accounts for another 11 percent.[14] However, a significant part of Japanese industrial aid actually consists of loans to Japanese corporations to subsidize investment abroad, particularly in the production of raw materials, called "development imports," needed by Japanese industry. Such aid to Japanese industry, if extended on sufficiently soft terms, is classified by Japan as ODA.[15] Clearly, it is more accurately viewed as subsidized foreign investment. Finally, a substantial and growing proportion of German aid consists of technical assistance rather than capital goods. When the total DAC figure for the industry, mining, and construction sectors is adjusted for these considerations, actual DAC aid for industrial projects is probably lower than the IFC's. The largest DAC aid program, that of the United States, has no formal industrial component at all anymore, and the relegation of financing for industrial development to the private sector will probably become even more complete under the new strategies formulated by donors in the 1970s and 1980s.

Some observers see the withholding of aid from industry as an effort by the advanced capitalist countries to deny industrialization to Third World countries. Albert Szymanski, for example, noting the small proportion of AID project funds going to the manufacturing and mining sectors, states:

> The official U.S. theory of economic development dictates that agriculture should have priority over industry. AID's efforts directly reflect this thinking, and, of course, the economic interest of the U.S. transnational corporations that want to avoid encouraging local competition.
>
> Not only are AID's projects concentrated on agriculture, but the local governments are often forced to devote an increased proportion of their effort to this same sector as a condition of receiving assistance. The U.S. economic assistance program acts to keep the economies of these countries supplemental to that of the United States.[16]

Payer, while rejecting "any inherent unwillingness on the part of the [World] Bank to finance industrial development," explains the low level of industrial lending by the "few opportunities for profitable investment in peripheral countries" that accept World Bank strictures against protective barriers.[17] This latter argument, however, is contradicted by the high level of private foreign investment in industry. The aid regime condones and supports industrial investment—of a specific type. Although generally withholding concessional financing for industrial investment from governments, it provides an array of supports for private, mainly foreign, industrial investment. In fact, the level of private foreign investment in industry and mining directly subsidized by the donor governments probably approaches the level of their aid to recipient governments for social and physical infrastructure projects.

The withholding of aid resources from industry and mining projects has had a dual purpose: to promote reliance on private capital and to prevent socialist or statist industrial development.[18] Sectoral withholding is a very limited strategy, however, given the always present possibility of fungibility—by itself, it can do little to stop the state from using its own resources for industrial development, including those resources freed up by the receipt of aid in other sectors. Hence, it is not surprising that the aid regime has evolved more active mechanisms for shaping industrial development as well. This chapter takes up four that have been particularly important: (1) the use of industrial project financing to shape industrial policy, (2) the provision of official subsidies for private foreign investment in industry, (3) support for development finance companies, and (4) the use of program aid to shape general economic policy.

Direct Aid for Industrial Projects

Although the amount of aid allocated for industrial projects has been small compared to aid to other sectors as well as to the total level of industrial investment, it is nonetheless worth analyzing this aid more closely. With the exception of the IFC, most industrial aid goes, in the first instance at least, to governments. What can we learn from the nature of the projects this aid finances?

Table 18 provides information on direct loans from the major multilateral development banks in the four fiscal years 1978–81 for projects involving the expansion of manufacturing production or mineral extraction, generally through the construction of new facilities or the modernization of existing ones.[19] The data reaffirm the previously noted scarcity of concessional external financing for industrial projects. Altogether, these MDBs made only forty-seven industrial loans over a four-year period to twenty-three countries. The majority of Third World countries received no MDB industrial loans. The World Bank was by far the most significant source of industrial loans, accounting for 74.5 percent of the total. If the IFC were included, the World Bank Group share would be even greater. For each MDB, industrial lending was concentrated among a few recipients. Brazil, Turkey, India, and Egypt accounted for three-fourths of total

TABLE 18   Multilateral Development Bank Loans for Industrial Projects, Fiscal Years 1978–81

Country	IBRD		IDA		IDB		ADB		AfDB		Total	
	Loans	$ m.	Loans	$ m.	Loans	$ m.	Loans	$ m.	Loans	$ m.	Loans	$ m.
Latin America												
Argentina					1	55.0					1	55.0
Bolivia			1	7.5							1	7.5
Brazil	3	433.0			2	170.5					5	603.5
Colombia	1	80.0									1	80.0
Honduras					1	15.0					1	15.0
Jamaica					1	57.2					1	57.2
Mexico	1	80.0			1	158.0					2	238.0
Peru	1	5.0			2	47.0					3	52.0
Africa												
Egypt	3	183.0							1	10.5	4	193.5
Mauritania	1	60.0							2	12.6	3	71.6
Morocco	1	50.0									1	50.0
Senegal									2	30.6	2	30.6
Tanzania	2	55.0	2	50.0							4	105.0
Tunisia	1	18.6									1	18.6
Uganda									1	11.6	1	11.6
Zambia									2	11.8	2	11.8
Near East/Asia												
Bangladesh			2	58.0							2	58.0
Burma							1	5.2			1	5.2
India	1	250.0	1	400.0							2	650.0
Jordan	1	35.0									1	35.0
Pakistan			1	55.0			3	138.6			4	193.6
Turkey	3	288.0									3	288.0
Yemen Arab Republic			1	7.0							1	7.0
Total	19	1537.6	8	577.5	8	502.7	4	143.8	8	77.1	47	2838.7

SOURCES: World Bank, *Annual Reports*, 1978–81; Inter-American Development Bank, *Annual Reports*, 1978–81; Asian Development Bank, *Annual Reports*, 1978–81; African Development Bank, *Annual Reports*, 1978–81.

NOTE: Loans to European LDCs (Portugal and Romania) have been excluded, as have loans for general research or preinvestment surveys, which do not involve direct expansion of industrial capacity.

IBRD industrial lending. India accounted for 69 percent of IDA industrial lending. Brazil and Mexico accounted for 65 percent of IDB industrial lending. Pakistan accounted for 96 percent of ADB industrial loans.

Relative to other types of aid, industrial aid is not only scarce but costly. The soft-loan windows of the MDBs engage in far less industrial lending than the hard-loan windows. Within the World Bank, "blend countries"—those eligible for both IBRD and IDA loans—appear to receive a higher proportion of their industrial loans from the IBRD than is the case for their aid as a whole. The IDB is even more strict, reserving all its industrial lending for its hard-loan window. All the African Development Bank's industrial loans likewise came from its hard-loan window. Given the even more onerous terms of borrowing from private sources, the scarcity of official financing for industrial purposes, and the costliness of what financing is available, underdeveloped countries have powerful incentive to rely more heavily on direct foreign investment or else to cut back levels of industrial investment.

The industrial loans the multilateral banks do make are almost always for large-scale projects. The mean industrial project loan for the IBRD in 1978–81 was $80.9 million; for the IDA, $72.2 million; for the IDB, $62.8 million; for the ADB, $36 million. The low mean of AfDB industrial loans ($9.5 million) reflects the comparative insignificance of AfDB lending in this area. These MDB loans often involve cofinancing, and total project cost estimates for the IBRD/IDA had a mean of $451.6 million.

MDB industrial lending for large-scale projects reflects an acceptance by the MDBs of the Third World thesis that certain large-scale investments are beyond the capacity or willingness of private capital to finance. It also probably reflects an awareness that, for a variety of political and economic reasons, LDCs are not likely to allow the lack of private capital to deter them from making these investments; therefore, only MDB participation in these projects can provide the MDBs with any leverage over their particular shape. Such participation may associate the MDBs with a large proportion of public sector industrial investment. For example, two projects that the World

Bank helped finance—a potash fertilizer project in Jordan and a paper pulp project in Tanzania—absorbed respectively one-third and one-quarter of these countries' public investment budgets over a five-year period.

Given the virtual inevitability of some degree of public industrial investment, the aid institutions may prefer that countries direct their own export earnings to the private sector and rely on external aid for the public sector. In Bangladesh, Rehman Sobhan observes:

> Virtually every new industrial project under execution in the public or private sector is tied to aid disbursements either directly to the project or through various public sector financing agencies. . . . The current practise appears to be to channel Bangladesh's own export earnings to the private sector but to leave the public sector dependent on commodity loans negotiated with the World Bank and other donors such as the U.S., U.K., FRG, Japan and the Scandinavians to keep the public enterprises operational.[20]

Compared to the 1950s, when the World Bank would lend to state-owned industries only if they were slated for transfer to private ownership, the acceptance of state ownership in large-scale MDB-assisted industrial projects represents a significant change. At the same time, MDBs do not finance small- and medium-range publicly owned industries. Virtually all MDB lending for small and medium industry is channeled through local development banks whose mandate is to loan only or primarily to the private sector.

The World Bank's acceptance of state ownership has been grudging. The Bank does not hide its preference for private ownership, and it has linked its critique of other aspects of development policy to the ownership issue. For example, the critique of import-substitution policies that the Bank developed during the 1970s was directed as well against state ownership. The Bank linked state ownership to import substitution by arguing that states favor, for a variety of reasons, capital-intensive industries serving the local elite market to labor-intensive export industries, which the Bank alleges are more likely to generate employment and contribute positively to the balance of payments.

Because Turkey has been a major recipient of World Bank loans for state-owned industries, a recent World Bank–sponsored study by a long-time Bank official provides a useful example of the Bank's continuing effort to demonstrate the superiority of private ownership. The study repeatedly takes the Turkish state to task for failing to enforce a 1938 law that mandated the state to turn over state-owned industries to the private sector once they were established.[21]

The World Bank uses its leverage to promote private ownership when it can. Loans often entail the restructuring of state enterprises, as indicated in the Bank's announcement of a 1980 loan for a textile project in Egypt:

> The $69 million project is designed to help transform the National Spinning and Weaving Company (National), located in Alexandria, into a financially viable and competitive enterprise capable of producing high quality products. A joint venture company will succeed National, a public sector company, to help achieve this objective.[22]

Similarly, the World Bank's description of an IDA loan of $30 million in 1982 to "rehabilitate the textile industry in Bangladesh" states:

> Reflecting government policy, seven specialized mills have been transferred from the Bangladesh Textile Mills Corporation to private ownership and another four units will shortly be also similarly transferred. The government plans to gradually introduce a free-market pricing system to all the mills operated by the corporation.[23]

The following year the World Bank reported in congratulatory terms that thirty-five jute and twenty-three textile mills had been returned to the private sector.[24]

The Bank promotes joint projects with foreign capital. A news release dated October 18, 1979, announcing an $80 million loan for a nickel project in Colombia, reports:

> Cerro Matoso, S.A. will be responsible for project execution with extensive technical support from Hanna Mining Company (U.S.). Cerro Matoso, S.A. was incorporated in March 1979. Its shareholders are an agency of the Colombian government, a subsidiary of Hanna Mining Company, and Billiton Overseas Limited, a member of the Royal Dutch Shell Group.

Marketing of the project's output would be assured through a long-term take-or-pay contract to be entered into between Cerro Matoso, S.A. and Billiton Metals and Ores International B.V., another member of the Royal Dutch Shell Group.

Besides the World Bank loan, additional long-term financing will be provided by the Chase Manhattan Bank ($120 million) and the U.S. Export-Import Bank ($25.6 million).[25]

In cases like this, where the joint company is established within months of the loan, its composition and structure result from the loan negotiation process.

Such negotiations can also result in important control shifts in preexisting joint companies, as illustrated by a World Bank loan of $98 million for an aluminum smelter project in Brazil in 1979.[26] During the loan negotiations, the company, Valesul Aluminio S.A., was owned predominantly by the state. But Cheryl Payer reports:

> In a shareholders agreement signed in conjunction with the loan papers, the government corporation was required to agree to reduce its stockholding in Valesul Aluminum from its currently held 61 percent to between 40 and 49 percent, that is, to reduce its majority holding to a minority, by selling shares to private Brazilian investors. This maneuver left Shell with the controlling interest in Valesul Aluminum.[27]

Although examples such as these show the World Bank's readiness to use its leverage to promote private ownership in the industrial projects it finances, state ownership remains the norm. The Bank and other donors may tolerate state ownership of the projects they finance because many of them function in effect as infrastructure for the private sector. Table 19 classifies MDB industrial lending in 1978–81 by industrial project. Fertilizer occupies first place, accounting for 35.3 percent of MDB lending. Although the World Bank and AID sought to use aid in the 1960s to force India to open its fertilizer industry to foreign private investment, fertilizer in most LDCs today constitutes a government-subsidized input to the agricultural sector, which is dominated by private producers. Steel, aluminum, cement, and some minerals similarly constitute basic materials supplied predominantly to private sector industries. Alcohol

TABLE 19 Multilateral Development Bank Loans for Industrial Projects, by Product, Fiscal Years 1978–81

Product	IBRD Loans	IBRD $ m.	IDA Loans	IDA $ m.	IDB Loans	IDB $ m.	ADB Loans	ADB $ m.	AfDB Loans	AfDB $ m.	Total Loans	Total $ m.
Fertilizer	4	490.0	4	513.0							8	1003.0
Minerals/gas	3	175.0	1	7.5	4	280.0	1	55.0	4	39.0	13	556.5
Steel, aluminum	4	262.0	3	57.0	1	55.0					8	374.0
Textiles, threads	5	225.6							3	32.3	8	257.9
Alcohol fuel	1	250.0			1	95.5					2	345.5
Petrochemicals	1	85.0			2	72.2					3	157.2
Cement							2	56.7	1	5.8	3	62.5
Other	1	50.0					1	32.1			2	82.1
Total	19	1537.6	8	577.5	8	502.7	4	143.8	8	77.1	47	2838.7

SOURCES: World Bank, *Annual Reports*, 1978–81; Inter-American Development Bank, *Annual Reports*, 1978–81; Asian Development Bank, *Annual Reports*, 1978–81; African Development Bank, *Annual Reports*, 1978–81.

production for fuel in Brazil is closely related to the energy sector. Significantly, the textile industry, which does not fit this infrastructure argument, is overwhelmingly privately owned in the countries aided by the Bank.

Payer's analysis of the Copesul petrochemical project in Brazil documents how the expensive and risky core materials sector was artificially separated from the more profitable downstream operations, with the former under state ownership and the latter under private ownership. Payer concludes:

> By taking part in the riskier first stage of what is really an inseparable project, the Bank was acting in a manner directly in line with its traditional infrastructure loans. . . . The infrastructure is often financed by government while the more profitable end remains under private control, (and) the core raw materials plant in these complexes is somewhat artificially separated, financially, from the whole for which it functions as infrastructure.[28]

MDB industrial lending (in this case, both the IBRD and IDB were involved) was an extension of its traditional emphasis on physical infrastructure.

In recent years, the World Bank has vigorously argued that the issue of private versus public ownership is less significant, in most cases, than how industrial enterprises are managed. According to Edward Mason and Robert Asher, "In its lending for public sector projects the Bank has, from the beginning, paid close attention to the form of organization within which the project was expected to operate, and it has frequently conditioned its loans on the willingness of the borrower to make organizational changes."[29] The shift in emphasis from ownership to management reflects the bilateral donors' realization in the mid 1960s that aid's effect on public policy outweighs its direct resource contribution. The basic themes of the World Bank's philosophy in this area emerge in many of its publications, but a particularly clear formulation may be found in a series of articles on the theme of economic development and the private sector published in the joint World Bank–International Monetary Fund magazine *Finance and Development* in 1981 and 1982. In particular, Barend A. de Vries's "Public Policy and the Private Sector" and Chauncey F.

Dewey and Harinder S. Kohli's "Market Factors in Large Industrial Development Projects" epitomize the Bank's approach.[30] All three authors are World Bank officials.

Dewey and Kohli start out by making the point that the public/ private distinction is not always straightforward. Some government-owned enterprises are run just like private businesses, and some private businesses are essentially controlled by government regulation.[31] Operating principles surpass ownership in importance. "Success with large industrial projects," Dewey and Kohli argue, "requires the marriage of sound economic policies, good administration, and market forces."[32] Of these three, market forces are paramount. Investment and operating decisions should be subordinated to "the signals of the market, adjusted as necessary to offset distortions . . . at every stage of the project cycle."[33] Good administration in the form of organizational autonomy and sound economic policies in the form of a commitment to financial viability are seen as preconditions for letting market forces do their work. It is worth examining these prescriptions in some more detail because they have profound implications for the kinds of industrial projects for which Third World countries can hope to get concessional external financing.

First, autonomy means autonomy from political processes in the government. But because prices in the market economy may be affected by government actions, the financial viability of proposed projects must be judged on the basis of adjusted prices. Departures from international market prices are treated as "distortions," and industrial projects depending on protective tariffs, subsidized interest rates, or other types of government support are rejected as uneconomic.

> When designing a project, to ensure its economic efficiency it is essential to use "economic" prices for inputs and outputs—that is, prices which do not reflect subsidies or other distortions. . . . Ideally, domestic prices of inputs and outputs should be in line with long-term international market prices. Similarly, the project ideally should be charged market rates for its financing. . . . In its continuing dialogues with country governments, the World Bank consistently favors the elimination of most direct and indirect subsidies to local industry—in order to restore

to the market its valuable role as indicator/enforcer of economic efficiency. In its lending for large industrial projects—even under long-term International Development Association (IDA) credits, which carry minimal charges—the Bank requires the borrowing government to relend the proceeds to the beneficiary organization at or close to market interest rates and with a maturity period of 12 to 15 years.[34]

Although couched in the technical language of project appraisal—shadow prices, economic rates of return, and so forth—these assumptions obviate efforts by Third World societies to insulate themselves from international market forces and to establish alternative priorities. The notion that international market prices may themselves be distorted is not entertained in these analyses. Organizational autonomy from political decision making and insistence on economic viability essentially mean the subordination of industrial investment and policy to external market forces over which Third World countries have little control. As de Vries puts it, "the Bank encourages the creation of independent—albeit publicly owned—organizations that are managed in most respects *as though they were private.*" (emphasis added)[35] Dewey and Kohli state: "Governments should allow even parastatal agencies maximum possible autonomy, and they should judge the performance of their managers mainly on the basis *of normal business and financial indicators.*" (emphasis added)[36] They note that when the Bank has loaned to countries with extensive state ownership in industry, "it has been the Bank's practice to lend *only to those state-owned industrial companies that in effect operate as commercial entities.*" (emphasis added)[37]

The political implications of these policies are profound. As Payer has observed, "If publicly owned undertakings are to be run exactly along capitalist lines, they can thus be effectively prevented from presenting any effective competition to private enterprise—either in the economic or the ideological sense."[38] The possibility of the state industrial sector pioneering an alternative mode of economic and political organization within an "intermediate" or "noncapitalist" regime is drastically undercut by recourse to external financing.

The World Bank, then, pursues a two-track strategy in its efforts to shape the nature of industrial enterprises: encouraging private ownership when it can, but always stressing the primacy of international market forces. A recent example is found in the recommendations in its detailed analysis of state enterprises in the 1983 *World Development Report*.[39] Its proposals in the chapter on managing state-owned enterprises are presented under the following headings:

1. "Control without interference"—the autonomy of enterprises
2. "Institutional links between government and enterprise"— which should "place government at arm's length" from the enterprises
3. "Holding managers accountable for results"—with the emphasis here on the use of shadow price accounting and other market-oriented standards of evaluation
4. "Liquidation"—closing down nonviable enterprises
5. "Divestiture"—transferring enterprises to the private sector

The list accurately reflects the Bank's central focus on management techniques but indicates also its continuing effort to cut back the public sector. The dual thrust is also evident in the Bank's 1981 report, *Accelerated Development in Sub-Saharan Africa: An Agenda for Action*, in which an "overextended public sector" is identified as one of three critical "domestic policy inadequacies" that have impeded economic growth.[40]

The World Bank has gone much further than the other MDBs in articulating a general development strategy and the norms governing access to its assistance. The lending behavior of the other MDBs, however, parallels that of the World Bank. The IDB, by far the most significant of the regional MDBs in terms of industrial lending, reserves all of its industrial lending for its hard-loan window; no loans for industry are made from the soft-loan Fund for Special Operations. Whereas manufacturing accounts for 26 percent of Latin American gross output, industrial loans account for only one-seventh of the IBD's loan portfolio, and only about half of this is for direct industrial projects.[41] The IDB's charter prevents it from using its regular resources for equity investments, but a portion of the Venezuelan Trust Fund, which the IDB administers, has been set aside for equity investments of up to $2 million in national or multinational Latin American companies. Although the level of these investments has been modest, the IDB has described the experience acquired as "invaluable for an expanded future action in this area."[42] The IDB is in the process of establishing an affiliate, the Inter-American Investment Corporation, which will make equity investments in and loans to private companies, much like the World Bank's IFC, and provide a variety of other services to the private sector as well. Like the IFC, this affiliate apparently will concentrate particularly on joint enterprises involving foreign capital.[43]

An IDB study has noted that, like other MDBs, the IDB's industrial lending "has been somewhat polarized, leaving an unintended gap of relatively little financing for medium-size projects in the $2 to $10 million range."[44] Unintended or not, the lack of IDB financing precludes countries from using external resources for public investment in this range, which is precisely the range of most foreign investments. Funding is available through development finance corporations for investments too small for foreign investors to be interested in and for large-scale investments that are either state owned or sufficiently large to require joint financing. But it is by and large withheld from projects in the intermediate range of most potential interest to single foreign investors. As the basic aid regime norms would allow, the major effort of the IDB to plug up this "gap" is to create an equity financing affiliate designed to cement alliances between foreign and local capital.

Official Subsidies for Private Foreign Investment in Industry

As we have seen, a major rationale for concessional assistance for social and physical infrastructure is that such investment paves the way for private investment. Infrastructure is the focus of most economic aid because it is unattractive to private investors yet necessary for the profitability of most private enterprises. Aid is generally withheld from the manufacturing and mining sectors, and the relatively small

amount of aid allocated directly for industrial projects generally is
structured to ensure that these projects do not challenge—and in fact
often support—the private sector.

Direct Financing of Private Investment

The support given to private enterprises is generally indirect. In
this section, we examine the major ways the aid regime provides official subsidies for private foreign investment in the Third World, particularly in industry. In the lexicon of the aid agencies, particularly
the World Bank, subsidy is a bad word, associated with "distortion."
"Incentives" is the preferred word for market interventions that are
positively viewed. Whatever term is used, our focus here is on the use
of official resources to facilitate flows of private foreign investment
that might not otherwise occur.

Subsidies currently operate primarily as part of bilateral aid programs with one major exception: the International Finance Corporation. In 1981, its twenty-fifth year, the IFC described itself as "one
of the major development institutions in the world today and the
leader in the private investment sector of development."[45] The IFC is
indeed the largest official source of loans to, and equity investments
in, private enterprises, although its loan and equity portfolio is
dwarfed by investment insurance portfolios of the bilateral agencies.

The IFC operates like the other international development banks,
using a combination of paid-in and callable capital subscriptions
from its members to support borrowing from international capital
markets. It then uses this borrowed capital to finance its activities. It
differs from the other arms of the World Bank in not requiring a host
government guarantee and in being empowered to make equity investments in private enterprises. Its authorized capital in 1981 was
$650 million, which it had leveraged into a $1,647 million portfolio
of loans ($1,374 million) and equity ($273 million) in 314 companies in 71 LDCs.[46] In 1981, it made $811 million in loan and
equity investments in projects estimated to have a total cost of $3,340

million. Although the IFC has attempted to diversify in recent years, most of its investments have always been in manufacturing and mining. The IFC announced in 1981 that for the first time fewer than half of its new investments were in manufacturing, but in terms of dollar amount, 73 percent were in manufacturing and another 8 percent in energy and minerals.[47]

In 1981, the IFC invested in thirty-five wholly private companies, twelve mixed companies, and nine wholly public entities designed to transfer resources to the private sector. Of the thirty-five wholly private companies, 67 percent involved foreign participation, reflecting the IFC's special interest in arranging joint ventures between local and foreign capital.[48]

Bilateral agencies, less burdened than the MDBs by considerations of creditworthiness, pioneered lending to private enterprises before the creation of the IFC and continue, in several countries, to finance a significant amount of foreign investment by their home multinationals. Direct loans to private enterprises to finance investments abroad were an innovative feature of the U.S. Development Loan Fund, established in 1958, and in its three years of operation, the DLF made $246.9 million of such loans, constituting 12 percent of all DLF loans. Between 1962 and 1970, AID made something over $500 million more of such loans.[49] In most cases, the loans involved a two-step repayment procedure: the companies repaid the loan in local currency to the host government, which in turn was required to repay AID in dollars. These loans, especially in the early 1960s, constituted a substantial proportion of AID industrial lending, amounting to 100 percent in one year. Around the end of the 1960s, however, direct loans to private companies were phased out in favor of investment guarantees, program lending, financing of local development banks, and support for the IFC. Similarly, the "Cooley" loans—loans of local currency generated by the sale of food aid—which provided $481.8 million for local currency costs of investments, primarily by U.S. corporations, were phased out in the 1970s.[50] There is evidence that Cooley loans were important tools facilitating the entry of U.S. corporations into the fertilizer sector in

India, and they probably played comparable roles in other sectors and elsewhere as well.[51] Although declining local currency sales of PL 480 foodstuffs influenced the phasing out of Cooley loans, the program contained the key to its own demise. Cooley loans helped finance the expansion of U.S. multinational banks abroad and thus helped make the cumbersome mechanism of the program, which required host government approval, unnecessary, since the multinational affiliates could then take over.

The phasing out of direct dollar and local currency loans to private enterprises by AID in the early 1970s also reflected the shift of several functions from AID to the Overseas Private Investment Corporation (OPIC), created by Congress in 1969 and operational since January 1971. Although the major function of OPIC has been to grant investment insurance, it also provides loans up to $4 million from its Direct Investment Fund and guarantees larger loans up to $50 million by private banks to finance foreign investments by firms in which U.S. investors account for at least 25 percent of the equity for loans or over 50 percent in the case of loan guarantees. OPIC generally restricts its lending to companies with private majority ownership, but it does provide that

> a guaranteed loan may be made to an entity in which local government ownership of voting shares represents the majority, if it is contractually agreed that management will remain in private hands, and there is a strong showing of direct U.S. interest in other respects. Wholly government-owned projects are not eligible.[52]

Between 1971 and 1981, OPIC authorized $502 million in loans and loan guarantees for eighty-nine projects in thirty-seven LDCs, with an estimated total cost of $2.2 billion. In fiscal year 1981 alone, OPIC authorized $101.3 million for twenty projects, a record amount. Of the total amount of these loans, 88.9 percent was for manufacturing and mining projects.[53] OPIC's outstanding finance portfolio came to $345.9 million in 1981.[54]

OPIC is formally separate from AID, but the head of AID is by statute the chairman of the board of OPIC. Since October 1979, both are part of the International Development Cooperation Agency. Although OPIC's achievements are extolled in foreign aid presentations to Congress, it is financially self-sufficient and does not require annual appropriations. Its commitments, however, are "backed by the full faith and credit of the United States."[55]

Other DAC governments provide loans to finance foreign investments by their home multinationals, but it is difficult to assess the magnitude of the effort. Japan probably provides the highest proportion of this type of financing. Its Export-Import Bank is empowered to provide up to 50 percent of the cost of approved overseas investments.[56] Apparently Japan also commonly finances the participation of foreign governments in joint ventures with Japanese firms.[57] The activities of the Export-Import Bank of Japan are complemented by Japan's Overseas Economic Cooperation Fund, which also makes loans to private firms investing overseas. Between 1969 and 1976, the Fund made eight loans totaling 1,700 million yen.[58] Depending on the terms negotiated with the Japanese firms, these loans may be included in Japan's accounting of its ODA. According to OECD, Japan in 1980 devoted $770.4 million in public funds "in support of private investment," well over twice the amount of ODA Japan provided for industry, mining, and construction projects.[59]

All the DAC countries have a variety of other ways to assume some of the costs of private foreign investment. OPIC, for example, will finance up to 50 percent of feasibility studies. AID's Bureau for Private Enterprise researches potential investment opportunities and advertises them to U.S. businesses. OPIC organizes tours of potential investors, and both AID and OPIC provide a variety of technical assistance and negotiating services. Other DAC countries provide similar services.

Insuring Private Investment

Although services and loans shift some of the costs of foreign investment from the multinationals to the state, cost is not the main obstacle to the expansion of foreign investment in the Third World. Concern with risk, especially political risk, is much more significant. In fact, one major appeal of the participation of IFC and bilateral agencies such as OPIC is that they lower the foreign investors' risk exposure by creating a direct interest of the World Bank or home governments in the investment. The host government is likely to avoid expropriation or other forms of contract abrogation with private investors because of potential ramifications on other flows of external financing.

DAC governments assume some of the risk of private foreign investors primarily through investment guarantee programs.[60] These programs provide insurance against a variety of political risks and occasionally more general business risks as well. In some countries, they are supplemented by tax provisions that subsidize foreign investment and allow companies to write off foreign losses. The first public investment insurance program was instituted by the Economic Cooperation Act of 1948, which provided for insurance through the ECA against currency inconvertibility (considered the major obstacle to investing in Europe at that time). A 1950 amendment to the act added guarantees against expropriation and confiscation, and the Mutual Security Act of 1956 added guarantees against losses due to war, revolution, and insurrection. The Foreign Assistance Act of 1961 added insurance against certain types of "business" risks as well, in addition to expanding the definition of "investment" to include loans, the provision of patents, and so forth. In 1963, Congress made the signing of the bilateral treaty necessary for instituting the Investment Guaranty Program (IGP), a prerequisite for economic aid.

The IGP made a slow start in the Third World. So safe did the loci of most U.S. foreign investment seem to U.S. investors that at the time of the Cuban Revolution, not a single one of the estimated $1.4 billion in investments expropriated by the Cuban government was insured under the IGP. After January 1960, the IGP was limited to underdeveloped countries, and during the 1960s, coverage expanded rapidly, from $0.4 billion in 1960 to $7.8 billion in 1970. The IGP was transferred to OPIC in 1971. Currently, "OPIC's insurance program provides coverage against: inconvertibility of local currency earnings and return of capital; expropriation and, in some cases, abrogation of contractual rights; and war, revolution and insurrection. The OPIC legislation of 1981 extends the program for coverage of certain types of civil strife."[61]

Despite the lesson of the Cuban Revolution, U.S. investors have continued to believe that some locations are safe from political risk. The 1979 OPIC report notes: "Because Iran was considered politically stable by most U.S. investors, OPIC's exposure in that country was relatively low and maximum liability of September 30, 1979, was $63.9 million."[62] Not surprisingly, the demand for political risk insurance has shot up, and OPIC reported that in the fourth quarter of fiscal year 1981, the volume of its new political risk insurance policies was the largest in its history.[63] OPIC's total insurance volume in 1982 exceeded $3 billion, doubling the previous year's record level.[64]

OPIC insurance is available for investments by U.S. citizens, corporations created under U.S. laws, and foreign businesses 95 percent owned by U.S. citizens or corporations. Coverage may be for up to 90 percent of new investments, but it may be extended to include earnings and interest on this investment up to 270 percent of the initial investment. Total outstanding coverage came to $9.6 billion in 1982.[65]

OPIC contracts are generally written for twenty-year periods. Thus, a contract written now will remain in force through a variety of changes in government, at a time when the bargaining power of Third World partners and governments is increasing. A study by the Center for International Policy suggests that these factors assure "the inherent instability of OPIC contracts."[66] Furthermore, OPIC has the right to assume the assets and liabilities of an expropriated company after it has paid the company's insurance claim (subrogation). Hence, an action against an OPIC-insured company by a Third World country could bring the country into direct conflict with the U.S. government. The United States, for example, pursued OPIC's subrogation claims against Iran through the Iran-U.S. Claims Tribunal.[67]

Although the great majority of Third World countries (ninety-eight as of 1982) have signed agreements with OPIC that recognize OPIC's subrogation rights, they have done so reluctantly at best. The Andean Pact of five Latin American countries in 1969 provided "that no instrument relating to foreign investment or technology transfer may contain clauses allowing subrogation by states of their national investor's rights or removing possible disputes from the jurisdiction of the recipient country."[68] OPIC withheld insurance to Andean group countries while the pact remained operative.

As in the case of OPIC loans and loan guarantees, the sectoral allocation of OPIC's investment insurance contrasts sharply with the sectoral allocation of concessional aid to governments. In 1970, 86.9 percent of outstanding IGP coverage was for investments in the manufacturing and mining sector. Expanding the concept of "investment" to include the supplying of materials, technology, and other services has resulted in some decline in the proportion of projects in actual manufacturing or mining production, but in fiscal year 1981, 68.6 percent of the investments insured were of this nature.[69]

A 1973 study prepared for the House Committee on Foreign Affairs found that 78 percent of IGP coverage went to corporations on the Fortune 500 list or to commercial banks among the largest fifty.[70] In its literature, OPIC takes pains to emphasize its orientation toward small businesses, which it defines as businesses not on the Fortune 1000 list. Using the narrower definition of the Fortune 500 list to produce results comparable to the House study, however, we find that thirty-five Fortune 500 corporations and Fortune 50 banks accounted for 63.8 percent of the investments insured by OPIC in fiscal year 1981. In terms of amounts of insurance, small businesses continue to play a relatively small role in OPIC's activities.

Determining whether investment guarantees are necessary for investments to be made is a complex matter. Without investment insurance, corporations might look for substitutes, such as a more aggressive foreign policy, rather than reduce their foreign investments. Such a foreign policy would be designed to increase the host countries' costs of expropriation or other unacceptable actions. Therefore, investment insurance cannot be considered apart from the wider framework of foreign policy and alternative forms of subsidy. However, the evidence does suggest that OPIC and similar agencies play a very important role. One study of investment plans turned down by OPIC found that 97 percent of their projected value was not subsequently invested. A 1971 *Business International* survey found 45.8 percent of OPIC customers saying that political risk insurance would be necessary for any future foreign investments.[71] A more recent, although rather limited, survey found lower levels of perceived OPIC importance among its customers: only 30 percent felt that the availability of OPIC insurance had an important impact on their investment decisions.[72] In a useful survey of OPIC's "mixed mandates," Jeffrey Burnham concludes:

> After thirty-five years of the incentive program's existence, it is still not possible to prove either that foreign investment is in fact beneficial for development, or that the program has been a major factor encouraging investment. Over the years, Congress has heard "expert" witnesses present arguments on all sides of both issues.[73]

Whatever the truth of the matter, from the host country's perspective, government-sponsored investment guarantees almost certainly raise the cost of potential policies that would activate insurance coverage. Because this coverage extends beyond directly "political" acts, such as nationalization, to issues of currency controls, taxation, and other more purely "economic" policies, the impact of investment guarantees can be very deep.

Twenty-one countries in addition to the United States have set up government investment insurance schemes. Between 1977 and 1981, around 20 percent of DAC net investment flows to developing countries were guaranteed under national programs. Within individual LDCs, the proportion of the accumulated stock of foreign investment covered varied from less than 1 percent to 87 percent.[74] World Bank President A. W. Clausen has reported that with political risks "so large that they cannot be handled by government entities or national investment institutions," the Bank is "exploring a multilateral investment insurance scheme that could build on the existing national and private schemes to set up a global scheme. The objective is to increase the flow of funds from the private sector."[75] A particularly significant feature of the World Bank's proposal is that it would cofinance guarantees with national agencies, thereby putting the status and power of the world's most powerful aid institution behind multinational corporate investments.

Development Finance Companies

In the last two sections, we have examined two ways in which assistance for industrial financing takes place within the aid regime. We saw that lending to governments for specific industrial projects is very limited and is concentrated in a small number of large-scale, generally state-controlled projects in a few countries. In contrast, the investment financing and insurance programs of the advanced capitalist countries support vastly greater amounts of foreign investment by multinational corporations in Third World countries.

In terms of aid dollars spent, however, both forms of assistance for industrial development have historically been surpassed by loans to intermediate credit institutions, known as Development Finance Companies (DFCs). DFCs are local versions of the International Finance Corporation. Relying to varying degrees on external financing, these institutions make loans to and equity investments in private enterprises within their own countries. Although most DFCs are not restricted to industrial investments, most have concentrated their activities in the manufacturing sector. In many countries, one or just a few DFCs constitute virtually the only source of medium- to long-term financing for private industrial enterprises.

The DFCs are important today because the international aid agencies have made them important, channeling the bulk of their aid for industrial development through them. The first such aid was a loan by the World Bank to the Development Bank of Ethiopia in 1950. "A principal reason for the International Bank's original interest in development banks was that they offered a practical solution to

the difficulties the Bank encountered in financing small private industrial projects directly."[76] These difficulties had involved the constitutional requirement of government guarantees of loans and a ban on
equity investments. Host governments guaranteed loans to DFCs,
which themselves were mostly private enterprises, and the DFCs, not
the Bank, made equity investments. DFCs could be expected to
know the local economic environment better than the Bank, although the latter nonetheless insisted on close supervision in the first
years of DFC operations. The charters of virtually all the DFCs aided
in the early years of the aid regime restricted DFC activities to the
private sector.

During the 1950s and 1960s, the World Bank, USAID, and, to a
lesser extent, the IDB all played active roles not only in financing but
also in promoting DFCs in Third World countries, many of them
newly independent. A World Bank study notes:

> During the first decades of international concern for development (1948–
> 1968), the many diagnostic missions sent to assess the potential and the
> needs of specific developing countries almost always identified inade-
> quate long-term credit as a central problem. Virtually all these missions
> recommended the creation or strengthening of a DFC as a principal
> means to its solution.
> . . . DFCs were created in large numbers—at least one for virtually
> every emerging sovereign entity and sometimes, as in Brazil and India,
> scores—to serve different regions or specialized clienteles.[77]

The World Bank claims to have "played a catalytic role by providing
the basic institutional design to be followed, or the basis for a major
reorganization, for about half of the DFCs which it has assisted."[78] It
played a particularly important role in India in the promotion of the
privately owned Industrial Credit and Investment Corporation of India (ICICI), fearing that otherwise all major channels for industrial
financing would be public.[79] Indeed, the capital structure of ICICI,
as well as of a comparable DFC in Pakistan, was designed by George
Woods, subsequently president of the World Bank.[80] Through 1981,
the World Bank lent $740 million to ICICI alone. As of 1980, the
Bank had provided 77 percent of the total foreign exchange resources

raised by the ICICI, with most of the rest coming from German, British, and U.S. bilateral sources.[81]

USAID also played a major role in promoting and reorganizing DFCs. The U.S. Development Loan Fund made 40 loans to DFCs between 1959 and 1961, amounting to $220 million. Between 1962 and 1970, USAID made 108 more loans to DFCs, totaling $790.6 million.[82] During this period, over two-thirds of MDB industrial lending was channeled through DFCs. Between 1961 and 1970, the World Bank loaned $1,078.9 million to DFCs, accounting for 73.9 percent of its industrial lending. Direct loans for specific industrial projects accounted for only 26.1 percent.[83] In those same years, the IDB loaned $367 million to DFCs in Latin America, accounting for 63.6 percent of its industrial lending.[84] The Asian Development Bank, opening its doors toward the end of the decade, made 60.1 percent of its industrial loans ($30 million) to DFCs between 1968 and 1970.[85]

Although USAID and the IDB were both willing to lend to government-controlled DFCs as long as they channeled the money to private enterprises, the World Bank persisted in its commitment to private ownership of DFCs themselves until the late 1960s. In 1965, a conference of Bank-assisted DFCs could be described as "a family affair" because of the private ownership of all the participants.[86] However, in a study financed by the Ford Foundation in the mid 1960s, two economists well connected with the aid establishment, Robert Adler and Raymond Mikesell, observed that the absence of private equity capital DFCs in most Third World countries meant that an increasing proportion of DFCs was going to be government owned. Clearly directing their words to the World Bank, they warned:

> The alternative to expanded equity participation [in government-owned DFCs] by external lending agencies may be industrialization dominated mainly by state enterprise. . . . Rapid industrialization is a primary goal of virtually all developing countries and will be achieved one way or another. What is at stake is whether it will be predominantly private or governmental in ownership and control. What we are suggesting, therefore, is that external assistance agencies (which are themselves public entities)

would be well advised to adopt whatever policies consistent with the productive use of their resources are required for the promotion of a predominantly private industrial sector, including willingness to work with and provide financing for public as well as private intermediate credit institutions and other government agencies dedicated to fostering rapid private industrial growth.[87]

In 1968, the World Bank agreed to finance government-owned DFCs as long as they served only the private sector. Subsequently, the Bank agreed to allow loans to government-owned enterprises "if this appeared appropriate in the circumstances, and if sound rules for making decisions were applied in financing such public enterprises."[88] Characteristically, having made the shift, the World Bank aggressively sought to establish relationships with government-owned DFCs, and by the mid 1970s, about half the DFCs it was assisting were government owned. Nonetheless, a 1976 Bank study estimated that the DFCs it assisted made 95 percent of their loans to private enterprises through 1975 and would make 85 percent to 90 percent between 1976 and 1980.[89] A 1983 Bank study reports that state-owned DFCs "still lend mainly to the private sector" and sees the Bank as having been successful in ensuring that "the DFC model originally exemplified in the private institutions has therefore carried over into state-owned institutions, which are now more prevalent."[90]

USAID has phased out its lending to DFCs, and the IDB has cut back its financing of DFCs in favor of a modest level of direct industrial project financing. Along with the three institutions of the World Bank Group, the Asian Development Bank and West Germany's Kreditanstalt für Wiederaufbau (KFW) currently constitute the most important sources of external funds for DFCs.

The World Bank originally insisted on approving all subprojects in which the Bank's funds would be used. Today it approves only larger subprojects for some DFCs. Paralleling this relaxation of direct control has been a diversification of the form DFC loans take. Although most are made directly to the DFC, with host government guarantee, some are made to government banks for distribution among a variety of types of credit institutions. Unlike other loans, these generally carry "a flexible amortization schedule, reflecting substantially the aggregate of the repayment schedules of the individual subloans."[91]

The World Bank's Sector Policy Paper on DFCs reports that the Bank provided almost $3 billion in financing to DFCs between 1950 and 1975. In fiscal years 1976 through 1981, the Bank loaned another $4.8 billion to DFCs, accounting for 56.7 percent of its industrial lending (DFCs and direct loans to industrial projects).[92] Although the DFC share has declined from the 1960s, it still is substantially greater than direct industrial project lending, and it is spread out over many more countries. Table 20 lists the countries receiving World Bank loans for DFCs and for industrial projects between 1978 and 1981.

Forty-six countries, plus the Caribbean Development Bank, received loans for DFCs. Of these, only fifteen received industrial project loans as well. Only one country received only industrial project loans. In terms of both geographical spread and dollar volume, aid for private enterprises through DFCs constitutes the major form of industrial lending by the MDBs. In 1980, the African Development Bank loaned $77.6 million for DFCs and only $52.8 million for industrial projects. The Asian Development Bank favored DFCs over industrial projects even more, lending $127 million for the former and $6.2 million for the latter in 1980. Only the IDB, in a reversal of its earlier lending priorities, now funds industrial projects at a higher level than DFCs.

In addition to channeling official financing to private enterprises, DFCs have been seen by aid agencies as a means of facilitating the emergence of a variety of features of a healthy and dynamic capitalism. Aid agencies have expected DFCs, through their insistence on real rates of interest combined with autonomous and professional management, to encourage and mobilize private savings for industrial investment. DFCs would help expand local markets in securities, aid agencies hoped, and bring about public policy changes favorable to the private sector. However, in the early 1970s, Mason and Asher concluded that World Bank–assisted DFCs had greater success "in channeling investment and entrepreneurship into financially viable enterprises than . . . in mobilizing domestic savings and

TABLE 20 World Bank Loans for DFCs and for Industrial Projects,
Fiscal Years 1978–81

| | Loans for DFCs[a] | | | | Loans for Industry |
| | IBRD | | IDA | | |
Country	Loans	$ m.	Loans	$ m.	$ m.
Bangladesh			2	57.0	58.0
Bolivia					7.5
Brazil	1	58.0			433.0
Burundi			1	3.4	
Colombia	3	265.0			80.0
Costa Rica	1	15.0			
Cyprus	1	5.0			
Ecuador	1	40.0			
Egypt	3	120.0			183.0
Gambia			1	3.0	
Ghana			1	19.0	
Haiti			1	7.0	
Honduras	1	15.0			
India	3	205.0			650.0
Indonesia	1	50.0	1	40.0	
Ivory Coast	1	12.6			
Jamaica	2	44.0			
Jordan	1	10.0			35.0
Kenya	1	30.0	1	10.0	
Korea	8	605.0			
Lesotho			1	4.0	
Madagascar			1	5.0	
Malawi	1	3.0			
Mauritania			1	8.0	60.0
Mauritius	2	13.5			
Mexico	3	322.0			80.0
Morocco	2	125.0			50.0

SOURCE: World Bank, *Annual Reports*, 1978–81.

[a]Excludes two IBRD loans to Portugal ($145 million), three IBRD loans to Yugoslavia ($210 million), and one IBRD loan to the Caribbean Development Bank ($23 million).

Continued on next page

TABLE 20—*continued*

Country	Loans for DFCs[a]				Loans for Industry
	IBRD		IDA		
	Loans	$ m.	Loans	$ m.	$ m.
Nicaragua	1	30.0			
Niger			1	5.0	
Nigeria	1	60.0			
Pakistan			1	40.0	55.0
Panama	2	35.0			
Paraguay	1	31.0			
Peru			1	60.0	5.0
Philippines	5	300.0			
Rwanda			1	5.2	
Solomon Islands			1	1.5	
Sri Lanka			2	24.0	
Tanzania	3	51.0			105.0
Thailand	1	30.0			
Tunisia	1	35.0			18.6
Turkey	4	250.0			288.0
Upper Volta			1	4.0	
Uruguay	1	30.0			
Yemen Arab Republic			1	12.0	7.0
Zaire			1	18.5	
Zambia	1	15.0			

contributing to the development of capital markets."[93] This seems to remain true. A study by Joseph Kane of a sample of thirty-one Bank-assisted DFCs, published in 1975, shows in detail that DFC dependence on external financing, rather than local savings, remains high. Despite the fact that twenty-eight of the thirty-one DFCs in his sample were wholly or partly privately owned, Kane found that only 17 percent of their resources came from the private domestic sector. For over half, the largest source of financing was external official aid, accounting for 46.8 percent of resources. In fact, as Kane points out, this figure understates the level of dependence significantly because most external official aid is provided on a line of credit basis, and portions are transferred only as they are committed to subborrowers. If all external official resources available to the DFC were included, the share of this sector would be substantially increased.[94] Although not providing figures, a 1983 Bank study of DFCs characterizes the record of DFCs in mobilizing domestic resources as "poor."[95]

Kane's study also demonstrates the high level of local government subsidy provided DFCs, even privately owned ones. For one thing, the government must guarantee loans by MDBs to the DFCs; in fact, as Kane notes, "virtually every infusion of external funds into the sample banks has as a necessary condition the active cooperation of domestic government."[96] In addition, governments commonly provide free or subsidized resources and services to the DFCs, as well as providing various types of guarantees reducing the risk of private investments in DFCs. Governments are the next most important source of DFC equity and debt capital, after external aid agencies, accounting for 31 percent of the total for the sample banks.

DFC dependence on government funds poses a dilemma for the World Bank and other aid agencies anxious to preserve the independence of the privately owned DFCs. Loan agreements with the World Bank commonly stipulate a debt/equity ratio of either 3:1 or 4:1. Given the limited initial capitalization of DFCs, combined with the difficulty of selling DFC shares, the only way to keep expanding lending is to expand the equity base by tapping government resources. This practice, however, opens the door to government control. An ingenious solution consists of a form of government altruism known as quasi equity. Kane describes the system:

> Quasi-equity is actually long-term debt funds that have been provided by government to the bank free of interest or bearing only a nominal rate. The main feature of such funds is that they are ranked either subordinate to equity in the event of liquidation or pari passu with it. Such funds have been requested by the World Bank for most of the banks it is associated with. These banks, being held ordinarily to a debt-equity ratio of 3:1, would be severely limited in their development impact if their total resources were only four times the equity base. But by government agreeing to stand on a par with or behind equity, such debt can then be

counted as quasi equity, expending the effective equity base and substantially increasing the borrowing potential of the bank.[97]

Quasi equity thus expands the DFC's equity base without giving the government corresponding shareholder control. It also enhances the profitability of the artificially narrow equity base. As Adler and Mikesell observe, quasi equity "provides the development company with a better chance of reaching a profitable stage fairly early in its operations and provides a cushion to protect shareholders during the period before adequate reserves have been accumulated."[98]

Since the early 1970s, the World Bank has stressed the importance of small-scale private enterprises, pointing out that small-scale enterprises (SSEs) tend to be more labor intensive than larger enterprises and are therefore more useful in addressing the basic problem of employment in societies where labor is abundant. The Bank's Sector Policy Paper on Small Enterprises put special emphasis on the role of DFCs in supporting such enterprises.[99]

In fact, most DFCs concentrate on considerably larger business than those defined as small-scale enterprises—businesses with fixed assets of $250,000 or less, excluding land. As of 1977, the Bank could retrospectively label only twenty-five projects in its history that could be said to have a substantial SSE impact. Eighteen of these consisted of loans for DFCs, but this was a small proportion of total loans for DFCs.[100] A study of a sample of Bank-assisted DFCs in 1970–72 indicates that 50 percent of the firms aided by the DFCs had assets over $300,000, and only 30 percent had assets under $100,000. Moreover, in terms of lending volume, firms with assets under $100,000 received only between 5 percent and 10 percent of total DFC lending.[101]

World Bank data through 1975 indicate that almost two-thirds of the DFCs it assisted made loans and equity investments averaging $300,000 or more. The Bank has estimated that DFCs provide on the average half the total cost of the investments they support, although the DFC share declines for larger projects. This means that the average investment supported by two-thirds of the DFCs was something over $600,000. Bank resources have been concentrated in

the DFCs making the larger subloans. Of Bank financing, 72.5 percent went for DFCs with average subloans of $500,000 or more.

Stacey Widdicombe, in a study of one DFC, the Jamaica Industrial Development Corporation (JIDC), found that overall the
JIDC had more success in sponsoring foreign investment than local
investment.[102] Unfortunately, none of the World Bank studies on
DFCs provides data on the degree to which DFC subloans go to
foreign firms, their affiliates, or joint ventures, but a high level of foreign involvement in DFCs seems taken for granted. Although Kane
found that only 5 percent of the resources of his sample of DFCs
came from external private sources, foreigners representing these
sources were routinely included on the boards of directors of most
DFCs. P. M. Mathew, summarizing discussions at the 1965 conference of World Bank–assisted DFCs, refers casually to the fact that
"much of the resources of private development companies is used to
support foreign-sponsored businesses."[103] And Mason and Asher
quote James Raj, former vice-president of the IFC, as saying: "Nearly
all [DFCs] have served as a focal point for introducing foreign investors to their countries and prompting these investors to begin serious explorations."[104] As in the case of the IFC, DFCs elicit foreign
investment less through their ability to provide financing—which although large in terms of local businesses is small by the standards of
multinational corporations—than through their role in arranging
joint ventures and in binding the host government to the terms of
the DFC agreements.

To test the "success" of the DFCs, Kane devised measures to see if
various financial functions of DFCs were growing relative to other
financial institutions. Using data from the 1960s and early 1970s, he
found that the DFCs were financing an increasing proportion of the
growth of stock of industrial capital; that they were playing an expanding role in both the supply of overall bank credit and in industrial credit; that commercial bank credit did not seem to be shifting
toward medium- or long-term assets, thus leaving the field to DFCs;
and that DFC financing was growing more rapidly than other non-
monetary financial intermediary institutions.[105] The 1970s, however,

witnessed a tremendous growth of multinational banks in the Third World, an expansion encouraged by the investment insurance of the aid regime. In 1981 alone, OPIC insured the creation or expansion of seventeen branches or affiliates of U.S. banks, almost all of them among the Fortune 50.[106] The expansion of bank affiliates abroad has to some degree reduced the role of the DFCs.

The World Bank is a tireless advocate of industrialization through labor-intensive export industries, and its loans for DFCs reflect this preoccupation. Most news releases it issues on its DFC loans emphasize their contribution to increasing exports. The export orientation has increasingly been written into loan agreements. For example, subprojects financed by a $150 million loan to various Philippine DFCs through the Central Bank of the Philippines "must be labor-intensive, export-oriented, and efficient in terms of resource utilization."[107] A 1981 loan to the Industrial Development Bank of Pakistan entails "priority to export-oriented, agro-based, labor-intensive projects."[108] A minimum of $14 million of a $70 million loan to Morocco's National Bank for Economic Development is to be set aside for "export-oriented industrial projects," and "priority will be given to those subprojects expected to export at least 20 percent of their incremental production."[109] Some loans not only push exports but are also linked to specific industrial sectors. A 1979 loan to two DFCs in Turkey, for example, specifically targets "private sector textile firms" and includes $1.2 million for "an extension service in industrial engineering and assistance in export marketing."[110] Ironically—and underlining the problematic nature of the World Bank's advocacy of export-led development—the United States in the same year signed an agreement with South Korea making the provision of PL 480 food aid contingent on "voluntary" restrictions by South Korea on its exports of textiles to the United States.[111]

Program Aid and Conditionality

The forms of assistance for industrial development discussed so far have all been examples of project aid. But there are also various forms of nonproject aid, which are not so easily sectorally identified. Several forms of nonproject aid clearly have only limited relevance for industry (for example, emergency and disaster relief and food aid, although the latter may be significant in keeping urban food prices and hence wages down). A substantial proportion of nonproject aid, however, takes the form of lines of credit for the financing of commodity imports or of balance of payments deficits. In 1980, such aid accounted for something over one-quarter of the total aid of those countries and institutions listed in Table 17. Not tied to specific projects, this aid might seem to offer more leeway than the forms of industrial aid we have been discussing.

Because of endemic balance of payments problems arising from their location in the world economy and because of the desire of recipient governments to determine the uses of aid, "program dollars are considered to be worth more than project dollars" in most Third World countries.[112] Precisely for that reason, however, recipient countries may be willing to accept conditions that they would otherwise be unwilling to accept. As one former aid official has concluded: "AID has thus far found loans for commodity imports the most powerful and flexible means of influencing macro-economic policies in those countries to which such loans are extended."[113] In return for flexibility in the utilization of this "free" foreign exchange, recipient governments commonly agree to bind themselves to a basic policy framework for development. This is accomplished not only through the conditions negotiated as part of the loan process but also through the structure of commodity aid programs themselves.

The basic structure of most commodity aid transfers was developed during the Marshall Plan, although the shift from grants to loans entailed significant additions. AID and its predecessor agencies have administered two major types of programs. The first is the Commodity Import Program (CIP), which has generally come under defense support programs, today called the Economic Support Fund (ESF). CIP was by far the largest commodity-financing program in the 1950s, but it was surpassed in size for most of the 1960s by program loans in support of development objectives. By the end of the 1970s, however, commodity import programs under the ESF resumed their dominant position, dwarfing the residual program lending remaining in the rest of the U.S. aid program. In addition, the U.S. government has administered a massive food aid program, which as late as the mid 1970s constituted almost half of U.S. commodity aid. Although these three commodity aid programs have had different official objectives, they have all shared the same basic structure, which is outlined for the case of program loans in the accompanying figure. Apart from the conditions often attached to such aid, the structure of commodity financing has in itself carried important implications for the development choices of Third World countries.

Some details vary with individual countries, but let us examine the basic chain of transfers involved in program loans. Following the figure, I will use the United States as a model, then note how commodity financing from other sources may vary from this.

Once an agreement with the recipient government has been reached, the U.S. government extends a line of credit for a certain dollar amount of goods. This line of credit is almost completely tied to the purchase of U.S. goods. In addition, official U.S. policy holds that commodity financing should not supplant exports that would have been purchased anyway by the recipient country; aid-financed goods should be "additional." During the 1960s, AID even prepared special "additionality" lists to promote U.S. goods that were underrepresented in Third World imports, although the basic reason for this underrepresentation was that the U.S. goods were not competitive with comparable goods from other sources. Technically, the tying provisions are suspended if the required goods are available in other underdeveloped countries, but in fiscal year 1978, less than 2 percent of U.S. commodity procurements of $1.08 billion involved non-U.S. producers.[114]

The next step is critical and is almost always written into the aid agreements. The line of credit is not available to the recipient government to use as it pleases, despite the fact that the government will be expected eventually to repay the loan, with interest. Instead, recipients must allocate most commodity financing according to market demand. To achieve this, the recipient is directed to sell the dollar

Flow of Transactions for Typical Commodity Aid Loan

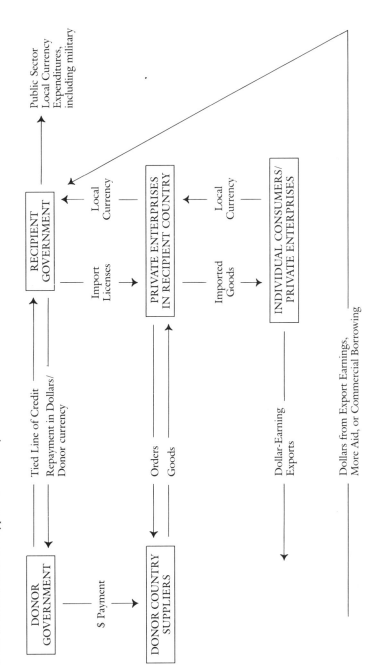

claims on U.S. goods to domestic importers and producers who pay for these dollar claims with local currency. Traditionally during the Marshall Plan and under the food aid programs, this local currency was divided between a small portion under complete control of the U.S. government and a larger portion under joint U.S.–recipient government control. In the case of India, local currency accumulated in the joint account this way eventually amounted to one-fourth of India's total money supply, an embarrassment to both sides.[115] An agreement in the 1970s essentially wrote the money off. With most commodity financing today, however, the recipient government retains full control of all or most of the local currency receipts.

The freedom of domestic importers and producers to use these import rights as they see fit varies with the program. Apart from the requirement of additionality, only minimal constraints have been placed on the CIP importers because a common goal of such aid is to placate urban elites and to lower military-induced inflation by flooding the market with imported consumer goods. Program loans may be restricted to specific sectors or types of goods; this is a matter of both donor objectives and recipient bargaining strength. At the margin, commodity financing shades into project aid; AID in the 1960s coined the phrase "sector loans" to refer to one version of this. The basic assumption, however, is that by transferring the rights to determine the content of the commodity imports to private enterprises, these enterprises and the role of the market within recipient societies are both strengthened.

The imported commodities are either sold directly to consumers or used to produce goods that will be sold to consumers or, occasionally, exported. Most food aid is likewise sold on the market. Consumers pay with local currency, which the domestic importers use to repay the government.

Apart from the possibilities for graft and the power (not politically insignificant) to grant import licenses and the like, the government is limited to an intermediary role and ends up mainly with its own local currency. Local currency can be useful in keeping down inflation (for example, by retiring public debt) and in financing the local currency costs of bureaucracies and armies, but it is useless for any kind of productive investment requiring foreign exchange. Commodity aid introduces external resources for production without in most instances expanding the state's role in production.

The recipient government is required, in the case of program loans and some CIP financing, to repay the loan with interest in dollars. This requirement structures into aid an incentive toward export-oriented development. To the extent that the commodities financed this way do not generate exports and hence foreign exchange, program lending requires recipients to use nonaid resources in a way consonant with one of the basic objectives of donor policy.

U.S. aid officials, unlike their counterparts in most other bilateral and in the multilateral agencies, must defend the intricacies of their programs before skeptical congressional committees. They have repeatedly justified this program aid structure in terms of strengthening the private sector. A USAID annual report states: "Program loans have proved to be the most effective way to get spare parts and needed equipment to private enterprise in the developing countries, helping to strengthen development of the private sector."[116] In Pakistan, "as existing foreign exchange budgetary procedures tended to treat the private sector as a residual element, commodity aid was deliberately directed to enlarging the flow of imports to that sector."[117] The shift from project to program aid weakened statist elements in the Pakistani government bureaucracy and strengthened the role of the promarket forces concentrated in the planning commission: "The Planning Commission's role increased in the Government as non-project aid assumed greater importance, since such aid gave the Planning Commission greater negotiating power with the rest of the Government."[118]

By relieving foreign exchange pressures, program aid also may lessen the temptation of governments to tap the foreign exchange currently lost through the repatriation of profits, dividends, service charges, and interests to foreign corporations and banks. Michael Barratt Brown has observed the "remarkable coincidence" that the outflow of investment income from the underdeveloped world is almost exactly balanced by the inflow of all forms of public capital, as calculated by the OECD.[119]

The basic structure of U.S. commodity aid programs has been adopted by most of the other bilateral and multilateral donors, with some exceptions. One important difference is that multilateral aid, and that of some of the bilateral aid donors, is untied. Because tying is estimated to lower the value of aid by up to 25 percent, untied loans are worth more in real terms, although the harder terms of most MDB loans offset this advantage.

Balance of payments assistance by the International Monetary Fund generally does not involve the previously described structure, partly because it is commonly devoted to financing deficits that have already been accrued. Although this IMF assistance lacks the structure of bilateral program aid, it constrains recipients with a high level of policy conditionality.

USAID pioneered both the rationale and the practice of conditional commodity financing in the 1960s. Commodity financing until then had almost always been within the context of defense support, with the combination of overriding military objectives and compliant client regimes generally making the issue of policy conditionality irrelevant or unproblematic. With the rapid expansion of development assistance to less dependent regimes in the late 1950s and early 1960s, however, USAID officials began to pay increasing attention to how aid could be used to influence broad economic policies. Development aid had mainly been project aid, and it was increasingly argued that project aid was inherently too limited, that program aid offered much greater possibilities: to influence not only the use of aid resources but of nonaid resources as well. Joan Nelson, who played a key role in elaborating USAID's rationale for conditional program lending, suggests that commodity financing offers a particularly effective means of influence for the following reasons:[120]

1. Commodity import loans are generally much larger than project loans.

2. Most donors are reluctant to finance commodity imports, al-

though this type of aid is badly needed by many Third World countries. "Therefore, commodity assistance is strongly desired and has high scarcity value."

3. The linking of program loans to broad economic policies "is more likely to seem reasonable to the recipient" because commodity imports feed into the economy as a whole.

4. Donors find reducing or cutting off project loan disbursements self-defeating, but commodity aid, in contrast, "can be increased or decreased at the margin or delayed in timing." This provides the donor with a credible threat or incentive lacking in the case of most project aid.

5. Commodity aid can finance the import cost of the kinds of policies (for example, import liberalization) that capitalist donors are likely to be pursuing.

The key term here is *scarcity*. To the extent that the LDC has alternative, less conditional, options, it is unlikely to solicit aid that both carries broad conditions and is dispensed in a way that effectively enforces these conditions. As we have seen, one type of scarcity is built into the aid regime via the norms of strategic nonlending and institutionalized noncompetition, both of which act to restrict the potential recipient's options. In addition, program lending has always concentrated in a few donors, although the balance between these donors has shifted over time. During the 1960s, the vast bulk of commodity financing came from USAID. Between 1966 and 1971, AID project loans came to about $2 billion; program loans and supporting assistance (mostly CIP) each came to about $3.6 billion. Program lending from other DAC countries was relatively insignificant, both because these programs were much smaller than USAID's and because the proportion going to commodity financing was much less. In 1970, the combined program aid of the next four largest DAC donors (France, Germany, U.K., and Japan) came to only about 40 percent of the U.S. commodity financing.[121] During the 1960s, the World Bank initiated program lending to India and Pakistan in an effort to exercise policy leverage that was, in retrospect, premature. The World

Bank subsequently drew back from program lending in the 1970s, but it has returned to it—under the label of "structural adjustment lending"—since 1979.

Table 21 presents data on nonproject aid from the major "Western" sources of aid for 1975, 1980, and 1981. The United States remains the largest source of DAC nonproject aid, although its level fluctuates considerably from year to year. Like OPEC nonproject aid, however, U.S. nonproject aid is highly concentrated in a few countries of special military significance. USAID program lending has virtually ceased; almost all nonproject financing is made through the ESF. Between 1975 and 1979, Israel and Egypt alone accounted for

TABLE 21   Nonproject Aid to LDCs from DAC Countries and Major Multilateral Sources, 1975, 1980, 1981 ($ millions)

Source	1975	1980	1981
DAC Bilateral			
United States	679.0	2014.1	1212.8
Japan	167.6	176.0	528.1
Germany	275.0	411.9	251.1
United Kingdom	319.5	87.2	175.9
Other DAC	589.5	706.2	676.8
Total	2030.6	3395.4	2844.7
World Bank Group[a]	520.0	522.5	1012.0
Regional MDBs (AfDB, ADB, IDB)[a]	27.8	0.0	0.0
International Monetary Fund[b]	2809.2	6007.7	8259.1
Total	5387.6	9925.6	12,115.8

SOURCES: Organization for Economic Cooperation and Development, *Development Co-operation: Efforts and Policies of the Development Assistance Committee, 1982 Review*, pp. 228–229; *1976 Review*, pp. 236–237; 1975, 1980, and 1981 annual reports of World Bank, International Finance Corporation, African Development Bank, Asian Development Bank, Inter-American Development Bank; International Monetary Fund, *Annual Reports*, 1975, p. 78; 1982, p. 75.

NOTE: This table excludes food aid.

  [a]Commitments.

  [b]Gross purchases, excluding reserve tranche, disbursements from administered accounts, and SDR allocations.

70.1 percent of the CIP and cash components of the ESF, which made up 70 percent of the ESF total.[122]

Table 21 indicates the growing importance of the International Monetary Fund and the World Bank for nonproject loans even before the debt crisis assumed worldwide proportions in 1982. Up through the early 1970s, USAID's nonproject aid alone far surpassed IMF lending and World Bank nonproject loans combined. In 1975, however, IMF lending was greater than the combined commodity aid of all the DAC countries, and in 1980, it was almost double. IMF lending tends to have a cyclical quality because there are formal limits on the amount of indebtedness its members can accrue, but the trend toward increased reliance on the IMF for nonproject assistance is clear. In fiscal year 1983, IMF assistance reached $11.1 billion and World Bank nonproject lending, $1.4 billion.[123]

The International Monetary Fund and the World Bank have come to monopolize nonproject financing for most countries, and internal shifts within both institutions have increased the level of conditionality of the aid. We explored in Chapter 3 how the slow growth of quotas, the establishment of new conditional facilities, and the creation of new access policies have greatly increased the proportion of IMF lending at high levels of conditionality. The World Bank has also expanded the conditionality of its lending. World Bank program loans, as noted earlier, have always been linked to a broad array of policy conditions. In 1980, however, the World Bank moved to formalize the inclusion of such conditions through the introduction of "structural adjustment" loans (SALs) specifically designed to "support major changes in policies and institutions of developing countries."[124] These loans come conceptually very close to IMF drawings under the extended financing facility and are in fact often linked to them. The Bank made the first two structural adjustment loans in fiscal year 1980, followed by twenty more between 1981 and 1983. Structural adjustment lending accounted for 71 percent of all World Bank nonproject lending in 1981, 86 percent in 1982, and 90 percent in 1983.

Although Third World countries have for years lobbied for more program lending by the World Bank, they have not clamored for structural adjustment loans. The Bank's 1981 *Annual Report* notes:

> Fewer than a dozen and a half countries, moreover, have adjustment programs that are either being supported under already approved structural-adjustment loans or for which preparatory work and discussions have begun—a number far smaller than the number of countries that need to implement such programs. The difficulty that governments find in gaining political acceptance for the adoption and implementation of structural-adjustment programs has been and continues to be the single most important obstacle to rapid progress by the Bank with structural-adjustment assistance.[125]

As of April 30, 1983, fourteen countries had received structural adjustment loans from the World Bank. All these countries had in addition standby or extended fund agreements with the IMF. Structural adjustment loans, like most other forms of program aid, are dispensed at regular intervals dependent on the recipient's fulfillment of specified conditions. Five countries have received more than one SAL, suggesting that single loans are deliberately set less than the cost of the total program. Indeed, the Bank has stated: "Structural adjustment lending . . . envisages the probability of multiyear programs being worked out and supported by a succession of loans."[126] The U.S. Treasury Department report discussed in the previous chapter spells out the implications:

> Given the structural and development situation of SAL recipients, the objective of attaining a sustainable deficit on current account can, in most cases, only be achieved in the medium-term. Thus, an important conditionality feature of the SAL program—which is premised on a series of loans to a country over a 5–7 year period—is leverage the Bank can exert to secure policy changes called for in a recipient's first SAL by withholding approval for a second SAL. For example, in the Malawi SAL, the Bank has made it clear there will be no second SAL until a fundamental reorganization of a dominant private holding company along lines prescribed by the Bank is achieved. A final judgment on the effectiveness of a given SAL program will often have to await, not the policy changes speci-

fied in a single SAL, but the anticipated economic results sought over the medium-term.[127]

World Bank policy currently limits structural adjustment lending to 10 percent of total lending, and a variety of vested interests will make it difficult for the Bank to raise this limit significantly. Accordingly, the Bank has undertaken an effort to convince bilateral donors to increase the level of their program aid. As one summary of a major World Bank report on Africa in 1981 put it:

> Donors should be prepared to provide these more flexible forms of support where they are satisfied that the recipient government is pursuing policies conducive to structural adjustment. One way to become satisfied on this point is to support, and allocate funds within the framework of, a structural adjustment programme negotiated and supervised by the World Bank and/or the IMF.[128]

World Bank efforts to line up bilateral cofinancing in advance, not tied to specific projects, represents an important part of this strategy.

Structural adjustment lending constitutes the World Bank's most potent weapon in its decade-long struggle against import substitution industrialization in favor of export-oriented development. In a typical statement, the Bank asserts:

> Most programs supported by assistance from the Bank, however, have included policy changes designed to initiate corrections of biases in incentive systems that deter exports and promote uneconomical import substitution. Structural-adjustment lending to the Philippines, for instance, has provided support for the beginning stages of a five-year program to correct such biases.[129]

"Outward-oriented policies with low protection" are the basic aim of structural adjustment lending.[130] Although the range of policy areas has varied among different SAL recipients, all have agreed to institute changes in trade policy designed to orient the economy more toward international market forces and toward exports.[131]

Noting that "often the need for structural adjustment is greatest in those countries that find it most difficult to adopt effective programs," the Bank has supported policy improvements on a more limited sectoral basis in the hope that they could be broadened gradually. The emphasis in these operations has been on reform of policies and institutions in priority sectors and subsectors of an economy—agricultural rehabilitation in Sudan and export rehabilitation in Tanzania, for example.[132]

The Bank's relatively few non-SAL program loans commonly seem to fall into this category. For example, the Bank's $110 million loan to Bangladesh in 1983 was "to finance essential imports in support of a broad range of improvements in public financial-resource mobilization and budgetary management, agricultural and food policies, and trade and industrial policies."[133]

Conclusion

The common perception that economic aid has mainly financed large-scale industrial projects is untrue; only a minute proportion of aid flows has been for this purpose, both in the past and currently. The alternative conclusion by some—that the withholding of aid from industrial projects represents an attempt to prevent industrialization—is also untrue. Aid has been structured to promote a certain type of industrialization, which is characterized by private ownership, openness to foreign capital, and reliance on market forces, and which is, increasingly, export oriented. Despite the small proportion of aid that has been directed to specific industrial projects, the aid regime has nonetheless played a major role in managing the process of industrial development in the Third World. Through the provision of direct financing for multinational investment, through insuring multinational investment, through sponsoring development finance companies that not only have been an important source of capital for the private sector but that have facilitated joint ventures between foreign and local capital, and through both the structure and conditionality of program assistance, regime norms have been implemented in a way promoting basic processes of dependent development.

The Aid Regime in Crisis

Introduction to Part Two: Crises of Dependent Development

The preceding chapters have emphasized the continuities of the economic aid regime. Despite the proliferation and diversification of aid sources, changes in fashion in development thinking, and significant shifts in the international balance of power, the bulk of economic assistance from the days of the Marshall Plan to the present has been structured to oppose the development both of national capitalism and of more radical, socialist departures from multilateral capitalism; to promote the expansion of the private sector, both domestic and foreign, and the dominance of market principles of exchange; and to encourage "outward-looking," export-oriented types of development. Changes in the aid regime have provided Third World countries some increased room for maneuver with respect to some issues, but the regime as a whole has made fundamental departures from these basic goals quite costly.

Elites in advanced capitalist countries have been divided about

191

how successfully the aid regime has promoted these goals. In the United States, the *Wall Street Journal* portrays the World Bank as run by dangerously utopian social experimenters. The newspaper opposed the 1983 quota increase for the International Monetary Fund. David Stockman, the Reagan administration's former budget director, accused the World Bank of placing "a major emphasis on programs fostering income redistribution," of supporting "state planning efforts in some countries," and of failing to "press recipients to redirect their economies toward a market orientation."[1] Conservative critics have for years published books with titles such as *The Great Giveaway*, attacking the efficacy of aid.[2] Somewhat ironically, the leftist critics of aid have generally attributed to it the most "success" in meeting the goals of the advanced capitalist countries.[3]

The fears of U.S. policymakers in the early days of the aid programs about the likelihood of noncapitalist development have not materialized, despite many reasons to believe that Third World societies would gravitate toward nationalist, statist, and perhaps socialist forms of development. Although donors have experienced some political setbacks and defeats, overall the aid regime has successfully promoted the basic goals of the United States and the other advanced capitalist countries. The very issues that define the agenda of development theory and practice today—the worldwide role of multinational corporations and banks, the problem of debt, the enormous increase in trade interdependence, the failure of market mechanisms to do much about rural poverty, the devastating consequences of recession in the West, the debate over IMF conditionality—testify to the success of the aid regime in promoting a multilateral capitalist world economy.

The success of the aid regime in promoting dependent development led to the emergence of two major problems during the 1970s that by the end of the decade prompted a pervasive sense of crisis. The first problem arose from the profoundly inegalitarian nature of the "development" promoted by the aid regime. As became increasingly clear in the 1970s, the benefits of worldwide dependent development were being distributed on a highly unequal basis, both among and within Third World countries. In response, in the mid 1970s, aid regime goals were overhauled in favor of "meeting basic needs." Although the goal of meeting basic needs was strongly asserted at the level of principle, its realization at the levels of norms, rules, and procedures was sharply limited. Nonetheless, some innovative initiatives were undertaken during the 1970s.

The second major problem was the crisis of debt that engulfed much of the Third World from the beginnings of the deep world recession in 1980 onward. The debt crisis is conventionally dated from Mexico's move to reschedule its debt in August 1982 and is seen as something to which the aid regime responded rather than contributed. In reality, a crisis of official debt was evident as early as 1979, and the operation of the aid regime was an important factor in the accumulation of commercial debt. For some countries, commercial borrowing constituted a means of escape from the traditional constraints of the aid regime. The debt crisis heightened the crisis in the aid regime itself, for traditional regime norms proved inadequate to deal with the depth of the problem. Despite apocalyptic warnings in the popular press, however, the era of debt crisis has been characterized not by institutional breakdown but by a restructuring of the aid regime that has reconsolidated the disciplinary functions weakened in the 1970s. Even those countries that successfully avoided debt renegotiation face an international context greatly altered by the debt crisis.

The problems of basic needs and of debt crisis have tended to focus attention on different geographical areas: basic needs primarily on Africa and South Asia, the debt crisis on Latin America and East Asia. But the issues are deeply interrelated, both stemming from a common process of worldwide development in which the aid regime has been an important determining element. The debt crisis is gradually extending to Africa and many of the low-income countries generally, and issues of basic needs are gaining new prominence in the wake of "adjustment" programs in many of the so-called middle-income countries.

The next chapter explores the origins and meaning of the basic needs approach and attempts to assess its effect on aid allocation. The overall theme is the limits of regime change. Furthermore, I argue that the impact of the world recession and the debt crisis—while unquestionably raising levels of poverty—has been to weaken the commitment to regime reforms focused on basic needs.

Chapter 6 explores in detail how the aid regime contributed to the buildup of debt in the Third World during the 1970s and how at the same time the availability of commercial financing weakened the aid regime's capacity to shape basic processes of development during the better part of a decade. The result, I argue, was an expansion of "state capitalist" development strategies that elicited increasing alarm among the aid institutions as time went by. By the beginning of the 1980s, however, state capitalist strategies were in crisis, as interest rates soared and both the volume and terms of trade plunged.

Chapter 7 details the process of aid regime restructuring and reconsolidation in the wake of the debt crisis in the 1980s. Although overall aid flows have been declining since 1981, an increasing proportion of other resource flows has been tied to aid regime functioning. The level of conditionality associated with aid and with these other flows has been substantially increased. A general reorientation of development aid has been brought about through the elaboration of an ideology and program of "structural adjustment." But whereas the aid regime has reconsolidated its disciplinary functions, it has done so in ways that could, under certain conditions, undermine its capacity to deal with future crises. This possibility is explored in the Epilogue.

5

Basic Needs and the Limits of Regime Change

One World Bank publication has referred to "a quiet revolution" in development thinking during the 1970s.[1] In fact, it was anything but quiet—the new orientation was announced with enormous fanfare. The U.S. Congress formally mandated a "New Directions" approach in 1973, involving, according to one observer, "priorities so different as to constitute a new official development assistance program."[2] At the World Employment Conference of the International Labor Organization in 1976, delegates "enthroned" a basic needs approach.[3] The Development Assistance Committee formally adopted a "basic human needs" approach in October 1977.[4] The World Bank has tirelessly expounded the new doctrine and sponsored major research efforts in support of it. The Bank's new approach has been hailed as "a far-reaching change in its development perspective" and as "a major new trend in lending that took concrete shape in the 1970s."[5]

In this chapter, I trace the origins of the crisis in development thinking that led to the elaboration of a basic needs approach and analyze the new approach's basic assumptions. I then assess the impact of basic needs thinking on aid allocation, noting that there has been a range of opinions about its operational implications. Analysis of changes in aid allocation in terms of countries, sectors, and policy conditionality indicates some modest changes in regime norms, rules, and procedures—though certainly falling short of the changes asserted at the level of regime principles. These changes, furthermore, can be accounted for largely by traditional regime norms; basic needs to some degree appears to constitute a humanitarian gloss on practices that would have existed anyway. The final section reviews the World Bank's analysis of its experience in this area and suggests that the basic needs approach is in decline.

Origins of the Basic Needs Approach

The change in development thinking in the early 1970s had a variety of sources. Undoubtedly the most important source was the very success of the aid regime in the 1950s and 1960s in promoting market-based, outward-oriented growth throughout the Third World. The United Nations had set a growth target of 5 percent per annum for the "development decade" of the 1960s, and overall this target was exceeded. Aid success was measured in terms of country growth rates, and individual projects were evaluated in terms of their contribution to overall growth rates.

By the early 1970s, however, those within the aid community increasingly recognized that the success of the development decade hid a more basic failure. The most famous indictment came from Robert McNamara, the relatively new president of the World Bank, before the board of governors in Nairobi in 1973:

> The basic problem of poverty and growth in the developing world can be stated very simply. The growth is not equitably reaching the poor. . . .

The data suggest that the decade of rapid growth has been accompanied by greater maldistribution of income in many developing countries, and that the problem is most severe in the countryside. . . . One can conclude that policies aimed primarily at accelerating economic growth, in most developing countries, have benefitted mainly the upper 40 percent of the population and the allocation of public services and investment funds has tended to strengthen rather than offset this trend.[6]

A year later an important Bank publication put the matter even more baldly:

It is now clear that more than a decade of rapid growth in underdeveloped countries has been of little or no benefit to perhaps a third of their population. . . . Paradoxically, while growth policies have succeeded beyond the expectations of the first development decade, the very idea of aggregate growth as a social objective has increasingly been called into question.[7]

Although insider accounts tend to treat this realization among development thinkers and their subsequent emphasis on basic needs as a natural process—a major World Bank theorist characterizing it as "no more, but also no less, than a stage in the thinking and responses to the challenges presented by development over the last 20 to 25 years"[8]—official aid institutions were led to adopt this new point of view by a number of other factors as well.

Of these other factors, the Vietnam War was perhaps the most crucial, especially given McNamara's metamorphosis from U.S. Secretary of Defense to president of the World Bank.[9] South Vietnam was touted in USAID literature in the 1950s and early 1960s as a major aid success story, but by 1967, only the presence of 535,000 U.S. troops could keep the South Vietnamese regime in power. Vietnam was by far the largest recipient of USAID assistance between 1962 and 1975, and the war as a whole is estimated to have cost the United States $168 billion—more than all economic aid from all sources to all LDCs during those years.[10] In Vietnam, the trickledown assumptions of capitalist growth theory did not work, and the specter of "two, three, many Vietnams" threatened the continued functioning of the aid regime.

As one sympathetic observer of the World Bank described the Bank's initiatives:

> The underlying political rationale behind the bank's poverty focus is the pursuit of political stability through what might be called defensive modernization. This strategy rests on an assumption that reform can forestall or pre-empt the accumulation of social and political pressures if people are given a stake in the system. Reform thus prevents the occurrence of full-fledged revolutions.[11]

The commitment to defensive modernization even led some aid officials to criticize previously lauded "models" of development. In 1971, Mahbub ul Haq, then senior adviser to the World Bank's Economic Department and soon to become director of policy planning and program review (until 1982), stated:

> In Pakistan, which increased a healthy growth rate during the 1960s, unemployment increased, real wages in the industrial sector declined by one-third, per capita income disparity between East and West Pakistan nearly doubled, and concentrations of industrial wealth became an explosive economic and political issue. And in 1968, while the international world was still applauding Pakistan as a model of development, the system exploded—not only for political reasons but for economic unrest. Brazil has recently achieved a growth rate close to 7 percent, but continuing maldistribution of income continues to threaten the very fabric of its society.[12]

In the context of this kind of critique, and with the United States moving to establish diplomatic relations with China, the World Bank and the other aid agencies could no longer ignore the development experience of China and other state socialist societies. Belated recognition of the achievements of these societies was a second factor contributing to the elaboration of an alternative to the traditional growth perspective. Mahbub ul Haq also observed in 1971:

> It appears that within a period of less than two decades, China has eradicated the worst forms of poverty; it has full employment, universal literacy, and adequate health facilities; it suffers from no obvious malnutrition or squalor. . . . China has proved that it is a fallacy that poverty can be

removed and full employment achieved only at high rates of growth and only over a period of many decades.[13]

The aid institutions, as we shall see, managed to assimilate the experience of China and other state socialist countries in a way that avoids revolutionary conclusions.

More difficult to trace is the effect of the critiques of aid and dominant patterns of development offered by dependency theorists and others on the Left during the late 1960s and early 1970s. By the mid 1970s, the establishmentarian modernization theory had been demolished within the academy—so much so that an article in the joint World Bank/IMF official journal *Finance and Development* insisted that the Bank "at no time embraced W. W. Rostow's stage theory of development and the 'takeoff into self-sustained growth.'"[14] Aid institutions were increasingly confronted by Third World representatives versed in these critiques.

The shift to basic needs in official development thinking implicitly acknowledged the validity of elements of these critiques, but it effectively shifted the focus of debate away from international to domestic factors. Although the basic needs approach drew on research carried out by Third World social scientists, many in the Third World viewed it as an attempt

> to shift back to the South the responsibility for problems of extreme poverty and deprivation. As used by Northern groups, the basic needs concept focuses more on internal inequalities in the South rather than on North-South disparities.[15]

The diffuseness of the "basic needs" approach has allowed numerous different programs and institutions to claim it. A U.S. Peace Corps document stated in 1978:

> "Basic human needs" means all things to all people or, more accurately, too few things to too few people. The Peace Corps is not the only organization that has had difficulty in reaching a common definition as to just what is meant by the concept.[16]

The DAC has called basic needs "a new employment-oriented approach to development."[17] Mahbub ul Haq of the World Bank has described its focus as "meeting the consumption needs of the entire population, not only in the customary areas of education and health, but also in nutrition, housing, water supply, and sanitation."[18] Aid donors have interpreted the new official DAC focus on basic needs variously. The 1978 *Review* of the Development Assistance Committee reported that "a number of DAC countries view their objectives as reasonably in line with the basic needs objectives and have seen little reason to change present policies for development assistance," characterizing the needed changes as mainly "tactical and procedural in nature." Steven Arnold's survey of five European aid donors, published in 1982, found little agreement about how the 1977 DAC resolution on basic needs should be implemented.[19]

Although some critics have dismissed the basic needs approach as an ideological smokescreen, it is more useful to see the basic needs approach as a genuine effort to respond to acutely perceived problems within the institutional and normative confines of the aid regime. Within these confines, one can detect incipient "Left" and "Right" versions of the basic needs strategy.[20] The most elaborated and dominant version is that of the World Bank. Accordingly, the following discussion focuses primarily, although not exclusively, on World Bank sources.

The basic needs approach developed in two stages. The first was the emergence in the early 1970s of the critique of growth measures as indicators of development and as goals of aid policy. McNamara's Nairobi speech was an important event in this process, but the U.S. Congress was already in the process of overhauling the structure of the U.S. aid programs under the title of "New Directions."[21] Given the key role the U.S. Congress plays in determining the level of resources flowing through the aid regime, the World Bank's new emphasis on absolute poverty from 1972 onward may have been in part a response to U.S. domestic politics. In 1973, the World Bank cosponsored a workshop in Bellagio and a conference at the University of Sussex on the subject of redistribution with growth and in the subsequent year published a book with that title that was the single most important document defining the new orientation during this

early period. Despite its title, *Redistribution with Growth* did not actually advocate redistribution of income or wealth. As a Bank senior
economist stated in the book:

> In espousing the general principle of redistributing the benefits of growth,
> an essentially political judgment was made, which is thematic to the vol-
> ume as a whole. This is that intervention which alters the distribution of
> the *increment* to the overall capital stock and income will arouse less hos-
> tility from the rich than transfers which bite into their existing assets and
> incomes.[22]

Because only the increment of growth was to be redistributed, the
strategy in effect placed as much emphasis on growth as the earlier
growth theories.

Although the articles in *Redistribution with Growth* did not hold to
a single line, they generally rejected the viability of strategies to re-
distribute existing assets. One article commented on "the danger of
economic retaliation which may involve significant economic costs in
terms of disruption of trade and capital flows"—it left unstated that
the World Bank itself would be one of the major agents of such economic retaliation.[23] Instead of redistribution of existing assets, "dynamic redistribution," or investment to raise the productivity of the
poor, was presented as the preferred strategy.[24] As McNamara put it
in 1975, "No degree of egalitarianism alone will solve the root problem of poverty. What is required are policies that will enhance the
productivity of the poor."[25]

The second stage saw a redefinition of what an assault on absolute
poverty would involve. International legitimization for this redefinition was provided by the basic needs resolutions of the World Employment Conference of the International Labor Organization in
June 1976.[26] In the hands of the World Bank, basic needs became
more of a consumption-oriented approach, although a production
component was also maintained. The main statement of the World
Bank's interpretation is *First Things First: Meeting Basic Human Needs
in Developing Countries*. Bank authors have published a wide range of
articles and booklets as well.[27]

The Bank's basic needs approach is an elaboration of the general strategy of "redistribution with growth." [28] Without prejudging the degree to which its theory has been translated into its project lending, the Bank's definition of this approach bears examination.

Assumptions of the Basic Needs Approach

As a theoretical orientation, the World Bank's interpretation of a basic needs approach has three dominant features. The first is the redefinition of absolute poverty in terms of unmet basic needs rather than income level and the attempt to devise programs and policies that will meet these basic needs directly. As Paul Streeten puts it: "The basic needs approach is concerned with particular goods and services directed at particular, identified human beings." [29] As yet, no agreement has been reached on the definition of either basic needs or the goods and services required to fulfill them, but *First Things First* proposes the following categories and indicators: [30]

BASIC NEED	INDICATOR
Health	Life expectancy at birth
Education	Literacy
	Primary school enrollment as a percentage of the population aged five to fourteen
Food	Calorie supply per head or calorie supply as a percentage of requirements
Water supply	Infant mortality per thousand births
	Percentage of population with access to potable water
Sanitation	Infant mortality per thousand births
	Percentage of population with access to sanitation facilities

Although the literature on basic needs varies considerably in the degree of sophistication about why such limited and minimal basic needs are not being met, the dominant imagery stresses the isolation and passivity of the poor, defined as "target groups." *First Things First* describes such target groups as typically "remote from the centers of economic activity," "distinct from those involved in the mainstream of economic activity," "weak and inarticulate," "not affected by the forces of economic progress," and as having "values . . . different from those of the planners and administrators."[31] McNamara repeatedly described the poor as having "remained largely outside the entire development effort"[32] and lying "beyond the reach of traditional market forces and present public services."[33]

The second feature involves the explicit juxtaposition of a basic needs approach with an approach that aims to reduce inequality, either domestic or international. Bank spokespersons argue that it is preferable to focus on meeting basic needs for a combination of normative, political, and economic reasons. The normative argument is presented in *First Things First*:

> First, equality as such is probably not an objective of great importance to most people other than utilitarian philosophers and ideologues. Second, this lack of concern is justified, because meeting basic human needs is morally a more important objective than reducing inequality.[34]

There is certainly reason to doubt the first statement, and the second may not be self-evident to all.[35] The crux of the issue is whether basic needs can be met without reducing inequality.

The only type of inequality the authors of *First Things First* discuss seriously is income inequality, and here they show no interest in income deciles, "for these are not sociologically, politically, or humanly interesting groups."[36] The logic of this position has pushed the Bank toward denial of sociological, political, or human significance of other forms of inequality as well. For example, the Bank's 1978 *World Development Report* disposes of the issue of tenancy in Asia in this way:

> While the problems created by tenancy are significant, they should not be exaggerated in the context of the development goals of accelerating growth and alleviating poverty. With some exceptions, tenancy prevails in only a small part of the agricultural sector, and most farmers are as likely

to lease land as to rent it. There is thus no sharp dichotomy between landlord and tenant in most areas in this region. Less than 6 percent of the
agricultural land in Bangladesh, India, and Indonesia is cultivated by tenants who do not also own or rent out land; in Pakistan, where the average
size of tenant holdings is considerably larger, the proportion is under
30 percent. Further, the area under tenancy has been declining in the last
decade or so. Where new technologies have penetrated, not only does the
scale of tenancy decline but the relations between landlord and tenant are
redefined, the sharing of input costs being a prominent example of changes
that take place.[37]

According to a study done under contract to AID, the proportion of
the rural labor force either landless or nearly so in the four countries
containing 75 percent of the world's absolute poor is 89 percent in
Bangladesh, 79 percent in India, 89 percent in Indonesia, and 88
percent in Pakistan. The Bank's own estimates of tenancy in its *Land
Reform* sector policy paper are as much as twice as high as the figures
presented in this passage.[38] By talking about proportion of land,
rather than people, and by eliminating tenants who themselves rent
out parcels of land, no matter how small and to whom (for example,
a relative), the Bank minimizes the importance of tenancy. One
might well argue, however, that the existence of leasing and renting
among the poor peasantry attests to the institutional pervasiveness of
tenancy, rather than its limited scope.

The Bank defends the basic needs approach on more explicitly
political grounds as well. First, Bank theorists argue that "reducing
inequality is a highly complex, abstract objective, open to many different interpretations and therefore operationally ambiguous" in contrast to basic needs objectives, which involve "concrete, specific
achievements judged by clear criteria."[39] More to the point, basic
needs objectives are more likely to be acceptable to existing Third
World governments. The 1980 *World Development Report* argues that
although "countries differ considerably in the priority they attach to
distributional objectives, there appears to be unanimity on the need
to reduce, and at some point eliminate, absolute poverty."[40] Similarly,
it is argued that people in the developed countries are more likely to

support aid aimed at meeting basic needs than aid designed to reduce inequality, either internal or international.

It is very doubtful whether closing the income gap [between rich and poor countries] in the near future is either desirable or possible. But closing the gap in terms of fulfilling basic needs as shown by such indicators as life expectancy, literacy rates, or nutrition levels is more desirable, feasible, and worthy of effort in international cooperation. . . . Therefore closing the basic needs gap is a more sensible and appealing objective than closing the income gap, and it should mobilize national and international support.[41]

The argument against promoting international equality spills over into the debate about a new international economic order. Basic needs theorists claim that their approach complements the reform of the international economic order. Nonetheless, *First Things First* argues that the benefits from trade and investment reforms envisioned by NIEO advocates would not necessarily reach the poor and that increased aid—allocated under donor control—would be more likely to contribute to the fulfillment of basic needs.[42] In fact, the literature is quite explicit in locating the main problem within the Third World: "The major obstacle to a better sharing of the benefits of growth is . . . the determination of developing countries to redefine the objectives of development, to reorient their policies, and to implement them."[43] The *Wall Street Journal* shared this sentiment in response to a 1983 World Bank report on Africa:

The bank's report flatly contradicts the conventional wisdom. The conventional wisdom (meaning what most people read or get preached at them on this subject) is that the poor state of economies in Africa is primarily *our* fault. Wrong, says the bank's report. After 10 years of extending $12.8 billion of loans to Africa, half of it without interest, the bank concludes that the problem is mostly *their* fault.[44]

In addition to these normative and political arguments, Bank theorists make a variety of economic arguments about why a basic needs approach is preferable to both traditional "trickle-down" approaches and to direct redistribution. Arguing that "growth is vital to reducing all aspects of absolute poverty," the Bank in *Poverty and Human Development* emphasizes how investment in "human capital" will promote growth through raising the productivity of the poor.[45] Although the human capital emphasis—particularly the stress on the importance of primary education—is much greater than it was in *Redistribution with Growth*, the approaches are linked by a common emphasis on raising productivity and growth rates.

The third central feature of the Bank's approach to basic needs is its resolute political indeterminacy. The Bank maintains that "political and economic systems among successful countries vary widely."[46] Therefore, "basic needs are not the monopoly of one creed."[47] The basic needs approach does not involve a "call to revolution," and "socialism is not a prerequisite" for meeting basic needs.[48] Such claims would be harder to substantiate if the goal of basic needs policy was reducing inequality or exploitation. South Korea and Taiwan, the two favored cases of outward-looking, export-oriented, rapid-growth countries, fare quite well on basic needs indicators, to the great satisfaction of World Bank officials. At the same time, the Bank's research on successful cases of basic needs fulfillment has forced it to speak positively of the strategies of countries it and other aid institutions have historically boycotted, such as Cuba and China, and to acknowledge the efficacy of subsidy policies, which it has consistently opposed as "inefficient" and as "distorting" market principles, in countries such as Sri Lanka and Tanzania.[49]

The Bank's indifference to larger social and political factors produces unusual bedfellows. The *World Development Report* analyzing agriculture in terms of bimodal versus unimodal agrarian structures lumps together China, Egypt, Malaysia, and South Korea in the "unimodal" single category.[50] A list of countries categorized as "doing well" on basic needs combines Taiwan, South Korea, the Philippines, Paraguay, Thailand, Sri Lanka, Cuba, Jamaica, Colombia, and Uruguay.[51] Taiwan and South Korea are described at one point as "fast growers with equality" and elsewhere as having "a relatively egalitarian distribution of income."[52] The poor are said to "have shared equitably in income growth" in Israel, Yugoslavia, Taiwan, Korea, Sri

Lanka, Costa Rica, and Tanzania.[53] Meeting the Bank's basic needs indicators has become a sign of "equity" and sometimes even "equality," without these terms ever being defined. What is cited as "equitable" and "egalitarian" development, moreover, appears to be compatible with increasing inequality in the distribution of income. In the Philippines, cited by the Bank as "doing well" on basic needs, income inequality is not only the highest in Southeast Asia but is also steadily increasing.[54]

Basic Needs and Aid Allocation

The development of the basic needs perspective has surely affected the intellectual work that goes on within the aid agencies. This perspective has in fact been associated with a major increase in the research operations of the agencies, most notably the World Bank. In addition to analyses of how to implement the approach within the context of individual institutions, there has been a substantial increase in research on income distribution, poverty, social policy, the effects of development on women, and other related issues. Virtually all aid organizations now take pains to distance themselves from previous "trickle-down" assumptions and to demonstrate their concern with poverty and basic needs. But as a former World Bank official comments: "This material has to be used with caution. Some staff members may be prolific writers, but it does not follow that they have much impact on Bank policy. The contrary conclusion could also be drawn: they have time to write so much because they have so few other responsibilities within the Bank!"[55]

In fact, changes in actual aid allocation have been considerably less striking. None of the regime assumptions discussed in Chapter 3 has been challenged; the changes that have taken place have been very much "norm-governed." Indeed, it may be argued that basic needs has provided a new, humanitarian rationale for developments always anticipated and justified by traditional regime norms. The changes in aid allocation involve (1) distribution among countries, (2) distribution among sectors, and (3) the degree and nature of policy conditionality.

Distribution Among Countries

One way of implementing a basic needs approach is to link economic aid to the basic needs record of recipient countries. Rejecting fears that a basic needs approach may mean the withholding of aid from industrial development, Mahbub ul Haq writes:

> Developing countries may well establish steel mills, or any other industry, and still remain consistent with their aim to reduce poverty so long as the benefits of the consequent growth are channeled to the poor. So the support of the donors for such projects should be based on their judgment of whether the overall development plans and policies of the country concerned are consistent with the objective of meeting basic needs, rather than on an evaluation of individual projects.[56]

He hopes that the donors' "overall policy signals can make clear that additional assistance will be given to those countries which commit themselves to giving higher priority to basic needs."[57] Among the bilateral donors, Sweden has been the most vocal and consistent advocate of this position. Sweden for years has pursued a policy of "partners, not projects," an approach reflected not only in its choice of recipients—the top four are Tanzania, Vietnam, India, and Mozambique—but also in the high proportion of assistance provided as program aid.[58]

The basic needs rationale may have strengthened the capacity of some leftist regimes to solicit new or increased aid from some European countries, but there is no evidence that aid allocation among countries overall has been significantly affected by the changes in development thinking discussed in this chapter. Among DAC countries, Tanzania, with a good basic needs reputation, received in 1979–80 the largest share of DAC ODA of any country in sub-Saharan Africa, but it was followed by Zaire, widely regarded as the opposite extreme.[59] Although a poor basic needs record has never resulted in

World Bank aid being withheld, failure to compensate expropriated foreign investors has (for example, in Ethiopia during the later 1970s and early 1980s).[60] The World Bank has refused new aid to Nicaragua since early 1982.[61] In 1979, it bowed to congressional pressure and agreed to withhold all aid from Vietnam in return for support for IDA funds.[62] Only the distribution of aid from the Scandinavian countries can be considered consistent with a policy of systematically rewarding basic needs performers, and this practice was well established even before basic needs came into vogue.

No clear relationship exists between aid allocation and the basic needs records of recipient countries not only for aggregate aid but also for "new style" projects ostensibly designed to alleviate poverty directly. A large proportion of World Bank rural and urban development loans has been directed to countries with notorious basic needs records (for example, Brazil, Bangladesh, Indonesia, and Zaire). To the extent that the aim of such lending is to support "defensive modernization," such a pattern is not surprising. But even an observer sympathetic to these aims, such as Robert Ayres, expresses the concern that the Bank has "fallen into one of its familiar habits, that of equating a country's willingness to undertake a poverty-oriented project with a wholesale change in sectoral policy in the country."[63]

A second way of linking basic needs to country aid allocation, one more consistent with the resolute political indeterminacy of the perspective, is focusing the most concessional forms of aid on the "neediest" countries. This view calls for an inverse relationship between level and concessionality of aid and "need," generally defined as per capita income. The World Bank formalizes this relationship by dividing recipients between its two arms, the IDA and the IBRD. (A similar division is found regarding the ordinary capital resources and the "special funds" of the regional development banks.) The IDA claims to take account of four main criteria—poverty (measured by per capita income), creditworthiness, economic performance, and population size—but per capita income level is critical. The IDA does not lend to any country with income over $730 per capita, and in fact between 1977 and 1982, 83 percent of its lending went to countries with per capita incomes below $410. The IBRD, in contrast, concentrates its lending on countries with per capita incomes above $730; such countries received 66 percent of IBRD loans between 1977 and 1982. In addition thirteen "blend" countries are eligible for both IDA and IBRD loans, accounting for 17 percent of IDA lending and 34 percent of IBRD lending between 1977 and 1983.[64] The $730 ceiling for the IDA is in real terms the same as the $250 ceiling established in 1964, so the IDA practice predates the basic needs perspective. Gross disbursements have increased much more rapidly for the IBRD than the IDA, however, growing by a factor of over three, compared to a factor of two for the IDA between 1975 and 1982.[65]

There have been some shifts in the roster of IDA recipients as a result of the IDA graduation policy dating back to 1964. Twenty-three countries had been graduated from IDA lending as of 1982. Apart from European countries, only Singapore and Venezuela have been formally graduated from the IBRD.[66] A consequence of IDA graduation policy has been the increasing proportion of sub-Saharan African countries in the IDA-only category. Between 1961–70 and 1977–82, sub-Saharan countries increased their share of IDA commitments from 16 to 26 percent. The main focus of IDA lending has always been South Asia, however; between these two time periods, South Asia's (mainly India, Bangladesh, and Pakistan) share declined only modestly from 63 percent to 60 percent.[67] In sum, although IDA's move out of some regions (Haiti and Guyana are the only remaining Latin American clients) and its increased emphasis on sub-Saharan Africa have often been presented as evidence of the basic needs approach, the IDA's actions can be equally well explained by the norms of creditworthiness, strategic nonlending, and institutionalized noncompetition, which date back to the origins of the aid regime. Both the DAC countries and the World Bank currently defend their low level of per capita assistance to India, the country with the largest number of absolute poor, on the grounds that India has access to and can afford commercial financing.[68]

Table 22 allows us to examine changes in DAC bilateral and multilateral aid allocations (including OPEC institutions) to the classes of

TABLE 22 Distribution of DAC Bilateral and Multilateral ODA and Total Official Flows, 1974 and 1980 (net disbursements)

Class of Country[a]	DAC Bilateral ODA		DAC Bilateral Total		Multilateral ODA		Multilateral Total	
	1974	1980	1974	1980	1974	1980	1974	1980
LLDCs								
$ m.	1181.7	3222.2	1182.3	4180.8	654.3	2030.0	671.8	2170.2
percentage	16.3	20.4	6.1	8.5	26.7	28.7	15.7	18.2
Other LICs								
$ m.	3125.2	5301.7	4379.5	8370.1	1020.5	3433.7	1060.1	4241.3
percentage	43.2	33.5	22.8	17.0	41.6	48.5	24.8	35.6
MICs								
$ m.	2365.7	6636.4	7051.8	15595.2	546.1	1490.2	1150.6	3577.1
percentage	32.7	41.9	36.7	31.7	22.3	21.0	26.9	30.0
NICs								
$ m.	403.7	401.0	6419.7	16002.5	150.0	59.6	1166.9	1802.7
percentage	5.6	2.5	33.4	32.6	6.1	0.8	27.3	15.2
OPEC[b]								
$ m.	160.2	270.0	187.0	4998.6	79.8	70.9	225.9	122.7
percentage	2.2	1.7	1.0	10.2	3.3	1.0	5.3	1.0
Total ($ m.)	7242.5	15831.3	19220.3	49147.2	2450.7	7084.4	4275.3	11914.0

SOURCE: Organization for Economic Cooperation and Development, *Geographical Distribution of Financial Flows to Developing Countries, 1977/1980* (Paris: OECD, 1981).

[a] See the Appendix for a list of countries in each category.
[b] Excludes Indonesia and Nigeria, which are included in the "Other LICs" and "MICs" categories, respectively.

countries distinguished by the OECD between 1974 and 1980. The table includes four types of data: (1) bilateral official development assistance (ODA) from DAC countries, (2) total bilateral net official flows from DAC countries (ODA plus other official flows of a less-concessionary nature), (3) ODA from multilateral institutions, and (4) total net flows from multilateral institutions. All figures refer to net disbursements.

The data in Table 22 support the position that the basic needs emphasis has not been associated with any fundamental redirection of aid flows. The proportion of ODA going to the least developed countries (LLDCs) has increased slightly, from 16.3 percent of the total to 20.4 percent for DAC bilateral ODA and 26.7 percent to 28.7 percent for multilateral ODA. But for DAC bilateral ODA, this increase has been offset by an overall decrease to low-income countries (LICs) overall. Clearly there has been no major reallocation overall either to LLDCs or to LICs.

These aggregate figures hide considerable variation among individual donors. Among the major DAC donors, France and the United States have by far the worst record regarding basic needs, with only 10.9 percent and 15 percent of bilateral ODA going to LLDCs in 1980 respectively. At the same time, the greater proportions of ODA allocated to LLDCs by some other donors reflect not so much a basic needs approach but the poverty of their ex-colonies, which have always absorbed a disproportionate part of their aid.

Table 23 allows us to examine the distribution of ODA among groups of LDCs by category of donor. Most IBRD and regional development bank lending does not qualify as ODA and is therefore not included in the table; such lending is heavily concentrated in the middle-income and newly industrializing countries. Even so, the data show the continuation of the "middle-income bias" documented in numerous aid allocation studies, although the degree of that bias for ODA alone seems to have declined.[69] The bias exists most strongly for OPEC and DAC bilateral ODA, least for multilateral ODA, reflecting the fact that multilateral agencies have the most formalized procedures of graduation.

TABLE 23   1980 Per Capita ODA Receipts of Different Groups of LDCs, by Category of Donor

Recipient Group	Population (millions)	Per Capita Income	ODA Receipts by Donor Group				
			DAC Bilateral[a]	Multilateral	OPEC Bilateral	Communist[b]	Total
LLDCs	268	$190	$13.60	$5.98	$3.07	$1.19	$23.84
Other LICs[c]	1129	$240	4.98	2.76	0.73	0.84	9.31
MICs	960	$418	16.29	3.12	9.66	1.05	30.12
OPEC[d]	105	$3,010	2.63	0.63	0.40	1.07	4.73
NICs	338	$2,140	1.17	0.12	0.05	0.05	1.34

SOURCE: Organization for Economic Cooperation and Development, *Development Co-operation: Efforts and Policies of the Members of the Development Assistance Committee, 1981 Review* (Paris, 1981), pp. 87, 236–238.

[a] Includes EEC.
[b] USSR and Eastern European countries only.
[c] Excluding China.
[d] Except Nigeria and Indonesia, which are included in the "MIC" and "Other LICs" categories, respectively.

The recipient group most out of line for all donors is the "other low-income countries" category. India, which accounts for 58 percent of the population in this category, received $3.36 per capita in 1980; Pakistan, in the same recipient group, received $15.23.[70] Although a variety of factors explains this disparity, several studies have demonstrated a "country size bias" in aid allocation, with smaller countries doing much better than larger countries. Regression results by Edelman and Chenery indicate that in 1973–74, doubling of population size meant a decrease of 35 percent in per capita aid and even more in terms of grant equivalents.[71] If China were included in the "other LICs" category in Table 23, the per capita aid receipts would be even more out of line. Unlike the bias in favor of middle-income countries, the bias against large population countries seems to be increasing.

Distribution Among Sectors

A second way to interpret the basic needs mandate is to focus on the sectoral allocation of aid. This has been the preferred approach of the World Bank and the majority of bilateral agencies. The basic needs literature clearly states that, theoretically, there is no automatic relationship between sectoral allocation and meeting basic needs. Aid to the agricultural sector, for example, does not automatically benefit the poor; aid for industry may benefit the poor if they receive an equitable share of the growth increment. Nonetheless, most claims about implementing a basic needs approach have relied mainly on evidence about the sectoral composition of aid.

The Functional Development Assistance Program of AID has restricted virtually all its aid to the categories of (1) agriculture, rural development, and nutrition; (2) population planning; (3) health; (4) education and human resources development; and (5) energy, private voluntary organizations, and selected development activities. No pretense is made, however, that the major part of the U.S. aid program, the Economic Support Fund, conforms to the "New Directions" or basic needs mandate.

The World Bank, summarizing the changes it instituted in support of "poverty alleviation" in the 1970s, reports that it

> increased its lending for sectors and subsectors widely considered to offer the most direct benefits to the poor—notably rural development, primary education, population, health and nutrition, small-scale industry, water supply and waste management, and urban development. Their share of IBRD/IDA lending has increased from 5 percent in 1968 to 30 percent in 1980, with major reductions in the shares—though not absolute amounts—of lending for electric power and the transportation sector.[72]

The changes in World Bank lending have themselves been an example of "redistribution with growth." Traditional types of Bank lending have not been cut back; in fact, they have grown in absolute terms. According to Robert Ayres, "it may be estimated that considerably more than one-half and perhaps as much as two-thirds or more of combined bank and IDA lending remained traditional at the end of the McNamara presidency."[73] New types of lending have come out of increments of growth.

In the early 1970s, the World Bank developed a concept of "new style" projects, which were supposed to deliver 50 percent or more of their benefits to the poor, at a low per capita cost, and in a way that could be reproduced in other areas. More recently, the Bank has distinguished between "poverty" and "nonpoverty" lending on the basis of "degrees of emphasis on activities especially likely to benefit poor people."[74] The Bank's classification of its own lending between 1968 and 1981 is presented in Table 24. For 1979–81, the Bank classified a little less than 30 percent of its lending as "directly poverty-oriented," a figure consistent with Ayres's estimate that more than two-thirds of Bank lending remains "traditional."

There are grounds for skepticism both about the degree of change that has taken place within Bank lending and about its claims that this lending changes the lives of the absolute poor. By far the most significant change in Table 24 is the increase in rural development lending, although the Bank has indicated that it expects the modest decline in the 1979–81 period to continue (partly due to greater bilateral aid in this area). The Bank defines a rural development project as one in which 50 percent of the benefits go to the rural poor. The

TABLE 24   World Bank Classification of Its Sector Lending by Poverty Focus
(percentage of total, three-year averages)

	Fiscal years			
Sector	1968–70	1971–73	1976–78	1979–81
Directly poverty-oriented				
Rural development	3.2	7.6	16.5	15.3
Education (primary and nonformal)	0.2	0.8	1.4	1.6
Population, health, nutrition	—	0.7	0.6	0.3
Small-scale industry	—	0.2	1.7	1.7
Urbanization	—	1.3	2.6	3.4
Water supply/ sewerage	1.6	4.7	4.6	6.7
Subtotal	5.0	15.3	27.4	29.5
Other				
Agriculture	16.1	13.3	15.8	13.4
Energy (power)	24.6	14.9	13.8	15.0
Energy (oil, gas, coal)	0.3	0.9	0.9	3.5
Industry (incl. DFCs)	15.7	16.4	16.5	13.5
Transportation	27.5	21.9	15.9	13.5
All other	10.9	16.3	9.6	11.6
Total	100.0	100.0	100.0	100.0

SOURCE: World Bank, *Focus on Poverty* (Washington, D.C., 1983), p. 6.

Bank often appears to count as "beneficiaries" everyone who lives in the project area, ignoring the well-documented fact that even projects as seemingly innocent as road building can have highly unequal effects on different social groups, worsening the position of some as they better that of others.[75] Other agencies make similar sweeping quantitative claims. For example, *Annual Report 1981* of the Asian Development Bank states: "During the year, the Bank approved 17 project loans, three program loans and two sector loans for agriculture which will boost the output of major staple crops and generate millions of new jobs for the rural poor." Two loans for fisheries are expected to benefit "over four million people."[76] Although the MDBs have published methodological treatises involving complex modeling for many sorts of subjects, they have not explained the methodology used to identify and count such "beneficiaries."

Analysis of the content of rural development projects also raises questions about how much is new. On the one hand, the projects tend to integrate different aspects of rural development more than previous projects. On the other hand, the projects include activities previously classified in other sectors. The sector showing the most significant decline is transportation. However, analysis of the descriptions of the sixty-seven agricultural and rural development projects listed in *Annual Report 1982* of the World Bank reveals that twenty of them explicitly mention the construction of roads or the provision of vehicles; a number of others may involve this as well.[77] Ayres reports that there were "road components" in 50 percent of the Bank's rural development projects between 1974 and 1979.[78] The sectoral changes indicated in Table 24 are probably less significant than they appear at first glance.

Table 25 presents sectoral data for ODA from combined DAC countries in 1971 and 1981. The data must be treated with caution because the DAC has revised its sectoral classifications in the intervening period. The most significant difference is the separate classification in 1971 of "technical assistance," probably involving projects mainly in agriculture and social infrastructure. Therefore, the disjunction between these latter two categories in 1971 and 1981 is probably overstated.

Aid to agriculture has increased, although the inclusion of agricultural technical assistance in a separate category in 1971 makes it difficult to tell how much. As a proportion of total aid, however, it remains substantially lower than agricultural and rural development lending by the World Bank. Energy and public utilities ODA has increased rather substantially, despite the common assumption that the basic needs approach has deemphasized large infrastructural projects. The share of nonproject aid has declined substantially. The proportion of aid for industrial projects has remained small.

The shift in DAC bilateral aid allocation toward agriculture is heavily influenced by the United States, which in 1980 accounted for

TABLE 25   Sectoral Distribution of DAC Bilateral ODA,
               1971 and 1981 (percentage)

Sector/Use	1971	1981
Agriculture	3.6	12.1
Industry/mining/trade/construction	4.6	6.9
Energy/public utilities	3.6	20.1
Transportation	3.8	—[a]
Social infrastructure	5.4	21.7
Other project	2.9	10.3
Technical assistance	22.7[b]	—[b]
Nonproject aid	39.6	26.3
Debt relief	9.2	2.6
Other	4.0	—
Total	100.0	100.0

SOURCE: Organization for Economic Cooperation and Development, *Development Co-operation: Efforts and Policies of the Members of the Development Assistance Committee, 1973 Review*, pp. 194–195; *1982 Review*, pp. 229–231.

[a]Apparently included in "Industry/mining/construction" and "Public utilities" categories.

[b]The "technical assistance" category for 1971 seems to involve project activities classified in 1981 mainly under "Agriculture" and "Social infrastructure."

well over one-third of the DAC total and in 1981, over one-fourth. Yet USAID, like the World Bank, has redefined sectoral categories so as to include a wide variety of projects in "agriculture."

> Many AID officials boast that over half of the agency's project funds now go for "Food and Nutrition." What we have discovered is that AID has turned "Food and Nutrition" into a catch-all category to include almost anything it finances outside the boundaries of major urban areas: electrification, roads, agricultural institutions and even "satellite application and training." . . . AID now lists electrification projects under the "Food and Nutrition" funding category. Rural electrification projects account for 40 percent of AID's "Food and Nutrition" lending in Asia.[79]

The new "poverty-oriented" categories of lending have contained virtually no projects of land reform. In 1975, a sector policy on land reform explained the Bank's "limited experience" in land reform:

In part, this may be because there have been relatively few cases of land reform, particularly in areas where the political situation was reasonably stable and otherwise conducive to World Bank involvement. But also relevant is the fact that the financial requirements of land reform tend to be relatively limited. Even where the land transferred is purchased from the previous owners, the amounts involved are usually small, especially where payments are in the form of bonds. In addition, such payments constitute an internal transfer (unless foreign owners are involved) and, thus, are not attractive for external financing.[80]

In light of the criteria of "new style" projects—that benefits be provided at low cost per unit—the justification of withholding aid for land reform because it does not cost enough is rather extraordinary. Although the sector policy paper called for more Bank support of land reform, Ayres reports that subsequent rural development projects have "made little or no attempt to deal with the basic fact about rural poverty in developing countries—the inequitable distribution of land. They largely accepted the existing land tenure situation as a given and accommodated themselves to it."[81] Bettina Hurni summarizes what appears to be the Bank wisdom:

> If the World Bank, through its "new style" projects, tries to change these structures more than just marginally, it encounters the opposition of the privileged, and if a socially oriented project goes too far in its "success," it will be hampered politically by the elite conservatives who fear political upheaval. As already mentioned, land reform is a good example of a structural change that is feared for its political consequences by the "power elite." Hence, the results of even successful "new style" projects have to remain moderately reformist politically and economically marginal, so that the existent power structure will be only slightly modified and will remain intact. As an outsider, the best the Bank can hope for is to not reinforce obvious, vicious circles of income distribution efforts, which somehow often seem to end up benefitting the rich.[82]

Policy Conditionality

While the basic needs literature denies any necessary connection between meeting basic needs and institutional structures, it nonetheless emphasizes the importance of specific government policies. Thus, the basic needs approach further supports the increased emphasis on general policy conditionality discussed in the previous chapters.

The World Bank reportedly threatened to cut off Morocco's entire lending program if it failed to undertake a slum upgrading project in Rabat. But aside from pressing governments to take on an occasional poverty-oriented project, basic needs considerations have apparently played a minor role in policy negotiations. A 1983 World Bank study of its antipoverty efforts concluded, with respect to "macroeconomic policy dialogue":

> Poverty issues have seldom featured significantly in such dialogues, and the analysis of structural adjustment programs has rarely considered who will carry the heaviest burdens of adjustment. . . . The Bank has often failed to raise, at the highest levels, politically sensitive issues of the impact that efficiency adjustments have on poverty. Seldom have poverty and related questions been discussed directly and in depth at Bank-led consortia and consultative groups.[83]

A separate internal analysis of the Bank's early experience with structural adjustment lending took the somewhat more positive view that such programs often involved improvement of "agricultural producer prices and the removal of widespread biases in incentive systems that favor capital-intensive industries and discourage exports."[84] Another Bank publication claims:

> Through direct involvement at the project level and more general dialogue and interchange, the Bank has exercised a marked influence on national policies and programs for rural development in many developing countries. There is now widespread acceptance that the rural sector is generally grossly undercapitalized and that greater emphasis on agricultural and food production is essential for balanced economic growth. Perhaps more significantly there has also been a growing adoption of the view that growth and equity in the rural areas can be served by raising the productivity of hitherto neglected small farmers and other low-income groups in the rural areas.[85]

The capacity of these sorts of policies to help the absolute poor is moot. It has been widely noted that improvement in agricultural prices may not benefit much of the rural population because the poor are often landless or near-landless and hence must make their living by wage labor and must purchase at least part of their food. Similarly, the absolute poor are seldom the immediate beneficiaries of the expansion of labor-intensive export industries, and the competitive logic of such industries has put the World Bank in the position of opposing wage increases. As with import substitution strategies, the Bank's critique of existing policies are often telling; whether the Bank's alternatives offer solutions for the problems of poverty and underdevelopment remains a subject of debate.[86]

In its review of its structural adjustment lending, the Bank admits that the programs it has financed have generally involved "reduced disposable incomes" and a reallocation of resources toward investment, away from consumption. It asserts that it "has been concerned to ensure that in designing structural adjustment programs, their impact on the poorest members of society and on programs of basic needs and human resource development are minimized." Looking to the future, the Bank says that future structural adjustment programs "will consider, as far as possible, how the burdens of adjustment are shared among income groups and how adverse effects on the poor, for example, through increased unemployment, higher prices of basic goods, or higher taxes, can be mitigated."[87] The language of "minimizing" and "mitigating" the impact suggests that at best such conditionality can be neutral; there has been no serious effort to build basic needs goals into the conditions for lending in a way to "maximize" the (positive) impact.

The only significant effort to date to make basic needs considerations a central focus of policy conditionality has been undertaken by the U.S. Congress. In bills authorizing the U.S. participation in the Supplementary Financing Facility of the IMF in 1978 and raising the U.S. quota in the IMF in 1980, Congress instructed the executive branch to work for stabilization programs emphasizing productive activities aimed at meeting basic needs and to ensure that standby arrangement policies do not have an adverse impact on basic needs. The bills lacked any enforcement mechanism apart from the requirement of annual reports to Congress, however, and had virtually no effect on U.S. positions within the IMF.[88]

Basic Needs and Regime Norms

The "revolution" in development thinking in the 1970s responded to real problems, but its effect on aid allocation has been limited. Although basic needs concepts could have been developed in a radical way—pointing to the necessity of fundamental redistribution of wealth and power—the aid institutions have domesticated them. Their approach has been thoroughly technocratic—a search for the correct mix of projects and policies, to be administered from above.[89]

The changes in overall patterns of aid allocation have been modest. There has been some shift of the more concessional types of aid toward the poorest countries and some shift in sectoral priorities, particularly toward agriculture. But these changes may not have resulted from the basic needs approach—arguing from the regime norms discussed in Chapter 3, we could say the changes would have occurred anyway.

With its emphasis on domestic responsibility for failures of basic needs fulfillment, the basic needs perspective has provided an additional rationale for the aid regime's bilateralism. Aid institutions have stressed the diversity of recipient's policies, not the similarities of their locations in the world economy.

Basic needs has also provided a "humanitarian" rationale for the withholding of aid from industrial development. As we have seen, the popular notion that aid in the past was largely devoted to industrial projects is false; basic needs rationalizes further industrial withholding. Despite the great increase in Third World industrialization over the last two decades, aid for industrial projects has remained a small and roughly constant proportion of total aid. Basic needs is a seemingly less ideological rationale than the refusal to allow public capital to compete with private. Furthermore, increased aid for agriculture has corresponded to the discovery by the multinational corporations of the profitability of both agricultural investment and of supplying inputs for commercialized peasant agriculture.

Basic needs has likewise reinforced the norm of institutionalized noncompetition among aid institutions, providing a humanitarian rationale for "graduating" countries from concessional financing as their creditworthiness increases, even if the gap between rich and poor countries is growing. Some observers have assumed that the increased correlation between level of per capita aid and per capita income indicates a shift from "foreign policy" to "humanitarian" motivations on the part of aid donors.[90] It is more accurate to view the formalization of graduation procedures as the fulfillment of long-standing regime norms. Concentration of the most concessional forms of external financing in the least creditworthy countries may be consistent with a "humanitarian" outlook, but it is also consistent with the norms of international capitalism.

Although basic needs have not themselves become a focus of conditionality, the basic needs perspective has provided an additional justification for conditionality in general. It has immeasurably enhanced the moral and political ground from which the Bank has mounted its attack on "domestic policy inadequacies."

Finally, basic needs has provided a vantage point for viewing the buildup of debt and the emergence of problems with servicing that debt as a kind of retribution for incorrect priorities and policies. It in no way has absolved recipients of their debt obligations. At the same time, the separating out of the poorest countries—often referred to as the Fourth World—has provided some donors with a non-precedent-establishing basis for writing off, on a purely unilateral basis, some of their more hopeless loans.

The Future of Basic Needs

Although basic needs defenders insist that the policy is not just another "fad" of the development community, there is evidence that its status as a distinctive approach is in decline. In this last section, I examine briefly the World Bank's analysis of its own experience and its evolving policy views.

In 1981–82, a task force of senior staff members reviewed the Bank's programs aimed at Third World poverty. In an internally cir-

culated report, the task force in early 1982 expressed concern over
the level of Bank commitment:

> Our discussions revealed widespread uncertainty about whether the com-
> mitment to poverty alleviation has been weakened or abandoned. The
> current concern with energy and structural adjustment, combined with
> the transition to a new chief executive, make many staff members ques-
> tion the Bank's commitment to this objective. New signals, real or imag-
> ined, are already affecting both policy dialogue and planned lending.[91]

No hint of this skepticism is contained in the version of this report,
entitled *Focus on Poverty*, that the Bank published for public distribution in 1983. In the language prevalent since McNamara, the
report claims that the Bank's rural projects have had 120 million
beneficiaries among the rural poor since 1974.[92] Despite its surface
optimism, the report is unusually frank about the limitations to date
of the Bank's poverty lending. Its rural development projects, the
centerpiece of its strategy, "have provided few direct benefits for the
landless, for tenants unable to offer collateral for loans, and for
the near-landless farmer who finds it hard to borrow, acquire inputs,
and take risks."[93]

> It has proved extremely difficult to benefit the very poorest groups
> who lack productive assets. These include most of the rural landless,
> urban jobless, adult illiterates, and female-headed households in develop-
> ing countries.[94]

The report even concludes that "a small minority of Bank projects" have worsened the plight of the landless—a startling admission
because the majority do not seem to have reached the landless at all.[95]
The report's analysis of the experience of some of the "poverty-
oriented sectors" identified in Table 24 raises questions about the
Bank's classification. Urban sites and services (the centerpiece of its
urbanization strategy) have not reached those in the bottom 20 percent of income distribution. By value, 70 percent of the benefits
of water supply and waste management projects, also identified as
"poverty-oriented projects," have gone to the nonpoor. Urban projects to increase employment and income have been "rather unsuccess-

ful." The most unambiguous claims are made for education projects, where it is reported that the proportion of lending for primary education has increased from 8 percent in 1969 to 33 percent currently. However, no data are provided to show that the poor are the direct beneficiaries of this lending.[96]

The Bank's conclusion that its rural and urban development projects have generally failed to benefit the poorest sectors of the population is supported by the most detailed independent study of its poverty lending to date, Robert Ayres's *Banking on the Poor: The World Bank and World Poverty*. Although Ayres, like the Bank itself, takes a very positive view of the Bank's record, he also admits that "virtually none of the projects were designed to reach the rural landless at all, nor were they principally oriented toward tenant farmers, sharecroppers, or squatters." He explains:

> The poorest of the poor in rural areas of developing countries were extremely difficult to find and, once found, to assist through Bank projects. The owner-operators were more locatable, and thus project benefits could be more readily targeted upon them.[97]

This is presumably a statement about the institutional limits of Bank projects rather than the geography of the rural poor. In the case of the urban development projects, Ayres shows how the Bank's insistence on cost recovery meant that "the very poorest could not be the target group of these projects."[98]

Focus on Poverty's admission that basic needs concerns have seldom played a role in general "policy dialogue" was cited earlier. The report concludes: "The experience of the 1970s suggests that Bank macroeconomic dialogues would more successfully support poverty alleviation if they stressed that poor people can benefit from the freeing of markets and similar actions only if concomitant structural changes provide the access, assets, or information the poor need to compete in the marketplace."[99] The implicit admission in this passage that the Bank has been more successful in "freeing markets" than in promoting structural changes that would allow the poor to protect themselves, as well as benefit, from market forces is probably an accurate statement of the success and failure of the aid regime as a whole.

The Bank's inability or unwillingness to move outside the traditional structure of regime norms has drastically limited the definition and the implementation of the basic needs perspective. Nonetheless, Bank officials have perceived themselves as being engaged in a struggle over the Bank's basic needs commitments. One of the leading members of the Bank's poverty task force, Mahbub ul Haq, director of policy planning, resigned in 1982 over "major policy differences" with the Bank's new president, A. W. Clausen. Clausen has emphasized the virtues of the private sector more insistently than his predecessor—although no more insistently than pre-McNamara Bank presidents. The Bank's language of "growth with distribution" and "meeting basic needs" has been largely replaced by the milder language of "growth with poverty alleviation."

Although changes in World Bank leadership and in some of the major aid-providing countries may have contributed to the apparent decline of the basic needs approach, the more fundamental problems reside in the strategy itself and in the institutional constraints within which the strategy was implemented. A sophisticated analysis of the limits of the World Bank's rural development projects, along with a revealing set of recommendations, is provided in a World Bank staff working paper by a consultant to the Bank (and former USAID official), Judith Tendler. Unlike *Focus on Poverty*, Tendler's analysis cannot be assumed to represent official policy; it probably represents the "left wing of the possible" within the institution. It nonetheless provides both an indicator of the Bank's self-awareness of problems and an example of the limits of reform within the constraints of the aid regime.

Tendler's *Rural Projects Through Urban Eyes: An Interpretation of the World Bank's New-Style Rural Development Projects* begins by arguing that a combination of institutional and ideological features of the World Bank has resulted, first, in the use of a growth justification for focusing on the rural poor and, second, in an attempt to reach the rural poor through projects dealing with agricultural production. Contrasting the Bank's shift toward rural development with the U.S.

"war on poverty" of the 1960s—the latter justified largely on equity grounds—Tendler notes:

> The move towards projects for the poor in the development field required a justification that did not represent a complete break with past thinking. Programs for the third-world poor, therefore, were conceived of as modified versions of growth policies—alternative ways of pursuing growth that were not as income-concentrating as the strategies of the past.[100]

Tendler argues that an economics-based, "output-increasing justification for the equity-oriented projects" made the latter respectable within the Bank while limiting these projects to trying to raise the productivity of direct agricultural producers. Given the Bank's method of calculating the economic rate of return for its projects, "the dependence of equity interventions on efficiency justifications" necessarily resulted in a concentration on projects involving more direct forms of agricultural investment over more indirect forms.[101]

Tendler goes on to argue that this production focus—as it has been conceived by the Bank in terms of its "smallholder strategy"—has necessarily resulted in the failure of the Bank's rural development projects to reach the very poor:

> The output preoccupation behind the new rural projects is also problematic because it requires that the project beneficiary be identified as a farmer-producer rather than as a wage worker in somebody else's enterprise. Project strategy is to improve the income of the poor by improving the circumstances of their own agricultural production—as owners or tenants. This working definition of the rural poor creates somewhat of a double bind. The lower one goes in the rural income distribution the less the share of a poor family's income that is derived from its own agricultural production. Even if one succeeds in reaching the poor with the services of this kind of project, then, one may still have little impact on their income. If a project is to have an impact on the income of the rural poor through their own agricultural production, in other words, then it may have to work with the less poor. This dilemma explains, in part, why the subsidized agricultural production services of the new projects frequently end up benefiting a less poor group than was intended.[102]

Alain de Janvry, in an exhaustive survey of agricultural reform in Latin America, draws very similar conclusions:

The programs of integrated rural development implemented within current agrarian structures can have only an extremely narrow clientele of
upper peasants. This is due to the advanced process of social differentiation whereby the large majority of rural poor are highly proletarianized
and more dependent on employment and wages for their subsistence
than on agricultural production.[103]

Even in sub-Saharan Africa, where rural social differentiation is less
advanced, the Bank has found that the better-off farmers and village
families have been the main beneficiaries of the Bank's projects.[104]

Tendler notes that this consequence has been evident from the
Bank's very first rural development project in northeast Brazil. Although sharecroppers and the landless represented at least 55 percent
of all farm families in the state involved, the project made no attempt
to reach them directly, partly because of its smallholder focus and
partly out of fear of alienating the local rural elite, whose cooperation
was deemed essential.

This latter reason—fear of elite reaction if its social relations of
production with the landless and sharecroppers are disturbed—
points to the second problem Tendler finds with the Bank's production focus. Tendler points out that even if a rural development project
is not designed to reach wage laborers, its success is likely to raise the
rural wage because smallholders will spend more time on their own
plots and will be less likely to join the pool of wage laborers. But
such "success" may prompt local landowners to use their power to
subvert the project:

> If the Bank succeeds in reaching the rural poor as producers, in sum,
> this is likely to increase the costs of production to the employer-landowner
> and to decrease the monopsonistic power of landowners over their ten-
> ants and employees. This political difficulty of assisting the poor in rural
> settings will often manifest itself in seemingly unrelated problems, like
> slow disbursement of project funds; the dissatisfaction of landowners
> will often surface as a waning of attention to the project by those in
> power. . . . Ironically, then, the very success of a project in reaching the
> rural poor and raising their incomes can lead to its undoing.[105]

For a variety of reasons, projects in such circumstances are unlikely
to have sufficiently powerful constituencies to protect them. Tendler

contrasts this political weakness of rural projects with urban ones, which she sees as fundamentally different. Urban projects, Tendler observes, have been justified mainly on equity, rather than growth, grounds. They have focused on infrastructure rather than on direct production. This infrastructure focus is seldom directly threatening to elites, and furthermore it generates powerful constituencies in favor of such projects—contractors, suppliers, politicians, and so forth. Thus, ironically, growth-oriented rural development projects are "more politically radical than urban projects" and are likely to be "particularly bereft of interest-group support."[106]

Although focusing primarily on Latin America and largely theoretical, Tendler's analysis is complex and fascinating; I have provided only a basic outline here. The nature of the conclusions she draws is equally interesting. Tendler's commitment to the rural poor and her desire for fundamental reform in the countryside are unassailable. But within the context of the World Bank, a sense of political realism leads her to propose recommendations that would appear to reduce further the limited redistributive content of World Bank programs.

The essential idea behind Tendler's recommendation is to learn from the less politically problematic urban projects. Specifically:

> The urban comparison suggests three ways in which one might improve the chances for rural projects to reach the poor: (1) by simulating the "targetability" of the urban poor—i.e., their physical concentration and isolation from the nonpoor; (2) by changing project designs in a way that causes less umbrage to the elites; and (3) by compensating for the lack of powerful and supportive interest groups behind project implementation.[107]

Tendler makes many concrete suggestions, but here I discuss only the two that seem most important overall. First, she proposes that rural development projects be located in geographical areas without powerful elites—in the language of the Bank mentioned before, in areas of unimodal rather than bimodal agriculture. Tendler does admit the obvious fact that "rural poverty . . . often goes hand in hand with land concentration" and that "choosing unimodal project areas . . . could turn out to limit considerably the number of potential project areas that have large concentrations of the poorest poor." She justifies this partly by noting that more equal areas tend to be found in "the more backward, less accessible areas of a country," which are "less blessed with development or potential for it."[108] But such a proposal does seem to admit defeat in the face of social inequality and injustice.

The other main proposal, also drawn from the urban experience, is to shift the Bank's focus from production to infrastructure in the rural areas. Although such investment has the potential to diminish the landlord's power over the peasant, "this impact will work itself out only over a longer run, and will not be perceived as so directly threatening as the production projects."[109] With proposals such as these, Tendler hopes that project "design can be modified with the purpose of decreasing opposition or eliciting more interest on the part of powerful groups."[110]

Tendler's staff working paper is in part a plea for the acceptance of equity goals, independent of growth-producing justifications. Recent World Bank theory and practice, however, seem to point in different directions. The language of basic needs has almost entirely disappeared from the World Bank's three recent reports on Africa, which locate the roots of Africa's development crises in "domestic policy inadequacies" of overvalued exchange rates, an overextended public sector, and biases against agriculture in pricing, taxation, and exchange rates. The reports prescribe greater reliance on market forces, including a "redefinition of the frontier between public and private sectors," as the centerpiece of revised development strategies.[111] As noted earlier, the Bank has placed increasing emphasis on "structural adjustment" programs, in which considerations of equity have been reduced to expressions of hope that adverse impacts on the poor can be "minimized" or "mitigated." Long-time World Bank consultant Bela Balassa has argued in a World Bank staff working paper that structural adjustment necessitates "a reordering of priorities as well as a reconsideration of policy instruments." He continues:

> To begin with, growth objectives will need to be given greater weight as compared to income distributional objectives. This is because the shocks suffered impose limitations on the ability of the government to pursue several objectives simultaneously, and economic growth is necessary to

provide the wherewithal for the alleviation of poverty that may be regarded as the appropriate income distributional objective.

The objective of regaining the pre-shock growth path also means that policies to alleviate poverty should give emphasis to measures that raise the productivity of the poor rather than increase consumption through the provision of public services or government subsidies.[112]

Structural adjustment has represented a return to growth-oriented, trickle-down theories of economic development, with the added argument that export-oriented growth will do more for the poor than antipoverty or redistributional programs. The *World Development Report 1982* implicitly overturns the basic needs approach by asserting: "Economic growth is the ultimate remedy for rural poverty."[113] Land reform, always receiving mixed reviews in Bank literature, receives its most negative summary to date:

> But land reform is more often preached than practiced—which can be highly damaging since it increases insecurity rather than reduces it. Among landlords, a general fear of reform and, in particular, concern that compensation will be inadequate may discourage them from making the most productive use of their land by leasing small parcels to sharecroppers and renters. This reluctance is most common, and most harmful, among large landowners. Discussion of land reform sometimes obscures the broader issue of security of tenure and leads to inaction on all fronts.[114]

Even discussion of land reform, the Bank seems to imply here, is not in the interest of the poor.

6

Aid, Debt, and the Crisis of State Capitalism

On August 30, 1982, Mexico stunned the world with its announcement that it was unable to meet the payments on the principal of almost $20 billion of its public sector debt, owed to about fourteen hundred foreign banks. By year's end, thirty-five countries were in arrears in their debt payments, and a record number of debt renegotiations were under way.[1] In 1982 and 1983, the World Bank reported, "almost as many developing countries have had to reschedule loans . . . as in the previous twenty-five years."[2] Arrears continued to accumulate in 1983, with forty-two countries owing $27 billion at the end of 1983.[3] Extensive rescheduling continued through 1984.

The apparent suddenness of the outbreak and rapid diffusion of the debt crisis throughout the Third World led to extensive and sustained media coverage in the West. Most of this coverage raised alarming specters of international financial collapse. In a representative cover story, *Time* magazine warned: "The global economy is sitting on a time bomb."[4] In contrast, representatives of the banks and of the official institutions sought from the beginning to downplay the crisis. The Development Assistance Committee, the World Bank, and the International Monetary Fund all insisted throughout that no "generalized" crisis existed at all; there were only "individual country problems." Bankers, agency officials, and the business press periodically announced that the crisis was over.[5]

Almost all analyses, whether alarmist or reassuring, have treated the debt crisis primarily as a matter of debt to commercial banks, emerging outside the aid regime. The aid institutions enter as part of the solution to the crisis, both through the provision of new financing and as enforcers of "adjustment" measures. In fact, the relationship between the aid regime and the debt crisis has been considerably more complex. The aid regime was itself a source of the crisis, in terms of both the behavior it was able to regulate and the incentive it provided Third World countries to use nonaid resources, when the occasion arose, to escape from the discipline of the aid regime. The debt crisis, in turn, both reflected and provoked a crisis in the aid regime, which has resulted in significant regime restructuring in the past several years.

This chapter explores the role of the aid regime in the origins of the debt crisis. It documents the existence of a widespread "official" debt crisis prior to the emergence of the more publicized crisis of debt to private creditors. In addition, by demonstrating that the accumulation of debt to private creditors has to be understood in part as a means of escaping unwanted regime discipline, it links the debt issue to development choices made in debtor countries. For a number of the major debtors, recourse to commercial lending made possible a range of development strategies that may be labeled "state capitalist." The final section of this chapter explores how changes in the world economy and in these countries' relationships to the aid regime produced a crisis of state capitalism as part of the crisis of debt.

The Aid Regime and Debt

Because the bulk of aid flows consists of loans, aid itself creates debt. According to OECD figures, a little over half of all official aid is dispensed in the form of loans, the rest as grants. This statistic is somewhat misleading, however, because the vast bulk of grant aid is in the form of technical assistance, the dollar value of which is often inflated and which is often of only limited interest to the recipient (who would in many cases prefer to go without such services rather than pay for them). Most capital and commodity aid creates debt. Although the terms of much of this debt are highly concessional by market standards, official debt by the early 1980s had come to be a considerable burden for many Third World countries, accounting for almost half of all long-term public debt in 1983. Regime norms excluded the most onerous part of this debt—loans from the hard-loan windows of the multilateral development banks—from renegotiation and even temporary payments moratoria. Despite the generally easier terms of bilateral aid, twenty Third World countries renegotiated their debt to bilateral official creditors between 1979 and 1983, an indication of the burden of even "highly concessional" official aid. Indeed, up through 1982, there were considerably more Paris Club reschedulings of debt to bilateral official creditors than there were reschedulings of debt to private creditors. Several years before Mexico's announcement, a widespread but little-noticed official debt crisis had emerged.

In addition, developments within the aid regime and in its relationship to other sources of external financing were important factors in the expansion of debt to private creditors. The following sections explore three reasons for this: (1) the increasing proportion of aid disbursements offset by official debt service, (2) the breakdown of regime graduation mechanisms, and (3) the desire to escape from regime discipline.

The Tendency Toward Net Transfer Decline

Aid increases during the 1970s fell short of increased financing needs of Third World countries. While official aid from all sources increased at an annual rate of about 5.8 percent in real terms during the 1970s, the proportion of current account deficits financed by official aid fell from 91.6 percent in 1970–72 to 44.4 percent in 1980.[6] The decline in aid's role was partly a question of political will in the North—appeals for larger aid increases by Third World lobbies (for example, the Group of 77) and by Northern commissions (for example, the Pearson and Brandt commissions) went unheeded. But also, as aid to official creditors grew and grace periods on past aid ran out, debt service increasingly came to offset new flows of aid.

Table 26 shows that while bilateral aid from the advanced capitalist countries increased rapidly enough to allow for a constant increase in absolute net transfer until 1983, the proportion of new aid offset by debt service increased fairly steadily over time, despite decreases in interest rates on ODA (from 2.5 percent overall in 1972 to 1.8 percent in 1982) and an increase in the proportion of ODA provided as grants. In 1968, the first year for which relatively full data are available, debt service as a proportion of gross disbursements (both loans and grants) came to 23.1 percent. With a few minor fluctuations, this proportion increased consistently until 1980: to 30.9 percent in 1970, 34.4 percent in 1975, and 39 percent in 1980. Seventeen Paris Club reschedulings between 1980 and 1982 helped lower this figure to 34.6 percent in 1982 and 31 percent in 1983. Still, close to one-third of official bilateral aid in 1983 simply covered repayment of past aid, compared with less than one-quarter in 1968.

A World Bank analysis that excludes grants but includes both bilateral and multilateral official loans shows a more complicated trend, but one similar in the long run. Because multilateral aid expanded more rapidly in the early to mid 1970s than bilateral aid and carried grace periods of four years or more, the proportion of new disburse-

TABLE 26   Gross and Net Official Bilateral Aid from Advanced Capitalist Countries, 1968–83

	1968	1969	1970	1971	1972	1973	1974	1975	1976	1977	1978	1979	1980	1981	1982	1983
Gross official disbursements ($ billions)	7.6	7.6	8.5	10.1	10.9	12.7	14.3	17.4	17.3	18.7	24.9	28.7	34.2	33.5	35.7	33.9
Net official transfer ($ billions)	5.8	5.4	5.9	6.7	7.1	8.3	9.3	11.4	11.2	11.6	16.1	16.7	20.8	22.3	23.4	23.4
Debt service as percentage of gross disbursements[a]	23.1	28.2	30.9	34.0	34.8	34.5	35.3	34.4	35.2	38.3	35.5	39.0	39.0	33.4	34.6	31.0

SOURCE: Organization for Economic Cooperation and Development, *Development Co-operation: Efforts and Policies of the Members of the Development Assistance Committee*, 1969–84 reviews.

NOTE: These are members of the DAC of the OECD. Figures are adjusted to exclude flows to multilateral organizations but to include interest payments, which are not included in the DAC concept of net flow. For some years, DAC data on interest payments are incomplete, and therefore net transfers are somewhat overstated.

[a] Calculated before rounding.

ments (on bilateral and multilateral loans combined) offset by debt service tended to decrease in the early 1970s, reaching a low of 35.7 percent in 1975. By 1979, however, as the growth of multilateral aid began to taper off and as repayments on loans made in the first part of the decade began to come due, debt service's share jumped sharply, to 53.5 percent in 1979.[7] Thus, by the end of the decade, over half of all new official loan disbursements were offset by debt service on previous official aid.

The tendency for net transfer to decline has been a particular problem for the hard-loan operations of the multilateral development banks. Table 27 shows that during the late 1960s, the IBRD suffered an absolute decline in its net transfers, which were actually negative in 1970.[8] According to Ronald Libby, the Bank's soft-loan subsidiary, the IDA, "was specifically designed for Bank use to enable its poorer major client countries to repay their loans."[9] Payer has argued:

> Unless the lending of the Bank, and the Bank, and the financial system as a whole, expands constantly, a point will come when it will be clearly more advantageous for a given country to repudiate its debts than to continue to pay them. This means that, in order to protect its considerable powers of leverage and its own strong but vulnerable record of no (highly visible) defaults, the Bank must constantly expand its volume of new loans in order to maintain a positive net transfer of resources. In this light, the radical expansion of Bank lending under McNamara's presidency, often viewed as the product of an idiosyncratic and even megalomaniac personality, can be seen rather as a systemic imperative.[10]

In 1972–73, when IBRD gross disbursements remained roughly steady, the proportion offset by debt service jumped from 70 percent to 84.19 percent. Similarly, when gross disbursements increased only marginally between 1977 and 1978, debt service's share rose from 67.5 percent to 77.4 percent. With debt service payments to the World Bank exceeding $5 billion in 1983—more than gross disbursements as late as 1979—it has been possible to raise absolute net transfers only by constantly increasing levels of new lending.

Net transfer as a proportion of gross disbursements by the World

TABLE 27   Gross Disbursements, Debt Service Receipts, and Net Transfer of IBRD and IDA, 1968–85

	1968	1969	1970	1971	1972	1973	1974	1975	1976	1977	1978	1979	1980	1981	1982	1983	1984	1985
IBRD																		
Gross disbursements ($ m.)	772	762	754	955	1182	1179	1533	1995	2470	2636	2787	3602	4363	5063	6326	6817	8580	8645
Debt service receipts ($ m.)	667	739	813	703	837	992	1141	1334	1505	1778	2156	2512	2922	3605	4100	4853	5780	6463
Net transfer ($ m.)	105	23	−59	252	345	187	392	661	965	858	631	1090	1441	1458	2226	2234	2800	2002
Net transfer as percentage of gross disbursements	13.6	3.0	−7.8	26.4	29.2	15.9	25.6	33.1	39.1	32.5	22.6	30.3	33.0	28.8	35.2	32.8	32.6	31.0
IDA																		
Gross disbursements ($ m.)	319	256	143	235	261	494	711	1026	1252	1298	1062	1222	1411	1878	2067	2596	2524	2491
Debt service receipts ($ m.)	8	10	12	14	16	24	33	44	55	68	80	89	104	124	149	187	115	151
Net transfer ($ m.)	311	246	131	221	245	470	678	982	1197	1230	982	1133	1307	1754	1918	2409	2409	2340
IDA & IBRD																		
Combined net transfer as percentage of combined gross disbursements	38.1	26.4	8.1	39.7	41.0	39.3	47.7	54.4	58.1	53.1	41.9	46.1	47.6	46.3	49.4	49.3	47.5	39.0

SOURCES: Edward S. Mason and Robert E. Asher, *The World Bank Since Bretton Woods* (Washington, D.C.: Brookings Institution, 1973), pp. 219–220; World Bank, *Annual Reports*, 1971–85.

Bank peaked in 1976, when it was close to 40 percent for the IBRD
and 58.1 percent for the IBRD and IDA combined. Between 1968
and 1985, there were only three years in which debt service to the
World Bank failed to offset over half of gross disbursements. Since
1983, over two-thirds of every dollar disbursed by the IBRD was offset by debt service on past IBRD loans; for the IBRD and IDA combined, over half of every dollar has been offset by debt service. With
the seventh replenishment of the IDA for 1984–87 falling far below
original projections (in real terms, only 60 percent of the sixth replenishment), a further decline in relative net transfer is inevitable.
Indeed, both IBRD and IDA absolute net transfers declined in 1985,
with debt service constituting a greater proportion of gross disbursements than in any year since 1970.[11]

Combined with "aid fatigue" in donor countries, debt service to
official creditors is now large enough to threaten the aid regime's capacity to maintain increases in net transfer, both absolute and relative. Both concessional (ODA) and nonconcessional net aid flows
have steadily declined since peaking in 1980. According to OECD
figures, total official net receipts from all sources declined from $64.2
billion in 1980 to $56.8 billion in 1983, a 12 percent decline.[12] The
World Bank reports that bilateral commitments fell 21 percent in
1982, to the lowest point since 1977, presaging further declines in
net receipts.[13]

In the case of the United States, economic aid has declined while
military aid has risen sharply. Yet despite the fact that a substantial
proportion of U.S. military aid is provided on either a grant or
highly concessional basis, military debt has assumed proportions
such that it too has compounded the debt problem. Interest payments on U.S. foreign military sales credits alone were estimated at
$2 billion in 1984.[14] Egypt, for example, had a $4.5 billion military
debt to the United States in 1984, and the interest payments on its
military debt were almost equal to its economic aid from the United
States. It was, furthermore, between $250 million and $300 million
in arrears in interest payments on its military debt in early 1985.[15]

Graduation, Planned and Unplanned

As noted in Chapter 3, the aid institutions can be ranked on a financial spectrum, merging into the private sector at one end and departing radically from market terms at the other. The concept of "graduation" is a central part of the operating logic of the regime—as countries become more creditworthy, they are expected to move along the spectrum in the direction of private sources of financing. Eventually, they are graduated from concessional financing altogether; in the meantime, they are graduated from greater to less concessional forms of financing.

As we have seen, the basic needs perspective has provided an additional rationale for formalizing graduation procedures. This formalization of graduation procedures has been done most consistently by the multilateral development banks with respect to their soft-loan operations. The World Bank, for example, has graduated twenty-seven countries from the IDA to the IBRD and thirteen to "blend" status, in which they are eligible for loans from both.[16] Some countries that previously received IBRD loans are now included in the IDA-only category, which suggests that if a country's debt-servicing position deteriorates, partly as a result of the relatively hard terms of the MDBs, its previous "graduation" may be revoked. Such cases have been somewhat rare, but if a debt-servicing crisis becomes sufficiently generalized, they could come to challenge the graduation logic of the aid regime.

Although the logic of graduation has been more formalized by the MDBs than by the bilateral agencies, the aid regime has progressively narrowed the difference between official aid and available private resources for an increasing number of Third World countries. In this sense, the introduction of institutional classifications of LDCs as "newly industrializing," "upper middle income," "lower middle income," "low income," and "least developed" should be considered as much prescriptive as descriptive. Such categories tend to indicate appropriate locations within an international financial structure as much as income levels.

During the 1970s, however, the graduation mechanisms of the aid regime broke down partially. First, the OPEC oil price increases and other upheavals in the world economy created financing needs that the aid regime was only partly able to fill. Second, in the expansionary and inflationary context of the world economy of the mid 1970s, the distinction between private and concessional financing became blurred. Countries still eligible for concessional financing found themselves aggressively solicited by commercial lenders, while worldwide inflation made real interest rates close to zero or even negative for several years. Third, graduation from concessional financing no longer had to mean reliance on private foreign investment; commercial lending offered an alternative that gave state elites much more control over investment decisions. Finally, the availability of commercial lending meant that instead of access to private financing being contingent on policies prescribed and certified by the aid institutions, private lending now became a means of avoiding the discipline of those institutions.

We explored in Chapter 2 some of the factors that led the international banks to look to the Third World for new customers in the late 1960s and in the 1970s. Let us now turn to the factors that produced a demand (or "pull") for this kind of financing. Arthur MacEwan has suggested:

> It is no exaggeration to say that the roots of this pull—the roots of Latin America's current debt problem—can be traced to the early colonial era, to the way Spanish and Portuguese America were connected to the international economy and to the types of social structures that were established in these Iberian colonies. . . . These two characteristics of the early era—external orientation of economic life and great inequality—have continued to exist in Latin American colonies, to one degree or another, down to the current period.[17]

The gist of this statement applies to most of the Third World and reminds us to place the events of the 1970s and 1980s in the historical context of dependency and world system change.

Many accounts cite the OPEC price increases in 1973–74 and 1979–80 as the events that triggered the accumulation of Third

World debt.[18] William Cline estimates that between 1974 and 1982, oil-importing Third World countries paid $260 billion more for oil imports than they would have if oil prices had simply risen at the rate of the U.S. wholesale price index.[19] This sum amounts to over half the increase in external indebtedness of these countries during these years. And as we saw earlier, the decision of OPEC countries to place the bulk of their surpluses on deposit with the major commercial banks fueled the expansion of the Euromarket, which led to the search for new borrowers in the Third World.

OPEC's role should not be overemphasized, however. Euromarket expansion predated the OPEC price rises and in most years even after 1973 was based much more on non-OPEC than on OPEC deposits. More important, the ability of the oil-importing Third World countries to pay for their oil imports was drastically weakened by the advanced capitalist countries' strategy of reducing their own deficits by deflating demand for Third World commodities while limiting aid and aggressively promoting exports. In this way, worldwide deficits increasingly shifted to the Third World. In 1973–76, the critical years in which real oil prices were the highest, decreases in export volume and prices played a much greater role than increases in import prices in worsening the trade deficits of oil-importing Third World countries.[20] In fact, for low-income countries, the increased cost in these years of food grain imports far exceeded the increased cost of oil imports.[21] In the 1978–81 period, the increase in oil prices was similarly less of a factor in the increase of current account deficits than changes in non-oil terms of trade.[22] The impact of the oil price increases was also mitigated for some countries by the spectacular expansion of OPEC aid after 1973, so that by 1975, OPEC countries and institutions accounted for one-quarter of all official aid.

In reality, bank lending to Third World countries had been on the rise before the OPEC price hikes. It had grown at an average rate of 37.7 percent between 1970 and 1972. An OECD study notes that "the major part of the expansion of the role of the banks in the financing of developing countries took place in the late 1960s and early 1970s, before the first oil shock."[23] The banks had already emerged by 1973 as Latin America's top creditor.[24] Peter DeWitt and James Petras suggest that, with the internationalization of their operations coinciding with stagnant credit demand in the industrial countries, "if the oil crisis had not existed, it would have had to be invented."[25] John Makin similarly comments that "the oil crisis of 1973–74 was the answer to the banker's prayer."[26] Certainly, the oil crisis came at a convenient time for the banks.

By 1975, the majority of Eurocurrency credits were being extended to LDCs, a situation that continued until 1980. So fierce was the competition among the banks for LDC borrowers that, as Table 28 shows, interest rates on LDC Euroloans approached and even temporarily went below rates on IBRD loans between 1975 and 1977. IBRD loans generally carried longer grace periods and maturities, and, importantly, fixed interest rates, but nonetheless the combination of the availability and cheapness of Euromarket financing undermined the traditional relationship between aid and nonaid resources. In 1976, Third World countries began to arrange loans over $1 billion and to negotiate spreads less than 1 percent over LIBOR. Although LIBOR subsequently rose sharply, some Third World countries were still arranging loans with spreads under 1 percent as late as mid 1982.

Even in years when Euromarket interest rates were markedly above those of the IBRD and other MDBs, worldwide inflation and the depreciation of the U.S. dollar made real interest costs "substantially negative" between 1973 and 1978.[27] An expanding world economy seemed to offer a way to bypass the key institutions of the aid regime.

The incentive to do this was not simply financial, however. Recourse to private bank lending during the 1970s represented an attempt to escape from the discipline of the aid regime. It was not an option open to all—thereby contributing to increased inequality within the Third World—but it was one grasped by most of the countries that had the opportunity. For a time, the aid regime's capacity to regulate the terms and timing of graduation was significantly compromised.

TABLE 28   Interest Rates on Loans to LDCs: Euroloans, World Bank,
Official Bilateral Loans, and Percentage Change in
Non-Oil LDC Export Unit Values, 1970–82

Year	Euroloans	IBRD Loans[a]	Official Bilateral Loans	Percent Change in NO-LDC Export Unit Values
1970	9.52	7.00	2.8	3.7
1971	8.02	7.25	3.6	−2.0
1972	6.82	7.25	3.8	5.1
1973	10.38	7.25	3.8	33.4
1974	12.24	7.25	4.0	36.1
1975	8.74	8.50	4.2	−1.0
1976	7.38	8.85	5.0	5.9
1977	7.64	8.20	4.6	15.0
1978	10.03	7.50	4.6	2.9
1979	12.30	7.90	4.6	16.5
1980	15.30	8.25	5.0	15.1
1981	17.40	9.60	5.8	−6.3
1982	17.50	11.60	6.1[b]	−6.6

SOURCES: 1970–78 Euroloan rates from Barbara Stallings, "Euromarkets, Third World Coun-tries and the International Political Economy," in Harry Makler, Alberto Martinelli, and Neil Smelser (eds.), *The New International Economy* (Beverly Hills: Sage Publications, 1982), p. 209. 1979–82 Euroloan rates from Organization for Economic Cooperation and Development, *External Debt of Developing Countries* (Paris, 1982), p. 31. IBRD rates from World Bank, *Annual Reports*, 1970–82. 1970–80 official bilateral rates from Nicholas C. Hope, *Developments in and Prospects for the External Debt of the Developing Countries: 1970–1980 and Beyond* (Washington, D.C.: World Bank Staff Working Paper No. 488, August 1981), p. 19. 1981–82 official bilateral rates calculated from data in DAC, *1982 Review*, pp. 178, 239. Change in export unit values from International Monetary Fund, *International Financial Statistics*, supplement on trade statistics, Supplement Series No. 4 (Washington, D.C., 1982), and *International Financial Statistics Year-book 1984*, p. 117.

[a] IBRD loans only; does not include IDA loans.

[b] 1982 figure assumes that ratio between official development assistance and other official flows is the same as for 1981.

Escape from Regime Discipline

Most capital and commodity aid, we have seen, comes in the form of project loans, tied to functionally and geographically specific uses. The relatively small proportion of aid available as program loans almost always carries high levels of conditionality. Euromarket loans in the 1970s usually differed from aid in both these respects, linked at most only vaguely to specific projects and carrying few explicit conditions apart from those dealing with repayment and potential default.[28] As one early account put it:

> Commercial bank loans have none of the irksome conditions relating to monetary management . . . frequently associated with International Monetary Fund standby facilities and credit tranche drawings and, indeed, loans from foreign governments. It is therefore understandable that monetary officials in many developing countries, wishing to allow themselves the greatest possible freedom of movement, are prepared to pay the higher cost (in terms of interest) of a Eurocurrency bank credit over an IMF drawing or a loan from a foreign government.[29]

Another source concluded that "developing countries have an important interest in this continuation and expansion of private bank lending that is characterized by competitiveness, free access, and depoliticization."[30]

The commercial banks' disinterest in imposing broad policy conditions on their loans was consolidated by their disastrous experience with Peru in 1976–77. The banks' attempt in the Peruvian case to impose and monitor broad policy changes independent of the IMF proved a divisive failure, and the banks have turned to the IMF in almost all cases since then.[31]

The banks' indifference to the uses to which their loans were put, as long as they were repaid, expanded Third World development options considerably. For one thing, socialist countries such as Cuba, long excluded from the aid regime, now had access to a form of financing from the advanced capitalist countries. (The main beneficiaries in this sense were the Eastern European countries, however, which accumulated an external debt to international banks of over $50 billion by the end of 1981.)

Of even greater importance was the way access to commercial bank financing enabled traditional users of aid to circumvent the regime norm of strategic withholding. As we saw earlier, strategic withholding of aid, particularly from the industrial sector, has been one of the aid regime's most effective mechanisms for influencing development policy. It has constituted a significant obstacle to the expansion of state ownership of industry and has virtually forced many states to rely on foreign investment. Although the extraordinary expansion of multinational corporations to virtually every corner of the Third World testifies in part to the aid regime's success, the rate of industrialization produced by foreign investment has long been considered insufficient by even the most hospitable Third World governments. Contrary to the expectations of Western policymakers in the early days of the aid regime, foreign investment flows have constituted over time a decreasing proportion of total resource flows, amounting to only 10.4 percent in 1980, down from 41 percent in 1956. In most years since 1975, the growth of foreign investment flows has not even kept up with inflation. Furthermore, the direct financial cost of this foreign investment has been high; in 1979, the outflow of profits and dividends on existing investment surpassed net investment flows by $1.5 billion.[32] Commercial bank loans offered new possibilities for expanding the public sector role in industry.

The availability of commercial financing was a major factor in the decline of IMF activities during the 1970s. Whereas the number of IMF standby agreements in effect ranged between twenty-four and thirty-two in the years between 1965 and 1970, the range fell to thirteen to nineteen between 1971 and 1979.[33] High-conditionality IMF lending declined to 19 percent between 1974 and 1976; only ten drawings beyond the first credit tranche were made by the entire Fund membership during these years.[34] Between 1974 and 1980, the IMF financed only about 4 percent of the deficits of non-oil LDCs. In fact, there was a net inflow of funds (purchases minus repurchases) to the IMF in each of the three years between 1978 and 1980. Between

1974 and 1982, international private banks financed about half the current account deficits of the Third World. As summarized by the IMF's managing director: "By 1981, private bank loans and international bond markets were financing slightly over one half of the current account deficits and reserve accumulations of the non-oil developing countries—a function that, even as recently as ten years ago, had been handled, though on a much smaller scale, primarily by official institutions and governments."[35] Although borrowing from the commercial banks was concentrated among a few LDCs, by January 1981, thirty-one countries owed private banks over $1 billion, and another thirty-two owed $250 million or more.[36]

Most of the major borrowers used commercial bank financing primarily to finance public sector industrial investment and advanced infrastructure. With capital raised on international markets, some governments were able both to insist on and to finance their share of joint ventures with foreign multinationals. Others used commercial bank loans to avoid the necessity of foreign investment in specific projects altogether. Although many multinationals entered into lucrative agreements with bank-financed public sector agencies, the overall effect of bank lending in the mid to late 1970s was to increase resources available for state-controlled industrial development and to decrease the level of reliance on direct foreign investment. The Inter-American Development Bank, for example, has observed for Latin America:

> In the 1970's, there was a significant change in the external financing of the region in favor of indebtedness and against foreign investment. Whereas in the period 1971–73 direct investment represented 24.4 percent of the flow of external capital, in 1974–80 it only represented approximately 17 percent. . . . In the 1970's, the low interest rates made indebtedness much more attractive than direct investment.[37]

These developments did not pass unnoticed. As early as 1973, when debt to private banks was only 7 percent of what it was in 1982, William S. Gaud, head of the IFC and former head of USAID, warned of "very real risks for the developing countries in borrowing so heavily in a market with no established lending standards and no overall surveillance to prevent unsound practices." Gaud warned particularly that the availability of such loans would lessen reliance on foreign investment. With the banks, he argued, there was no meaningful "partnership" (as there was with the multinationals) because "the lenders have no direct involvement in the enterprise in which their funds are ultimately invested."[38] The following year, Antonio Ortiz Mena, president of the IDB, sounded a similar alarm, noting:

> Obviously, such practices can lead to the excessive use of credit and to an improper allocation of financial resources. . . . This observation is even more to the point if it is kept in mind that the countries sometimes resort to the euro-currency market to finance the total cost of the investment.

For Ortiz, the outdistancing of the role of the multilateral development banks by the private banks suggested "the advisability of broadening the Bank's activities."[39]

This conclusion was ironic, given the aid regime's historic norm of institutionalized noncompetition with the private sector. It reflected a belief, increasingly expressed by the aid institutions as the decade progressed, that the banks' activities were compromising the functioning of the aid regime. The International Finance Corporation complained that the "apparent low cost of private international borrowing undoubtedly contributed to the relative stagnation of net private direct investment flows to the developing countries during the 1970s" and speculated that the availability of such loans "may have led developing countries to adopt a less welcoming policy toward direct (foreign) investors."[40]

The Development Assistance Committee warned in its 1979 report:

> A vicious circle has developed in that some developing countries have tried to avoid the onerous Fund conditions (especially in higher credit tranches) by first exhausting their recourse to private bank lending. . . . Ample alternative private financing has thus tended to weaken the role of the IMF, and a major part of its resources remains idle.[41]

The same concern was reiterated in the following year's report, in which "the virtual absence of 'conditionality'" of private bank lending was noted.[42] In 1981, the DAC observed:

> These institutional developments have been so significant as to have changed completely the environment within which balance-of-payments strategies and general economic policies are formulated. The supply of international liquidity has not acted as a constraint on economic policies. Indeed, it may be said that the supply of finance has come to be determined by demand. In this situation the constraint facing individual capital-importing countries is not the availability of finance but the ability to sustain the servicing costs and, ultimately, the credibility of domestic economic policies.[43]

The World Bank cited "an inverse correlation between access to finance and structural adjustment in non-oil developing countries," and a Fund economist expressed concern that "the present institutional arrangements do not assure proper reconciliation between adjustment and financing."[44]

The use of commercial loans to escape the discipline of the aid regime was only possible for LDCs with significant access to international private capital markets; the rest remained firmly implanted within the traditional logic of the aid regime. But what was the significance of this partial escape from regime norms?

External Financing and State Capitalism

The changes in the aid regime in the 1970s discussed in the previous sections increased both the appeal and the viability of a range of strategies that, despite their diversity, may be called "state capitalist." Ironically, the commercial banks in the advanced capitalist countries made possible statist and nonmarket forms of development that the aid regime had historically obstructed. A diversity of state capitalist strategies produced record levels of industrial growth during the 1970s in a number of Third World countries, but by the early 1980s, these strategies were in crisis. The debt crisis abruptly ended the temporary escape from the discipline of the aid regime.

The concept of state capitalism is highly contentious, and I shall not attempt to delineate its boundaries precisely.[45] In general, proponents of the concept assert that the role of the state in certain societies goes qualitatively beyond the state intervention in the economy that is characteristic of all modern societies, yet the fundamental domestic framework and international context of these societies remain "capitalist." James Petras has defined state capitalism as "a social system in which the principal sources of surplus production are owned and directed by the state and in which the state becomes the principal source of capital accumulation within a market economy."[46] Given enabling conditions, state capitalism may in many contexts be considered virtually an "overdetermined" outcome in the sense that it is a response to a multiplicity of external and internal factors. Fitzroy Ambursley and Robin Cohen note: "The expanded role of the state in numerous countries of the capitalist periphery does not necessarily reflect any radicalization of these regimes, but corresponds rather to the exigencies of national capital accumulation and to the realities of the present-day world economy."[47] The specific forms that state capitalism takes vary widely, however.

Historically, Third World state capitalism was based on nationalization of extractive industries, hitherto foreign owned—acts that ran the risk of making the country an international outcast. With Euromarket expansion, a number of states discovered a new way of becoming the principal source of capital accumulation: foreign borrowing. Despite the reservations of the aid institutions, it was now possible to base state capitalism on a "respectable" financial mechanism.

Although the potential of escape from regime discipline that came to exist in the 1970s increased the viability of state capitalist options, not all major borrowers pursued them. Two categories of countries can be separated out immediately. First, for a few borrowers, most notably Zaire, the level of personalism and corruption, general mismanagement, and foreign influence ruled out any coherent statism.

Zaire's President Mobutu is reputed to have stashed away in foreign bank accounts assets equal to his country's entire external debt. Zaire was one of the first major borrowers from the banks in the 1970s to run into serious debt-servicing problems; by the end of 1978, it had accepted foreign control over both its central bank and its finance ministry.[48] Second, there were several borrowers, most notably post-Allende Chile and post-1976 Argentina, in which monetarist, free-market policies encouraged private sector borrowing from international banks in an ideologically inspired effort to reduce the state's role in the economy. In such cases, borrowing was often used for luxury consumption and financial speculation. Argentina's extensive borrowing was devoted almost exclusively to speculating in foreign currencies, luxury imports, and arms purchases.[49] (Argentina's President Alfonsin has characterized Argentina's debt as the only one with no assets to show for it.)[50] In Chile, luxury goods imports, largely financed by foreign borrowing by private companies, were 491 percent higher in 1979 than in 1970; imports of industrial machinery were up only 3 percent. Foreign loans were also used to buy over four hundred state enterprises sold off by the government at "attractive terms" to a handful of private financial/industrial groups in Chile. Whereas in 1975 the private sector accounted for 11 percent of Chile's external debt, in 1982 it accounted for over one-half.[51]

Most of the major borrowers from the international banks, in contrast, fall on a state capitalist continuum that may be separated into two groupings, with considerable diversity and overlap within each. The poles of the continuum correspond to Kuniko Inoguchi's distinction between the financial (banking) and entrepreneurial functions of state capitalist regimes.[52] States stressing the banking role tend to be more ideologically conservative and to occupy a less competitive position vis-à-vis the private sector; the exemplar of this type of state capitalism is South Korea. This type of state shapes the process of development primarily through its central role in the mobilization and allocation of investment capital, largely through state-owned financial institutions. The ability of states to do this has depended crucially on access to international capital markets. In

South Korea, government borrowing has far exceeded foreign investment (which accounted for only 7.9 percent of capital inflows between 1972 and 1976) and has been critical for the government's role in providing about two-thirds of all financial intermediation. South Korea's foreign debt was $37.4 billion in mid 1983.[53] During the 1970s, one government development bank alone provided half of all lending to the country's capital goods industry. In addition, the government routinely guaranteed private sector borrowing, with the result that Korean companies are the most highly leveraged in the world. Public sector industries are by no means insignificant in Korea, but the main mechanism of state control in Korea and similar cases has been through financial intermediation.[54]

Brazil represents an intermediate case, in which the state's entrepreneurial function is more pronounced. Nine of the ten largest firms and one-third of the largest one hundred firms in Brazil are state enterprises. An estimated eight hundred enterprises are characterized by varying degrees of state ownership in Brazil.[55] But as in South Korea, the banking function of the state predominates. Three-quarters of all investment capital to the private sector is provided by state institutions, and even private banking is strictly controlled. According to Inoguchi's calculations, domestic lending by the Brazilian state in 1979 was almost twice the level of government capital expenditure.[56] Pakistan illustrates this pattern also; public financial institutions account for more than 75 percent of financial sector value added, and state enterprises account for less than 10 percent of manufacturing value added.[57]

Countries such as Mexico and Peru provide an entrepreneurial contrast to this financial emphasis; their capital expenditures were, respectively, four and three times their domestic lending in 1980.[58] This state capitalist grouping, which also includes such countries as Turkey, Venezuela, Indonesia, Tunisia, India, and Algeria, is distinguished by the greater predominance of the productive public sector, particularly in industry. In Mexico, there were 740 state-owned corporations in 1976, and the public sector accounted for 45 percent of GDP.[59] There were three hundred firms with varying degrees of state ownership in Venezuela at the end of the 1970s, and the public sector accounted for 67.9 percent of GDP in 1981.[60] In Algeria, which represents the "left" boundary of the state capitalist category, the state held 88 percent of industrial assets in 1977, and state enterprises accounted for 68 percent of all fixed capital formation between 1978 and 1981.[61]

Euromarket borrowing was crucial to the state capitalist strategies of these countries during the 1970s. In contrast to most foreign aid, international financial markets enabled states to expand their role in direct production. The fears expressed by the major aid agencies, discussed in the previous section, were realized. In its 1982 annual survey, *Social and Economic Progress in Latin America*, the Inter-American Development Bank concluded that "the public sector—or its plans, in the case of publicly guaranteed investment credits to the private sector—has been favored with the reappearance of the international private capital markets."[62] Nonfinancial state enterprises accounted for 28 percent of all Euromarket borrowing in 1980.[63] State enterprises in the Third World as a whole increased their share of gross domestic product by almost 50 percent during the 1970s, from 6.8 percent to about 10 percent.[64] Although there was variation, countries that borrowed heavily expanded public sector industrial investment considerably more rapidly than those without access to this form of financing. The share of GDP accounted for by state enterprises rose between 1970 and 1980 from 10.3 percent to 22.8 percent in Mexico, from 4.2 percent to 32.3 percent (1981) in Peru, and from 17.4 percent to 46.9 percent in Venezuela.[65]

The unconditional nature of most Euromarket loans, alongside the issue of fungibility, makes it difficult to specify the precise impact of Euromarket borrowing. A range of studies, however, has established a positive relationship between indebtedness and investment in most of the major borrowers. In an early quantitative study, Robert Solomon found that capital formation as a proportion of total absorption increased in most of the major borrowers between 1970 and 1975; my updated calculations using 1979–81 data show further increases.[66] Using somewhat different procedures, the IMF's

1983 *World Economic Outlook* similarly concluded that "increases in the indebtedness of the non-oil developing countries have reflected primarily an exchange of debt instruments for additional physical capital."[67] Citing that study, the IMF's managing director summarized:

> Further evidence is given by a recent Fund study, covering the 20 non-oil developing countries with the largest debt service payments in 1982. This shows that the increased indebtedness of these countries over the past decade or so has been primarily reflected in an increase in investment outlays rather than in spending for consumption. The median investment ratio for these countries rose from about 19 percent of GNP in 1968–72 to 22 percent in 1974–77 and further to nearly 24 percent in 1978–81.[68]

Crude measures of this nature say little about the appropriateness or effectiveness of such investment. Although debt-financed investments may have been productive in a narrow economic sense, they were often far from socially optimal. In some countries, Euromarket borrowing did little more than offset capital flight, which is estimated at $55 billion for Latin America between 1977 and 1983, 30 percent of new borrowing.[69] Both the World Bank and the Inter-American Development Bank report a significant decline in the rate of return on investment in the major debtor countries at the end of the 1970s.[70] Other critics raise questions about the appropriateness of state investment decisions and about the class interests served by them. Brazilian economist Celso Furtado attacks the "techno-authoritarian system," insulated from democratic pressures.[71] In the case of Venezuela, Petras and Morley contend: "The principal beneficiaries of state ownership have been the big manufacturers, large commercial farmers and ranchers, bankers, construction contractors and real estate interests and the large export-importers who have received the bulk of investment funds and credits."[72] They demonstrate further that this type of state capitalism has been compatible with a considerable expansion in the absolute size of foreign investment.

Nonetheless, as one account of domestic criticism of the technocrats who ran up Brazil's external debt notes:

Few Brazilians would undo much of the work of the technocrats. They have constructed one of the developing world's most sophisticated networks of roads, banking, telecommunications and electric power to service a widely diversified industrial base that could enable Brazil to outperform most other countries in a world upturn.[73]

Furthermore, as we have seen, Euromarket borrowing enabled Third World countries to decrease the *relative* importance of multinationals. For Latin America, foreign investment's share of external capital inflows fell by 30 percent 1971–73 and the rest of the decade.[74] A World Bank study of South Korea has similarly documented how the availability of external bank financing enabled South Korea to limit quite drastically the penetration of foreign multinationals even while pursuing an export-oriented, high-growth strategy. Direct foreign investment accounted for only 4.4 percent of Korea's external liabilities in 1983.[75]

Even in Brazil, where foreign investment was more welcome, Euromarket borrowing allowed high levels of industrial development to be accompanied by a relative decline in the role of foreign direct investment. In his classic study of Brazilian dependent development, Peter Evans made this prophetic observation:

> The entire success of the dependent development is predicated on multinationals willing to invest, international bankers willing to extend credit, and other countries willing to consume an ever increasing volume of Brazilian exports. The emphasis here has been on the internal elite structures that made the triple alliance possible. Yet the formation of these internal structures could not have taken place in the absence of an environment in which international capital, both financial and industrial, was anxiously pursuing new opportunities in the periphery and in which Brazil stood out as an ideal investment climate. The process of accumulation in Brazil is still vulnerable to the effects of disruptions in the international economy, and that vulnerability constitutes the most obvious limitation of the triple alliance.[76]

As we shall see, that vulnerability appeared with a vengeance in the early 1980s. First, however, we briefly examine the implications of

Euromarket borrowing for the internal structure of the Third World itself.

Consequences of Unequal Access

Unequal access to Euromarket financing has both reflected and accentuated differences among Third World countries. Table 29 details the differences among non-oil LDCs in the growth of their debt to private banks. The newly industrializing countries (NICs) have monopolized this borrowing all along, accounting for 73.9 percent of total accumulated debt in 1982. Over two-thirds of NIC public debt was to private banks in 1982. Most of the rest of non-oil developing country borrowing has been concentrated among the middle-income countries (MICs). Only 6 percent of the debt of low-income countries (LICs), amounting to about $6.6 billion, was owed to private banks in 1982; this amounted to only 1 percent of the net international claims of commercial banks worldwide.[77]

The comparative smallness of LIC debt to private creditors should not be interpreted as being inconsequential. Using the more restricted World Bank low-income category, Max Mmuya and I have found that twenty-seven low-income countries owed on average 17 percent of their external debt to private creditors in 1982, accounting for 36.4 percent of their total debt service. Debt service to private creditors was the largest category of debt service for almost half these countries. Despite its comparatively small size, therefore, debt to private creditors was a significant factor in the early emergence of a debt crisis among the low-income countries.[78]

Growth rates reflected in the data in Table 29 indicate a widening of the differences between country groupings. Between 1975 and 1980, LIC debt to private banks grew by 85.7 percent, MIC debt by 288.8 percent, and NIC debt by 162.7 percent. Between 1980 and 1982, however, LIC debt to private banks grew by 26.9 percent, MIC debt by 24.6 percent, and NIC debt by 42.8 percent. MICs were no longer approaching NICs in private borrowing as quickly as they had been.

TABLE 29   Distribution of Debt to Private Banks of Non-Oil LDCs, by Income Group, 1971, 1975, 1980, 1982 ($ billions and as percentage of total public debt)

Income Group	1971		1975		1980		1982	
	Bank Debt	% Total Debt	Bank Debt	% Total Debt	Bank Debt	% Total Debt	Bank Debt	% Total Debt
LICs	0.4	2	2.8	7	5.2	6	6.6	6
MICs	3.5	14	11.6	29	45.1	38	56.2	39
NICs	12.2	38	47.5	60	124.8	65	178.2	67

SOURCE: Organization for Economic Cooperation and Development, *External Debt of Developing Countries* (Paris, 1982), p. 34.

Table 30 provides details on the twenty largest Third World debt-ors to private banks as of December 1982. The data illustrate the concentration of Euromarket lending in a relatively few countries. Only one country designated as a non-oil low-income country by the OECD was among the top twenty. Among the top ten, seven were NICs or OPEC countries. Although the bulk of Euromarket lending

TABLE 30   Twenty Largest Third World Debtors to Private Banks as of December 1982

Debtor	Debt to Private Banks ($ billions)	Country Grouping
1. Mexico	62.9	NIC
2. Brazil	60.5	NIC
3. Venezuela	27.5	OPEC
4. Argentina	25.7	NIC
5. So. Korea	23.3	NIC
6. Philippines	12.6	MIC
7. Chile	11.6	MIC
8. Indonesia	10.0	OPEC/LIC
9. Malaysia	8.7	MIC
10. Nigeria	8.5	OPEC/MIC
11. Algeria	7.7	OPEC
12. Taiwan	6.6	NIC
13. Colombia	6.3	MIC
14. Kuwait	6.2	OPEC
15. Saudi Arabia	5.5	OPEC
16. Peru	5.4	MIC
17. Egypt	4.9	LIC
18. Thailand	4.9	MIC
19. United Arab Emirates	4.8	OPEC
20. Ecuador	4.5	OPEC
Total	308.1	

SOURCE: "The Banker's Guide to LDC Debt," *The Banker* 133,694 (December 1983): 62–63.

NOTE: Both public and private debt are included in these figures.

is concentrated in these twenty countries, there were sixty-eight Third World countries with debt to private banks over $100 million in 1981 and another thirteen functioning as offshore banking centers.[79]

Although uneven access to international capital markets interacts with numerous differences between individual countries and country groups, the evidence that indebtedness is associated with increased investment suggests that differential access to private capital markets is very likely one of the factors explaining the increasing gap between the low-income countries and the middle-income and newly industrializing countries. Table 31 documents some of these growing disparities among Third World countries. The low-income countries, accounting for close to half the world's population, suffered declines in their share of world GNP, the ratio of their per capita income to that of the United States, and their share of world merchandise exports. Both categories of middle-income countries made advances in the first two indicators, but not in the third. Only the NICs advanced in all three.

Unequal access to international capital markets played a major role in the responses to the oil price increases in 1973–74 and 1979–80. As Dell and Lawrence have shown, the ability to borrow in private capital markets allowed some countries to avoid deflation and to shift the counterpart deficits of OPEC's surpluses elsewhere.[80] This has been a continuing process. *IMF Survey* acknowledged in December 1982 that "the burden of adjustment in the international economy has shifted further to the non-oil developing countries."[81] As Dell and Lawrence argue convincingly, not only have structural deficits been shifted increasingly to the weakest countries, but these countries have also been unable, relative to the more creditworthy countries, to escape the discipline of the IMF:

> Fund resources form a much higher proportion of the total balance of payments financing available to the weakest and—in terms of the narrow criteria of private capital markets—least creditworthy countries than they do for other Fund members. The weakest countries are those that can least afford to hold full-owned reserves and thus, most likely to require

TABLE 31   Developing Country Groups: Selected Indicators, 1955 and 1980

Country Group	Share in World Population		Share in World GNP		Per Capita Income as % U.S. Per Capita Income		Share of World Merchandise Exports	
	1955	1980	1955	1980	1955	1980	1955	1980
LICs	44.7	47.1	8.1	4.8	2.7	2.2	5.6	1.9
Non-Oil MICs	6.7	8.0	3.8	4.0	8.4	10.9	6.9	3.9
Oil-exp. MICs	9.6	11.2	3.7	5.0	5.8	9.7	8.0	7.6
NICs	7.1	7.3	5.1	7.7	10.7	22.9	6.8	8.0
All LDCs	68.1	73.6	20.7	21.5	4.5	6.4	27.3	21.4

SOURCE: World Bank, *World Development Report 1982*, pp. 22, 26.

Fund assistance requiring them to come under Fund surveillance. They are, therefore, in multiple jeopardy—they tend, through the process of shifting mentioned earlier, to attract more than their share of the pressure exerted by structural current account surpluses in the system, as well as a less than proportional share of the capital flows that these surpluses generate; they are least likely to be able to finance such deficits out of owned reserves or by borrowing from nonofficial sources; they are, therefore, most likely to have to comply with constraints upon their economies, the extent of which is a function of the inadequacy of available official financing; and they have the least capacity for adjustment because of the rigidity and lack of diversification of their economies.[82]

Most of the major borrowers successfully avoided the IMF during the 1970s. Brazil, Colombia, Venezuela, Algeria, and Nigeria managed to avoid credit tranche purchases altogether in the 1970s; Indonesia did after 1973. South Korea made only minor credit tranche drawings in three years between the late 1960s and 1979. Mexico and Chile made substantial credit tranche purchases in two years and a lesser purchase in another year, but otherwise refrained from such borrowing. Thailand refrained from credit tranche purchases up to 1979. In contrast, the great majority of low-income countries made repeated IMF drawings. It is at least a moot question whether the greater submission to IMF discipline during those years by low-income countries, as compared to middle-income and newly industrializing countries, better prepared these countries for the traumatic events of the early 1980s.

The capacity of the major borrowers to resist the discipline and constraints of the aid regime collapsed between 1979 and 1983. By the end of 1983, virtually all the major debtors were deeply enmeshed in the aid regime, with new implications for the future of state capitalism in the Third World.

International Debt and the Crisis of State Capitalism

One central constraint was always built into the nature of external indebtedness: the need to earn foreign exchange to service the debt.

As a commercial bank economist and World Bank consultant noted, "The emphasis on foreign exchange earnings to repay debts means that countries need to emphasize their export sector more than they might otherwise wish. But if foreign savings are to be used to develop the economy, this bias must be accepted."[83] The cost of this bias did not seem unduly large in the 1970s. Worldwide inflation made real interest rates on commercial loans negative or just slightly positive for much of the decade. Export prices increased at a rate in most years that enabled countries either to keep up with increasing debt service or to attract new loans to pay off old ones. If negative or low real interest rates and rising export prices had continued, there would have been no generalized debt crisis in 1982.

Variable interest rates and reliance on exports to pay for debt service drastically increased the vulnerability of Third World countries to changes in the world economy. This in turn increased their vulnerability to decisions by the governments of the major capitalist countries that largely determine the health of the world economy. Decisions by these governments, particularly the United States, created the drastically altered international conditions giving rise to the debt crisis.

Few foresaw either these decisions or their consequences. Walter Wriston, the aggressive chairman of Citibank who symbolized the new banking style of the 1970s, predicted in 1978 that the growth in world trade would continue unabated and that world trade would double in the next ten years. Five years later Wriston explained, "I don't know anyone that knew Volcker was going to lock the wheels of the world."[84]

I shall not attempt to explore here why these policies evolved or how they led to the most serious downturn in the capitalist world economy in fifty years. What follows is instead a look at the three major immediate causes of the debt-servicing crisis—the hardening terms of debt, the decline in the volume and terms of trade, and the advent of negative transfers—along with a consideration of how the debt crisis challenged the viability of state capitalist strategies.

Hardened Terms of Debt

As we have seen, the structure of LDC debt changed dramatically in the 1970s. For all non-OPEC LDCs, the proportion of public debt accounted for by ODA declined from 41 percent in 1971 to 23 percent in 1982; debt to private banks rose from 20 percent in 1971 to 46 percent in 1982. For the newly industrializing countries, 67 percent of their total debt was owed to private banks.

Table 32 shows that debt service on long-term loans more than quadrupled between 1975 and 1982, to a total of almost $110 billion. The proportion of debt service devoted to interest increased steadily, reaching 47 percent in 1983. Among official creditors, the most rapidly growing category of debt service between 1975 and 1983 was multilateral debt service, which, as we have seen, is excluded by regime norms from renegotiation or rescheduling. Overall, however, debt service on bank loans rose by far the most, from $7.8 billion in 1975 to $52 billion in 1982. At least from 1980 onward, about half the increase in debt service on loans from private banks was due to increases in the variable interest rates on previous debt.[85]

Table 32 does not include short-term debt, contracted for less than one year. Such debt traditionally has been excluded from debt statistics on the grounds that it is generally "self-liquidating," usually being used to finance trade. By 1982, however, short-term debt was being used increasingly to roll over long-term debt and had come to constitute 20 percent of all LDC debt.[86] It was not self-liquidating.

Interest rates on debt to private banks rose both because of increases in LIBOR and, to a lesser degree, because of increased spreads over LIBOR (sometimes disguised as a shift to the U.S. prime rate, generally about half a percentage point higher). LIBOR rose from 5.5 percent in 1972 to 9.25 percent in 1978 to 17 percent in 1981. It averaged just over 16 percent in 1982 and fell sharply to an average of 10.6 percent in 1983. It jumped 2 percent in the first half of 1984, then declined to about 10 percent by early 1985. The nominal decline after 1981 was largely offset by the decline in inflation, how-

TABLE 32   Long-Term Debt Service of LDCs, by Source of Lending, 1971, 1975–83 ($ billions)

Source of Lending	1971	1975	1976	1977	1978	1979	1980	1981	1982	1983
Advanced capitalist countries[a]										
Bilateral ODA[b]	1.3	1.7	1.9	2.0	2.3	2.6	2.8	2.8	2.9	3.0
Export credits	4.9	10.4	11.9	15.9	19.6	23.9	28.1	32.4	33.0	31.2
Bank loans	1.9	7.8	10.2	13.6	22.5	31.3	36.3	47.0	52.0	41.0
Other private	0.8	1.6	2.3	3.2	4.1	4.8	5.1	5.5	6.6	6.5
Multilateral organizations	0.9	1.6	2.0	2.5	3.2	3.8	4.6	5.7	6.8	8.0
USSR and Eastern Europe	0.6	0.8	0.9	1.1	1.3	1.7	1.8	2.0	2.2	2.5
OPEC countries	—	0.2	0.2	0.6	0.9	1.2	1.5	1.9	2.4	3.0
Other	0.3	1.0	1.3	1.3	1.4	1.9	2.0	2.6	3.9	3.6
Total debt service	10.5	25.1	30.8	40.1	55.3	71.2	82.3	100.0	109.8	98.8
Interest	3.2	8.8	10.2	12.7	17.4	25.5	35.2	43.2	50.3	46.8
Amortization	7.3	16.3	20.6	27.4	37.9	45.7	47.1	56.8	59.5	52.0

SOURCE: Organization for Economic Cooperation and Development, *Development Co-operation: Efforts and Policies of the Members of the Development Assistance Committee, 1983 Review*, p. 213.

[a] Members of the DAC of the OECD.
[b] Official development assistance.

ever, and the IMF estimates that real rates on long-term debt actually increased in 1983.[87]

The translation of nominal into real interest rates depends very much on the deflator used. The usual choice is between a U.S. price index and an index of LDC export prices. Using one version of the latter, the IMF has estimated that real interest rates on commercial loans to LDCs moved from a range of minus 7 percent to minus 11 percent during 1973–78 to a range of plus 7 percent to plus 10 percent in 1981.[88] According to the World Bank, the real rate of interest in 1982, using LDC export prices as the deflator, was 19.4 percent (7.1 percent if U.S. prices are used).[89] At the same time, average maturities on bank loans declined from 9 years in 1978 to 7.5 years in 1981.[90] Average maturities on loans to Latin America were 4.74 years in 1982.[91]

Another way of examining the burden of increased interest rates is to compare real rates with historical norms. The IMF estimates that real interest rates at the end of 1983 were four percentage points higher than those "at a comparable stage in previous postwar cycles." This spread "can be seen as representing almost a fifth of the total current account deficit of non-oil developing countries."[92] With each percentage point costing LDCs about $4 billion in additional debt service, this unprecedented spread results in the transfer of around $16 billion from the Third World to the commercial banks—roughly the amount of all multilateral aid. Between 1978 and 1981, increased interest payments exceeded the increased cost of net oil imports by over one-third.[93]

Rapidly increasing debt service not only made it difficult for LDCs to sustain positive capital inflows, but it also altered the profitability of investments already undertaken. De Larosière has observed: "Investment projects financed at variable interest rates that appeared profitable at very low real interest rates can quickly become unprofitable when real interest rates increase sharply."[94] The Inter-American Development Bank concluded:

> For example, in 1980, an investment project to be financed with external debt, without resort to subsequent refinancings, would have to generate

an income stream that would permit the debt to be paid in the first three and a half years. Very few projects in the countries of the region could be launched under those conditions.[95]

Hardened terms of debt undermined the debt-servicing calculations upon which state capitalist industrialization had been based. By the end of the 1970s, most new borrowing by Third World countries was simply refinancing past debt, rather than adding new resources.

Decline in Volume and Terms of Trade

Burdensome as the hardened terms of debt were, they did not in themselves unleash the debt crisis. Loss of export income because of the decline in the volume and terms of trade was much more important, particularly for the low-income countries. Despite the fact that 69 percent of their debt in 1982 remained ODA, down only 5 percent from 1971, and that their overall debt service was increasing gradually, twenty-six out of thirty-four Paris Club reschedulings between 1979 and 1983 were carried out by low-income countries (as defined by the OECD). Because of the particularly devastating impact of the world recession on the low-income countries, the proportion of their exports devoted to servicing debt in 1982 was almost identical to that of the newly industrializing countries.[96]

The volume of world trade, after growing rapidly in most of the 1970s, barely increased (1.5 percent) in 1980, stagnated in 1981, and fell 3.6 percent in 1982. LDC export prices fell 16 percent in 1981 and 14 percent in 1982. World trade rose 2 percent in volume in 1983 but declined 2 percent in value.[97] Although the increase in the volume of world trade was greater in 1984, the rate of increase in LDC commodity prices declined sharply, and overall these prices remained 18 percent below what they had been in 1980. Non-oil commodity prices declined sharply in the latter part of 1984 and remained depressed in early 1985.[98]

The IMF's *Annual Report 1982* observed that in real terms, "non-oil primary commodity prices in mid 1982 were lower than at any other time for more than three decades, and 21 percent lower than in the recession year 1975."[99] Changes in the terms of trade were negative in each of the successive years between 1981 and 1983.[100] In 1983, Nicaragua had to export 11.2 tons of coffee to purchase a tractor it could get with 4.4 tons in 1977.[101] To buy a truck in 1981, Tanzania had to produce four times as much cotton, three times as much coffee, three times as many cashews, or ten times as much tobacco as five years earlier.[102]

William Cline has estimated that non-oil LDC export losses due to the decline in the volume of world trade came to $21 billion in 1981–82, and losses due to worsening terms of trade came to $79 billion, for a total of $100 billion for the two years.[103] This sum is greater than all the debt service paid to commercial banks during these two years.

Negative Bank Transfers

For many countries, the combination of rising debt service and falling export revenues meant that the only way to pay for old loans was to secure new ones. New loan disbursements had to exceed rising debt service. For Latin America to maintain a constant net inflow of roughly $20 billion, gross loan disbursements had to increase from $31.4 billion in 1976 to $72 billion in 1981.[104]

Table 33 allows us to analyze the increasing tendency for debt service to offset new lending. Although all the data are from the World Bank, the series 1970–79 and 1980–83 may not be strictly comparable because the Bank has strengthened its debt-reporting system in the past several years. The data up through 1979 probably understate the level of private bank lending, particularly in the earlier years. Although the earlier data appear to be less comprehensive, they are probably sufficient to indicate the general trend of bank transfers.

Table 33 shows that gross disbursements on new bank loans increased rapidly enough to result in a steady increase in net transfer only until 1978. After declining slightly in 1979, net transfers

TABLE 33   Private Bank Lending to LDCs: Gross Disbursements, Debt Service, and Net Transfers, 1970–84 ($ billions)

	1970	1971	1972	1973	1974	1975	1976	1977	1978	1979	1980	1981	1982	1983	1984
Gross disbursements	2.6	4.2	6.3	9.5	13.2	17.1	22.9	28.7	42.8	50.3	72.0	88.1	74.1	78.3	71.8
Amortization	1.2	1.6	2.1	3.0	3.7	3.8	4.8	8.2	16.4	19.8	36.3	38.5	40.5	38.3	33.2
Interest	0.5	0.6	0.8	1.2	2.1	3.0	3.7	5.2	7.7	12.4	26.8	34.6	40.5	39.3	47.3
Debt service	1.7	2.2	2.9	4.2	5.8	6.8	8.5	13.4	24.1	32.2	63.1	73.1	81.0	77.6	80.5
Net transfer	0.9	1.9	3.5	5.2	7.4	10.3	14.4	15.3	18.7	18.1	8.9	15.0	-6.9	0.7	-8.7

SOURCES: 1970–79 data from Nicholas C. Hope, *Developments in and Prospects for the External Debt of the Developing Countries: 1970–80 and Beyond* (Washington, D.C.: World Bank Staff Working Paper No. 488, August 1981), pp. 15–16; 1980–83 data from World Bank, *Annual Report 1984*, p. 39; 1984 data from World Bank, *Annual Report 1985*, p. 43.

NOTE: Although all data are from the World Bank, the 1970–79 and the 1980–83 series may not be strictly comparable, mainly because of expanded reporting.

plunged in 1980, rose again in 1981, and then turned negative in 1982. In 1983, new disbursements and debt service almost exactly canceled each other out; net transfer turned negative again in 1984. Between 1970 and 1976, the proportion of gross disbursements offset by debt service declined to a low of about 37 percent. By 1978, over half of new lending was eaten up by debt service, and in 1980, 88 percent. Debt service was 109 percent of new disbursements in 1982.

The apparent improvement in 1983 net transfer was entirely due to increased borrowing by oil-exporting LDCs, whose gross disbursements jumped from $27.8 billion in 1982 to $40.2 billion in 1983. Gross disbursements to oil-importing LDCs fell from $46.3 billion in 1982 to $22.4 billion in 1983; their net transfer in 1983 was minus $14.2 billion.[105] In Latin America, net transfer was minus $17.2 billion in 1983; at least for Brazil, net transfers have been negative since 1981.[106] Taking into account all types of capital flows, the Cartagena group of eleven Latin American nations estimates an outflow from Latin America as a whole of $55 billion in 1983–84 combined.[107] For the Third World as a whole, UNCTAD economists have estimated that for every dollar from all sources in 1980–82, LDCs repaid eighty-two cents.[108]

The debt-servicing crisis that erupted in the wake of worsening terms of debt, declining volume and terms of trade, and negative bank transfers meant that the easing of aid regime constraints on development policy was over. No longer could strategically located countries escape from the constraints and discipline of the aid regime. At the same time, the magnitude of the debt crisis created a crisis in the aid regime itself. The next chapter chronicles the process by which the aid regime has been restructured and reconsolidated in the early 1980s.

7

Regime Restructuring and Reconsolidation

The debt crisis both reflected and greatly accentuated crisis in the aid regime. As we have seen, the emergence of the debt crisis was partly rooted in the breakdown of aid regime discipline in the 1970s; the major aid institutions perceived this breakdown as a threat several years before the debt crisis became generalized. With the rapid spread of debt-servicing problems in the Third World, especially after mid 1982, traditional regime norms proved no longer sufficient.

The use of Paris Club reschedulings of official debt to safeguard the privileged status of multilateral development bank (MDB) loans and private bank loans could no longer work in 1982, when debt service on ODA from DAC countries accounted for only 2.6 percent of total debt service.[1] Even when debt service on official export credits was added, the saving resulting from Paris Club reschedulings fell considerably short of the debt service due private creditors. Furthermore, with MDB loans excluded from rescheduling, despite the fact that the bulk of MDB loans carried harder terms than bilateral loans, a much larger amount of bilateral aid had to be rescheduled to provide the same potential level of debt relief as a much smaller amount of MDB debt.

The demands of the debt crisis represented one more in a series of external shocks raising the external financing needs of Third World countries and thereby, in the absence of a radical expansion of aid resources, threatening to make the aid regime irrelevant. As aid officials quickly recognized, the scale of the financial problems facing debtor countries dwarfed the resources of the aid institutions. Unless those resources, or others the aid regime could claim to "unlock," could be increased substantially, aid institutions would be in a weaker position than ever to restore regime discipline. At the same time, the advent of negative transfers to the commercial banks and the increasing proportion of aid offset by debt service threatened to make default or repudiation attractive options, despite the formidable array of penalties sure to be imposed on a defaulting or, especially, a repudiating country. Even a limited default would trigger a generalized boycott by most aid institutions, thereby threatening a continued role for those institutions themselves.

More generally, there was the possibility that the debt crisis might be taken as an indictment of the entire regime-sponsored model of outward-oriented development, particularly if rising protectionism among the industrial countries undermined the premises of outward-oriented development strategies. The debt crisis offered both opportunity for new influence and the danger of irrelevance for the major aid institutions.

Despite its unprecedented nature, the debt crisis did not evoke any fundamental departures from practices evolved during the formative years of the aid regime. One account in March 1984 could assert, with only slight exaggeration, that "in practice, no new idea has been tested; both creditors and debtors continue to deal with the debt through traditional methods that have prevailed since the creation of the IMF after World War II to help Western nations remain solvent."[2] World Bank and IMF officials repeatedly insisted that no generalized crisis existed at all and that individual country debt problems remained "manageable," best dealt with on a "case by case" basis.[3] Leaders of the advanced capitalist countries at the Williamsburg, London, and Bonn economic summits in 1983, 1984, and 1985 rejected calls for radical reforms and reiterated their confidence in existing institutions and procedures. Despite preliminary press speculation about major new initiatives in the wake of spreading default in Africa and renewed economic crisis in Latin America, U.S. proposals at the annual World Bank/IMF meetings in Seoul in October 1985 were similarly restrained, tinkering with regime rules and procedures rather than altering principles or norms. No fundamental regime change has occurred.

Nonetheless, the need for more modest adjustments in the aid regime has been widely recognized and acted upon. Although some of these changes have been supported by Third World nations, the collective function of the adjustments as an alternative to fundamental change reflects the success of the major creditor countries and banks in guiding and limiting the process of regime change. This chapter surveys these changes and suggests that they represent a reconsolidation of the aid regime's historic capacity to shape the basic contours of Third World development. Four themes emerge from this survey: (1) the increased linkage between aid and nonaid resources, (2) the altered balance between different types of aid flows, (3) the increased level of conditionality characterizing financial flows overall, and (4) the elaboration of a common "agenda" of conditionality in the concept of structural adjustment. The first three themes are discussed in this chapter; the fourth is dealt with in the Epilogue.

Increased Linkage Between Aid and Nonaid Resources

As we saw in the previous chapter, aid flows have been declining since the early days of the debt crisis. In this context, increased linkage between aid flows and other resource flows has had two main functions. First, it has increased the level of nonaid resources or at least, more commonly, prevented these resources from declining as much as they would have otherwise. Second, it has increased the leverage of the major aid institutions by increasing the "critical mass" of financing at their disposal. It has also done this by increasing the proportion of total external financing linked to aid regime norms and procedures. The following sections explore five mechanisms through which this increased linkage has been achieved: (1) debt renegotiations, (2) the IMF's "bailing in" the banks, (3) bridge financing, (4) cofinancing and loan guarantees, and (5) new ways of promoting foreign direct investment.

Debt Renegotiations

Table 34 traces the history of the two major types of debt renegotiation since 1974: reschedulings of bilateral official debt, generally under Paris Club auspices, and renegotiations of public debt owed to private sources, generally commercial banks. Until 1982, the latter generally involved refinancing rather than rescheduling, but increasingly debt renegotiation has come to include a package of rescheduling, refinancing, and, on occasion, new loans.

The data in Table 34 suggest that the debt crisis really dates to 1979, when as many debt renegotiations occurred as in the previous three years combined and when renegotiations with private creditors took a particularly sudden leap. The next major increase took place in 1981, followed by a virtual explosion of debt renegotiations in 1983 and 1984. Between 1981 and 1984, over twice as many Paris Club renegotiations took place as between 1974 and 1980. Furthermore, the thirty in 1983–84 were two and one-half times the number in 1981–82. The increase in renegotiations with private creditors was even more striking, with over five times as many renegotiations occurring between 1981 and 1984 as between 1974 and 1980. Likewise, the thirty-six renegotiations in 1983–84 were three and one-half times the number in 1981–82. Debt renegotiations with both

TABLE 34   Renegotiations of Debt to Official and Private Creditors,
1974–84 ($ millions)

Year	Official Creditors	Private Creditors
1974	Chile (509) Ghana (190) India (179) Pakistan (650)	
1975	Chile (216) India (157)	
1976	India (169) Zaire (211)	Argentina (970)
1977	India (110) Sierra Leone (27) Zaire (236)	
1978	Gabon (105) Peru (478) Turkey (1223)	
1979	Sudan (373) Togo (170) Turkey (873) Zaire (1147)	Guyana (29) Jamaica (126) Peru (821) Turkey (2640) Zaire (402)
1980	Liberia (30) Sierra Leone (41) Turkey (2600)	Nicaragua (582) Togo (68) Zaire (402)
1981	Central African Republic (55) Liberia (25) Madagascar (142) Pakistan (263) Senegal (77) Togo (92) Uganda (56) Zaire (574)	Bolivia (444) Jamaica (103) Nicaragua (188) Sudan (638) Turkey (3100)

SOURCES: 1974 data from World Bank, *World Development Report 1983* (New York: Oxford University Press, 1983), p. 23; 1975–84 data from World Bank, *World Development Report 1985* (New York: Oxford University Press, 1985), p. 28, with the following exceptions: 1983 Cuban figure from *South* 32 (June 1983): 70; 1982 Polish figure from *World Development Report 1983*, p. 23; 1983 Polish figure from *New York Times* (September 19, 1983), p. D1; 1984 Polish figure from *New York Times* (April 27, 1984), p. D7.

NOTE: 1984 private creditor debt renegotiation data include some cases in which agreement in principle was reached in 1984 but final signing did not occur until 1985.

Continued on next page

TABLE 34—*continued*

Year	Official Creditors	Private Creditors
1982	Madagascar (103)	Guyana (14)
	Malawi (24)	Liberia (27)
	Romania (234)	Nicaragua (102)
	Senegal (84)	Poland (4600)
	Sudan (174)	Romania (1598)
	Uganda (22)	
1983	Brazil (3478)	Brazil (4532)
	Central African Republic (13)	Chile (3400)
	Costa Rica (97)	Costa Rica (1240)
	Ecuador (200)	Cuba (1200)
	Liberia (18)	Dominican Republic (497)
	Malawi (30)	Ecuador (1835)
	Mexico (1550)	Malawi (59)
	Morocco (1225)	Mexico (23,625)
	Niger (33)	Nigeria (1920)
	Peru (450)	Peru (380)
	Romania (195)	Poland (2600)
	Senegal (64)	Romania (567)
	Sudan (502)	Togo (74)
	Togo (114)	Uruguay (815)
	Yugoslavia (988)	Yugoslavia (1586)
	Zaire (1317)	
	Zambia (285)	
1984	Ivory Coast (153)	Argentina (23,241)
	Jamaica (106)	Bolivia (536)
	Liberia (17)	Brazil (5350)
	Madagascar (120)	Ecuador (5065)
	Mozambique (200)	Guyana (24)
	Niger (22)	Honduras (148)
	Peru (1000)	Ivory Coast (306)
	Philippines (685)	Jamaica (148)
	Sierra Leone (88)	Liberia (71)
	Sudan (245)	Madagascar (195)
	Togo (55)	Mexico (48,725)
	Yugoslavia (500)	Morocco (530)
	Zambia (150)	Niger (28)
		Peru (1415)
		Philippines (4904)
		Poland (1900)
		Senegal (97)
		Sierra Leone (25)
		Venezuela (20,750)
		Yugoslavia (1246)
		Zambia (75)

official and private creditors continued at a high but somewhat diminished rate in 1985.

Perusal of the list of countries in Table 34 challenges the widely shared misconception that the debt crisis is essentially a matter of a few "newly industrializing" or "middle-income" countries. In an article published as late as July 1985, Rudiger Dornbusch asserts: "The debt problem is primarily a Latin American problem and not a problem of African or Asian less developed countries. . . . It is not a problem of most LDCs, and especially not of the 'poor' LDCs."[4] However true this statement if the "problem" is defined solely in terms of the threat posed to commercial banks, it nevertheless fails to convey the extent of debt crisis within the Third World and the profound changes it has wrought. Over two-thirds of the fifty-one Paris Club reschedulings between 1979 and 1984 involved low-income countries (as defined by the OECD). Low-income countries even accounted for one-third of private creditor debt renegotiations, if the European cases in Table 34 are excluded from consideration. Indeed, with debt service obligations of low-income African countries expected to be double in 1985–87 over what they were in 1981–82, the World Bank has warned:

> When Africa's arrears are taken into account, its debt service outlook is even more dismal. Servicing obligations in 1984 would jump about 30 percent if all arrears were paid in that year. Unless corrective measures are taken, the external resource position of sub-Saharan Africa is likely to become disastrous in the next few years.[5]

The seriousness of the crisis was reflected in the accumulation of arrears by low-income African countries to the IMF in 1984 and 1985, a virtually unprecedented situation. Six African countries owed over $400 million to the IMF in late 1985. Barring new regime initiatives, African arrearages were expected to double in 1986.[6]

Debt renegotiations increased not only in number in the early 1980s but also in size. Although generally true of Paris Club reschedulings, this increase was particularly true of renegotiations of debt to private creditors. Between August 1982 and the spring of 1983, negotiations were initiated to restructure between $90 billion and $100 billion of debt to commercial banks.[7] This amount dwarfed all previous reschedulings, both public and private. Multi-year reschedulings have subsequently involved sums as high as $48.7 billion in a single agreement.

Before 1982, private creditors generally preferred to refinance debt rather than reschedule payments. In essence, refinancing had been taking place—on an ad hoc and informal basis—for many countries from the end of the 1970s. The unwillingness of a growing number of banks, particularly the smaller, regional ones, to continue to increase exposure in this way led to the shift to short-term lending, which played an important part in triggering the debt crisis in 1982. Most subsequent debt renegotiations have involved the formal rescheduling of principal; however, the traditional norm that interest must be kept up to date and may not be rescheduled has been adhered to in almost all cases. Some countries have been able to negotiate new loans that in effect refinance old loans without a formal rescheduling under club auspices. Hence, the list of private creditor debt renegotiations in Table 34 understates the number of cases in which debt has effectively been restructured.

The debt renegotiation process has involved a struggle between debtors and creditors over who will bear the burden of record high interest rates and the far-reaching deterioration of trade relations. The banks insist that they have borne much of the cost. For example, William S. Ogden, vice-chairman of Chase Manhattan Bank, asserted in early 1983: "Already the penalty—in the form of reschedulings, nonperforming assets and loss of flexibility—is a large one. To add to it through new and unnecessary punitive measures will diminish the ability of the banks to furnish needed new credits."[8] Although the banks have had tense moments in the debt renegotiations and have not always gotten precisely what they wanted, analysis of the new norms that came out of the debt-restructuring agreements in 1982–84 indicates a high level of bank success in defending their interests. Debt has become a means by which aid regime discipline has been reconsolidated.

The first such norm involves central government responsibility for the debts of all state enterprises, regardless of the circumstances under which such ·debt was contracted. In a number of countries, state enterprises were able to borrow abroad with minimal central government supervision, and the loan agreements with them were not officially guaranteed by the central government. This situation was known to the lenders and was presumably taken into account in setting the terms of the loans. In fact, in some cases, the banks actively cooperated with individual state enterprises to escape central government supervision. In Venezuela, international banks knowingly aided state enterprises in circumventing Venezuelan law prohibiting state enterprises from incurring long-term debt without congressional approval by extending short-term credits just short of the prescribed limits.[9] As a consequence, Venezuela ended up with a uniquely high proportion of short-term debt.

According to U.S. government regulations, banks are not supposed to lend more than 10 percent of their capital to any single borrower. When the U.S. comptroller of the currency sought to enforce this rule in 1978, both the banks and the borrowing countries argued that a government and its state enterprises were separate borrowers and ·that the rule should apply only to individual borrowers.[10] The banks' view prevailed, despite the fact that two years earlier the banks and the U.S. government combined had successfully forced Indonesia to assume the debts of its relatively autonomous state oil company, Pertamina.

In the debt negotiations of 1982–84, debtor countries maintained the position, until recently shared with the banks, that central government debt and the debts of state enterprises were different things. The banks now insisted that, regardless of the circumstances, central governments had to assume the debts of state enterprises. The bank position prevailed in all cases. The most striking case involved Yugoslavia. Yugoslav law explicitly releases the central government from responsibility for foreign debts incurred by enterprises or by the central banks of the country's constituent republics. *The Banker* reported in July 1983:

> Prime Minister Milka Planic had at first balked at western demands that the federal government and national bank should guarantee the loans—

which were negotiated with regional banks who, according to Yugoslav law, are therefore solely responsible for this repayment. Ultimately, however, the government had little choice but to accept the terms.[11]

The norm was consolidated in such cases as Mexico, Brazil, Argentina, and Venezuela. Consolidation of the norm means that bank loans to such state enterprises are not dependent on the solvency of the enterprises or the projects, but carry the unconditional backing of the entire government.

The Inter-American Development Bank and other commentators have expressed concern that the assumption of state responsibility for debt biased international capital markets in the 1970s toward the public sector. The consolidation of the norm that central governments are responsible for the debt of all state enterprises might seem to increase this bias. However, a second new regime norm extends the responsibility of Third World governments to the debts of private enterprises in their countries as well.

Official lending to private enterprises, with the exception of the International Finance Corporation (IFC), has almost always carried a government guarantee. Commercial bank loans to the private sector have almost never carried such guarantees, however. Nonetheless, as the debt crisis became increasingly serious, the banks began to insist that debtor governments assume responsibility for private sector debt in addition to public sector debt. Private sector debt constituted between one-third and one-half of total debt. Rescheduling countries universally resisted the inclusion of private sector debt within debt-restructuring agreements but found progress on renegotiating public sector debt contingent on accommodation on this issue.

The two most important early cases were Mexico and Chile. A *Euromoney* account entitled "The Mexican Crisis Blurred the Lines Between Public and Private Sector Debt" stated:

> After Mexico, banks will not only be more cautious; they will be less willing to distinguish between public and private sector loans. In the past six months of negotiations, the $14 billion debt of the Mexican private sector became the issue upon which all else depended.
> Since companies—even healthy ones—relied on the central bank for

dollars to service their loans and were unable to obtain any, their debt became the equivalent of poor quality public sector debt. The public sector debtors, meanwhile, were allotted dollars to keep interest payments current. And in the financial rescue package which has now taken shape, private sector debt is effectively lumped into the overall rescheduling of the country's debt.[12]

In the case of Mexico, the agreement reached stopped short of a formal government guarantee of private sector debt, but it did include detailed provisions guaranteeing foreign exchange at preferential rates to private enterprises to service their foreign debts. The agreement involved an unprecedented degree of external influence in defining the relationship between the Mexican public and private sectors.

In Chile, particularly after many of the leading debtor banks in the private sector collapsed in the deep recession of 1982–83, the international creditor banks successfully held out for a formal guarantee. After initial declarations that the government would not take over the debts of the private banks, the Chilean government backed down in May 1983 and assumed the debts of its private banking sector. Although Argentina's military government did not reach final agreement with its creditors before the 1983 elections brought a civilian government back to power, the military government likewise offered to assume responsibility for the country's private debt.

Private sector debt was included in seven restructuring agreements in 1983, with governments assuming varying degrees of responsibility for it.[13] The Mexican case appears to have become the norm, with new bargaining centering on how preferential an exchange rate indebted companies should be allowed and which private debt should be included. The banks have continued to make the restructuring of public sector debt contingent on agreement about private sector debt; for example, conflict over the issue delayed Venezuela's multiyear rescheduling of its public sector debt until May 1985.

Because a substantial proportion of private sector borrowing from abroad "was funneled straight out again" as capital flight, particularly in Argentina, Chile, Mexico, and Uruguay, the establishment of regime norms forcing governments to assume responsibility for this debt has been particularly onerous. The World Bank commented in its 1985 *World Development Report:*

> All these difficulties have been compounded by the recent tendency in debt reschedulings to include even nonguaranteed debt as part of government obligations. The public sector shoulders the transfer risk associated with servicing foreign debt contracted by the private sector, even though the assets acquired with this debt are usually held outside the country, where they provide scant benefit to the local economy.[14]

A third new norm involves the economic penalty imposed on the debtor for rescheduling debt. Official debt renegotiations in the past have often softened the terms of aid, primarily by stretching out the repayment period while retaining low fixed interest rates. Earlier private creditor debt renegotiations generally refinanced debt at comparable or, in a few instances, at slightly softer terms than those at which the debt had been contracted. In the 1982–83 renegotiations, however, the banks successfully insisted on a substantial hardening of the terms of their loans, even though, unlike official loans, these loans were already at variable interest rates. Table 35 provides information on how the terms of renegotiated debt hardened substantially for ten Latin American countries in 1983.

Table 35 indicates the continuation of a number of traditional regime norms, such as the "short-leash" norm allowing the rescheduling of only that portion of debt immediately due. As of mid 1983, only about 15 percent of the debt of the ten countries in Table 35 had been rescheduled; larger, multiyear rescheduling was initiated in 1984 and was limited to a few select countries. The banks remained unwilling to reschedule interest payments. The major new feature was the degree to which the terms of rescheduled debt and of new loans worsened, both because of increased spreads over LIBOR and because of new front-end fees. Refinancing fees and front-end fees on new loans alone for Mexico, Brazil, Chile, Ecuador, and Cuba came to $588.9 million in 1983.[15] A study by M. S. Mendelsohn for the Group of 30 in 1983 concluded that, on average, "restructured debt is yielding banks about 2 percent a year more than the terms on

TABLE 35 Terms of Renegotiated Debt and New Loans in 1983 and Average Terms on Bank Loans in 1979 for Ten Latin American Borrowers

		Renegotiated Debt		New Loan		
Country	External Debt	Amount	Terms	Amount	Terms	Normal Terms in 1979
Argentina	\$39.0 b.	\$5.5 b.	8½ years 3 years grace 2⅛% over LIBOR	\$1.5 b.	5 years 1⅝% over LIBOR 1⅛% front-end fee ½% commitment fee	⅝% over LIBOR 10 years 5 years grace ⅝% fee
Brazil	\$89.0 b.	\$4.7 b.	8 years 2½ years grace 2½% over LIBOR 1½% refinancing fee	\$4.4 b.	8 years 2½ years grace 2⅛% over LIBOR 1½% front-end fee ½% commitment fee	¾% over LIBOR 12 years 7 years grace ½% fee
Chile	\$17.2 b.	\$3.4 b.	8 years 4 years grace 2⅛% over LIBOR 1¼% refinancing fee	\$1.3 b.	7 years 4 years grace 2¼% over LIBOR 1¼% front-end fee ½% commitment fee	⅞% over LIBOR 20 years 2 years grace ⅝% fee
Costa Rica	\$4.0 b.	\$0.655 b.	8½ years 3 years grace 2¼% over LIBOR			⅞% over LIBOR 10 years 4 years grace ⅝% fee

Cuba	$3.2 b.	$0.140 b.	8½ years 3½ years grace 2¼% over LIBOR 1¼% refinancing fee			1% over DM LIBOR 3 years grace ½% fee
Ecuador	$6.5 b.	$2.9 b.	8 years 2 years grace 2¼% over LIBOR 1¼% refinancing fee	$0.45 b.	2¼% over LIBOR	¾% over LIBOR 10 years 5 years grace ½% fee
Mexico	$83.0 b.	$19.7 b.	8 years 4 years grace 1⅞% over LIBOR 1¼% refinancing fee	$5.0 b.	6 years 3 years grace 2¼% over LIBOR 1¼% front-end fee ½% commitment fee	⅝% over LIBOR 10 years 4 years grace ½% fee
Nicaragua	$2.8 b.	$0.562 b.	12 years 5½ years grace ½% over LIBOR			
Peru	$11.5 b.	$0.320 b.	8 years 3 years grace 2¼% over LIBOR	$0.43 b.	2¼% over LIBOR	1⅜% over LIBOR 3½ years grace ⅝% fee
Uruguay	$4.0 b.	$0.786 b.	6 years 2 years grace 2¼% over LIBOR	$0.24 b.	6 years 2 years grace 2¼% over LIBOR	⅞% over LIBOR 10 years 2 years grace ½% fee

SOURCE: *South* 33 (July 1983): 63.

which most of that debt was originally contracted." Mendelsohn estimated that debt restructuring under way at the time would yield an
extra $1.75 billion over what bank earnings would have been with-
out restructuring.[16]

This figure actually understated the profitability of debt restructuring because the international banks used the debt crisis as an ex-
cuse for raising the spreads and fees on *all* new loans to Third World
countries, whether they were having debt-servicing difficulties or
not. Indeed, there is evidence that restructuring proved so profitable
that it set the norm for new borrowing. According to one account in
1983: "Bankers are extracting front-end fees of around 1.5 percent
for Latin American reschedulings, and have come to expect this level
of profitability for the whole of the region." The same author noted
in the case of Asian borrowers:

> Recent Asian syndicated loans have met with cool receptions in the euro-
> market and have not been easy to arrange, in spite of carrying higher
> spreads and shorter maturities. Knowing that these countries will have to
> come to the market for more funds soon, many bankers are waiting for
> loans offering them higher profits.[17]

In fact, there is evidence that on occasion banks withheld new lending in order to force debtor countries (for example, Peru in 1983) to
restructure existing debt on terms more attractive to the banks.

In 1984, the terms of rescheduled debt eased somewhat, dropping
from the 1.88 to 2.5 percent range over LIBOR characteristic of
agreements in 1982–83 to 1.5 to 2 percent over LIBOR. In the context of multiyear agreements, a few major borrowers did even better;
the 1984 Mexican agreement carried graduated spreads starting at
0.87 percent and rising to 1.25 percent.[18] These modest improvements must be qualified in several ways, however. First, the better
terms have been reserved for only a few, better-off countries. Second,
while spreads have declined slightly, real interest rates have risen
steadily. Third, interest rates have risen particularly rapidly on long-
term lending. Fourth, the proportion of LDC debt denominated in
dollars has risen steadily, from 66.8 percent in 1979 to 76.3 percent
in 1983.[19] The appreciation of the dollar on this increased portion of

dollar-denominated debt alone has probably more than offset the slight reduction in spreads over LIBOR.

A fourth set of new regime norms involves the altered relations among the banks themselves and between the banks and the International Monetary Fund. As the larger banks took over some of the debt of the smaller banks and did most of the new lending, the proportion of debt owed to the largest banks increased significantly. Combined with increased coordination with the IMF and with the Bank for International Settlements (BIS), the international banking system became, in the words of one observer, increasingly "cartelised."[20]

Debtor country agreement with the IMF, generally in the form of a standby arrangement, had long been a condition for most debt renegotiations, both official and private. In 1982 and 1983, this linkage was extended to provide for accelerated repayment should the debtor become ineligible to draw under an arrangement with the Fund during the life of the agreement. Through 1985, only Mozambique, Nicaragua, Cuba, Nigeria (uninsured short-term debt only), and Venezuela had succeeded in renegotiating debt without an IMF agreement.

The urgency and complexity of the debt renegotiation process necessitated several important changes in 1982. First, the BIS and the treasuries and central banks of creditor countries found it necessary to play a "bridging" role, providing temporary financing immediately while agreement with the IMF was worked out. In the Mexican case, the U.S. government and the BIS came up with $2.5 billion within two days of Mexico's initial request for rescheduling. The World Bank's *World Development Report 1983* commended the BIS for helping countries avoid "unilateral reschedulings or moratoria" and for providing "an opportunity for the more orderly renegotiation of debt."[21] In December 1983, the BIS announced it was formally establishing a $3.1 billion fund for the IMF to draw on, thus increasing its role.[22]

Second, the IMF realized during the Mexican crisis that its access policies would not allow it to offer Mexico sufficient resources to convince Mexico to accept its brand of conditionality. Accordingly, on November 16, 1982, IMF Managing Director Jacques de Larosière

called together officials from the leading creditor banks and told
them he would refuse to recommend the Mexican accord to the IMF
board unless the banks agreed to come up with an additional $5 bil-
lion in new loans (the IMF loan was for $3.9 billion). "He read the
riot act," one banker at the meeting is reported to have said.[23] Although some bankers resented de Larosière's heavy-handed pressure,
the incident illustrated both how dependent the IMF was on linking
other resources to its own and how dependent the banks were on the
IMF to enforce discipline upon debtors. Previously, IMF agreements
had functioned to "unlock" access to other forms of financing subsequently; what was new was the active role of the IMF in lining up
"debt-restructuring packages" that themselves included the provision
of new financing. As a *Euromoney* article put it, the IMF was no
longer simply drawing up adjustment programs but was

> now orchestrating the activities of commercial banks and other providers
> of cash, while itself getting involved in countries on a longer-term basis.
> . . . There has never been a tighter collaboration between the Fund, the
> governments and central banks of the industrial countries and the com-
> mercial banks.[24]

Bailing the Banks In

The new relationship between the IMF and the commercial banks
forged in the Mexican crisis and carried over into subsequent debt
restructurings has elicited considerable debate. On the one hand, the
IMF has been accused of "bailing out" the banks. Indeed, liberals
and conservatives taking this position came close to defeating legislation in the U.S. Congress increasing the U.S. quota in the IMF in
1983. On the other hand, IMF officials have insisted that, to the contrary, they were using their resources to "bail the banks in," to prevent them from withholding new lending.

In a sense, both interpretations are correct. On the one hand,
without the IMF's success in mobilizing new financing and in making
that financing contingent both on "adjustment" and on observance

of debt-servicing obligations, the banks would probably not have been able to avoid debt repudiation entirely and formal default almost completely. Furthermore, the banks' success in 1983–84 in imposing severe penalties on debtors in the renegotiation process, in the form of increased spreads over LIBOR, front-end fees, and shorter maturities, clearly depended on the negotiating framework and extra financing provided by the IMF.

On the other hand, IMF loans have been far too small to finance directly much debt service. Mexico got the maximum allowable commitment from the Fund—slightly less than $4 billion over three years—but Mexico's interest payments to the banks in 1983 alone came to about $11 billion. The IMF has definitely strong-armed the banks into maintaining a higher level of new lending than they ideally would have preferred. Commercial bank exposure in the non-oil LDCs increased by $25 billion in 1983.[25]

Because much of this new lending has been linked to IMF agreements and/or debt restructurings, it has been variously referred to as "nonspontaneous," "forced," and "involuntary." These terms are misleading, however. Increased bank exposure necessarily followed from the banks' decision to harden the terms of restructured debt. As an IMF study comments pointedly:

> Regarding the terms of restructuring of bank debt, banks remained unwilling to reschedule payments at less than market-related interest rates. However, owing to the magnitude of the external payments disequilibrium in a number of recent cases, debt restructuring on market terms appeared feasible only if the banks were willing to provide additional financing or at least assure maintenance of their existing "exposure." The banks firmly decided to restructure debt on commercial terms, while recognizing that this might require continued growth in their exposure to some countries. . . . For some countries, the weight of scheduled interest payments has proved to be so burdensome that any rescheduling of principal payments on commercial terms has required a commitment of new funds if interest were to be paid as scheduled.[26]

The explicit linkage between new commercial lending and IMF conditionality represents a profound transformation of the situation in the mid to late 1970s, when commercial lending enabled borrowers to avoid the IMF altogether. Even where new lending has not been linked to adjustment programs, there is evidence that the commercial banks have increasingly concentrated their lending on trade and project-related finance, particularly of an export-oriented nature. Indeed, an IMF study reports: "In some cases, financing projects creates the possibility of directly pledging the project's revenue to meet related debt service."[27]

Bridge Financing

The debt crisis elicited a new type of official aid, known as bridge financing: short-term loans, "arranged in haste, and made available without policy conditions."[28] The purpose of bridge financing has been to assist debtor countries to continue debt-servicing payments while negotiating agreement with the IMF for additional, longer term financing. A more general function has been to reassure capital markets that necessary official support will be forthcoming. Bridge financing in most cases has been provided by an array of official institutions, often in concert: government central banks, export agencies, and the Bank for International Settlements. There have also been some instances of commercial bank bridge financing, most notably a $1.1 billion syndicated bridge loan to Argentina in the fall of 1982. The banks' experience with Argentina, which took two years to reach agreement with the IMF and then sought to reschedule the bridge loan, led them to look to official sources for bridge financing in most subsequent cases.

From the perspective of the dominant aid regime institutions, the trick has been to structure bridge financing so that it provides an incentive, not a disincentive, for coming to terms with the IMF and with creditor countries and banks. The issue has been complicated by the U.S. banks' concern with their quarterly profits. Such concern lay behind the unique bridge financing provided Argentina in late March 1984, consisting of $300 million from Mexico, Brazil, Colombia, and Venezuela and of $100 million from commercial banks, guaranteed by the U.S. Treasury. As part of the package, the United States offered Argentina a $300 million loan once agreement with the IMF was reached. The offer was extended for a month at the end of April and then again for fifteen days at the beginning of June. But when Argentina temporarily broke off negotiations with IMF staff and sought to present the Fund with a take-it-or-leave-it proposal, the United States withdrew its offer. Brazil, Colombia, Mexico, and Venezuela extended the repayment deadline one month at the end of June but refused to do so beyond then. Although the U.S. government, the banks, the four Latin American debtor/lenders, and Argentina all sought to pursue their own ends through the bridge loan, Argentina appears to have successfully used everyone else's fear of default to extend the time available for its negotiations with the IMF, with whom it reached agreement in late September.

U.S. unwillingness to provide direct bridge financing in the Argentinian case appears to reflect a decreased readiness on the part of official creditors to provide bridge financing. Instead, as Cline has suggested:

> Temporary interest arrears provide an alternative vehicle for financing prior to completion of the arrangements, because they equal or exceed the formal financing that is to be mobilized. Arrears also place pressure on the country to come to terms with the IMF and the banks.[29]

One form of that pressure is the likelihood that such arrears will activate the withholding of official aid. Although bridge financing remains a regime option, it has receded in importance as temporary arrears have come to be accepted as not intrinsically threatening and as carrying a more effective form of incentive for agreement.

Cofinancing and Loan Guarantees

The practice of linking aid regime resources with each other and with nonaid resources predates the debt crisis but has been given new impetus by it. The most significant mechanism has been co-financing, the association of financing from one official agency with funds either from other official agencies (generally either aid institutions or export-promotion agencies) or from private sources, mainly commercial banks. The World Bank and the regional MDBs, particularly the Inter-American Development Bank (IDB) and the Asian Development Bank (ADB), have been the most active organizers of cofinancing because of their structural position in the aid regime, which allows them to extend their preferred creditor status. Between 1973 and 1984, the World Bank mobilized $17.2 billion from other official sources (primarily bilateral aid programs and the regional MDBs), $11.9 billion in export credits (generally guaranteed by official export-promotion agencies), and $10.2 billion from private sources (mainly commercial banks). In fiscal year 1984, 42 percent of World Bank projects (IBRD and IDA) were cofinanced, linking $6 billion of Bank funds with an additional $4.1 billion. Although the absolute amount of cofinancing was down in 1984 from the peak in 1982, a record proportion of Bank projects was cofinanced in 1984. A slightly higher proportion (44 percent) was cofinanced in 1985.[30]

Cofinancing with other aid institutions dates to the early days of the aid regime, but cofinancing with private financial institutions dates only to 1974 and attained significant scale, in terms of overall World Bank lending, only in 1980. In that year, private sources accounted for $1.8 billion of $6.5 billion in cofinancing, or about 32 percent. In 1982, private cofinancing rose to $2.2 billion but fell, amid the general cutback of bank lending in 1983, to just over $1 billion.[31]

Under its traditional practices, the World Bank and cofinancing institutions sign separate agreements with the borrower. Both agreements contain cross-default clauses. In addition, in the case of cofinancing with private banks, a separate "memorandum of agreement" is signed between the World Bank and the commercial banks, which "assures greater-than-usual access by private lenders to the wealth of country and project information that the World Bank collects and analyzes in the normal course of its activities." The memorandum also commonly appoints the World Bank to be the billing agent for the private lender.[32]

Partly in response to the drastic decline in private cofinancing in fiscal year 1983, the World Bank adopted a new set of cofinancing techniques aimed at luring more commercial funds into World Bank projects and programs. In these, the World Bank becomes a direct participant in loan syndication and attempts to trade its protection against default and rescheduling for terms better than the market's. Specifically, these new techniques include (1) World Bank participation in the later maturities of a commercial loan, so that the Bank is repaid only after the commercial banks are repaid; (2) World Bank financing of any difference that arises between a fixed debt service schedule for the borrower and variable interest rates; and (3) World Bank guarantee of later maturities of commercial loans made in conjunction with Bank loans.[33] In addition, the Bank now also sells to commercial banks participation in some of its loans.

In fiscal year 1984, the World Bank made nine of these new types of cofinanced loans (which it refers to as "B-loans").[34] Four of these were to the National Bank of Hungary. Of the other five, only three actually involved direct World Bank funding: a $34 million loan to Thailand with a World Bank participation of $8.5 million and two loans totaling $200 million to Colombia with Bank participation of $30 million. The Colombian loans, according to the Bank, represented "something of a breakthrough, as the loans are among the first new market operations (outside of reschedulings) in Latin America since the emergence of the debt crisis, and the first syndicated loans to Colombia since 1983."[35] In the other two loans during 1984, the World Bank did not actually provide any financing at all, and its direct role was quite limited. In the case of a cofinanced loan to Paraguay, the Bank agreed to finance any unpaid maturity at the end of the loan resulting from the difference between a fixed repayment schedule of eleven equal semiannual payments and a specified return to the commercial banks based on variable interest rates. Even with the Bank's participation, the spread over LIBOR was set at 2.25 percent for the first five years and 2.37 percent for the second five years—a rate over twice as high as the prevailing rate a few years earlier.[36] In the case of a $60 million loan to Brazil, the World Bank simply guaranteed 40 percent of the repayments in the last year and half of a ten-year loan by the European Coal and Steel Community to a Brazilian mining company.[37] Such minimal World Bank involvement demonstrates that the Bank is offering under its new cofinancing program not financing but protection under its preferred creditor status. The appeal of the new cofinancing techniques is reflected in the fact that all new cofinancing in fiscal year 1984 with private creditors involved the new B-loans; no traditional cofinancing arrangements were concluded with private creditors. This pattern continued in 1985, when five B-loans totaling $922 million were made.[38]

Like the World Bank, the IDB and the ADB have been expanding cofinancing with private banks in recent years, although progress has been uneven and the proportion of total lending much less. IDB cofinancing from private sources, known as "complementary financing," was $85 million in 1981 and $99 million in 1982, but it fell to $30 million in 1983. Cumulative complementary financing came to $642 million at the end of calendar year 1983.[39] ADB cofinancing from private banks was $260.6 million in 1982 and $180.4 million in 1983.[40] It increased 145 percent to $442 million in 1984, out of a total of $1,164 million for all ADB cofinancing.[41] Both institutions are exploring new mechanisms to increase cofinancing, and like the World Bank, the ADB began to participate in commercial loan syndications during fiscal year 1983.

Although cofinancing has prevented new bank lending from dropping more than it has, and in some cases has at least probably softened the terms of commercial loans, the growing importance of cofinancing could represent a future dilemma for the aid regime. Cofinancing mechanisms that link the MDBs with commercial loans remove the latter from potential default and rescheduling, thus reducing the capacity for debt restructuring precisely when the debt structure is worsening. As a staff attorney for the IDB has noted, in comments that apply to the other MDBs as well, any default on the complementary loan is unquestionably a default against the IDB, which is the lender of record. Borrowing countries are very reluctant to jeopardise their relations with the MDBs because of the importance they attach to projects financed by these institutions and the favourable terms under which these loans are extended. This explains why member countries of the IDB have accorded to complementary loans the same special status as other IDB loans and have not sought to include them in debt rescheduling. From the standpoint of the private banks, this "umbrella" protection is the most attractive feature of this programme.[42]

In the short run, this practice provides ironclad guarantees to the private lenders, but in the long run it could have destabilizing effects on the aid regime. Currently their ability to renegotiate non-MDB debt helps debtor countries avoid formal default and maintain their debt service to the MDBs, thereby preserving the latter's preferred creditor status. If a substantial proportion of debt to private creditors acquires the same status as MDB debt, both the privileged status of MDB debt and the aid regime's capacity to respond to future debt crises could be seriously compromised. This problem would be even further compounded if, as was widely discussed at the time of the 1985 Seoul meetings of the IMF and World Bank, the World Bank were also to guarantee loans not falling under cofinancing arrangements.[43]

Foreign Direct Investment

The implications of the debt crisis for the private sector in general and foreign investment in particular have been complex. On the one hand, both Latin and North American observers have described the private sector and the multinationals as the "forgotten victims" of the debt crisis.[44] Unequal competition with the state sector for scarce foreign exchange and contractional stabilization policies have brought a substantial portion of the private sector to the verge of bankruptcy, and several multinationals have made widely publicized pullouts. One line of analysis predicts increased statism in response to the current period of crisis and uncertainty.[45]

On the other hand, the debt crisis has provided new leverage for the major aid institutions to promote foreign direct investment. IMF Managing Director de Larosière stated in June 1984:

> Expanded flows of direct investment to the developing countries are in everybody's interest. . . . The developing countries should be encouraged to remove obstacles to such flows and to place greater emphasis on policies designed to attract foreign direct investment as part of their development strategy.[46]

This idea is not new, but a number of the mechanisms used by the aid regime in the era of debt crisis to promote foreign investment are.

First, as we have already seen, the debt-restructuring agreements have themselves in a number of countries been used to safeguard the status of private sector debt and to provide privileged access by private enterprises to foreign exchange. In addition, the IMF agreements upon which most debt restructurings have been contingent have commonly involved cutbacks in restrictions on foreign investment. IMF stabilization programs have frequently involved privatization of state enterprises, simplification of approval procedures for foreign investment, and elimination of restrictions on profit repatriation. The renewed emphasis on promoting foreign investment has been reflected in the various annual reports of the major aid institutions. Even the IDB, traditionally the least ideologically conservative of the multilateral development banks, advised in its 1985 report *Social and Economic Progress in Latin America*:

> In general, the role of the public sector in the economy should be re-examined, with a view to limiting its scope to the more traditional areas of providing basic social and economic infrastructure, creating a propitious environment for private investment, and satisfying basic social needs. . . . Direct investment, both foreign and domestic (with adequate public regulation), should become an increasingly important source of investment capital because of its advantages over debt financing, particularly with respect to transfer of technology and responsiveness to local economic conditions.[47]

Second, the aid regime has been expanding what had previously been a relatively minor component of official financing: equity investments in, and loans to, private enterprises in Third World countries. As we saw in Chapter 4, this type of financing dates from the 1950s. While other types of aid have been stagnating or declining, however, this type has been expanding rapidly in the 1980s. Loans and investments by the International Finance Corporation (IFC), the World Bank affiliate that deals directly with private sector enterprises, increased by a record 38 percent in 1983, to $845 million. In addition, the IFC attracted another $418 million from commercial banks by syndicating eighteen of its loans.[48] In fiscal year 1984, the IFC increased the number of approved projects to sixty-two in thirty-seven countries, although the aggregate of its loans and investments fell to $696 million. Syndicated cofinancing remained roughly the same, at $415 million. Since 1985, the IFC has been in the midst of a major expansion. Its board of governors approved a doubling of its capital base in June 1984, which is expected to result in IFC loans and equity investments of $7.4 billion between July 1985 and July 1990—an average of almost $1.5 billion per year. This is expected to be supplemented by $3 billion in syndications over the same five-year period; overall, the IFC hopes to provide the catalyst for about $30 billion in private sector investment in the Third World.[49] This amount exceeds the estimated total project costs of $27 billion of the first twenty-nine years of the IFC's existence. Because most IFC recipient enterprises involve at least partial foreign ownership, the IFC program could have a substantial impact on overall levels of foreign investment and ownership. IFC investments approved in 1985 rose sharply to $937.2 million.[50]

Several other aid institutions have been initiating or expanding IFC-type operations. The Asian Development Bank initiated equity investments in December 1983.[51] The Inter-American Development Bank completed negotiations in late 1984 for the establishment of a new affiliate, the Inter-American Investment Corporation, which will function like the IFC and will supplement current IDB equity investments under the Venezuelan Trust Fund. Its initial capitalization will be $200 million, and it is expected to get under way in 1986.[52]

Third, investment insurance programs covering political risks, administered by or in conjunction with aid institutions, have also been expanded in the wake of the debt crisis. The United States Overseas Private Investment Corporation (OPIC) doubled its insurance volume in 1982, to over $3 billion, increased it to almost $4 billion in 1983, and enlarged it to $4.3 billion in 1984. Between 1981 and 1984, OPIC insured or helped finance 508 investment projects in over sixty countries.[53] Twenty-two capital-exporting countries have official investment insurance programs.[54] In 1982, World Bank President A. W. Clausen announced that with political risks "so large that they cannot be handled by government entities or national institutions," the World Bank was "exploring a multilateral investment insurance scheme that could build on the existing national and private schemes to set up a global scheme. The objective is to increase the flow of funds from the private sector."[55] Details of the Bank's proposal for a Multilateral Investment Guarantee Agency (MIGA) were published in December 1984. In addition to direct investment, the proposal envisions the possibility of insuring such things as management and turnkey contracts, portfolio investments, and even straight project loans. The agency would coguarantee investments with national agencies where the agencies were already heavily exposed or the investments were unusually large or multinationally financed.[56] Although a World Bank vice-president has asserted that multilateral guarantees would not discriminate against domestic investment because they would protect only existing rights rather than create new rights for the investor vis-à-vis the host country,[57] linking foreign investments directly to the World Bank in this way would clearly increase the protection of the former in much the same way that cofinancing removes commercial loans from potential default or rescheduling. The likelihood of expropriation, unilateral contract changes, or even the initiation of government policies affecting transfer or other risks covered by the insurance program would seem greatly diminished by the simple fact of formal World Bank involvement. The provision for subrogation by MIGA—raising the specter of direct conflict with the World Bank—would seem to give foreign investment an almost untouchable status. The expansion of MDB loans to and equity investments in private enterprises would appear to have the same result. MIGA was approved by the World Bank's board of governors in October 1985 and is expected to come into existence in 1986.

Potentially the most radical development has been the emergence of proposals for the exchange of debt for equity holdings in debtor country enterprises. Given the scale of external debt, which for the non-oil LDCs was almost five times the stock of foreign direct investment in 1983, implementation of these proposals could result in large-scale denationalization of industry. Governments of debtor countries have to date shown little enthusiasm for the idea, but there have been several cases of exchange of private company debt for equity in Mexico. For example, in December 1984, Mexico's largest private company, Grupo Industrial Alfa, reached agreement with its foreign creditors to exchange 30 percent of its foreign debt of $2.5 billion for equity in the form of stock.[58] Proposals for such exchanges have been propounded by such leading banking officials as the presidents of the Bank for International Settlements and the New York Federal Reserve. At the end of 1984, the International Finance Corporation was negotiating with four Latin American countries to implement a debt to equity conversion scheme for private sector external debt.[59]

As of 1984, these regime innovations had probably succeeded in linking a greater proportion of private investment flows to the aid regime, but not in increasing the level of these flows. According to World Bank figures, net foreign direct investment to LDCs rose from $10.6 billion in 1980 to $15 billion in 1981, then declined steadily to $9.4 billion in 1984.[60] These figures include reinvested earnings but not expansion financed by local borrowing in the host country, which in fact has long been the primary mechanism of multinational expansion. In the deflationary conditions of debtor countries, figures on international private investment flows may vastly understate the real expansion of multinational holdings. Quite apart from the fact that the dollar's appreciation means that it buys more than before, Citicorp's senior adviser for international operations has noted that in the major debtor countries that have experienced large-scale economic contraction, "you can buy for a song most of the valuable industrial capacity that exists in these countries."[61] Even if proposals for the conversion of debt into equity are not implemented, aggressive purchasing by the multinationals could result in large-scale denationalization of debtor country industry.

Restructuring of Regime Resources

In addition to being increasingly linked to nonaid flows, aid regime resources themselves have been restructured in the wake of the debt crisis. The IMF has come to play a much more central role, and its resources are among the few that have been substantially increased. Most bilateral aid flows have stagnated, and within the MDBs, there has been a shift in resources away from the soft-loan windows (which depend on bilateral contributions) to the hard-loan windows. MDBs have also acted to increase the speed of their disbursements by loosening some of their traditional norms, such as the reluctance to finance too large a share of local costs. This section details these restructurings of regime resources and explores some of their implications.

Centrality of the IMF

Despite some grumbling about "involuntary lending," bankers have welcomed what one refers to as the "IMF's triumphant return" in the 1980s.[62] Although it is a gross exaggeration to suggest that the IMF ever went away, we have seen that some countries were able to escape its discipline during the 1970s. During the 1950s, the IMF concluded fifty-seven standby agreements—its major mechanism of conditionality—with its members for a total of $4 billion. In the 1960s, the IMF's role in imposing formal conditions on its members expanded substantially; 231 standby agreements were signed for a total of $14 billion. During the 1970s, in contrast, the number of standby and related agreements fell to 177, covering about $17.6 billion, a sharp decrease in real terms, despite a substantially enlarged membership and the shocks first of the end of the Bretton Woods monetary system and then of the oil price rises and the deterioration of the terms of trade.[63] As we saw in the previous chapter, the Development Assistance Committee was moved to complain in 1979 that the IMF role had been "weakened" and that "a major part of its resources remains idle."[64]

The DAC complaint provides a stark contrast to the IMF's situation in late 1983, when the Fund estimated that by year's end its loan commitments would exceed by $6.3 billion its capital on hand unless a general quota increase was forthcoming.[65] Between 1980 and 1983, the worldwide recession and the debt crisis forced a record number of Third World countries to turn to the IMF. During fiscal years 1980, 1981, 1982, 1983, and 1984, there were 164 operative standby or extended fund agreements involving seventy-one countries, sixty-nine of them LDCs. These "adjusting" countries accounted for three-quarters of the combined GDPs of all LDCs.[66] Gross purchases by developing countries jumped from $2.8 billion in calendar year 1979 to $6 billion in 1980, and then to $8.4 and $8 billion in 1981 and 1982. During the first six months of 1983, gross purchases by LDCs amounted to a record $7 billion, almost equal the annual levels of the previous two years. Gross purchases were $13.2 billion for the entire year, 70 percent over 1982.[67] Although purchases declined to about $7.5 billion in 1984, they still constituted the fourth largest amount in the Fund's history.[68]

Forty-three countries had standby or extended fund agreements with the IMF at the end of 1983, and thirty-three agreements were in effect at the end of 1984.[69] The balance between different forms of IMF assistance has shifted decisively toward the high-conditionality side, with 88 percent of total purchases in 1984 consisting of credit tranche and extended fund drawings.[70] The IMF has been tough in holding its members to its agreements; in mid 1982, it had "interrupted" drawings on ten of the thirty-four standby arrangements then in effect because of failures to meet performance criteria. The fund's early hard-line position appears to have paid off; it reported only two inoperative arrangements in its *Annual Report 1983* and only one in 1984.[71]

In early 1984, the IMF's managing director proudly reported: "Adjustment is now virtually universal. . . . Never before has there been such an extensive yet convergent adjustment effort."[72] The statement accurately reflected the broad sweep of IMF conditionality; the Fund has probably never been in a stronger position for imposing its particular set of ideals. Nonetheless, its bargaining power has varied considerably in different cases. The IMF has negotiated the most demanding performance criteria with authoritarian military regimes; recognition of political limits in more democratic countries has forced the Fund to settle for somewhat less stringent criteria. De Larosière has warned: "Some countries are already approaching the limits of social and political tolerance of their adjustment process."[73]

In fact, the issue of differential performance criteria—for example, differences in the relative sizes of allowable budget deficits—has become a political issue in countries that have accepted more demanding criteria.[74] The Fund has been forced in several cases to grant waivers for certain performance criteria and to modify others. Although these waivers indicate a degree of bargaining power for the Third World countries involved, the waivers themselves have come only after new rounds of negotiation, and their importance underlines the enormously powerful position of the Fund. For example, when the IMF announced in November 1983 that it was waiving and revising certain performance criteria for Brazil, it indicated that the waiver "unlocks a financial package" involving (1) rescheduling debt service to commercial banks in 1984, (2) continued disbursement of new commercial loans previously agreed to, (3) new export credits,

(4) Paris Club rescheduling of debt to official creditors, and (5) further drawings from the Fund.[75]

The renewed centrality of the IMF has depended not only on the readiness of Third World countries to approach the IMF but also on the IMF having sufficient resources to finance adjustment programs. As we have seen, the IMF has for specific countries built up a "critical mass" of financing by linking its aid to other sources of financing. But in addition, in 1983 and early 1984, overall IMF resources were significantly expanded in two ways. First, quotas were expanded by 47.5 percent, increasing Fund resources by $30 billion. The quota increase was implemented, however, in a way that increased overall Fund resources without proportionately increasing individual country access. The call for an increase was approved by the IMF's board of governors in March 1983 and was virtually unanimously supported by Third World governments, although many had originally sought a larger increase. At the annual meetings of the IMF and the World Bank in September, probably the most bitter in the two institutions' histories, Third World countries discovered that their access to Fund resources would not necessarily increase at all. Led by the United States, the dominant advanced capitalist countries succeeded in substituting for the existing maximum access policy of 150 percent of quota a two-tiered system of 102 percent and 125 percent. The 102 percent access policy reduced borrowing limits for 108 of the IMF's 146 members while enabling the Fund to finance a greater number of adjustment programs. Access limits were further reduced in September 1984, to 95 percent and 115 percent, again over bitter Third World opposition, and then again in September 1985 to 90 percent and 110 percent of the quota. Access limits for the compensatory financing facility and the buffer stock facility were also reduced in 1983, and the reduced limits were reaffirmed in 1984 and 1985. The yearly review of access limits, and pointed reminders that they "are not to be regarded as targets,"[76] demonstrate to Third World countries that continued access to financing is not guaranteed.

Of almost equal importance in expanding the Fund's resources was a series of agreements negotiated in late 1983 and early 1984 enabling the Fund to borrow money to finance adjustment programs in the Third World. Historically, borrowing arrangements have allowed the IMF to increase its resources without increasing member quotas (and thereby individual country access). The general arrangements to borrow (GAB), involving ten advanced capitalist countries, were increased from $6.7 billion to almost $18 billion, supplemented by $1.6 billion from Saudi Arabia. In an important departure from past practice, the IMF was now empowered to use this money to finance adjustment programs for non-GAB participants. Similar borrowing arrangements were subsequently negotiated with Belgium, Japan, the Saudi Arabian Monetary Agency, and the Bank for International Settlements, for another $6.3 billion. These arrangements supplemented the $30 billion quota increase with a further $26 billion.[77]

Together, the quota increase and the new borrowing arrangements increased IMF resources by 89 percent, greatly increasing the proportion of official external financing channeled through the IMF. At the same time, the new access policy, limiting individual country access to levels below or at best only slightly higher than previously, made the IMF's capacity to mobilize other sources of financing more critical than ever.

Shifting Hard-Loan/Soft-Loan Balance

The increased significance of IMF lending has meant a hardening of the terms of official financing because IMF loans must be repaid within a few years and at relatively high interest rates. This process has been reinforced by the shifting balance between the resources available through the hard- and soft-loan windows of the multilateral development banks.

One would expect, on the basis of regime norms discussed in Chapter 3, that the balance of regime resources would shift over time in a market direction as an increasing number of countries graduated from the more concessional forms of external financing. This expectation does not explain the current trend, however. The shift toward hard-loan operations of the MDBs since around 1980 reflects, on the one hand, the political unpopularity of foreign aid in the donor countries and, on the other hand, disagreement among donor governments and institutions about how graduation norms should be implemented.

The World Bank and the majority of donor governments have insisted on the need for continued high levels of ODA through the soft-loan windows of the MDBs and have expressed concern about premature graduation of countries to financing that carries harder terms. However, the Reagan administration has successfully hastened the shift toward the hard-loan windows. Its basic rationale was outlined in a 1982 Treasury Department report that recommended reducing U.S. support for soft-loan operations of the MDBs as a way of forcing countries to turn to the private sector or to more conditional forms of concessional financing.[78] In the subsequent negotiations for the seventh replenishment of the International Development Association (IDA), the United States supported a decrease of IDA resources on the grounds that "excessive concessional assistance can drive down domestic mobilization of resources" and "cause countries to relax their own efforts to pull themselves up by the bootstraps."[79] IDA was refunded at a level 40 percent in real terms below the sixth replenishment, with the United States, Britain, West Germany, and Sweden all reducing their shares in the program. IDA's share of total new World Bank commitments had already fallen from 32 percent in fiscal years 1979 and 1980 to 23 percent in 1983 and 1984, and its share will decline even more sharply in the years ahead.

The same type of shift has occurred in the other MDBs as well. In 1980, the Inter-American Development Bank increased its hard-loan capacity by $8 billion and its soft-loan capacity by $1.75 billion—18 percent of the total increase. In 1983, it increased its resources respectively by $15 billion and $703 million—4 percent of the total increase.[80] The 1983 replenishment of the Asian Development Fund, the soft-loan window of the Asian Development Bank, involved no real increase and a decrease relative to total ADB lending. In fiscal year 1984, the ADB's loans from ordinary capital resources increased by 30.3 percent while its soft loans from the ADF declined by 2.7 percent.[81]

The burden of this shift toward the MDB hard-loan windows has been accentuated by the adoption of variable interest rates by the MDBs. The World Bank switched over from fixed to variable interest rates on its loans in July 1982 (it began to levy front-end fees in January of that year). As two Bank financial analysts note: "Both the front-end fee and the variable lending rate system permit the Bank to pass through to borrowers the consequences of adverse interest rate movements."[82] The rate is adjusted twice a year and is set at 0.5 percent above the cost of Bank borrowing. The Bank's executive board suspended front-end fees in 1985. The IDB instituted variable interest rates on its regular loans in 1983, and the IFC did so in 1984.

Accelerated Disbursement

The major MDBs all took steps to increase the pace of disbursement on existing aid commitments in 1983. In February, the World Bank announced a "special action program" (sometimes referred to as the "special assistance program"), under which an extra $2.25 billion in disbursements in fiscal years 1983 through 1985 was contemplated. The program involved several ways of speeding up disbursements, including financing more local costs and setting aside previous country limits on structural adjustment loans, the most rapidly disbursed form of World Bank aid.[83] Such benefits were to be conditional; World Bank President A. W. Clausen stated that the most important aspect of the program was "increased attention to policy reform" and that the Bank would "accelerate disbursements only to those countries that indeed take needed policy action to overcome their economic difficulties."[84] In the case of Brazil, both approval of new World Bank project loans and continuation of accelerated disbursements under the special action program were made contingent on agreement with the IMF.[85] The IBRD attributed most of its 26 percent increase in disbursements in fiscal year 1984 to the special action program, which involved 260 projects in forty-four countries through fiscal year 1985.[86] The special action program's success in accelerating disbursements in 1983 and 1984 probably contributed to the decline in World Bank disbursements in 1985; the program was discontinued at the end of the fiscal year.

In March 1983, the IDB instituted a similar program, known as the "special operating program," also designed to speed up disbursements and conclude high-priority projects. Thirty-nine loans were affected in 1983 and 138 in 1984.[87] A somewhat different approach was taken by the ADB, which instituted a new category of "special assistance loans," new loans of foreign exchange designed to generate local currency revenues needed for the completion of high-priority, Bank-sponsored projects and, presumably, to aid countries in debt servicing. Four loans of this type, totaling about $60 million, were made in 1983.[88]

Although these special MDB programs were instrumental in helping MDB lending rise in 1983 and 1984, in contrast to most other forms of aid, they pose an obvious problem. To the extent that they simply speed up disbursements without increasing commitments, a future dip in MDB aid is inevitable. This has been recognized by the World Bank, which notes in its *Annual Report 1984*: "This increment, however, resulting from both accelerated disbursements on ongoing projects and substitution of [special action program] operations for more traditional projects, represents advances of post-fiscal 1986 disbursements."[89] As we have seen, IBRD disbursements and net transfer declined in 1985 and will continue to do so unless a capital increase takes place.

Increased Conditionality

The survey so far of the processes of regime restructuring has shown that (1) nonaid capital flows have been increasingly linked to aid regime functioning and (2) more-conditional and less-concessional forms of aid have expanded at the expense of less-conditional and more-concessional forms of aid, both at the overall regime level and within individual aid institutions. Together these processes have both reduced alternatives to high-conditionality assistance and aggregated in the hands of coordinating aid institutions a "critical mass" of financing sufficient to induce compliance with regime norms. By themselves, therefore, they have gone a long way to restore the discipline of the aid regime. In addition, three other developments have increased the conditionality associated with access to aid: (1) the strengthening of mechanisms of donor coordination, (2) the IMF's new two-tier access policy, and (3) the inducement of multiyear debt rescheduling.

Strengthened Donor Coordination

As we saw in Chapter 3, coordination between donors has traditionally been achieved through consultative groups and consortia and through the mechanisms of the Paris Club, which has maintained a secretariat since 1974. The strengthening of mechanisms of donor coordination has involved both a revitalization and expansion of these institutions and a renewed emphasis on general policy influence.

In a survey of aid coordination in its 1983 annual report, the Development Assistance Committee called on donors to "become more involved in the policy consultative process" and to adjust their programs to the resultant outcomes.[90] Five countries during 1983 requested new World Bank–sponsored consultative groups, alongside the twenty currently active ones, in addition to two others sponsored by, respectively, the Netherlands and the OECD. (Of lesser significance were twenty-one UNDP-sponsored "round tables" and one recipient-led group.) Together, these countries participating in one or another type of coordinating group received about 50 percent of all aid in 1983.[91]

The DAC's 1984 annual survey reported further progress in aid coordination:

Aid co-ordination, which was advocated in the first of these annual reports, for 1961, gained wider and more committed adherence during the past year. . . . The DAC High-Level Meeting of 28th–29th November 1983 sparked a renewal of interest in co-ordination at the country level as a means of enhancing the effectiveness of development programmes. Directors of DAC member institutions largely resolved their reservations about accepting the limitations implied by serious coordination. They endorsed a process of consultation with governments of developing countries and multilateral agencies looking to the strengthening of existing mechanisms of co-ordination and the initiation of new ones.[92]

In a discussion of Africa, the DAC explicitly linked this coordination with IMF and World Bank policy advice:

Economic recovery in the next several years can best be assisted in the context of structural adjustment programmes designed with the help of the World Bank and the IMF. Where such a framework of policies and measures to accelerate economic growth is not in place, its adoption or completion should be advocated and assisted by development institutions.[93]

The World Bank has proposed the creation of six to seven new consultative groups for sub-Saharan African countries as well as the establishment of resident missions in every sub-Saharan African country receiving significant World Bank aid.[94] Both the IMF and the World Bank have expanded resident representatives and missions in the Third World; as of mid 1984, the IMF had twenty-three and the World Bank, thirty-one. These supplement frequent visiting missions, which in the case of the World Bank can amount for a single country to over one hundred per year.[95] In Washington, the Bank has expanded the operations of the Economic Development Institute (EDI), which in fiscal year 1985 hosted twenty-eight hundred participants, largely civil servants from the Third World, in seminars and courses both in the United States and abroad. The EDI has become an increasingly important means of World Bank influence and informal coordination, but it has been little studied. It receives only passing notice, for example, in Payer's detailed critique of Bank operations.[96]

World Bank officials and reports have increasingly stressed the

Bank's "nonfinancial role," with Stanley Please going so far as to claim a "comparative advantage" for the Bank in the policy area.[97] Please, a former bank official, sees this function obstructed and entitles his book *The Hobbled Giant*, but the events of the past several years have gone far to unleash the giant.

IMF Access Policy

As we saw earlier, access limits for IMF members were reduced at the time of the 1983 quota increase and were set at two levels, 102 percent and 125 percent, which were further reduced in 1984 and 1985. The new access policy was bitterly assailed at the 1983 IMF/World Bank meetings by almost all Third World countries. Bangladesh's minister of finance and planning charged that it would "nullify the quota increase," and China's minister of finance declared tht "the quota increase will become mostly meaningless."[98] From a regime perspective, however, the new access policy ensured that the new resources generated for the IMF would enable the IMF to finance adjustment programs in more countries and at the same time provide a new inducement for compliance, in the form of the two-tier access policy.

Two years later the Fund had yet to spell out the conditions that determine one or the other level of access. The chairman of the Interim Committee of the board of governors stated in 1983 that the adoption of two access limits was "intended to be an incentive for countries to adopt serious adjustment policies," and an Interim Committee communiqué stated that determination of the appropriate access limit would depend "on the seriousness of the balance of payments needs and the strength of the adjustment effort."[99] The discretionary power of the IMF's board of governors was further underlined by the provision for financing above the access limits "in exceptional circumstances."[100] Because such exceptional financing is likely to involve IMF borrowing under the GAB arrangements discussed earlier, the power of the leading advanced capitalist countries, already disproportionate because of the IMF's weighted voting system, would appear to be further enhanced.

Multiyear Debt Rescheduling

Another incentive for compliance with the policy conditions of the major aid institutions involves rescheduling. In the first phase of the post-1982 debt crisis, severe penalties were imposed on all renegotiating countries. Even countries that were servicing their debts on schedule found their market positions seriously eroded, although terms for a small number of countries perceived as "safe" eased in the course of 1984, prompting some observers to speak of an increasingly segmented international capital market. As rising interest rates in the first half of 1984 elicited renewed concern over the possibility of a debtors' cartel, the major Western governments began to pressure the banks to bend regime norms for a few particularly cooperative and influential countries, most notably Mexico and Brazil. The London summit of leaders of seven advanced capitalist countries endorsed for the first time in June 1984 the concept of multiyear rescheduling for those countries that had successfully undertaken adjustment programs.[101]

Coming shortly before the Cartagena conference of Latin American debtors in June 1984, the new policy enunciated by the London summit nations was widely seen as an effort to split off the cooperative from the recalcitrant countries (particularly Argentina) and to block the formation of a debtors' cartel. To date, the strategy appears to have been successful. The Cartagena group has not expanded its membership, and it has limited itself to the traditional (largely ineffectual) lobbying role of Third World international groupings. Multiyear debt-restructuring agreements for such countries as Mexico, Brazil, Ecuador, Venezuela, and Argentina have provided better terms than those obtained by most other Third World countries and have divided the Third World not only along an axis of resistance and compliance but also along one of bargaining power—such terms have not been available to weaker and poorer countries, no matter how compliant they have been. Debt, which many saw as a possible new basis of Third World solidarity, has seemingly become a new basis of differentiation and competition.

Conclusion

"The most remarkable thing about government debts," John Makin observes in his historical survey of earlier debt crises, "is the consistency with which they are repudiated by war, inflation, simple fiat, or the disappearance or reconstitution of the government that issued them." [102] What is remarkable about the current era of debt crisis is how little this statement applies to it. Despite predictions of default, repudiation, and financial collapse from all sorts of observers, not a single case of debt repudiation has occurred. Even those countries that have fallen far behind in interest payments have refrained from formal declarations of default and have made periodic payments to demonstrate goodwill. The "grim scenario was not played out. . . . The strategy has been working," IMF Managing Director de Larosière announced with considerable satisfaction in February 1985. [103]

We have seen in this chapter that the strategy has worked at least in part because of the reconsolidation of aid regime discipline. In the process, the links between North and South have been considerably transformed. In a speech before the United Nations General Assembly, Argentine President Alfonsin declared that the world economic order was "becoming a financial order exclusively." [104] Alfonsin's statement accurately reflects the degree to which North-South relations have become focused on financial issues, particularly debt, and the increasingly dominant role of a few major financial institutions.

The aid institutions understand fully that they must do more than safeguard the status of debt and that the critical question in the long run will be the kind of development that emerges from regime functioning. It would be foolhardy to make hard and fast predictions about a world in which the aid regime is only one among numerous factors shaping world development. But it is instructive to explore the basic outlines of the kind of development promoted under the auspices of structural adjustment programs and to note how some of the mechanisms of regime reconsolidation discussed in this chapter could, under certain conditions, become a source of instability and new crisis in the future. These two issues constitute the subject of the Epilogue.

EPILOGUE: REGIME CONDITIONALITY AND DEVELOPMENT CHOICES IN THE 1980s

The very recession that demonstrated more powerfully than ever the external vulnerability of Third World societies also facilitated a process of regime reconsolidation that strengthened the aid institutions' capacity to foster outward-oriented strategies in debtor nations. The recession and debt crisis might have convinced Third World countries of the dangers of tying their fates too closely to the policies of the advanced capitalist countries; rather, these events have been used effectively by the aid institutions to promote further "adjustment" to external economic and political forces and to increase the overall dependence of individual countries on the health of the world economy as a whole and on the unstable fortunes of their location within it.

The IMF has insisted that there is no alternative to adjustment and that the only choice is between delayed but painful versus immediate but less painful adjustment. The issue is presented as a technical, not a political, one. As John White has noted of multilateral development institutions generally:

> They have to argue . . . that there is no room for debate, that their prescriptions are the only possible prescriptions, that there is some single process called "development" which is the process which their activities are self-evidently designed to promote and that any departure from their recommendations in support of this process constitutes a dilution of the developmental character of aid.[1]

"The IMF has to operate under a reality which is not a happy one," IMF Managing Director Jacques de Larosière replied to a question about the impact of adjustment programs on living standards in

1983.[2] It is not part of the political or organizational culture of the aid regime to question the constraints imposed by that unhappy reality, either internationally or domestically. Although aid institutions have demonstrated considerable technical virtuosity in operating within these constraints (for example, finding new ways to mobilize capital), they have displayed little interest in exploring their role in upholding that reality.

The Structural Adjustment Agenda

The concept of structural adjustment has become the central category in the development lexicon of both the World Bank and the IMF. In its emphasis on "adjustment," the concept takes as given the domestic and international constraints on alternative development strategies, and in its emphasis on "structure," it indicates the depth of adjustment dictated by these constraints. It assumes not only the viability but also the necessity of dependent development.

The World Bank and the IMF have published extensively on the concept of structural adjustment.[3] Much of this literature is devoted to demonstrating the superiority of outward, export-oriented development strategies to inward, self-reliant or import substitution strategies. These studies raise a number of controversial issues of measurement, classification, and sampling, as well as questions of potential fallacy of composition—the latter illustrated by Paul Bairoch's observation that if all nonsocialist LDCs had exported manufactured goods at Hong Kong's per capita rate in 1970, these exports would have been more than three times total world exports.[4]

But the relevant point here is that the historical functioning of the aid regime has practically precluded real inward-oriented, self-reliant strategies and that the classification of countries into two groups is really a classification of different modes of outward orientation. The World Bank's and IMF's critique of what they call inward-oriented strategies constitutes a critique of a development model that they themselves shaped in important ways and is based on an overstated contrast between countries whose policies had much in common, partly due to the functioning of the aid regime. Countries such as Brazil and the Philippines, now criticized for excessive inward orientation, were only a few years ago extolled by aid institutions. Citing South Korea, a recent World Bank publication observes that "the history of economic development has been full of surprises."[5] Yet the statism and strict control over foreign capital underlying South Korea's success is consistently downplayed in World Bank publications, and similar efforts elsewhere would almost certainly be undermined by structural adjustment policies. The Korean "surprise" might well be impossible to achieve under present circumstances.

As an outline of a new development strategy, the structural adjustment agenda combines both old and new themes. These may be reduced to two major ones, the first dealing with the relationship to the world economy and the second with the nature of the domestic economy.

The first and most traditional theme recommends pursuit of comparative advantage in international trade as the centerpiece of development strategy. Time-honored arguments in favor of export-led development are supplemented by a new twist of the basic needs approach—the thesis that outward-oriented strategies, by relying on cheap labor in manufacturing as a country's comparative advantage, thereby generate more employment and do more to alleviate poverty than inward-oriented strategies, which are said to result in more capital-intensive investment providing less new employment.[6]

The second theme involves an assault on attempts by Third World countries to insulate their economies from international market forces. Departures from "pure market functioning" are attacked as "distortions"—except when they promote goals compatible with outward-oriented development, in which case they are generally called "incentives." The preference for a market economy is hardly a new theme, but the World Bank in particular has in the past several years aggressively identified a range of "domestic policy inadequacies" that it proposes to remedy through greater responsiveness to international market signals. The structural adjustment literature attacks "distorted" domestic pricing, non-market-based interest rates, infant industry protectionism, and favoritism toward domestic, against foreign, capital.[7] It has provided a rationale for greatly expanding the range of aid conditionality.

In the context of regime reconsolidation discussed in the previous chapter, adjustment programs have constituted an assault on deep-rooted state capitalist tendencies in Third World countries. They also constitute a considerable gamble in the context of the current world economy.

Between 1980 and mid 1984, sixty-nine LDCs were covered by a total of 161 high-conditionality adjustment agreements with the International Monetary Fund. Fifteen of these countries also had structural adjustment agreements with the World Bank. Although full details of most of these agreements have not been made public, those details that are available indicate an attack on the institutional foundations of state capitalist strategies. In particular, the role of public enterprises, state control of credit allocation, and restrictions on foreign capital have come under sustained attack. Individual country outcomes will depend ultimately on the domestic balance of forces, but the reconsolidation of aid regime discipline favors those forces supporting more market-based, outward-oriented approaches based on alliance with foreign capital.

"First and foremost," de Larosière asserted in May 1984, "debt problems in the great majority of cases were the result of overexpansionary fiscal and monetary policies over a number of years."[8] Adjustment programs in many countries have borne the imprint of this analysis. Drastic decreases in the level of public investment were centerpieces of adjustment programs in a wide range of countries, including Brazil, Mexico, Turkey, Bangladesh, Peru, and Togo.

Cutbacks in public sector investment have in many cases been linked to privatization of state enterprises and to the reallocation of credit to the private sector. In Bangladesh, the combination of privatization and credit reallocation "provided room for a significant growth in credit to the private sector, even as total domestic credit expansion deteriorated sharply."[9]

The pressure for privatization has extended beyond productive enterprises to social services as well. The World Bank reports, for the
case of housing:

> In Zimbabwe, the Bank is proposing to lend to building societies for fi-
> nancing private housing. In the Ivory Coast, basic reforms of housing
> policy are to be adopted in the SAL II program which provide for major
> reductions in subsidies, sale of government-owned units to private owners
> and a shift from the public sector to the private sector in house construc-
> tion. A housing loan is under preparation to implement these reforms.[10]

A similar approach is being implemented in Malawi. Indeed, the
Bank goes so far as to propose, for the distribution of drugs in the
rural areas, limiting "the public sector role to training, certification,
and supervision" of paraprofessionals and then letting them set up
private practices in the villages.[11]

Protectionism and restrictions on foreign investment have come
under particularly strong attack. Mexico, Brazil, Chile, Indonesia,
Malaysia, and a variety of other countries have moved to eliminate or
reduce restrictions on profit repatriation and on allowable levels of
foreign ownership.

These various elements may be seen together in the case of South
Korea, which somewhat paradoxically has been held up as a model by
the international institutions at the same time it has been under enormous pressure to modify its policies fundamentally. Because of the
export-oriented nature of its development and because of its "dimin-
ishing comparative advantage in low-wage, labor-intensive products"
as other, poorer countries followed its lead, South Korea was hit especially hard by the initial phase of the world recession, with its gross
national product declining in real terms by 6.2 percent in 1980.[12]
Debt service in that year accounted for over three-quarters of its current account deficit. Since then, South Korea has negotiated three
standby agreements with the IMF and two structural adjustment
loans with the World Bank. These contained many of the usual
elements: import liberalization, fiscal moderation, wage restraint, exchange rate flexibility, and promotion of private investment. In addi-

tion, the state banking sector, which was identified as the key institutional underpinning of Korean state capitalism in Chapter 6, became a target of IMF/World Bank adjustment. In a description of the 1981 program, *IMF Survey* described a set of financial policies "aimed at eliminating distortions in the banking and tax systems" and reported: "To reinforce the market mechanism in the financial sector, two more commercial banks were denationalized, bringing the total to four since 1980."[13] The report went on to observe that in 1982:

> To stimulate foreign direct investment, the number of industries in which foreigners could invest was increased substantially, approval procedures were simplified greatly, and restrictions on repatriation and dividends were removed. Despite rising protectionism around the world, the import liberalization ratio was increased to 77 percent from 75 percent in 1981.[14]

Structural adjustment policies in South Korea in 1983, under agreements extending into 1985, included denationalization of the last commercial bank and further liberalization of imports and foreign investment.[15] A report by a Fund economist summing up Korea's experience stated:

> The pace of structural reform was quickened in 1982–83. Within the financial sector, the Government denationalized all nationwide commercial banks . . . and authorized two new commercial banks and numerous nonbank financial institutions. To stimulate foreign direct investment, the number of industries in which foreigners can invest was increased substantially, approval procedures were simplified, and restrictions on repatriation of capital and dividends were removed. . . . Korea has also continued to liberalize imports.[16]

These changes must be seen as the outcome of interaction between the aid regime and domestic struggles over development strategy, not as the simple imposition of discipline on an unwilling country.[17] Nonetheless, the aid regime has played a critical role in these changes, which would appear to spell the end of a state role that deserves to be called "state capitalist."

At the other end of the ideological spectrum, and largely outside the boundaries of the aid regime, Cuba has also been forced by the

debt crisis to reorient its policies in a more outward-looking direction. Cuba is not a member of the IMF; therefore, its rescheduling
agreement with private creditors in 1983 included policy provisions
left in other cases to the IMF. A number of these were similar to the
standard IMF gamut: reduction of industrial imports, cutbacks in
social services, increased consumer prices, and significantly expanded
exports. At the same time, operating outside the institutional context
of the aid regime, Cuba succeeded in obtaining a number of unusual
concessions. As one account reports:

> The conditions agreed to by Cuba with its creditors are significantly dif-
> ferent from those often imposed by the International Monetary Fund, in
> that they link the fulfillment of the rescheduled payments to the avail-
> ability of western credit lines and to a normalisation of trade with the
> creditor countries. This linkage is seen by analysts as protecting not only
> Cuba, but also as providing the creditors with some protection against
> U.S. pressures.[18]

In the early period of the debt crisis, a number of Third World leaders
expressed the hope that debt renegotiation could be linked to broader
questions of trade and aid relations. Argentine officials stressed the
need to raise the question of commodity prices and tariff and non-
tariff barriers to Third World exports in any debt negotiations. Tan-
zanian President Julius Nyerere and others mused about the potential power of debt.[19] Through 1985, Cuba's modest success in
linking debt repayment to trade and credit access remained an iso-
lated case; debt renegotiations remained compartmentalized, and
hopes for "global negotiations" to address Third World needs had
been dashed.[20] Debt had not proven able to provide significant bargaining power for the Third World as a whole.

Potential Contradictions and the Politics of Debt

Using regime conditionality to extend the outward orientation of
Third World countries constitutes a considerable gamble in the current world context. Aid officials frankly acknowledge that the policies

of structural adjustment they promote with their expanded leverage will work only if certain conditions are met: most notably, that the advanced capitalist countries achieve and sustain a high rate of growth and avoid protectionism. De Larosière has warned: "The advice we give to these countries—to diversify their productive base and shift the orientation of their economies toward exports—is meaningless if the industrial countries succumb to protectionist pressures."[21] Noting that a 3 percent growth rate for the industrial countries will be necessary for the financial problems of developing countries to be manageable, de Larosière states: "Central to these projections is the assumption that the industrial countries will face up to the formidable structural problems they themselves are confronting."[22] A GATT study likewise observes that "if the industrial countries remained preoccupied with 'safeguarding vital industries,' 'reconquering domestic markets,' and 'eliminating intolerable bilateral deficits,' the best policy reforms that the debtor countries could devise for themselves could not be very promising."[23] Similarly, having outlined its familiar prescriptions for outward-oriented development, the World Bank's *World Development Report 1983* comments soberly: "For them to bear full fruit, however, the world economy must regain the momentum it achieved in 1976–78. Without that, the developing countries' prospects are bleak indeed."[24] The report predicts "catastrophic consequences for the developing countries" if "the industrial countries' recovery were to taper off into a decade of very slow growth" (that is, 2.5 percent per year).[25] A U.S. government report in early 1983 concluded that the debt crisis would be solved by recovery in the West, which it optimistically estimated to average 4.2 percent through the mid 1980s. It admitted the problem would not be resolved with growth rates much less than this.[26]

Warnings about the inevitable failure of Third World outward-oriented policies if the industrial countries should fail to restore and maintain high growth rates, restructure their economies to allow for increased imports, and avoid protectionism are aimed solely at the industrial countries. To their Third World clients, the aid institutions maintain a resolute optimism about the virtues of outward-oriented development. "The benefits of international economic linkages are too great," de Larosière has proclaimed, "to risk by a policy strategy based on insulating the domestic from the international economy."[27] The World Bank's *World Development Report 1984* calls on Third World countries to eschew proposals for delinking and instead to ride "the world economy rollercoaster" efficiently.[28]

Increasingly, however, these institutions have been caught between their deep commitment to a certain model of development and their recognition that the necessary conditions for that model are very likely in the process of decline. The recovery in 1984, which arrived two years later than the World Bank and the IMF predicted, has been limited in scope and tenuously based on unprecedented levels of deficit financing, which in turn have driven up international interest rates, aggravating the debt crisis. The IMF finds itself in the paradoxical position of lavishing praise on the United States as the engine of recovery while attacking the "expansionary fiscal policies" and "unprecedented absorption of global savings" that have made the recovery possible.[29] The United States became a net debtor in 1985, and its projected external debt by 1990 is expected to surpass that of all underdeveloped countries combined.[30]

The problem of growth is complicated by the widely noted fact that simultaneous adjustment across the Third World has imparted a deflationary bias to the world economy. As one European official has commented: "The IMF was not set up to deal with the world as a system, and it does not treat the effects of its policies globally."[31] The decline of OECD exports to non-OPEC LDCs is estimated to have cost three hundred fifty thousand jobs in 1982 alone.[32]

The IMF's faith that debtor countries can "export their way out of debt" presupposes growing access to the markets of the advanced capitalist countries; the IMF projects an average real growth of LDC exports of 5.5 percent per annum as necessary for a "workable outcome."[33] Yet protectionism has risen rapidly in the developed countries. Between 1980 and 1983, products restricted by tariffs or other barriers grew from 20 percent of total consumption of manufactured goods in the United States and Europe to 30 percent and kept climbing in 1984.[34] Although the IMF and the World Bank have succeeded in inducing substantial import liberalization in adjusting Third World countries, the institutions have been powerless to do more than apply moral suasion to the developed countries. The IMF's *Annual Report 1983* struck an almost desperate note in warning the industrial countries that "restrictions against the exports of developing countries penalize most severely those countries that have adopted outward-looking growth strategies and the liberalization of their domestic economies advocated by the Fund."[35] Yet these institutions can do little more than scold the industrial countries about their moral obligations or express pious hopes, as the IMF does in its *Annual Report 1984*, that "conditions should be propitious" for a serious attack on protectionism.[36] The World Bank's analysis in its *Annual Report 1984* seems considerably more prescient: "There would be an inherent contradiction between the financial pressure on borrowers to generate outflows of net resources and possible resistance in industrial countries against accepting a corresponding trade deficit." Yet the World Bank is unable to do much more than cite this as an "unresolved problem."[37]

Bank for International Settlements President Fritz Leutwiler stated in June 1984 that the Western central banks had developed a contingency plan to deal with the possibility of default.[38] Yet the aid institutions have refused to sanction contingency planning on the part of Third World countries should the premises of outward-oriented development turn out to be wrong. The World Bank, while admitting that "there are valid reasons for fearing increased protection," nonetheless insists that "inward-oriented policies are not warranted."[39] So committed are the major aid institutions to a particular model of development that they not only have failed to encourage contingency planning but also have actively opposed it.

The gamble that the structural adjustment agenda represents points to a potential vulnerability of the regime changes discussed in the previous chapter: the concentration of power in the hands of the IMF and the World Bank makes the whole world economy feel the effects of their decisions. If, as some have claimed, the IMF is making the

Third World pay for the fiscal irresponsibility (and military buildup) of the Reagan administration and undermining conditions for future growth, the process of regime reconsolidation could be short-lived.[40]

In addition to the issue of the concentration and content of conditionality, there are potential contradictions built into some of the mechanisms by which the aid regime has dealt with the debt crisis. The first stems from the increasing linkage between nonaid capital flows and the MDBs. As noted earlier, this linkage has functioned to remove an increasing proportion of debt—and potentially foreign equity holdings as well—from the possibility of default, rescheduling, or unilateral contract changes. This could threaten both the privileged creditor status of the MDBs and the ability of debtors to avoid formal default in future debt crises because the proportion of debt available for renegotiation will be much smaller.

A second contradiction stems from the practice of stepping up disbursements by the MDBs. As noted earlier, in the absence of substantial capital increases, this practice is likely to accelerate the decline of aid in the future. In addition, the atrophy of traditional forms of World Bank cofinancing with the private banks in favor of its new B-loans suggests that new cofinanced commercial flows are likely to substitute for previous forms of financing, not supplement them. Thus, not only are overall levels of financing likely to continue to decline, but an increasing proportion will also be more tightly than ever locked into the MDBs' privileged status.

A third contradiction stems from the fact that aid levels are being maintained at such high levels partly through the worsening of terms of aid. As we have seen, the MDBs have been forced to channel an increasing proportion of their aid through their hard-loan facilities, which carry interest rates about three-quarters of market rates. In addition, these loans in the cases of the IBRD and the IDB now carry variable interest rates, recalculated every six months like commercial bank loans, which increase borrowers' vulnerability to the kinds of interest rate increases that played a major role in bringing on the early 1980s debt crisis.

From the point of view of Third World debtors, the "resolution" of the debt crisis has required putting foreign creditors' claims ahead of citizens' claims. Neither the figures on reschedulings nor the rosy IMF descriptions of "successful adjustment" convey the social devastation that has accompanied the debt crisis. In Latin America, per capita income fell between 1981 and 1983 and stagnated in 1984. According to the Inter-American Development Bank:

> By 1982, seven countries of the region saw a full decade of rising incomes wiped out, as their per capita GDP's fell to 1972 levels or lower. Estimates indicate that for the region as a whole per capita GDP levels in 1983 were lower than they were in 1977, and in some countries as low as in the 1960s.[41]

In low-income Africa, per capita incomes fell 2.7 percent in 1981 and 2.1 percent in 1982. The World Bank expects per capita incomes in low-income African countries to be lower by the end of the 1980s than they were in 1960.[42] Although Asian countries overall have fared better, per capita incomes in 1983 either stagnated or declined in Bangladesh, Indonesia, Nepal, and the Philippines. With the exception of the Philippines, however, virtually all Asian countries increased per capita incomes in 1984.[43]

All the ills of the Third World cannot of course be blamed on the accumulation of debt or the response to the debt crisis. But issues of debt unquestionably lie at the center of North-South relations, and indebtedness has become the major mechanism of surplus appropriation from the Third World. Since 1981, annual debt service by LDCs has been in the realm of $100 billion, more than all aid. The thirteen largest debtors repaid $21 billion more in 1983 than they received in new loans. Net financial transfers for Latin America have been substantially negative since 1982. LDC debt has increased steadily, from $545.8 billion in 1982 to $686.5 billion in 1984.[44]

In the North, this outflow of resources from the Third World has been accepted as natural by policy analysts. William Cline asserts: "The basic concept that must be recognized . . . is that for an interim period the excessively indebted countries must indeed make outward transfers of resources if their debt levels are to be reduced relative to exports and if their creditworthiness is to be restored."[45] Cline's view reflects the assumption, stated as fact by the Inter-American Development Bank, that "debt service constitutes an inflexible claim on the balance of payments, normally the most rigid of all."[46]

Whether this claim will continue to be upheld, and how long Third World countries can sustain negative financial transfers, will depend in large measure on the impact of the debt crisis and regime reconsolidation on politics in the Third World, both within and between countries. "If you had asked me six months ago what one factor most likely will upset this already shaky debt-restructuring effort," a U.S. banker told the *Wall Street Journal* in the fall of 1983, "I probably would have said a weak U.S. economic recovery. Now I would say it is the internal politics in these countries."[47] Another banker and former U.S. assistant secretary of state for economic affairs observed: "There are political forces that in many cases can be the Achilles' heel of working out the debt problem."[48] "The politics of debt," the *New York Times* noted in March 1984, "is rapidly becoming the dominant politics of Brazil"—a statement that applies to an increasing number of Third World countries.[49]

The Cartagena conference of eleven Latin American debtors in June 1984 marked a substantial increase in the conscious politicization of the debt crisis. Despite its limited immediate outcome, it represented a far cry from the situation fourteen months earlier at the Group of 77 summit meeting in Buenos Aires, where, it was reported:

> Private debt and rescheduling were the main topics of conversation outside the Buenos Aires conference hall. Inside, it was handled gingerly, particularly by the major Latin American debtors, who were under considerable pressure from the US, the EEC and the IMF/World Bank not to entertain any idea of a "debtors' cartel," or even to exchange and coordinate information.[50]

Predictions of whether Cartagena will in retrospect be seen as a step toward a more effective challenge to the management of the debt crisis by the creditor countries, banks, and institutions lie beyond the scope of this book. But the politics of debt will clearly continue to be shaped by and respond to the regime structures and policies this book has discussed.

It also seems clear that political as well as economic contradictions are entailed in the adjustment strategy. For a number of countries, the debt crisis has come at a time of political liberalization or crisis of an authoritarian government. Whether the adjustment policies of the IMF, World Bank, and commercial banks are compatible with continued political liberalization is an open question. It has often been argued that the kind of export-oriented strategy favored by these institutions necessitates a high level of political repression—to keep wages competitively low and to provide the "stable investment climate" necessary for multinational investment.[51] However, the austerity demands imposed on Third World countries have been so devastating in their social consequences that it is unclear whether most governments can continue to implement them without some form of new "social contract" with the rest of society—a contract almost sure to involve the expansion of political rights as the trade-off for economic concessions. Democratization in turn is almost inevitably bound to produce support for tougher bargaining stances by debtor governments.

The capacity of new political forces to develop creative responses to the debt crisis and to the larger crisis of development will rest not only on domestic political developments but also on how Third World political forces interact with one another internationally. If the debt crisis should provide impetus for new forms of Third World solidarity, this could turn out to be its most enduring and important legacy.

APPENDIX:
OECD CLASSIFICATION OF
LESS DEVELOPED COUNTRIES

Low-Income Countries (LICs)

LEAST DEVELOPED COUNTRIES
(LLDCS)

Afghanistan
Bangladesh
Benin
Bhutan
Botswana
Bourkina Faso
Burundi
Cape Verde
Central African Republic
Chad
Comoros
Ethiopia
Gambia
Guinea
Guinea-Bissau
Haiti
Laos
Lesotho
Malawi
Maldives
Mali
Nepal
Niger
Rwanda
Somalia
Sudan

OTHER LICS

Angola
Bolivia
Burma
China
Djibouti
Egypt
El Salvador
Equatorial Guinea
Ghana
Honduras
India
Kampuchea
Kenya
Liberia
Madagascar
Mauritania
Mayotte
Mozambique
Pakistan
St. Helena
Sao Tome & Principe
Senegal
Sierra Leone
Solomon Islands
Sri Lanka
Togo

Low-Income Countries (LICs)—*continued*

Tanzania
Uganda
Western Samoa
Tonga
Yemen Arab Republic
Yemen, People's Democratic
    Republic of

Tokelau Islands
Tuvalu
Vanuatu
Vietnam
Zaire
Zambia

Middle-Income Countries (MICs)

Bahamas
Bahrain
Barbados
Belize
Bermuda
Brunei
Cameroon
Chile
Colombia
Congo
Cook Islands
Costa Rica
Cuba
Cyprus
Dominican Republic
Falkland Islands
Fiji
Gibraltar
Guadeloupe
Guatemala
Guiana, French
Guyana
Israel
Ivory Coast
Jamaica
Jordan
Kiribati
Lebanon
Macao
Malaysia
Malta

Martinique
Mauritius
Morocco
Nauru
Netherlands Antilles
New Caledonia
Nicaragua
Niue Island
Oman
Pacific Islands
Panama
Papua New Guinea
Paraguay
Peru
Philippines
Polynesia, French
Reunion
St. Pierre & Miquelon
Seychelles
Surinam
Swaziland
Syria
Thailand
Trinidad & Tobago
Tunisia
Turkey
Uruguay
Wallis & Futuna
West Indies[1]
Zimbabwe

Newly Industrializing Countries (NICs)

Argentina	Portugal
Brazil	Singapore
Greece	Spain
Hong Kong	Taiwan
South Korea	Yugoslavia
Mexico	

Organization of Petroleum-Exporting Countries (OPEC)

Algeria	Libya
Ecuador	Nigeria (MIC)
Gabon	Qatar
Indonesia (LIC)	Saudi Arabia
Iran	United Arab Emirates
Iraq	Venezuela
Kuwait	

SOURCE: Organization for Economic Cooperation and Development, *External Debt of Developing Countries, 1982 Survey* (Paris, 1982), p. 122.

[1]West Indies includes Anguilla Antigua, Cayman Islands, Dominica, Grenada, Montserrat, St. Kitts-Nevis, St. Lucia, St. Vincent, Turks and Caicos Islands, and the British Virgin Islands.

NOTES

Introduction

1. Joseph Marion Jones, *The Fifteen Weeks* (New York: Harcourt, Brace and World, 1955), pp. 262–263.

2. Paul G. Hoffman, *Peace Can Be Won* (New York: Doubleday, 1951), p. 130.

3. See, for example, Townsend Hoopes, *The Limits of Intervention* (New York: David McKay, 1969).

4. Editorial: "The Real Shame in Foreign Aid," *New York Times* (October 31, 1983), p. A18.

5. Organization for Economic Cooperation and Development, *Development Co-operation: Efforts and Policies of the Members of the Development Assistance Committee, 1984 Review* (Paris, 1984), p. 131. This annual publication is hereafter referred to as DAC, *Review*.

6. De Larosière reports that IMF conditional financing has the effect of "unlocking access by the country concerned to additional external finance. It has been estimated that every dollar of fund financing in support of adjustment programs has in the recent past generated an additional four dollars of new commercial lending"; *IMF Survey* (March 7, 1983), p. 74.

7. DAC, *1981 Review*, p. 31. A useful sampling of the statistical literature on the relationship between aid and development is contained in Mitchell A. Seligson (ed.), *The Gap Between Rich and Poor: Contending Perspectives on the Political Economy of Development* (Boulder: Westview Press, 1984).

8. For discussions of the issue of fungibility, see David A. Baldwin, "Foreign Aid, Intervention, and Influence," *World Politics* 21,3 (April 1969) : 425, 447; and Charles Wolf, Jr., *Foreign Aid: Theory and Practice in Southern Asia* (Princeton: Princeton University Press, 1960). Joan Robinson argues

331

that there are very few cases where foreign aid could not be substituted for by reduced consumption in *Economic Philosophy* (Chicago: Aldine, 1962), p. 121.

9. See, for example, the way "humanitarian" and "recipient need" variables are counterposed to "foreign policy" and "donor interest" variables in such works as R. D. McKinlay and R. Little, "A Foreign Policy Model of U.S. Bilateral Aid Allocation," *World Politics* 30,1 (October 1977):58–86; and R. McKinlay, "The German Aid Relationship: A Test of the Recipient Need and the Donor Interest Models of the Distribution of German Bilateral Aid 1961–1970," *European Journal of Political Research* 6 (1978):313–331.

10. Fernando Henrique Cardoso and Enzo Faletto, *Dependency and Development in Latin America* (Berkeley and Los Angeles: University of California Press, 1979), p. 212.

11. Quoted in Robert A. Pastor, *Congress and the Politics of U.S. Foreign Economic Policy 1929–1976* (Berkeley and Los Angeles: University of California Press, 1980), p. 254.

12. Pierre Uri, *Development Without Dependence* (New York: Praeger, 1976), p. 36.

13. For interpretations of the various traditions converging in world systems theory, see Walter L. Goldfrank, "Karl Marx as a World-System Thinker," paper presented at the annual meeting of the American Sociological Association, Detroit, September 2, 1983; and Daniel Chirot and Thomas D. Hall, "World System Theory," *Annual Review of Sociology* 8 (1982):81–106. A useful summary of the world systems perspective is Christopher Chase-Dunn and Richard Rubinson, "Toward a Structural Perspective on the World System," *Politics and Society* 7,4 (1977):453–476.

14. Peter T. Bauer and Basil S. Yamey go so far as to claim that "the concept of the Third World and the policy of official aid are inseparable. Without foreign aid there is no Third World. Official aid provides the only bond joining together its diverse and often antagonistic constituents." Their implicit denial of any common structural location of Third World countries within the world economy is the antithesis of the approach taken here, even if they are right in seeing aid and Third World status as closely related. See their "Foreign Aid: What Is At Stake?" in W. Scott Thompson (ed.), *The Third World: Premises of U.S. Policy* (San Francisco: Institute for Contemporary Studies, 1983), pp. 115–135.

15. Immanuel Wallerstein, "Crisis as Transition," in Samir Amin, Giovanni Arrighi, Andre Gunder Frank, and Immanuel Wallerstein, *Dynamics of Global Crisis* (New York: Monthly Review Press, 1982), p. 13.

16. Andre Gunder Frank, "Global Crisis and Transformation," *Development and Change* 14,3 (July 1983): 332.

17. Theda Skocpol stresses the autonomy of state structures and of the interstate system in her classic review, "Wallerstein's World Capitalist System: A Theoretical and Historical Critique," *American Journal of Sociology* 82,5 (1977): 1075–1090. For a sampling of critiques stressing the primacy of class relations at the national level, see various essays in Ronald H. Chilcote (ed.), *Dependency and Marxism: Toward a Resolution of the Debate* (Boulder: Westview Press, 1982); Ronald H. Chilcote and Dale L. Johnson (eds.), *Theories of Development: Mode of Production or Dependency?* (Beverly Hills: Sage Publications, 1983); and P. Limqueco and B. McFarlane (eds.), *Neo-Marxist Theories of Underdevelopment* (London: Croom Helm, 1983). A useful middle position is provided by Dale L. Johnson, "Class Analysis and Dependency," in Chilcote and Johnson, *Theories of Development*, pp. 231–255.

18. Robert Keohane and Joseph Nye, *Power and Interdependence: World Politics in Transition* (Boston: Little, Brown, 1977).

19. For a useful set of articles from a special issue of *International Organization* on international regimes, see Stephen D. Krasner, *International Regimes* (Ithaca: Cornell University Press, 1983).

20. Robert O. Keohane, *After Hegemony: Cooperation and Discord in the World Political Economy* (Princeton: Princeton University Press, 1984), p. 13.

21. For a perceptive analysis of how organizational imperatives of aid institutions themselves can undercut regime norms, see Judith Tendler, *Inside Foreign Aid* (Baltimore: Johns Hopkins University Press, 1975). Carter's fitful human rights policies can be seen as a largely unsuccessful effort to introduce new regime norms; see Lars Schoultz, *Human Rights and U.S. Policy Toward Latin America* (Princeton: Princeton University Press, 1981). Schoultz's fine study shows that Congress and the Carter administration did succeed in introducing (what have turned out to be strictly temporary) changes in U.S. foreign aid policy, but that attempts to introduce human rights considerations at the level of regime norms were unsuccessful. Not one of the ninety-nine multilateral development bank loans the United States opposed on human rights grounds between 1976 and 1980 was actually blocked. See also Lars Schoultz, "Politics, Economics, and U.S. Participation

in Multilateral Development Banks," *International Organization* 36,3 (Summer 1982):537–574.

22. Goran Ohlin, *Foreign Aid Policies Reconsidered* (Paris: OECD Development Centre, 1966), p. 10.

23. Office of Planning and Budgeting, Agency for International Development, *U.S. Overseas Loans and Grants and Assistance from International Organizations, Obligations and Loan Authorizations, July 1, 1945–September 30, 1983.*

24. Jones, *The Fifteen Weeks*, p. 162.

25. Stephen Kinzer, "With Economic Woes Deepening, Managua Sees Years of Shortages," *New York Times* (October 22, 1984), p. A10. In his speech to the United Nations on October 21, 1985, Nicaraguan President Daniel Ortega Saavedra estimated that eleven thousand Nicaraguans had died and five thousand more had been wounded in the U.S.-supported insurgency; *New York Times* (October 22, 1985), p. A13.

26. For the impact of military aid, see Miles D. Wolpin, *Militarism and Social Revolution in the Third World* (Totowa, N.J.: Rowman and Allanheld, 1982); Miles D. Wolpin, *Military Aid and Counterrevolution in the Third World* (Lexington, Mass.: Lexington Books, 1972); and Michael T. Klare, *War Without End: American Planning for the Next Vietnams* (New York: Vintage Books, 1972).

27. For useful discussions of concessionality in foreign aid, see David A. Baldwin, *Economic Development and American Foreign Policy 1943–1962* (Chicago: University of Chicago Press, 1965), Introduction; and John White, "The Evaluation of Aid Offers," *Development and Change* 7,3 (July 1976):233–248.

28. The grant element, as calculated by the Development Assistance Committee, expresses the benefit over normal market terms (assumed to be 10 percent) accruing to the recipient from aid's concessionality. For a loan to meet the DAC's "official development assistance" (ODA) standard of a grant element of over 25 percent, it must generally have a maturity of over ten years and an interest rate below 5 percent. The face value of a loan multiplied by its grant element yields the "grant equivalent" of the loan.

29. DAC, *1984 Review*, p. 202.

30. Thomas C. Schelling, "American Aid and Economic Development: Some Critical Issues," in American Assembly, *International Stability and Progress* (New York: American Assembly, 1957), p. 158.

31. Office of Planning and Budgeting, Agency for International Development, *U.S. Overseas Loans and Grants*, various issues.

32. Denis Goulet and Michael Hudson, *The Myth of Aid* (Maryknoll, N.Y.: Orbis Books, 1971), pp. 85–92.

33. DAC, *1982 Review*, p. 171.

34. Baldwin, *Foreign Aid and American Foreign Policy: A Documentary Analysis* (New York: Praeger, 1966), p. 120.

35. *Foreign Assistance and Related Agencies Appropriations for 1971*, hearings before a subcommittee of the Committee on Appropriations, H.R., 91st Congress, 2nd Session, Part 2, p. 14.

36. *World Bank News*, 2,35 (September 15, 1983) : 3.

37. The Third World oil-exporting, aid-providing countries obviously differ as a group in significant ways from the oil-importing, aid-receiving countries. Yet the differences should not be overdrawn. Some oil exporters (most notably Iraq and Iran) have alternated suddenly between being aid providers and recipients, and the oil exporters' position within the overall aid regime (for example, their influence in the multilateral development banks) remains ambiguous. The main focus of this study, however, is on the oil-importing Third World countries.

Introduction to Part One

1. Joyce and Gabriel Kolko, *The Limits of Power: The World and United States Foreign Policy, 1945–1954* (New York: Harper and Row, 1972); and Fred L. Block, *The Origins of International Economic Disorder: A Study of United States International Monetary Policy from World War II to the Present* (Berkeley and Los Angeles: University of California Press, 1977).

2. Dean Acheson, *Present at the Creation* (New York: W. W. Norton, 1969), p. 308.

3. Theodore A. Wilson, *The Marshall Plan 1947–1951* (New York: Foreign Policy Association, 1977), p. 12.

4. William A. Brown, Jr., and Redvers Opie, *American Foreign Assistance* (Washington, D.C.: Brookings Institution, 1953), pp. 405–406. During this period, the World Bank loaned in addition $100 million to Australia, $329 million to Latin America, and $254 million to Africa and Asia.

5. J. Keith Horsefield (ed.), *The International Monetary Fund 1945–1965* (Washington, D.C.: IMF, 1969), p. 397. See also Imanuel Wexler, *The*

Marshall Plan Revisited: The European Recovery Program in Economic Perspective (Westport, Conn.: Greenwood Press, 1983), pp. 130–133.

6. John Lewis Gaddis, *Strategies of Containment* (New York: Oxford University Press, 1982), p. 4.

7. For studies dealing with the intricate relationship between economic and military aid during this period, see Amos A. Jordan, *Foreign Aid and the Defense of Southeast Asia* (New York: Praeger, 1962); John D. Montgomery, *The Politics of Foreign Aid: American Experience in Southeast Asia* (New York: Praeger, 1963); American Assembly, *International Stability and Progress* (New York: American Assembly, 1957); and Charles Wolf, Jr., *Foreign Aid: Theory and Practice in Southern Asia* (Princeton: Princeton University Press, 1960).

8. Hollis B. Chenery, "Objectives and Criteria for Foreign Assistance," in Robert A. Goldwin (ed.), *Why Foreign Aid?* (Chicago: Rand McNally, 1963), p. 42.

9. Mutual Security Agency, *Report to the Congress on the Mutual Security Program for the Fiscal Year 1961*.

10. Gaddis, *Strategies*, pp. 43, 65–71.

11. See, for example, Thomas G. Paterson (ed.), *Cold War Critics* (Chicago: Quadrangle Books, 1971).

12. David Baldwin, *Economic Development and American Foreign Policy 1943–1962* (Chicago: University of Chicago Press, 1966).

13. Ibid., p. 212.

14. Ibid., p. 66.

15. Gustav Ranis, "Alternative Resource Transfer Mechanisms and the Development Process: Research Issues," in National Science Foundation, *International Economic Policy Research: Papers and Proceedings of a Colloquium Held in Washington, D.C., October 3, 4, 1980* (Washington, D.C.: National Science Foundation), p. II-98.

16. Studies of the role of Congress in aid policy formation include Hadley Arkes, *Bureaucracy, the Marshall Plan, and the National Interest* (Princeton: Princeton University Press, 1972); Baldwin, *Economic Development*; Theodore Geiger and Roger D. Hansen, "The Role of Information in Decision Making on Foreign Aid," in Raymond A. Bauer and Kenneth J. Gergen (eds.), *The Study of Policy Formation* (New York: Free Press, 1978); Richard Gerster, "The IMF and Basic Needs Conditionality," *Journal of World Trade Law* 16, 6 (November-December 1982): 497–517; William L. Morrow, "Legislative Control of Administrative Discretion: The Case of

Congress and Foreign Aid," *Journal of Politics* 30,4 (November 1968): 985–1011; Michael K. O'Leary, *The Politics of Foreign Aid* (New York: Atherton Press, 1967); Robert A. Pastor, *Congress and the Politics of U.S. Foreign Economic Policy 1929–1976* (Berkeley and Los Angeles: University of California Press, 1980); Leroy Rieselbach, "The Demography of the Congressional Vote on Foreign Aid, 1939–1958," *American Political Science Review* 58,3 (September 1964): 577–588; Jonathan Sanford and Margaret Goodman, "Congressional Oversight and the Multilateral Development Banks," *International Organization* 29,4 (Autumn 1975): 1055–1064; Lars Schoultz, "Politics, Economics, and U.S. Participation in Multilateral Development Banks," *International Organization* 36,3 (Summer 1982): 537–574; and Kenneth Waltz, *Foreign Policy and Democratic Politics: The American and British Experience* (Boston: Little, Brown, 1967), chap. 6. For an official factual account, see *Congress and the Nation: 1945–1964: A Review of Government and Politics in the Postwar Years* (Washington, D.C.: Congressional Quarterly Service, 1965), pp. 160–186, and subsequent issues.

17. Harold van B. Cleveland, "If There Had Been No Marshall Plan . . . ," in Stanley Hoffmann and Charles Maier (eds.), *The Marshall Plan: A Retrospective* (Boulder: Westview Press, 1984), pp. 59–64. Cleveland nonetheless described the Marshall Plan as "a most extraordinarily successful operation" because of its political consequences. A somewhat similar conclusion is drawn by Alan Milward, *The Reconstruction of Western Europe, 1949–51* (Berkeley and Los Angeles: University of California Press, 1984), pp. 469–470.

18. See "Discussion" in Hoffmann and Maier, *The Marshall Plan*, p. 65.

19. Ibid., p. 66.

20. In contrast, "American planners in the spring of 1947 moved quickly from the notion of case-by-case aid to a coherent West European strategic concept"; Charles S. Maier, "Supranational Concepts and National Continuity in the Framework of the Marshall Plan," in ibid., p. 30.

21. See, for example, Jacques de Larosière, "Current Policies of the IMF: Fact and Fiction," *IMF Survey* (January 9, 1984), p. 3.

Chapter 1

1. Until relatively recently, the main works on the actual operation of the Marshall Plan were the two early classics, William Adams Brown, Jr., and

Redvers Opie, *American Foreign Assistance* (Washington, D.C.: Brookings Institution, 1953); and Harry B. Price, *The Marshall Plan and Its Meaning* (Ithaca: Cornell University Press, 1955). Book-length analyses of the origins of the Marshall Plan include Hadley Arkes, *Bureaucracy, the Marshall Plan, and the National Interest* (Princeton: Princeton University Press, 1972); and John Gimble, *The Origins of the Marshall Plan* (Stanford: Stanford University Press, 1976). Two important recent books that reassess the actual functioning of the Marshall Plan are Alan S. Milward, *The Reconstruction of Western Europe, 1945–51* (Berkeley and Los Angeles: University of California Press, 1984); and Imanuel Wexler, *The Marshall Plan Revisited: The European Recovery Program in Economic Perspective* (Westport, Conn.: Greenwood Press, 1983). However, neither of these addresses either the role of the underdeveloped areas in the Marshall Plan or the ERP's impact on these areas.

2. Robert A. Packenham, *Liberal America and the Third World: Political Development Ideas in Foreign Aid and Social Science* (Princeton: Princeton University Press, 1973), p. 34.

3. David Wall, *The Charity of Nations: The Political Economy of Foreign Aid* (New York: Basic Books, 1973), p. 37. For a similar conception of the Marshall Plan as simply a "repair job," see Tibor Mende, *From Aid to Recolonization* (New York: Pantheon, 1973), p. 36. Similar views are found in Doris A. Graber, "Are Foreign Aid Objectives Attainable?" *Western Political Quarterly* (March 1966): 70; and Tom S. Soper, "External Aid," *African Affairs* (April 1966): 149.

4. Joyce and Gabriel Kolko, *The Limits of Power: The World and United States Foreign Policy, 1945–1954* (New York: Harper and Row, 1972), esp. chap. 17, "The Failure of the Marshall Plan, 1949–1950," pp. 453–476.

5. For analyses of the emergence of Eastern Europe as a peripheral area and as the first "Third World," see Immanuel Wallerstein, *The Modern World System: Capitalist Agriculture and the Origins of the European World-Economy in the Sixteenth Century* (New York: Academic Press, 1974), chap. 2; and L. S. Stavrianos, *Global Rift: The Third World Comes of Age* (New York: William Morrow, 1981), chap. 3.

6. United Nations, Economic Commission for Europe, *Economic Bulletin for Europe*, second quarter, 1949, vol. 1, no. 2 (Geneva, October 1949), p. 27.

7. By 1952, Western European trade was a tiny fraction of what it

had been in 1938. West German exports to Eastern Europe declined from 13.1 percent of total exports to 1.2 percent, its imports from 12.9 percent to 2.3 percent. U.K. exports declined from 4.5 percent to 0.6 percent and imports from 5.8 percent to 2.7 percent. United Nations, Economic Commission for Europe, *Economic Bulletin for Europe*, second quarter, 1952, vol. 4, no. 3 (Geneva, November 1952), p. 35.

8. Organization for European Economic Co-Operation, *European Recovery Programme: Second Report of the O.E.E.C.* (Paris, 1950), p. 140.

9. U.S. Department of State, *Foreign Relations of the United States 1950* (Washington, D.C.: Government Printing Office, 1977), vol. 1, p. 840. This annual publication is hereafter referred to as *FRUS*.

10. Organization for European Economic Co-Operation, *European Recovery Programme*, p. 140.

11. *U.S. News and World Report* (August 13, 1948), p. 32, (September 17, 1948), p. 26.

12. D. F. Fleming, *The Cold War and Its Origins, 1917–1960* (Garden City, N.Y.: Doubleday, 1961), p. 438.

13. Organization for European Economic Co-Operation, *European Recovery Programme*, p. 140.

14. Economic Cooperation Administration, Special Mission to the United Kingdom, *The Sterling Area: An American Analysis* (London: Economic Cooperation Administration, 1951), p. 68.

15. Organization for European Economic Co-Operation, *European Recovery Programme*, p. 149.

16. John H. Williams, *Economic Stability in a Changing World* (New York: Oxford University Press, 1953), p. 175.

17. Quoted in Daniel Yergin, *Shattered Peace: The Origins of the Cold War and the National Security State* (Boston: Houghton Mifflin, 1977), p. 307.

18. Gabriel Kolko, *The Politics of War: The World and the United States Foreign Policy, 1943–1945* (New York: Vintage, 1970), p. 283.

19. Milward, *The Reconstruction of Western Europe*, p. 55.

20. Warren Leroy Hickman, *Genesis of the European Recovery Program: A Study of the Trend of American Economic Policies* (Geneva: Imprimeries Populaires, 1949), pp. 26–27. This book, published in 1949, foreshadows much of the contemporary "revisionist" historiography of this period.

21. Lloyd C. Gardner, *Architects of Illusion: Men and Ideas in American Foreign Policy, 1941–1949* (Chicago: Quadrangle, 1970), p. 22.

22. Ibid., p. 57.

23. Hickman, *Genesis of the European Recovery Program*, p. 79.

24. William Appleman Williams, *The Tragedy of American Diplomacy* (New York: Delta, 1962), pp. 236–237. Williams has explored the long-term social roots of the belief in the necessity of export markets in *The Roots of the Modern American Empire: A Study of the Growth and Shaping of Social Consciousness in a Marketplace Society* (New York: Vintage, 1969). For a variety of other statements by U.S. officials linking reliance on exports to avoiding a postwar depression, see J. Fred Rippy, "Historical Perspective," in James Wiggins and Helmut Schoeck (eds.), *Foreign Aid Reexamined* (Washington, D.C.: Public Affairs Press, 1958).

25. For example, see Yergin, *Shattered Peace*, p. 309.

26. Hickman, *Genesis of the European Recovery Program*, pp. 138, 208.

27. David Eakins, "Business Planners and America's Postwar Expansion," in David Horowitz (ed.), *Corporations and the Cold War* (New York: Monthly Review Press, 1969), p. 160. See also David Eakins, "The Development of Corporate Liberal Policy Research in the United States, 1885–1965" (Ph.D. dissertation, University of Wisconsin, 1966).

28. *U.S. News* (July 4, 1947), p. 13.

29. *U.S. News and World Report* (February 27, 1948), p. 21.

30. Jacob A. Rubin, *Your Hundred Billion Dollars: The Complete Story of American Foreign Aid* (Philadelphia: Chilton, 1964), p. 41.

31. *U.S. News* (September 26, 1947), p. 19.

32. President's Committee on Foreign Aid, "European Recovery and American Aid: A Report" (Harriman committee report), in James P. Warburg, *Put Yourself in Marshall's Place* (New York: Simon and Schuster, 1948), p. 69.

33. The wide-ranging efforts of the United States to influence the Italian elections of 1948 are described in part in Howard K. Smith, *The State of Europe* (New York: Knopf, 1949).

34. For example, see Kolko and Kolko, *The Limits of Power*; Kolko, *The Politics of War*; and Fernando Claudin, *The Communist Movement: From Comintern to Cominform*, pt. 2 (New York: Monthly Review Press, 1975).

35. Kolko and Kolko, *The Limits of Power*, p. 367.

36. Michael J. Hogan, "European Integration and the Marshall Plan," in Stanley Hoffmann and Charles Maier (eds.), *The Marshall Plan: A Retrospective* (Boulder: Westview Press, 1984), pp. 4, 6.

37. Fred L. Block, *The Origins of International Economic Disorder: A Study of United States International Monetary Policy from World War II to the Present* (Berkeley and Los Angeles: University of California Press, 1977), p. 9.

38. Warburg, *Put Yourself in Marshall's Place*, p. 46.

39. "The Stake of the Businessman in the European Recovery Program," address by George C. Marshall to Pittsburgh Chamber of Commerce, January 15, 1948; *Department of State Bulletin* 28,447 (January 25, 1948): 111.

40. President's Committee on Foreign Aid, *European Recovery and American Aid: A Report* (Washington, D.C., 1947).

41. Economic Cooperation Administration, *France: Country Study* (Washington, D.C., February 1949), p. 39.

42. Hoffman's shift from seeing U.S. private investment as a primary instrument of European recovery to seeing it as an indication that recovery had been achieved is described in Arkes, *Bureaucracy*, pp. 250–255.

43. *Balance of Payments of the United States, 1949–1951*, a supplement to the *Survey of Current Business* (Washington, D.C.: U.S. Department of Commerce, 1952), p. 160.

44. John E. Orchard, "ECA and the Dependent Territories," *Geographical Review* (January 1951): 67.

45. William C. Mallalieu, *British Reconstruction and American Policy* (New York: Scarecrow Press, 1956), p. 196.

46. *Extension of E.R.P.*, hearings before the Committee on Foreign Affairs, H.R., 81st Congress, 1st Session (February 1949), p. 25.

47. Williams, *Tragedy of American Diplomacy*, p. 173.

48. For example, see Economic Cooperation Administration, *Eighth Report to Congress*, quarter ending March 31, 1950, p. 4; *Ninth Report to Congress*, quarter ending June 30, 1950, pp. 14–15; *A Report on Recovery Progress and United States Aid* (Washington, D.C., 1949), pp. 13, 16, 46.

49. Economic Cooperation Administration, *Twelfth Report to Congress*, quarter ending March 31, 1951, p. 21.

50. *U.S. Foreign Policy for a Post-War Recovery Program*, hearings before the Committee on Foreign Affairs, H.R., 80th Congress, 1st and 2nd Sessions (December 1947–February 1948), pp. 206–207.

51. Economic Cooperation Administration, *Sixth Report to Congress*, quarter ending September 30, 1949, p. 30.

52. Economic Cooperation Administration, *Country Data Book: France* (March 1950), p. 4.

53. Organization for European Economic Co-Operation, *Interim Report on the European Recovery Programme*, vol. 2 (Paris, December 1948), p. 293.

54. Kolko and Kolko, *The Limits of Power*, p. 448.

55. Economic Cooperation Agency, *A Report on Recovery Progress and United States Aid* (Washington, D.C., February 1949), pp. 232–236.

56. Economic Cooperation Agency, *Thirteenth Report to Congress*, quarter ending June 30, 1951, p. 2; and J. J. Joseph, "The Failure of the Marshall Plan," *Science and Society* (Winter 1949–50): 56.

57. J. Fred Rippy, "Historical Perspective," in Wiggins and Schoeck, *Foreign Aid Reexamined*, p. 13.

58. Mutual Security Agency, *The Overseas Territories in the MSP* (March 31, 1952), p. 2.

59. Nelson A. Rockefeller, "Widening Boundaries of National Interest," *Foreign Affairs* 29,4 (July 1951): 527.

60. Fritz Sternberg, "Partners in Reaction," in Walter M. Daniels (ed.), *The Point Four Program* (New York: H. W. Wilson, 1951), p. 185.

61. Kolko and Kolko, *The Limits of Power*, p. 558.

62. Ibid.

63. *Mutual Security Program Appropriations for 1952*, hearings before a subcommittee of the Committee on Appropriations, H.R., 82nd Congress, 1st Session, p. 750. This point is reiterated in the *Second Report to Congress on the Mutual Security Program* (June 30, 1952), p. 24: "Increased emphasis was placed on building up the national armies of the Associated States of Indochina. . . . As the national armies become stronger, the French will be able to transfer from Indochina to Europe the trained professional officers, non-commissioned officers and enlisted men who are much needed for the build-up of NATO forces."

64. Richard M. Freeland, *The Truman Doctrine and the Origins of McCarthyism* (New York: Knopf, 1972). For a recent popular account, see Charles L. Mee, Jr., *The Marshall Plan: The Launching of the Pax Americana* (New York: Simon and Schuster, 1984).

65. *Emergency Foreign Aid*, hearings before the Committee on Foreign Affairs, H.R., 80th Congress, 1st Session (November 1947), pp. 239, 255.

66. Cited in Dean Acheson, *Present at the Creation: My Years in the State Department* (New York: Signet, 1969), p. 398.

67. Fredrich J. Dobney (ed.), *Selected Papers of Will Clayton* (Baltimore: Johns Hopkins University Press, 1971), pp. 223–224.

68. The argument that Latin American countries would benefit from the

U.S. focus on European recovery is found in "ERP to Aid in Industrial Development in Latin America," statement of U.S. delegate to Economic and Social Council of the Pan American Union on January 30, 1948, *Department of State Bulletin* 28,449 (February 8, 1948): 184; and "Interdependence of the Americas," address by George C. Marshall to Ninth International Conference on American States, Bogotá, April 1, 1948, *Department of State Bulletin* 28,458 (April 11, 1948): 469—473. Internal State Department correspondence was less sanguine; a letter from a division chief in Washington to the U.S. ambassador in Argentina states, for example: "The whole ERP is in a very real sense discriminatory against Latin America. While an attempt is made to confine this discrimination within the bounds of necessity and to balance it with programs assisting Latin America, some discrimination is inherent and unavoidable." *FRUS* 1949, vol. 2, p. 480.

69. Acheson, *Present at the Creation*, pp. 350—351.

70. *FRUS* 1949, vol. 2, p. 560.

71. Samuel P. Hayes (ed.), *The Beginning of American Aid to Southeast Asia: The Griffin Mission of 1950* (Lexington, Mass.: D. C. Heath, 1971), p. 5.

72. *Extension of European Recovery—1950*, hearings before the Committee on Foreign Relations, U.S. Senate, 81st Congress, 2nd Session (February-March 1950), p. 94.

73. David A. Baldwin, *Economic Development and American Foreign Policy* (Chicago: University of Chicago Press, 1966), p. 79.

74. Ibid., p. 102.

75. Louis J. Halle, *The Society of Man* (New York: Harper and Row, 1965), pp. 21—30.

76. Through December 1951, there were 105 Point Four projects in Latin America, 21 in the Near East and Africa, and 16 in South Asia. U.S. Department of State, Technical Cooperation Administration, *Point 4 Projects, July 1 through December 31, 1951* (Washington, D.C., March 1952).

77. Kolko and Kolko, *The Limits of Power*, p. 623.

78. Economic Cooperation Administration, *The Netherlands: Country Study* (Washington, D.C., February 1949), p. 5.

79. *FRUS* 1949, vol. 4, p. 414.

80. Economic Cooperation Administration, *Sixth Report to Congress*, quarter ending September 30, 1949, p. 12.

81. Economic Cooperation Administration, *Ninth Report to Congress*, quarter ending June 30, 1950, pp. 14—15.

82. Organization for European Economic Co-Operation, *Economic Progress and Problems of Western Europe* (Paris, June 1951), p. 123.

83. Economic Cooperation Administration, *Twelfth Report to Congress*, quarter ending March 31, 1951, p. 21.

84. Organization for European Economic Co-Operation, *Europe—The Way Ahead*, fourth annual report of the OEEC (Paris, December 1952), p. 47.

85. Ibid., p. 261.

86. Data from *Balance of Payments of the United States, 1949 – 1951*, a supplement of the *Survey of Current Business* (Washington, D.C.: U.S. Department of Commerce, 1952), pp. 128–131; *Survey of Current Business* 33,6 (June 1953).

87. Organization for European Economic Co-Operation, *Interim Report on the European Recovery Programme, Report of the Overseas Territories Committee* (Paris, 1948), p. 10.

88. Ibid., p. 11.

89. Ibid., p. 38.

90. Economic Cooperation Administration, *A Report on Recovery Progress*, p. 16.

91. *Balance of Payments*, pp. 128–133; *Survey of Current Business* 33,6 (June 1953).

92. Economic Cooperation Administration, *The Sterling Area*, p. 66; see also Economic Cooperation Administration, *Country Data Book: United Kingdom* (March 1950), p. 7.

93. Philip W. Bell, *The Sterling Area in the Postwar World: Internal Mechanism and Cohesion, 1946 – 1952* (London: Oxford University Press, 1956), pp. 56–57.

94. Bob Fitch and Mary Oppenheimer, *Ghana: End of an Illusion* (New York: Monthly Review Press, 1966), pp. 43–44.

95. Mallalieu, *British Reconstruction*, p. 185.

96. Susan Strange, *Sterling and British Policy* (London: Oxford University Press, 1971), p. 67.

97. "Department of State Policy Statement on Indochina, September 27, 1948," *FRUS* 1948, vol. 6, p. 46.

98. Andrew Kamarck, *Economics of African Development* (New York: Praeger, 1967), p. 201.

99. Economic Cooperation Administration, *Eleventh Report to Congress*, quarter ending December 31, 1950, p. 47.

100. Price, *The Marshall Plan*, p. 151.

101. Economic Cooperation Administration, *Eleventh Report to Congress*, quarter ending December 31, 1950, pp. 47–48.

102. Mutual Security Agency press release no. 21, "Big U.S. Tractors to Aid Malaya in Fight Against Community Bands," April 12, 1952.

103. National Planning Association, "The Foreign Aid Programs and the United States Economy," in Special Senate Committee to Study the Foreign Aid Program, *Foreign Aid Program: Compilation of Studies and Surveys* (Washington, D.C.: Government Printing Office, 1957), p. 935.

104. See *FRUS* 1948, vol. 6, pp. 43–49.

105. Hayes, *The Beginning of American Aid*, p. 98.

106. Ibid., pp. 50–51.

107. *FRUS* 1948, vol. 6, pp. 613–616.

108. Ibid., p. 345.

109. Ibid., pp. 345–346.

110. Price, *The Marshall Plan*, p. 217.

111. Kolko and Kolko, *The Limits of Power*, p. 470. The OEEC, always under pressure from the United States to put the best face on things, took a quite contradictory stance in its official publications. On the one hand, it warned as early as 1950 that the best Europe could hope for by 1952 was a dollar deficit of $2.25 billion and concluded, "It is clear . . . that a serious problem will exist after 1952." The OEEC then went on to argue that this problem would be "generally manageable" if certain assumptions were met—most notably major U.S. tariff reductions and increases in imports from Europe. It was evident by this time, however, that such a course was not politically practical in the United States; therefore, the necessary assumptions were not going to be met. See Organization for European Economic Co-Operation, *European Recovery Programme*, second report of the OEEC (Paris, 1950), pp. 21–25, 247–249.

112. J. K. Galbraith, "European Recovery: The Longer View," *Review of Politics* (April 1950): 166–167.

113. Kolko and Kolko, *The Limits of Power*, p. 473.

114. Acheson's confidential memorandum to Truman in February 1950 attests to the growing alarm within the State Department. See *FRUS* 1950, vol. 1, pp. 834–837. Fred Block details the attempts of various agencies of the U.S. government to devise a solution in *The Origins*, chap. 4.

115. Williams, *Tragedy of American Diplomacy*, p. 168; Wexler, *The Marshall Plan Revisited*, p. 252.

116. Economic Cooperation Administration, *Tenth Report to Congress*, quarter ending September 30, 1950, p. 4.

117. Kolko and Kolko, *The Limits of Power*, chap. 17, "The Failure of the Marshall Plan, 1949–1950," pp. 453–476. Although Wexler, *The Marshall Plan Revisited*, sees the Marshall Plan as successfully fulfilling some of its goals, his analysis lends support to the Kolkos' conclusions for the areas they emphasize.

118. Agency for International Development, *U.S. Overseas Loans and Grants and Assistance from International Organizations: Obligations and Loan Authorizations, July 1, 1945–June 30, 1970*. The figures cited include Greece but not Turkey.

119. *Report to the President on Foreign Economic Policies* (Gray Report), (Washington, D.C.: Government Printing Office, November 10, 1950), pp. 4, 10.

120. *FRUS* 1950, vol. 1, pp. 834–835.

121. Ibid., p. 836.

122. For an analysis of this critical decision and of the role of the document of the National Security Council known as NSC-68, see Fred Block, "Economic Instability and Military Strength: The Paradoxes of the 1950 Rearmament Decision," *Politics and Society* 10,1 (1980): 35–58.

123. Ibid., pp. 46–47.

124. Block, *The Origins*, p. 107.

125. Paul G. Hoffman, *Peace Can Be Won* (New York: Doubleday, 1951), p. 91.

Chapter 2

1. There is no complete annual inventory of aid flows. By far the most complete survey is the annual report of the Development Assistance Committee of the Organization for Economic Cooperation and Development, *Development Co-operation: Efforts and Policies of the Members of the Development Assistance Committee*. This is hereafter referred to as DAC, *Review*.

2. See, for example, Dewan C. Vohra, *India's Aid Diplomacy in the Third World* (New Delhi: Vikas, 1980).

3. For an alternative periodization, see John White, *The Politics of Foreign Aid* (New York: St. Martin's Press, 1974), pp. 195–237.

4. John Franklin Cooper, *China's Foreign Aid: An Instrument of Peking's Foreign Policy* (Lexington, Mass.: D. C. Heath, 1976), p. 12; Janos Horvath,

"Economic Aid Flow from the USSR: A Recount of the First Fifteen Years," *Slavic Review* 29,4 (December 1970): 630.

5. See U.S. Department of State, *The Sino-Soviet Economic Offensive in the Less Developed Countries* (Washington, D.C.: Government Printing Office, 1958); updated and republished under various titles in subsequent years, for example, *The Threat of Soviet Economic Policy* (1961).

6. Leo Tansky, *U.S. and U.S.S.R. Aid to Developing Countries: A Comparative Study of India, Turkey, and the U.A.R.* (New York: Praeger, 1967), p. 5.

7. R. P. Sinha, "Soviet Aid and Trade with the Developing World," *Soviet Studies* 26,2 (April 1974): 277–278.

8. The decade of the 1950s was also critical in laying the basis for the "success" of several countries currently promoted as models of development by the major aid institutions, most notably Taiwan and Korea. These countries' relatively good performances on "basic needs" almost certainly stem from the land reform programs carried out under U.S. auspices during these years.

9. Samuel P. Hayes (ed.), *The Beginning of American Aid to Southeast Asia: The Griffin Mission of 1950* (Lexington, Mass.: D. C. Heath, 1971), pp. 12–13.

10. For the evolution of Soviet aid policy, see Roger Kanet (ed.), *The Soviet Union and the Developing Nations* (Baltimore: Johns Hopkins University Press, 1974).

11. William J. Lederer and Eugene Burdick, *The Ugly American* (New York: W. W. Norton, 1958).

12. For descriptions of U.S. and IBRD efforts to head off the establishment of SUNFED by creating first the International Finance Corporation and then the International Development Association, see James Baker, *The International Finance Corporation* (New York: Praeger, 1968), pp. 24–28; David A. Baldwin, *Economic Development and American Foreign Policy 1943–1962* (Chicago: University of Chicago Press, 1966), pp. 95–99; Edward S. Mason and Robert E. Asher, *The World Bank Since Bretton Woods* (Washington, D.C.: Brookings Institution, 1973), pp. 345–350, 381–389; B. E. Matecki, *Establishment of the International Finance Corporation and United States Policy* (New York: Praeger, 1957), pp. 97–108, 123–128, 159; and James H. Weaver, *The International Development Association* (New York: Praeger, 1965), pp. 5, 26–47.

13. For a comparative analysis of the development of regional development

banks, see John White, *Regional Development Banks* (New York: Praeger, 1972).

14. Ronald T. Libby, "International Development Association: A Legal Fiction Designed to Secure an LDC Constituency," *International Organization* 29,4 (Autumn 1975): 1065–1072.

15. Ibid.

16. John Syz, *International Development Banks* (Dobbs Ferry, N.Y.: Oceania, 1974), p. xxvii.

17. World Bank, *Annual Report 1981*, p. 176.

18. Stephen D. Krasner, "Power Structures and Regional Development Banks," *International Organization* 35,2 (Spring 1981): 311, 317, 325.

19. Two useful brief surveys of EEC/Third World relations are Diddy R. M. Hitchens, "Europe and the Third World," paper presented at the 1984 annual meeting of the American Political Science Association, Washington, D.C., 1984; and Miles Kahler, "Europe and Its 'Privileged Partners' in Africa and the Middle East," *Journal of Common Market Studies* 21,1–2 (September/December 1982): 199–218. For more exhaustive detail, see Christopher Stevens (ed.), *EEC and the Third World: A Survey*, vols. 1–3 (London: Overseas Development Institute/Hodder and Stoughton, 1981, 1982, 1983).

20. Richard C. Robarts, *French Development Assistance: A Study in Policy and Administration* (Beverly Hills: Sage Publications, 1974), pp. 17–18.

21. For an analysis of the changing assumptions underlying U.S. aid policy in the 1950s and 1960s, see Robert E. Wood, "Foreign Aid and Social Structure in Underdeveloped Countries: U.S. Economic Aid Policies and Programs, 1948–1970" (Ph.D. dissertation, University of California at Berkeley, 1976), chap. 5.

22. A survey of the administrative structures of the major DAC programs is contained in George Cunningham, *The Management of Aid Agencies: Donor Structures and Procedures for the Administration of Aid to Developing Countries* (London: Croom Helm in association with the Overseas Development Institute, 1974). For Japan, not covered by Cunningham, see Gerald Holtham, "A Rising Sum? Japanese Resource Flows to LDCs," *ODI Review* 1(1974): 46–49; and Alan Rix, *Japan's Economic Aid: Policy-Making and Politics* (New York: St. Martin's Press, 1980).

23. Interpretations of United States foreign aid policy emphasizing the link between "development aid" and counterinsurgency goals include Richard J. Barnet, *Intervention and Revolution* (New York: Meridian, 1968);

Noam Chomsky and Edward S. Herman, *The Washington Connection and Third World Fascism* (Boston: South End Press, 1979); Melvin Gurtov, *The United States Against the Third World: Antinationalism and Intervention* (New York: Praeger, 1974); Michael T. Klare, *War Without End: American Planning for the Next Vietnams* (New York: Vintage, 1972); Harry Magdoff, *The Age of Imperialism* (New York: Monthly Review Press, 1969); Lynn Richards, "The Context of Foreign Aid: Modern Imperialism," *Review of Radical Political Economics* 9,4 (Winter 1977): 43–75; and Richard J. Walton, *Cold War and Counter-Revolution: The Foreign Policy of John F. Kennedy* (Baltimore: Penguin Books, 1972). Many detailed analyses of U.S. aid programs from this perspective may be found in North American Congress on Latin America, *NACLA Newsletter* (subsequently *NACLA Report on the Americas*). For example, see Hector Melo and Israel Yost, "Funding the Empire: U.S. Foreign Aid," *NACLA Newsletter* 4,2 (April 1970): 1–13; Israel Yost, "The Food for Peace Arsenal," *NACLA Newsletter* 5,3 (May-June 1971): 1–7; and the special issue "A.I.D. Police Programs for Latin America 1971–72," *NACLA Newsletter* 5,4 (July-August 1971).

24. Robert L. Ayres, "Breaking the Bank," *Foreign Policy* 43 (Summer 1981): 111; and Robert L. Ayres, *Banking on the Poor: The World Bank and World Poverty* (Cambridge: MIT Press, 1983), pp. 226–228.

25. Recent surveys of OPEC aid include Organization for Economic Cooperation and Development, *Aid from OPEC Countries* (Paris, 1983); and two articles by Zubair Iqbal on Arab institutions in *IMF Survey* (March 21, 1983): 85–87, and (April 4, 1983): 98–100. For discussions of the evolution of OPEC aid institutions, see Edith Hodginson, "OPEC Aid: The Programme of the Newly Rich," *ODI Review* 2 (1975): 15–24; Ibrahim F. I. Shihata and Robert Mabro, "The OPEC Aid Record," *World Development* 7,2 (February 1979): 161–173; Ali A. Mazrui, "The Cultural Aspects of Foreign Aid," *ODI Review* 1 (1978): 1–14; and Ibrahim F. I. Shihata, *The Other Face of OPEC: Financial Assistance to the Third World* (London: Longman Group, 1982).

26. DAC, *1978 Review*, pp. 148, 153.

27. DAC, *1981 Review*, pp. 81, 109.

28. D. N. Prasad, *External Resources in Economic Development of India* (New Delhi: Sterling, 1972), p. 318.

29. Edward S. Mason and Robert E. Asher, *The World Bank Since Bretton Woods* (Washington, D.C.: Brookings Institution, 1973), pp. 219–220.

30. *IMF Survey*, supplement on the Fund (November 1982), p. 15.

31. The literature on Euromarket lending to Third World countries is already vast and is rapidly growing. Useful introductions include George C. Abbott, *International Indebtedness and the Developing Countries* (London: Croom Helm, 1979); Jonathan David Aronson (ed.), *Debt and the Less Developed Countries* (Boulder: Westview Press, 1979); David Gisselquist, *The Political Economics of International Bank Lending* (New York: Praeger, 1981); Lawrence G. Franko and Marilyn J. Seiber (eds.), *Developing Country Debt* (New York: Pergamon Press, 1979); Charles Lipson, "The International Organization of Third World Debt," *International Organization* 35,4 (Autumn 1981): 603–632; Marilyn J. Seiber, *International Borrowing by Developing Countries* (New York: Pergamon Press, 1982); and Eugene Versluysen, *The Political Economy of International Finance* (New York: St. Martin's Press, 1981).

32. Irving S. Friedman, *The Emerging Role of Private Banks in the Developing World* (New York: Citicorp, 1977), p. 86.

33. Benjamin J. Cohen, with Fabio Basagni, *Banks and the Balance of Payments* (London: Croom Helm, 1981), p. ix.

34. Organization for Economic Cooperation and Development, *External Debt of Developing Countries: 1983 Survey* (Paris, 1984), p. 16.

35. *New York Times* (December 21, 1977), p. 53.

36. Richard Bernal, "Transnational Banks, the International Monetary Fund and External Debt of Developing Countries," *Social and Economic Studies* 31,4 (December 1982): 76.

37. DAC, *1980 Review*, p. 161.

38. John H. Makin, *The Global Debt Crisis: America's Growing Involvement* (New York: Basic Books, 1984), p. 4.

39. Ibid.

40. Overall, U.S. banks derive over half their profits from overseas operations. See Peter DeWitt and James F. Petras, "The Political Economy of International Debt," in James F. Petras, with A. Eugene Havens, Morris H. Morley, and Peter DeWitt, *Class, State and Power in the Third World* (Montclair: Allanheld, Osmun, 1981), p. 98.

41. Limited access to Soviet aid is formalized in official ideology by a distinction between countries that are anti-imperialist and even sometimes of a "socialist orientation" and those actively engaged in socialist construction. The USSR accepted Cuba as a "socialist state" in 1972, but virtually all other Third World revolutionary states have been classified in the first cate-

gory. The USSR has explicitly said that assistance to the Third World cannot be allowed to impede the progress of the socialist community. For an excellent discussion of Soviet ideology in relationship to Chile under Allende, see Joseph L. Nogee and John W. Sloan, "Allende's Chile and the Soviet Union: A Policy Lesson for Latin American Nations Seeking Autonomy," *Journal of Interamerican Studies* 21,3 (August 1979) : 339–368.

42. DAC, *1971 Review*, pp. 190–191.

43. Organization for Economic Cooperation and Development, *Geographical Distribution of Financial Flows to Less Developed Countries 1966–1967* (Paris, 1969).

44. DAC, *1981 Review*, p. 106.

45. Ibid., p. 97; Adrian Hewitt, "European Aid Donors," *ODI Review* 2 (1977): 91.

46. DAC, *1981 Review*, p. 93.

47. Ibid., p. 113.

Chapter 3

1. For comparative studies of the management of different aspects of the world economy, see Joan Edelman Spero, *The Politics of International Economic Relations* (New York: St. Martin's Press, 1977).

2. Robert O. Keohane and Joseph S. Nye, *Power and Interdependence: World Politics in Transition* (Boston: Little, Brown, 1977), p. 19.

3. Charles Lipson, "The Transformation of Trade: The Sources and Effects of Regime Change," *International Organization* 36,2 (Spring 1982): 417.

4. Donald J. Puchala and Raymond F. Hopkins, "International Regimes: Lessons from Inductive Analysis," *International Organization* 36,2 (Spring 1982): 247.

5. Stephen D. Krasner, "Structural Causes and Regime Consequences: Regimes as Intervening Variables," *International Organization* 36,2 (Spring 1982): 186.

6. Puchala and Hopkins, "International Regimes," pp. 246–247. Although patterned behavior is said to alert one to the existence of a regime, Puchala and Hopkins (p. 246, fn.) make it clear that regimes are defined by subjectivity, not behavior: "The reality of a regime exists in the subjectivity of individuals who hold, communicate, reinforce, or change the norms and authoritative expectations related to the set of activities and conduct in question."

7. Ibid., p. 270.

8. Oran R. Young, "Regime Dynamics: The Rise and Fall of International Regimes," *International Organization* 36,2 (Spring 1982): 277–279.

9. Stephen D. Krasner, "Regimes and the Limits of Realism: Regimes as Autonomous Variables," *International Organization* 36,2 (Spring 1982): 499.

10. Benjamin J. Cohen, "Balance of Payments Financing: Evolution of a Regime," *International Organization* 36,2 (Spring 1982): 457–478; Charles Lipson, "The International Organization of Third World Debt," *International Organization* 35,4 (Autumn 1981): 603–631.

11. John Gerard Ruggie, "Political Structure and Change in the International Economic Order: The North-South Dimension," in J. G. Ruggie (ed.), *The Antinomies of Interdependence* (New York: Columbia University Press, 1983), pp. 435–436, fn., p. 465.

12. For a sophisticated discussion of how this occurs, see Robert O. Keohane, *After Hegemony: Cooperation and Discord in the World Political Economy* (Princeton: Princeton University Press, 1984).

13. John White, *Regional Development Banks: The Asian, African and Inter-American Development Banks* (New York: Praeger, 1972), p. 12.

14. Even studies of aid from this perspective tend to find evidence of less asymmetry of power than is usually assumed. See Anthony D. Moulton, "On Concealed Dimensions of Third World Involvement in International Economic Organizations," *International Organization* 32,4 (Autumn 1978): 1019–1035.

15. Young, "Regime Dynamics," pp. 282–285.

16. Because of aid's quantifiable nature, the literature on its allocation is vast. Unfortunately, the sophistication of the statistical techniques employed contrasts with the modesty of the results obtained. The studies fall into three rough categories. First, there are studies that try to develop models identifying those factors that predict actual aid allocation. These include Kenneth D. Auerbach, "The Distribution of Multilateral Assistance: A Five Organization Study," *Social Science Quarterly* 57,3 (December 1976): 645–659; Jagdish N. Bhagwati, "Amount and Sharing of Aid," in Charles R. Frank, Jr., et al., *Assisting Developing Countries: Problems of Debts, Burden-Sharing, Jobs and Trade* (New York: Praeger, 1972), pp. 67–281; William R. Cline and Nicholas P. Sargen, "Performance Criteria and Multilateral Aid Allocation," *World Development* 3,6 (June 1975): 383–391; Michael Davenport, "The

Allocation of Foreign Aid: A Cross Section Study," *Indian Economic Journal* 16,4 (April-June 1969): 458–475; Leonard Dudley, "Foreign Aid and the Theory of Alliances," *Review of Economics and Statistics* 61,4 (November 1979): 564–571; Leonard Dudley and Claude Montmarquette, "A Model of the Supply of Bilateral Aid," *American Economic Review* 66,1 (March 1976): 132–142; John A. Edelman and Hollis B. Chenery, "Aid and Income Distribution," in Jagdish N. Bhagwati (ed.), *The New International Economic Order: The North-South Debate* (Cambridge: MIT Press, 1977), pp. 27–49; J. Stephen Hoadley, "Small States as Aid Donors," *International Organization* 34,1 (Winter 1980): 121–137; Paul Isenman, "Biases in Aid Allocations Against Poorer and Larger Countries," *World Development* 4,8 (August 1976): 631–641; Masakatsu Kato, "A Model of U.S. Foreign Aid Allocation: An Application of a Rational Decision-Making Scheme," in John E. Mueller (ed.), *Approaches to Measurement in International Relations* (New York: Appleton-Century-Crofts, 1969), pp. 198–215; Michael Lipton, "Aid Allocation When Aid Is Inadequate: Problems of the Non-Implementation of the Pearson Report," in T. J. Byres (ed.), *Foreign Resources and Economic Development* (London: Frank Cass, 1972), pp. 157–182; William Loehr, David Price, and Satish Raichur, *A Comparison of U.S. and Multilateral Aid Recipients in Latin America, 1957–1971* (Beverly Hills: Sage Professional Papers in International Studies, 1976); R. D. McKinlay, "The Aid Relationship: A Foreign Policy Model and Interpretation of the Distributions of Official Bilateral Economic Aid of the United States, the United Kingdom, France and Germany, 1960–1970," *Comparative Political Studies* 11,4 (January 1979): 411–463; R. McKinlay, "The German Aid Relationship: A Test of the Recipient Need and the Donor Interest Models of the Distribution of German Bilateral Aid 1961–1970," *European Journal of Political Research* 6 (1978): 235–257; R. D. McKinlay and R. Little, "A Foreign-Policy Model of the Distribution of British Bilateral Aid, 1960–1970," *British Journal of Political Science* 8,3 (July 1978): 313–331; R. D. McKinlay and R. Little, "A Foreign Policy Model of U.S. Bilateral Aid Allocation," *World Politics* 30,1 (October 1977): 58–86; R. D. McKinlay and R. Little, "The U.S. Aid Relationship: A Test of the Recipient Need and the Donor Interest Models," *Political Studies* 27,2 (June 1979): 236–250; Alfred Maizels and Machiko K. Nissanke, "Motivations for Aid to Developing Countries," *World Development* 12,9 (1984): 879–900; Kul B. Rai, "Foreign Aid and Voting in the UN General Assembly, 1967–1976," *Journal of Peace Research* 17,3 (1980): 269–277; Edward Thomas Rowe, "National Attributes Associated with

Multilateral and US Bilateral Aid to Latin America: 1960–1971," *International Organization* 32,2 (Spring 1978): 463–475; Pierre Uri, *Development Without Dependence* (New York: Praeger, 1976), chap. 4; and Eugene R. Wittkopf, *Western Bilateral Aid Allocations: A Comparative Study of Recipient State Attributes and Aid Received* (Beverly Hills: Sage Publications, 1972).

A second group of studies focuses on domestic factors in the donor country determining the donor's total level of aid. These include Michael Beenstock, "Political Econometry of Official Development Assistance," *World Development* 8,2 (February 1980): 137–144; and Francis X. Colaco, *Economic and Political Considerations and the Flow of Official Resources to Developing Countries* (Paris: Development Centre, OECD, 1973).

A third type of study has been less concerned with actual aid levels and allocations than with specifying proper ones on the basis of various theoretical assumptions. These include John Conlisk and Donald Huddle, "Allocating Foreign Aid: An Appraisal of a Self-Help Model," *Journal of Development Studies* 5,4 (July 1969): 245–251; J. C. H. Fei and D. S. Paauu, "Foreign Assistance and Self-Help: A Reappraisal of Development Finance," *Review of Economics and Statistics* 47 (August 1965): 251–267; and R. I. McKinnon, "Foreign Exchange Constraints in Economic Development and Efficient Aid Allocation," *Economic Journal* 74 (June 1964): 388–409.

17. Puchala and Hopkins, "International Regimes," p. 270.

18. For the concept of "norm-governed" regime change, see John Gerard Ruggie, "International Regimes, Transactions and Change: Embedded Liberalism in the Postwar Economic Order," *International Organization* 36,2 (Spring 1982): 379–415.

19. Guy Gran, *Development by People* (New York: Praeger, 1983), p. 28.

20. White, *Regional Development Banks*, p. 91.

21. For example, the OPEC Gulf States insisted that Egypt reach agreement with the IMF for a rescheduling agreement to be completed. See Robert N. McCauley, "A Compendium of IMF Troubles: Turkey, Portugal, Peru, Egypt," in Lawrence G. Franko and Marilyn J. Seiber (eds.), *Development Country Debt* (New York: Pergamon Press, 1979), pp. 168–173.

22. Cohen, "Balance of Payments Financing," p. 478.

23. Spero, *The Politics*, provides a useful overview of these efforts. See also Ankie M. M. Hoogvelt, *The Third World in Global Development* (London: Macmillan, 1982); and Robert L. Rothstein, *Global Bargaining: UNCTAD*

and the Quest for a New International Economic Order (Princeton: Princeton University Press, 1979).

24. Commission on Foreign Economic Policy, *Report to the President and the Congress* (Washington, D.C., January 23, 1954), p. 9.

25. For a view of STABEX and the Lomé Convention as "innovative and ground-breaking," see Isebill V. Gruhn, "The Lomé Convention: Inching Towards Interdependence," *International Organization* 30,2 (Spring 1976): 241–262.

26. Organization for Economic Cooperation and Development, *Development Co-operation: Efforts and Policies of the Members of the Development Assistance Committee, 1982 Review* (Paris, 1982), p. 141. This annual publication is hereafter cited as DAC, *Review*. The trade estimate is from the World Bank and is cited in L. C. Raghavan, "It's Now or Never," *South* 30 (April 1983): 15.

27. International Monetary Fund, *Annual Report 1985*, p. 66.

28. Brian Tew, "The Position and Prospects of the International Monetary System in Historical Context," in Tony Killick (ed.), *Adjustment and Financing in the Developing World: The Role of the International Monetary Fund* (Washington, D.C.: International Monetary Fund, 1982), p. 195.

29. It is official U.S. policy, stated by the National Advisory Council on International Monetary and Financial Policies, that "debt relief should not be given as a form of development assistance." Consistent with this position, the United States and most other advanced capitalist countries have argued that questions of debt relief lie outside the province of UNCTAD. See Marilyn J. Seiber, *International Borrowing by Developing Countries* (New York: Pergamon Press, 1981), pp. 128–129, 155.

30. Rosemary E. Galli, "The United Nations Development Program, 'Development,' and Multinational Corporations," *Latin American Perspectives* 3,4 (Fall 1976): 67–78. For a critique of UN agricultural development programs in terms of their penetration by private interests, see Susan George, *How the Other Half Dies: The Real Reasons for World Hunger* (London: Penguin, 1976), esp. chap. 9.

31. Gruhn, "The Lomé Convention."

32. Congressional Research Service, Library of Congress, *Soviet Policy and United States Response in the Third World*, report prepared for the Committee on Foreign Affairs, U.S. House of Representatives (Washington, D.C.: Government Printing Office, March 1981), pp. 257–258.

33. See, for example, Joanna Moss and John Ravenhill, "Trade Developments During the First Lomé Convention," *World Development* 10,10 (October 1982): 841–856; and Constantine V. Vaitsos, "From the Ugly American to the Ugly European: The Role of Western Europe in North-South Relations," in Harry Makler, Alberto Martinelli, and Neil Smelser (eds.), *The New International Economy* (Beverly Hills: Sage Publications, 1982), pp. 167–190.

34. World Bank, *Annual Report 1982*, pp. 11–14.

35. Paul N. Rosenstein-Rodan, "The Consortia Technique," in Richard Gardner and Max Millikan (eds.), *The Global Partnership: International Agencies and Economic Development* (New York: Praeger, 1968) pp. 223–230.

36. One study of the OECD-sponsored consortium for Turkey shows how the Turkish government was able to use the pledging process to put donors on the defensive. See Milton J. Esman and Daniel S. Cheever, *The Common Aid Effort* (Columbus: Ohio State University Press, 1967), pp. 261, 298–303.

37. For a useful analysis of the functioning of one consultative group, see Just Faaland (ed.), *Aid and Influence: The Case of Bangladesh* (New York: St. Martin's Press, 1981).

38. Isenman, "Biases in Aid Allocations."

39. Quoted in David A. Baldwin, *Economic Development and American Foreign Policy, 1943–1962* (Chicago: University of Chicago Press, 1966), p. 79.

40. Testimony of Peter McPherson, *Foreign Assistance Legislation for Fiscal Year 1982*, pt. 1. Hearings before the Committee on Foreign Affairs, H.R., 97th Congress, 1st Session, March 1981, pp. 250–251.

41. Baldwin, *Economic Development*, p. 37.

42. David Baldwin, "Foreign Aid, Intervention, and Influence," *World Politics* 21,3 (April 1969): 425–447. See also David Baldwin, "The International Bank in Political Perspective," *World Politics* 18,1 (October 1965): 68–81.

43. John Syz, *International Development Banks* (Dobbs Ferry, N.Y.: Oceana, 1974), p. 175.

44. Marina Von Neumann Whitman, *Government Risk-Sharing in Foreign Investment* (Princeton: Princeton University Press, 1965).

45. For examples, see Cheryl Payer, *The World Bank: A Critical Analysis* (New York: Monthly Review Press, 1982), esp. chap. 5.

46. U.S. Department of the Treasury, *United States Participation in the*

Multilateral Development Banks in the 1980s (Washington, D.C.: Department of the Treasury, 1982), pp. 28–30, 2, 7.

47. For a detailed exploration of this issue, see Robert E. Wood, "Foreign Aid and the Capitalist State in Underdeveloped Countries," *Politics and Society* 10,1 (1980): 1–34.

48. Whitman, *Government Risk-Sharing*, p. 256.

49. Organization for Economic Cooperation and Development, *Resources for the Developing World: The Flow of Financial Resources to Less Developed Countries, 1962–1968*, p. 199.

50. *IMF Survey* (April 18, 1983), p. 115.

51. Andres Federman et al., "Troubled Matchmaker Seeks a Formula for Security," *South* 27 (January 1983): 67.

52. *World Bank News* 2,35 (September 15, 1983): 3.

53. Peter Heller, "The Underfinancing of Recurrent Development Costs," *Finance and Development* 16,1 (March 1979): 41.

54. Joan M. Nelson and Gustav Ranis, *Measures to Ensure the Effective Use of Aid* (AID Discussion Paper No. 12, September 1966), p. 8. See also Clarence S. Gulick and Joan M. Nelson, *Promoting Effective Development Policies: AID Experience in the Developing Countries* (AID Discussion Paper No. 9, September 1965); and Joan M. Nelson, *Aid, Influence, and Foreign Policy* (New York: MacMillan, 1968).

55. U.S. Department of the Treasury, *United States Participation*, p. 78.

56. Ibid., pp. 35–36.

57. Joseph Gold, *Conditionality* (Washington, D.C.: IMF Pamphlet Series No. 31, 1979), pp. 2, 5.

58. Ibid., p. 9.

59. David Gisselquist, *The Political Economics of International Bank Lending* (New York: Praeger, 1981), p. 197.

60. Sidney Dell, "Stabilization: The Political Economy of Overkill," *World Development* 10,8 (August 1982): 603.

61. See "Guidelines on Conditionality," adopted March 2, 1979, in International Monetary Fund, *Annual Report 1979*, pp. 136–138.

62. Despite the IMF managing director's assurance that "the Fund does not rely on any particular model or approach" and that "it would be impossible to devise any one model of adjustment that could apply across the board to all Fund members" (*IMF Survey*, November 1982 supplement on the Fund, p. 2), official IMF documents explicitly prescribe the particular model for which the Fund has become justly famous. See, for example,

Gold, *Conditionality*, pp. 30–34; Manuel Guitian, *Fund Conditionality: Evolution of Principles and Practices* (Washington, D.C.: IMF Pamphlet Series No. 38, 1981), esp. pp. 14–16, 30–40; A. W. Hooke, *The International Monetary Fund: Its Evolution, Organization and Activities* (Washington, D.C.: IMF Pamphlet Series No. 37, 2nd ed., 1982), esp. pp. 33–35; and Andrew Crockett, "Issues in the Use of Fund Resources," *Finance and Development* 19,2 (June 1982): 10–15. Outside observers who see a basically unchanged IMF approach to conditionality include Dell, "Stabilization"; Sidney Dell and Roger Lawrence, *The Balance of Payments Adjustment Process in Developing Countries* (New York: Pergamon Press, 1980); and Tony Killick, Graham Bird, Jennifer Sharpley, and Mary Sutton, "IMF Policies in Developing Countries: The Case for Change," *The Banker* 134,698 (April 1984): 31–36.

63. Richard S. Eckaus, "Observations on the Conditionality of International Financial Institutions," *World Development* 10,9 (September 1982): 777.

64. Quoted in Cheryl Payer, *The Debt Trap: The International Monetary Fund and the Third World* (New York: Monthly Review Press, 1974), p. 11.

65. For an excellent discussion of the normative content of these seemingly technical concepts, see Cheryl Payer, *The World Bank: A Critical Analysis* (New York: Monthly Review Press, 1982), chap. 3.

66. Organization for Economic Cooperation and Development, *Geographical Distribution of Financial Flows to Developing Countries* (Paris, 1981), pp. 230–231.

67. For a discussion of different definitions and reporting systems of Third World debt, see Seiber, *International Borrowing*, p. 34.

68. Lipson, "The International Organization of Third World Debt." See also Charles Lipson, "The IMF, Commercial Banks and Third World Debts," in Aronson, *Debt and the Less Developed Countries*, pp. 317–333.

69. Stephen D. Cohen, with Jerel A. Rosati, "The Political Economy of US Policy on LDC Debt Relief: Executive-Legislative Relations, 1977–1980," *World Development* 10,2 (February 1982): 147–160.

70. Quoted in Gisselquist, *The Political Economics*, p. 191.

71. Ibid., p. 192.

72. Friedman, *The Emerging Role of Private Banks*.

73. Lars Schoultz, "Politics, Economics, and U.S. Participation in Multilateral Development Banks," *International Organization* 36,3 (Summer 1982): 556.

74. Seiber, *International Borrowing*, Appendix 1, p. 155.

75. McCauley, "A Compendium of IMF Troubles," pp. 148, 176.

76. DAC, *1983 Review*, p. 213.

77. "World Bank's Graduation Policy Reaffirmed," *Finance and Development* 19,2 (June 1982): 3.

Chapter 4

1. The major omissions from the data summarized here and in Table 17 are communist aid, UN aid, EEC multilateral aid, and OPEC multilateral aid.

2. See Zubair Iqbal, "Arab Institutions Provide Development Finance; Supplement Capital Flows to Developing Nations," *IMF Survey* (March 21, 1938), pp. 85–87; and "Arab Regional, Multilateral Finance Institutions Channel Assistance to the Developing Countries," *IMF Survey* (April 4, 1983), pp. 98–100.

3. Congressional Budget Office, *Assisting the Developing Countries: Foreign Aid and Trade Policies of the United States* (Washington, D.C.: Government Printing Office, 1980), pp. 50–51.

4. Organization for Economic Cooperation and Development, *Development Co-operation: Efforts and Policies of the Members of the Development Assistance Committee, 1982 Review* (Paris,1982), pp. 228–231. This annual publication is hereafter referred to as DAC, *Review*.

5. EEC food aid disbursements were $437 million; WFP commitments were $296 million. DAC, *1981 Review*, p. 96; World Food Programme, *Report of the Ninth Session of the United Nations/FAO Committee on Food Aid Policies and Programmes, Rome, 13–24 April 1980*, and *Report of the Tenth Session . . . 13–21 October 1980*.

6. DAC, *1981 Review*, p. 113.

7. Organization for Economic Cooperation and Development, *Geographical Distribution of Financial Flows to Developing Countries, 1977/1980* (Paris, 1981), pp. 70–71.

8. Frances Moore Lappé, Joseph Collins, and David Kinley, *Aid as Obstacle: Twenty Questions about our Foreign Aid and the Hungry* (San Francisco: Institute for Food and Development Policy, 1980), p. 15.

9. U.S. Agency for International Development, *U.S. Overseas Loans and Grants and Assistance from International Organizations: Obligations and Loan Authorizations, July 1, 1945–September 30, 1983*, pp. 4, 13, 18.

10. Shada Islam, "Keeping EEC Aid on the Straight and Narrow," *South* 32 (June 1983): 37.

11. World Bank, *The World Bank and International Finance Corporation* (Washington, D.C., 1983), p. 33.

12. See *Operations Reports* of AID and its predecessors.

13. International Finance Corporation, *Annual Report 1980*, p. 2.

14. DAC, *1982 Review*, pp. 230–231.

15. See Gerald Holtham, "A Rising Sum? Japanese Resource Flows to LDCs," *ODI Review* 1 (1974): 49; and Alan G. Rix, "The Misugoro Project: Japanese Aid Policy and Indonesia," *Pacific Affairs* 52,1 (Spring 1979): 56.

16. Albert Szymanski, *The Logic of Imperialism* (New York: Praeger, 1981), pp. 239–240.

17. Cheryl Payer, *The World Bank: A Critical Analysis* (New York: Monthly Review Press, 1982), p. 118. Perhaps the strangest explanation of the avoidance of industrial projects by the aid agencies is offered by John White, who argues that it results from "the desire to avoid embarrassment—in the sense of taking on projects where profitability offers a clear standard of success or failure"; John White, "International Agencies: The Case for Proliferation," in G. K. Helleiner (ed.), *A World Divided: The Less Developed Countries in the International Economy* (Cambridge: Cambridge University Press, 1976), p. 279. On this basis, one would have to argue that the IFC is braver than its parent institution.

18. For the implications of this strategy for the nature of the state itself, see Robert E. Wood, "Foreign Aid and the Capitalist State in Underdeveloped Countries," *Politics and Society* 10,1 (1980): 1–34.

19. The official data on industrial sector lending by MDBs have been adjusted in Table 18 in several ways. First, loans to European LDCs (Portugal and Romania) have been excluded. Second, loans for general research or pre-investment surveys, which do not involve direct expansion of industrial capacity, have also been excluded. Third, credit schemes for individual producers, elementary food processing, and a few other projects of questionable industrial relevance have also been excluded.

20. Rehman Sobhan, *The Crisis of External Dependence: The Political Economy of Foreign Aid to Bangladesh* (Dhaka: University Press, 1982), p. 37.

21. Bertil Walstedt, *State Manufacturing Enterprise in a Mixed Economy: The Turkish Case* (Baltimore: Johns Hopkins University Press, for the World Bank, 1980).

22. World Bank, Bank News Release No. 80/86 (May 1, 1980), "World Bank Approves $69 Million Loan to Egypt for Second Textile Project."

23. World Bank, IDA News Release No. 82/32 (February 4, 1982), "Bangladesh Textile Mills to be Rehabilitated with IDA Assistance."

24. World Bank, *World Development Report 1983*, p. 86.

25. World Bank, Bank News Release No. 80/15 (October 18, 1979), "World Bank Lends $80 Million for Nickel Project in Colombia."

26. World Bank, Bank News Release No. 79/50 (March 8, 1979), "World Bank Lends $98 Million for Aluminum Project in Brazil."

27. Payer, *The World Bank*, p. 121.

28. Ibid., p. 146.

29. Edward S. Mason and Robert E. Asher, *The World Bank Since Bretton Woods* (Washington, D.C.: Brookings Institution, 1973), pp. 252–253.

30. Barend A. de Vries, "Public Policy and the Private Sector," *Finance and Development* 18,3 (September 1981): 11–15; Chauncey F. Dewey and Harinder S. Kohli, "Market Factors in Large Industrial Development Projects," *Finance and Development* 19,2 (June 1982): 28–32.

31. Dewey and Kohli, "Market Factors," p. 29.

32. Ibid., p. 30.

33. Ibid., p. 29.

34. Ibid., p. 31.

35. De Vries, "Public Policy," p. 13.

36. Dewey and Kohli, "Market Factors," p. 32.

37. Ibid., p. 32.

38. Payer, *The World Bank*, p. 112.

39. World Bank, *World Development Report 1983*, pp. 78–87; see also Mary M. Shirley, *Managing State-Owned Enterprises* (Washington, D.C.: World Bank Staff Working Paper No. 577, 1983).

40. World Bank, *Accelerated Development in Sub-Saharan Africa: An Agenda for Action* (Washington, D.C., 1981), p. 4.

41. Inter-American Development Bank, *The Role of the Bank in Latin America in the 1980's* (Washington, D.C., April 1981), p. 13.

42. Ibid., p. 14.

43. "Progress Made on Investment Corporation," *IDB News* (July 1983), p. 3; "Shares Allocated for Investment Corporation," *IBD News* (December 1984), p. 1.

44. Inter-American Development Bank, *The Role of the Bank*, p. 13.

45. International Finance Corporation, *Annual Report 1981*, p. 2.

46. Ibid., pp. 4, 6–7, 15.

47. Ibid., pp. 18–19.

48. Ibid., p. 15.

49. Marina Von Neumann Whitman, *Government Risk-Sharing in Foreign Investment* (Princeton: Princeton University Press, 1965), p. 2; and *Foreign Assistance Program: Annual Report to Congress*, 1962–1970. The Inter-American Development Bank, which unlike the World Bank does not require a government guarantee of all loans, also made direct loans to private enterprises during this period. See Sidney Dell, *The Inter-American Development Bank: A Study in Development Financing* (New York: Praeger, 1971), pp. 131–133.

50. Whitman, *Government Risk-Sharing*, p. 281; *Foreign Assistance Program: Annual Report to Congress*, 1964–1970.

51. Over one-third of Cooley loans in the Near East and South Asia were made to U.S. fertilizer companies. For a discussion of how Cooley loans were used to "break the barrier" of Indian resistance to foreign private investment in this sector, see the testimony by William Gaud in *Foreign Assistance, 1965*, hearings before the Committee on Foreign Relations, U.S. Senate, 89th Congress, 1st Session, pp. 543–544.

52. Overseas Private Investment Corporation, *Finance Handbook* (Washington, D.C., May 1980), pp. 6–7.

53. Overseas Private Investment Corporation, *Annual Report 1981*, pp. 51–52.

54. Ibid., p. 46.

55. Overseas Private Investment Corporation, "Background Information Release, RJ/589," p. 7.

56. Sukehiro Hasegawa, *Japanese Foreign Aid: Policy and Practice* (New York: Praeger, 1975), p. 139.

57. Holtham, "A Rising Sum?" pp. 49–51.

58. Rix, "The Misugoro Project," p. 58.

59. DAC, *1981 Review*, pp. 152–153, 202.

60. Although it arrived too late to be used in this discussion, readers interested in the historical evolution of U.S. investment guarantees should consult the important recent study by Charles Lipson, *Standing Guard: Protecting Foreign Capital in the Nineteenth and Twentieth Centuries* (Berkeley and Los Angeles: University of California Press, 1985).

61. *The Foreign Assistance Program: Report to the Congress, Fiscal Year 1970*,

p. 71; and Overseas Private Investment Corporation, "Background Information Release," pp. 3–4.

62. Overseas Private Investment Corporation, *Annual Report 1979*, p. 37.

63. Overseas Private Investment Corporation, *Annual Report 1981*, p. 5.

64. Overseas Private Investment Corporation, *Annual Report 1982*, p. 22.

65. Ibid., p. 1 insert.

66. Cynthia Arnson and William Goodfellow, "OPIC: Insuring the Status Quo," *International Policy Report* 3,2 (September 1977): 5.

67. Iran in August 1983 agreed to repay in full its loans to the Export-Import Bank, in arrears since the hostage crisis in 1979, including interest, which had been accruing at a rate of $66,000 a day. The total was $419.5 million (*New York Times* [August 24, 1983], p. A1). OPIC's claims remain before the Iran-U.S. Claims Tribunal.

68. Arnson and Goodfellow, "OPIC," p. 6.

69. Overseas Private Investment Corporation, *Annual Report 1981*, pp. 53–56.

70. *Overseas Private Investment Corporation: A Critical Analysis*, report prepared for House Committee on Foreign Affairs (Washington, D.C.: Government Printing Office, 1973), p. 89.

71. Ibid., pp. 45–46.

72. Robert Mandel, "The Overseas Private Investment Corporation and International Investment," *Columbia Journal of World Business* 19,1 (Spring 1984): 91.

73. Jeffrey B. Burnham, "OPIC's Mixed Mandates: A Case Study of the Impact of Pluralism on Congress' Ability to Contribute to Foreign Policy Formulation," paper presented at the 1984 annual meeting of the American Political Science Association, Washington, D.C., August 30–September 2, 1984, p. 20.

74. World Bank, *World Development Report 1983*, p. 17; and Ibrahim F. I. Shihata, "Increasing Private Capital Flows to LDCs," *Finance and Development* 12,4 (December 1984): 8.

75. "A Conversation with Mr. Clausen," *Finance and Development* 19,4 (December 1982): 7.

76. Shirley Boskey, *Problems and Practices of Development Banks* (Baltimore: Johns Hopkins University Press, for the International Bank for Reconstruction and Development, 1959), p. 4.

77. David L. Gordon, *Development Finance Companies, State and Privately Owned: A Review* (Washington, D.C.: World Bank Staff Working Paper No. 578, 1983), pp. 3, 8.

78. World Bank, *Development Finance Companies: Sector Policy Paper* (Washington, D.C., April 1976), p. 11.

79. Wolfgang Friedman et al., *International Financial Aid* (New York: Columbia University Press, 1966), p. 222.

80. Gordon, *Development Finance Companies*, p. 47.

81. World Bank, Bank News Release No. 82/15 (October 8, 1981), "India Receives World Bank Loan for Industrial Credit"; and Bank News Release No. 80/92 (May 15, 1980), "World Bank Lends $100 Million for Development Finance Company in India."

82. Whitman, *Government Risk-Sharing*, p. 275; *Foreign Assistance and Related Agencies Appropriations for 1970*, hearings before a subcommittee of the Committee on Appropriations, H.R., 91st Congress, 1st Session, part 2, pp. 317–319; *Foreign Assistance Program: Annual Report to Congress, Fiscal Year 1970*, pp. 54–68.

83. Mason and Asher, *The World Bank*, p. 834.

84. Inter-American Development Bank, *The IDB's First Decade and Perspectives for the Future* (Washington, D.C., 1970), p. 27.

85. Asian Development Bank, *Annual Report 1980*, p. 33.

86. William Diamond (ed.), *Development Finance Companies: Aspects of Policy and Operation* (Baltimore: Johns Hopkins University Press, 1968), p. 2.

87. Robert W. Adler and Raymond F. Mikesell, *Public External Financing of Development Banks in Developing Countries* (Eugene: Bureau of Business and Economic Research, University of Oregon, 1966), p. 61.

88. World Bank, *Development Finance Companies*, p. 14.

89. Ibid.

90. Gordon, *Development Finance Companies*, p. 39.

91. World Bank, Bank News Release No. 78/116 (June 19, 1978), "World Bank Approves $60 Million for Industrial Development in Nigeria."

92. World Bank, *Development Finance Companies*, p. 3; and World Bank, *Annual Reports 1976–1981*.

93. Mason and Asher, *The World Bank*, p. 362.

94. Joseph A. Kane, *Development Banking: An Economic Appraisal* (Lexington, Mass.: D. C. Heath, 1975), pp. 100–102, 110.

95. Gordon, *Development Finance Companies*, p. 16.

96. Kane, *Development Banking*, p. 114.

97. Ibid., p. 97.

98. Adler and Mikesell, *Public External Financing*, p. 39.

99. World Bank, *Employment and Development of Small Enterprises: Sector Policy Paper* (Washington, D.C., February 1978), pp. 7–8, 31–32, 53.

100. Ibid., pp. 18, 53.

101. World Bank, *Development Finance Companies*, p. 5.

102. Stacey H. Widdicombe, Jr., *The Performance of Industrial Development Corporations: The Case of Jamaica* (New York: Praeger, 1972).

103. P. M. Mathew, "Relations Between Governments and DFCs," in Diamond, *Development Finance Companies*, pp. 98–99.

104. Mason and Asher, *The World Bank*, p. 365.

105. See Kane, *Development Banking*, chap. 5.

106. Overseas Private Investment Corporation, *Annual Report 1981*, pp. 53–56.

107. World Bank, Bank News Release No. 81/84 (May 11, 1981), "World Bank to Assist Industrial Sector in the Philippines."

108. World Bank, IDA News Release No. 82/15 (November 5, 1981), "IDA Approves Credit to Pakistan."

109. World Bank, Bank News Release No. 82/6 (July 16, 1981), "Morocco Receives Two World Bank Loans for Industrial Development."

110. World Bank, Bank News Release No. 80/7 (September 6, 1979), "World Bank Provides $80 Million in Loans for Private Sector Textile Project in Turkey."

111. Congressional Budget Office, *Assisting the Developing Countries*, p. 24.

112. Mason and Asher, *The World Bank*, p. 431.

113. Joan M. Nelson, *Aid, Influence and Foreign Policy* (New York: Macmillan, 1968), p. 77.

114. Congressional Budget Office, *Assisting the Developing Countries*, p. 34.

115. Norman Palmer, *South Asia and United States Policy* (Boston: Houghton Mifflin, 1966), p. 156.

116. *Foreign Assistance Program: Annual Report to the Congress, Fiscal Year 1964*, p. 4.

117. J. Russell Andrus and Azizali F. Mohammed, *Trade, Finance and Development in Pakistan* (Stanford: Stanford University Press, 1966), p. 48.

118. Stephen Lewis, *Pakistan, Industrialization and Trade Policies* (London: Oxford University Press, 1970), p. 35.

119. Michael Barratt Brown, *The Economics of Imperialism* (Harmondsworth, Middlesex: Penguin, 1974), p. 226.

120. Nelson, *Aid, Influence and Foreign Policy*, pp. 77–78.

121. DAC, *1972 Review*, pp. 218–219, 228–229.

122. Congressional Budget Office, *Assisting the Developing Countries*, p. 20.

123. IMF, *Annual Report 1983*, p. 85; and World Bank, *Annual Report 1983*, p. 131.

124. World Bank, *Annual Report 1981*, p. 69.

125. Ibid., p. 70.

126. World Bank, *Annual Report 1980*, p. 68.

127. U.S. Department of the Treasury, *United States Participation in the Multilateral Development Banks in the 1980s* (Washington, D.C.: Department of the Treasury, 1982), p. 177.

128. Philip Daniel, "Accelerated Development in Sub-Saharan Africa: An Agenda for Structural Adjustment Lending?" *Bulletin, Institute of Development Studies, Sussex*, 14,1 (January 1983): 13.

129. World Bank, *Annual Report 1981*, p. 70.

130. For a defense of "outward-oriented policies with low protection" by an economist long associated with the World Bank, see Bela Balassa, "Shifting Patterns of World Trade and Competition," World Bank Reprint Series No. 231.

131. See the list of "key components of structural adjustment operations" for eight countries in Pierre M. Landell-Mills, "Structural Adjustment Lending: Early Experience," *Finance and Development* 18,4 (December 1981): 19. For a case study of the Bank's approach to an industrial sector, see Barend A. de Vries and Willem Brakel, *Restructuring of Manufacturing Industry: The Experience of the Textile Industry in Pakistan, Philippines, Portugal, and Turkey* (Washington, D.C.: World Bank Staff Working Paper No. 558, 1983).

132. World Bank, *Annual Report 1981*, p. 70.

133. World Bank, *Annual Report 1983*, p. 118.

Introduction to Part Two

1. Robert L. Ayres, "Breaking the Bank," *Foreign Policy* 43 (Summer 1981): 106.

2. Eugene W. Castle, *The Great Giveaway: The Realities of Foreign Aid* (Chicago: H. Regenery, 1957). For an academic critique from the Right, see P. T. Bauer, *Dissent on Development* (Cambridge: Harvard University Press, 1972), pp. 96–112; P. T. Bauer and B. S. Yamey, "The Pearson Report: A Review," in T. J. Byres (ed.), *Foreign Resources and Economic Development* (London: Frank Cass, 1972); and P. T. Bauer and Basil S. Yamey, "Foreign Aid: What Is At Stake?" in W. Scott Thompson (ed.), *The Third World: Premises of U.S. Policy* (San Francisco: Institute for Contemporary Studies, 1983), pp. 115–135.

3. For a sampling of critiques of aid from the Left that assume the efficacy of aid, see Walden Bello, David Kinley, and Elaine Elinson, *Development Debacle: The World Bank in the Philippines* (San Francisco: Institute for Food and Development Policy, 1982); Robert Carty and Virginia Smith, *Perpetuating Poverty: The Political Economy of Canadian Foreign Aid* (Toronto: Between the Lines, 1981); K. T. Fann and Donald C. Hodges (eds.), *Readings in U.S. Imperialism* (Boston: Porter Sargent, 1971); Susan George, *How the Other Half Dies: The Real Reasons for World Hunger* (Harmondsworth, Middlesex: Penguin Books, 1976); Felix Greene, *The Enemy: What Every American Should Know About Imperialism* (New York: Vintage, 1970); Teresa Hayter, *Aid as Imperialism* (Harmondsworth, Middlesex: Penguin Books, 1971); Frances Moore Lappé, Joseph Collins, and David Kinley, *Aid as Obstacle: Twenty Questions about Our Foreign Aid and the Hungry* (San Francisco: Institute for Food and Development Policy, 1980); Cheryl Payer, *The World Bank: A Critical Analysis* (New York: Monthly Review Press, 1982); Robert I. Rhodes (ed.), *Imperialism and Underdevelopment* (New York: Monthly Review Press, 1970); and Steve Weissman et al. (eds.), *The Trojan Horse: A Radical Look at Foreign Aid* (San Francisco: Ramparts Press, 1974).

Chapter 5

1. Mahbub ul Haq, "Changing Emphasis of the Bank's Lending Policies," in World Bank, *The World Bank and the World's Poorest* (Washington, D.C.: World Bank, 1980), p. 4.

2. Jasper Ingersoll, "Anthropologists and the Agency for International Development (A.I.D.): An Old Hate Relationship and a New Love Affair," *Anthropological Quarterly* 50,4 (October 1977): 201.

3. Richard Jolly, "The World Employment Conference: The Enthronement of Basic Needs," *ODI Review* 2 (1976): 31–44. The United States

voted against the basic needs theme at the ILO conference but soon adopted the basic needs language. See Harlan Cleveland, "Introduction: Toward an International Poverty Line," in John McHale and Magda Cordell McHale, *Basic Human Needs: A Framework for Action* (New Brunswick, N.J.: Transaction Books, 1978), p. 10.

4. Organization for Economic Cooperation and Development, *Development Co-operation: Efforts and Policies of the Members of the Development Assistance Committee, 1978 Review* (Paris, 1978), Annex 1, "Statements by DAC Members on Development Co-operation for Economic Growth and Meeting Basic Human Needs." This annual publication is hereafter referred to as DAC, *Review*.

5. Bettina S. Hurni, *The Lending Policy of the World Bank in the 1970s: Analysis and Evaluation* (Boulder: Westview Press, 1980), p. 5.

6. Quoted in Peter J. Henriot, "Development Alternatives: Problems, Strategies, Values," in Charles K. Wilber (ed.), *The Political Economy of Development and Underdevelopment* (New York: Random House, 1979), p. 9.

7. Hollis Chenery, "Introduction," in Hollis Chenery et al., *Redistribution with Growth* (New York: Oxford University Press, for the World Bank, 1974), p. xiii.

8. Paul Streeten, "From Growth to Basic Needs," in World Bank, *Poverty and Basic Needs* (Washington, D.C.: World Bank, 1980), p. 5.

9. According to Ho Kwon Ping: "McNamara's own disenchantment with the war and American inability to suppress national liberation movements militarily led to his transformation from war minister to aid-giver, and to the liberal view that the best and only effective way to combat revolution in the Third World is to provide development assistance to weak governments"; "End of the McNamara Era," *Far Eastern Economic Review* 109,39 (September 19, 1980): 106.

10. *Indochina Newsletter* (November-December 1982), p. 12.

11. Robert L. Ayres, "Breaking the Bank," *Foreign Policy* 43 (Summer 1981): 111. See also Robert L. Ayres, *Banking on the Poor: The World Bank and World Poverty* (Cambridge: MIT Press, 1983), pp. 226–227.

12. Quoted in Escott Reid, *Strengthening the World Bank* (Chicago: Adlai Stevenson Institute, 1973), p. 34.

13. Ibid., p. 179.

14. John H. Adler, "Development Theory and the Bank's Development Strategy—A Review," *Finance and Development* 14,4 (December 1977): 33.

15. Graciela Chichilnisky, *Basic Needs and the North/South Debate* (New York: Institute for World Order, 1982), p. 9.

16. Peace Corps, Office of Programming and Training Coordination, *Working Draft Discussion Papers: Basic Human Needs Perspectives of Peace Corps Programming* (Washington, D.C., 1978), p. 1.

17. DAC, *1977 Review*, p. 9.

18. Mahbub ul Haq, "Foreword," in Paul Streeten et al., *First Things First: Meeting Basic Human Needs in the Developing Countries* (New York: Oxford University Press, for the World Bank, 1981), p. vii.

19. DAC, *1978 Review*, p. 30. Steven H. Arnold, *Implementing Development Assistance: European Approaches to Basic Needs* (Boulder: Westview Press, 1982).

20. For an outline of a "Left" version of basic needs, see David Seddon's report on the struggle for basic needs in Nepal in United Nations Research Institute for Social Development, Popular Participation Programme, *Dialogue About Participation* 2 (Geneva: UNPISD/82/C.6, 1982), pp. 129–134.

21. For a discussion of the origins of the "New Directions" approach, see the volume by Donald R. Mickelwait, Charles F. Sweet, and Elliott R. Morse: *New Directions in Development: A Study of U.S. AID* (Boulder: Westview Press, 1979).

22. C. L. G. Bell, "The Political Framework," in Chenery et al., *Redistribution with Growth*, p. 56.

23. Montek S. Ahluwalia, "The Scope for Policy Intervention," in ibid., p. 79.

24. Ibid., pp. 80–81.

25. Robert W. McNamara, *Address to the Board of Governors* (Washington, D.C.: World Bank, September 1, 1975), p. 14.

26. International Labor Organization, *Employment, Growth and Basic Needs: A One-World Problem* (Geneva, 1976).

27. *First Things First: Meeting Basic Human Needs in the Developing Countries* was written by Paul Streeten, with Shahid Javed Burki, Mahbub ul Haq, Norman Hicks, and Frances Stewart. Streeten describes the book as a "personal document, reflecting the view of the author," but also as an attempt "to distill the lessons of the World Bank's work on basic needs that started early in 1978." Streeten and his colleagues have produced as well a voluminous array of articles on basic needs, some of them providing more technical and quantitative support for the arguments in *First Things First*. A number of these have been published in *World Development*, which Streeten edits.

28. For an analysis that emphasizes the differences between a basic needs approach and a "redistribution with growth" approach, see Ayres, *Banking on the Poor*, pp. 83–91. Continuing differences within the World Bank are

also emphasized in William Ascher, "New Development Approaches and the Adaptability of International Agencies: The Case of the World Bank," *International Organization* 37,3 (Summer 1983): 415–439. For an analysis that contrasts, perhaps overly neatly, the World Bank's approach to rural development with that of AID and the United Nations, see Dennis A. Rondinelli and Kenneth Ruddle, "Coping with Poverty in International Assistance Policy: An Evaluation of Spatially Integrated Investment Strategies," *World Development* 6,4 (April 1978): 479–497.

29. Streeten, "From Growth to Basic Needs," p. 7.

30. Streeten et al., *First Things First*, p. 93.

31. Ibid., p. 52.

32. Robert W. McNamara, "Introduction," in World Bank, *Poverty and Basic Needs*, p. 3.

33. Robert W. McNamara, "Introduction," in World Bank, *The World Bank*, p. 3.

34. Streeten et al., *First Things First*, p. 17.

35. The literature on peasant revolutions is replete with discussions of peasant egalitarianism, sometimes viewed as a threat to the revolutionary process envisioned by urban revolutionary elites. For example, see James C. Scott, "Revolution in the Revolution: Peasants and Commissars," *Theory and Society*, 7,1–2 (March 1979): esp. 120–123.

36. Streeten et al., *First Things First*, p. 16.

37. World Bank, *World Development Report 1978*, p. 43.

38. Milton J. Esman and Associates, *Landlessness and Nearlandlessness in Developing Countries* (Ithaca: Rural Development Committee, Center for International Studies, Cornell University, 1973), pp. 182, 330. This study was contracted by AID. Substantially higher tenancy figures may also be found in World Bank, *Land Reform: Sector Policy Paper* (Washington, D.C.: World Bank, 1975), p. 61.

39. Streeten et al., *First Things First*, p. 17; Streeten, "From Growth to Basic Needs," p. 7.

40. World Bank, *World Development Report 1980*, p. 32.

41. Streeten et al., *First Things First*, pp. 160–161.

42. Ibid., pp. 166–167.

43. Chenery, "Introduction," p. xix.

44. Editorial: "Paper Principles," *Wall Street Journal* (September 26, 1983), p. 28.

45. World Bank, *Poverty and Human Development* (New York: Oxford University Press, for the World Bank, 1980).

46. Frances Stewart, "Country Experience in Providing for Basic Needs," in World Bank, *Poverty and Basic Needs*, p. 12.

47. Streeten et al., *First Things First*, p. 27.

48. Ibid., pp. 55–56, 182.

49. Contrast, for example, the basically favorable treatment of Sri Lanka by World Bank official Paul Isenman, "Basic Needs: The Case of Sri Lanka," *World Development* 8 (1980): 237–258 (available as World Bank reprint no. 197), with the wholesale attack on Sri Lanka's "administered controls" and "subsidy regime" by IMF official Deena Khatkhate in "Anatomy of Financial Retardation in a Less Developed Country: The Case of Sri Lanka, 1951–1976," *World Development* 10,9 (September 1982): 829–840.

50. World Bank, *World Development Report 1978*, p. 63.

51. Streeten et al., *First Things First*, p. 97.

52. Ibid., p. 31; *World Development Report 1979*, p. 90.

53. Chenery, "Introduction," p. xv.

54. Walden Bello, David Kinley, and Elaine Elinson, *Development Debacle: The World Bank in the Philippines* (San Francisco: Institute for Food and Development Policy, 1982).

55. Aart van de Laar, *The World Bank and the Poor* (The Hague: Martinus Nijhoff, 1980), p. 7.

56. Mahbub ul Haq, "An International Perspective on Basic Needs," in World Bank, *Poverty and Basic Needs*, p. 33.

57. Ibid.

58. Steven H. Arnold, *Implementing Development Assistance: European Approaches to Basic Needs* (Boulder: Westview Press, 1982), p. 126.

59. DAC, *1982 Review*, p. 189.

60. For details on World Bank aid withholding from Ethiopia, see Stanley Please, *The Hobbled Giant: Essays on the World Bank* (Boulder: Westview Press, 1984), pp. 87–89.

61. Diana Johnstone, "Leftists Fight World Bank Blockade," *In These Times* (August 10–23, 1983), p. 8.

62. William Clark, "Robert McNamara at the World Bank," *Foreign Affairs* 60,1 (Fall 1981): 181.

63. Ayres, *Banking on the Poor*, p. 166.

64. World Bank, *IDA in Retrospect* (New York: Oxford University Press, for the World Bank, 1982), p. 30.

65. Ibid., p. 28.

66. "World Bank's Graduation Policy Reaffirmed," *Finance and Development* 19,2 (June 1982): 2–3.

67. World Bank, *IDA in Retrospect*, p. 25.

68. For example, see Shahid Javed Burki, "UNCTAD VI: For Better or For Worse?" *Finance and Development* 20,4 (December 1983): 18.

69. The fullest exploration of middle-income bias in aid allocation is Paul Isenman, "Biases in Aid Allocation Against Poorer and Larger Countries," *World Development* 4,8 (August 1976): 631–641.

70. DAC, *1981 Review*, p. 87.

71. John A. Edelman and Hollis B. Chenery, "Aid and Income Distribution," in Jagdish N. Bhagwati (ed.), *The New International Economic Order: The North-South Debate* (Cambridge: MIT Press, 1977), p. 32.

72. World Bank, *Focus on Poverty: A Report by a Task Force of the World Bank* (Washington, D.C.: World Bank, 1983), pp. 4–5.

73. Ayres, *Banking on the Poor*, p. 232.

74. Hurni, *The Lending Policy*, p. 47; World Bank, *Rural Development: Sector Policy Paper* (Washington, D.C.: World Bank, February 1975), pp. 60–61; World Bank, "Focus on Poverty," p. 5.

75. A comprehensive survey of the unequal impact on different social groups of infrastructural projects may be found in Cheryl Payer, *The World Bank: A Critical Analysis* (New York: Monthly Review Press, 1982). Payer's most provocative thesis, however, is that the World Bank's "new style" projects may be more harmful for the poor than its traditional infrastructural projects.

76. Asian Development Bank, *Annual Report 1981*, pp. 32, 33.

77. World Bank, *Annual Report 1982*, pp. 97–103.

78. Ayres, *Banking on the Poor*, pp. 98–99.

79. Frances Moore Lappé, Joseph Collins, and David Kinley, *Aid as Obstacle: Twenty Questions about Our Foreign Aid and the Hungry* (San Francisco: Institute for Food and Development Policy, 1980), p. 35.

80. World Bank, *Land Reform*, p. 11.

81. Ayres, *Banking on the Poor*, p. 104.

82. Hurni, *The Lending Policy*, p. 111.

83. World Bank, *Focus on Poverty*, p. 28.

84. World Bank, *Annual Report 1982*, p. 40.

85. Montague Yudelman, "Impact of the Bank's Rural Development Lending," in World Bank, *The World Bank*, p. 31.

86. The debate is joined, for example, in Bello, Kinley, and Elinson, *Development Debacle*.

87. World Bank, *Annual Report 1982*, pp. 40–41.

88. Richard Gerster, "The IMF and Basic Needs Conditionality," *Journal of World Trade Law* 16,6 (November-December 1982): 497–517.

89. Ayres frankly admits that the Bank's approach has been "basically top-down." The technocratic bias is strikingly evident in a later passage: "In confronting political considerations more directly in this chapter, it is assumed that macroeconomists can reconcile the competing claims of growth and distribution, producing redistribution with growth. It is also assumed that agricultural economists can design viable strategies for small-scale, subsistence farms; that scientists, engineers, and technicians can develop appropriate technology; and that urban and regional planners can devise ways to make the urban environments in which the poor live more humane and prevent hyperurbanization in ways that are economically efficient (without resorting to simplistic administrative fiats)"; Ayres, *Banking on the Poor*, pp. 65, 210. Hurni, in her admiration for the World Bank, goes so far as to assert: "The correct strategy mix of traditional 'hard' projects and the more socially oriented ones was found in the 1970s"; Hurni, *The Lending Policy*, p. 127.

90. This dichotomy between foreign policy, or "donor-interest," motivations, versus humanitarian, or "recipient-need," motivations, is most explicit in the work of R. D. McKinlay and R. Little. See R. D. McKinlay, "The Aid Relationship: A Foreign Policy Model and Interpretation of the Distributions of Official Bilateral Economic Aid of the United States, the United Kingdom, France and Germany, 1960–1970," *Comparative Political Studies* 11,4 (January 1979): 411–463; R. McKinlay, "The German Aid Relationship: A Test of the Recipient Need and the Donor Interest Models of the Distribution of German Bilateral Aid 1961–1970," *European Journal of Political Research* 6 (1978): 235–257; R. D. McKinlay and R. Little, "A Foreign-Policy Model of the Distribution of British Bilateral Aid, 1969–70," *British Journal of Political Science* 8,3 (July 1978): 313–331; R. D. McKinlay and R. Little, "A Foreign Policy Model of U.S. Bilateral Aid Allocation," *World Politics* 30,1 (October 1977): 58–86; and R. D. McKinlay and R. Little, "The U.S. Aid Relationship: A Test of the Recipient Need and the Donor Interest Models," *Political Studies* 27,2 (June 1979): 236–250. The validity of the dichotomy, if not their conclusions, is assumed by a critic in Paul Mosley, "Models of the Aid Allocation Process: A Comment on McKinlay and Little," *Political Studies* 29,2 (June 1981): 245–253.

91. Ayres, *Banking on the Poor*, p. 230.

92. World Bank, *Focus on Poverty*, p. 11.

93. Ibid., pp. 12–13.

94. Ibid., p. 34.

95. Ibid., p. 13.

96. Ibid., pp. 18–22.

97. Ayres, *Banking on the Poor*, pp. 102–103.

98. Ibid., p. 164.

99. World Bank, *Focus on Poverty*, p. 29.

100. Judith Tendler, *Rural Projects Through Urban Eyes: An Interpretation of the World Bank's New-Style Rural Development Projects* (Washington, D.C.: World Bank Staff Working Paper No. 532, 1982), p. 3.

101. Ibid., pp. 4, 7.

102. Ibid., p. 6.

103. Alain de Janvry, *The Agrarian Question and Reformism in Latin America* (Baltimore: Johns Hopkins University Press, 1981), p. 263.

104. Tendler, *Rural Projects Through Urban Eyes*, p. 6, fn.

105. Ibid., p. 24.

106. Ibid., p. iii.

107. Ibid., p. iv.

108. Ibid., pp. 52–53.

109. Ibid., p. 55.

110. Ibid., p. iv.

111. World Bank, *Accelerated Development in Sub-Saharan Africa: An Agenda for Action* (Washington, D.C.: World Bank, 1981), pp. 4, 37. See also World Bank, *Sub-Saharan Africa: Progress Report on Development Prospects and Programs* (Washington, D.C., 1983); and World Bank, *Toward Sustained Development in Sub-Saharan Africa: A Joint Program of Action* (Washington, D.C., 1984).

112. Bela Balassa, *Structural Adjustment Policies in Developing Countries* (Washington, D.C.: World Bank Staff Working Paper No. 464, July 1981), pp. 1–2.

113. World Bank, *World Development Report 1982*, p. 5.

114. Ibid., p. 85.

Chapter 6

1. "Payments Arrears Incurred by Fund Members More than Doubled in 1982, Study Reports," *IMF Survey* (August 8, 1983), p. 231.

2. World Bank, *Annual Report 1983*, p. 34.

3. "World Recovery Failing to Reverse Restrictions on Trade and Payments," *IMF Survey* (July 16, 1984), pp. 210, 215.

4. Jay Palmer, "The Debt-Bomb Threat," *Time* (January 10, 1983), p. 42.

5. For the official institutions, see World Bank, *World Debt Tables*,

1982–83 ed., pp. vii, xvi; Organization for Economic Cooperation and Development, *External Debt of Developing Countries: 1982 Survey* (Paris, 1982), p. 8. For the bankers' "hurrah tactic," see "The Global Financial Crisis: Can Recent Emergency Measures Succeed?" *International Currency Review* 15,4 (December 1983): 39; and "What Debt Crisis?" *Wall Street Journal* (April 20, 1983), p. 28.

6. Tony Killick and Mary Sutton, "An Overview," in T. Killick (ed.), *Adjustment and Financing in the Developing World: The Role of the International Monetary Fund* (Washington, D.C.: International Monetary Fund, 1982), p. 10.

7. Nicholas C. Hope, *Developments in the Prospects for the External Debt of the Developing Countries: 1970–1980 and Beyond* (Washington, D.C.: World Bank Staff Working Paper No. 488, August 1981), p. 15.

8. Net transfer to LDCs alone in 1970 was positive, however.

9. Ronald T. Libby, "International Development Association: A Legal Fiction to Secure an LDC Constituency," *International Organization* 29,4 (Autumn 1975): 1067.

10. Cheryl Payer, *The World Bank: A Critical Analysis* (New York: Monthly Review Press, 1982), p. 50.

11. Barring an expansion of the Bank's capital base, this decline had been expected, but not until 1986. See Gerald Rice, James Corr, and Susan Fennell, "Maintaining Financing for Adjustment and Development," *Finance and Development* 20,4 (December 1983): 46.

12. "Increase in Bilateral Aid in 1983 Was Offset by Contraction in Multilateral Contributions," *IMF Survey* (August 6, 1984), p. 229.

13. World Bank, *Debt and the Developing World* (Washington, D.C.: World Bank, 1984), p. xiii.

14. Harry J. Shaw, "U.S. Security Assistance: Debts and Dependency," *Foreign Policy* 50 (Spring 1983): 105–123.

15. Judith Miller, "Egypt Said to Lag on Paying U.S. Arms Debt," *New York Times* (February 14, 1985), p. A8.

16. World Bank, *World Development Report 1984*, p. 49.

17. Arthur MacEwan, "The Current Crisis in Latin America and the International Economy," *Monthly Review* 36,9 (February 1985): 3.

18. See, for example, Paul S. Nadler, "Troubled Foreign Loans in Perspective," *Bankers Monthly* (February 15, 1984), pp. 10–12.

19. William R. Cline, *International Debt and the Stability of the World Economy* (Washington, D.C.: Institute for International Economics, 1983), pp. 20–21.

20. Sidney Dell and Roger Lawrence, *The Balance of Payments Adjustment Process in Developing Countries* (New York: Pergamon Press, 1980), p. 11.

21. Shahid Javed Burki, "The Prospects for the Developing World: A Review of Recent Forecasts," *Finance and Development* 18,1 (March 1981): 21.

22. World Bank, *IDA in Retrospect* (New York: Oxford University Press, for the World Bank, 1982), p. 29.

23. Organization for Economic Cooperation and Development, *External Debt of Developing Countries: 1983 Survey* (Paris, 1984), p. 16.

24. Inter-American Development Bank, *External Debt and Economic Development in Latin America* (Washington, D.C., 1984), p. 15.

25. R. Peter DeWitt and James F. Petras, "Political Economy of International Debt: The Dynamics of Financial Capital," in Jonathan David Aronson (ed.), *Debt and the Less Developed Countries* (Boulder: Westview Press, 1979), p. 194.

26. John H. Makin, *The Global Debt Crisis: America's Growing Involvement* (New York: Basic Books, 1984), p. 111.

27. J. de Larosière, "The Impact of Interest Rates on International Finance and Trade," *IMF Survey* (November 15, 1982), p. 360.

28. The conditions governing repayment and default were commonly very wide-ranging. For example, a loan agreement between Citicorp and Jamaica states that the borrower is in default if "an extraordinary situation occurs which gives reasonable grounds to conclude in the judgement of the Majority Banks, that the borrower will be unable to perform or observe in the normal course its obligations under this Agreement." For this and other examples, see Richard Bernal, "Transnational Banks, the International Monetary Fund and External Debt of Developing Countries," *Social and Economic Studies* 31,4 (December 1982): 71–101.

29. Kevin Pakenham and Josslyn Gore-Booth, "The Eurocurrency Markets as a Source of Finance for the Developing World," *ODI Review* 2 (1974): 22.

30. William A. Noellert, "The International Debt of Developing Countries and Global Economic Adjustment," in Lawrence G. Franko and Marilyn J. Seiber (eds.), *Developing Country Debt* (New York: Pergamon Press, 1979), p. 273.

31. For details on Peru, see Barbara Stallings, "Peru and the U.S. Banks: The Privatization of Financial Relations," in Richard Fagen (ed.), *Capitalism and the State in U.S.–Latin American Relations* (Stanford: Stanford University Press, 1979), pp. 217–253.

32. Organization for Economic Cooperation and Development, *Development Co-operation: Efforts and Policies of the Members of the Development Assis-*

tance Committee, 1980 Review (Paris, 1980), pp. 163–164. This annual publication is hereafter referred to as DAC, *Review*.

33. International Monetary Fund, *Annual Reports*, 1965–1979.

34. Dell and Lawrence, *The Balance of Payments*, p. 114.

35. Killick and Sutton, "An Overview," p. 11; International Monetary Fund, *Annual Report 1982*, p. 109; and de Larosière, "The Impact of Interest Rates," p. 361.

36. Staff team headed by Richard C. Williams, *International Capital Markets: Developments and Prospects, 1982* (Washington, D.C.: IMF Occasional Paper No. 14, July 1982), p. 12.

37. Inter-American Development Bank, *Economic and Social Progress in Latin America, 1982 Report*, p. 58.

38. Quoted in Carlos Diaz-Alejandro, "The Post-1971 International Financial System and the Less Developed Countries," in G. K. Helleiner (ed.), *A World Divided: The Less Developed Countries in the International Economy* (Cambridge: Cambridge University Press, 1976), p. 191.

39. Quoted in ibid.

40. International Finance Corporation, *Annual Report 1981*, p. 12.

41. DAC, *1979 Review*, p. 96.

42. DAC, *1980 Review*, p. 161.

43. DAC, *1981 Review*, p. 59.

44. David Williams, "Opportunities and Constraints in International Lending," *Finance and Development* 20,1 (March 1983): 26. See also World Bank, *World Development Report 1981*, chap. 6.

45. For discussions of varying approaches to state capitalism, see Alex Dupuy and Barry Truchil, "Problems in the Theory of State Capitalism," *Theory and Society* 8,1 (July 1979): 1–38; Berch Berberoglu, "The Nature and Contradictions of State Capitalism in the Third World," *Social and Economic Studies* 28,2 (June 1979): 341–363; James Petras, "State Capitalism and the Third World," in James Petras, *Critical Perspectives on Imperialism and Social Class in the Third World* (New York: Monthly Review Press, 1978), pp. 84–102; and Samir Amin, *Unequal Development* (New York: Monthly Review Press, 1976), pp. 343–350. For a parallel discussion of the "entrepreneurial state," see Raymond D. Duvall and John R. Freeman, "The State and Dependent Capitalism," *International Studies Quarterly* 25,1 (March 1981): 98–118.

46. James Petras, with Morris H. Morley, "The Venezuelan Development 'Model' and U.S. Policy," in Petras, *Critical Perspectives*, p. 230.

47. Fitzroy Ambursley and Robin Cohen, "Crisis in the Caribbean: In-

ternal Transformations and External Constraints," in Fitzroy Ambursley and Robin Cohen (eds.), *Crisis in the Caribbean* (New York: Monthly Review Press, 1983), p. 4.

48. Jonathan David Aronson, "The Politics of Private Bank Lending and Debt Renegotiations," in Aronson, *Debt and the Less Developed Countries*, p. 293.

49. Andrew Thompson, "Debt: Argentina's Generals Get Ready to Pass the Buck," *South* 34 (August 1983): 72.

50. Tony Emerson, "Argentina's Debt: The View from Buenos Aires," *The Banker* 134,698 (April 1984): 25.

51. Maria Elena Hurtado, "Fiesta to Fiasco: Chile's Free Market Hangover," *South* 31 (May 1983): 25; "Chile: Goodbye Chicago?" *The Banker* 133,684 (February 1983): 69; and Inter-American Development Bank, *External Debt*, p. 12. For why Chilean policies led to the accumulation of debt, see Philip O'Brien, "Authoritarianism and Monetarism in Chile, 1973–1983," *Socialist Review* 77 (September-October 1984): 45–79.

52. Kuniko Inoguchi, "Third World Statism and Indebted Growth," paper presented at the annual meeting of the American Political Science Association, Washington, D.C., August 1984.

53. Steve Lohr, "Seoul's Effort to Industrialize," *New York Times* (August 16, 1983), p. D4.

54. For an excellent analysis of the Korean state and its role in development, see Stephan Haggard and Chung-in Moon, "The South Korean State in the International Economy: Liberal, Dependent, or Mercantile?" in John Gerard Ruggie (ed.), *The Antinomies of Interdependence* (New York: Columbia University Press, 1983), pp. 131–189. See also Jeff Frieden, "Third World Indebted Industrialization: International Finance and State Capitalism in Mexico, Brazil, Algeria, and South Korea," *International Organization* 35,3 (Summer 1981): 407–431.

55. Inter-American Development Bank, *External Debt*, p. 160.

56. Inoguchi, "Third World Statism," p. 30.

57. Mary M. Shirley, *Managing State-Owned Enterprises* (Washington, D.C.: World Bank Staff Working Paper No. 577, 1983), pp. 9–10.

58. Inoguchi, "Third World Statism," p. 30.

59. Frieden, "Third World Indebted Industrialization," p. 413–418.

60. Jeffrey Hart, "The Constraints on Associative Development in a Privileged Developing Country: The Case of Venezuela," in Ruggie, *The Antinomies*, p. 205; Inter-American Development Bank, *External Debt*, p. 148.

61. Frieden, "Third World Indebted Industrialization," p. 422; and World Bank, *World Development Report 1983*, p. 49.

62. Inter-American Development Bank, *Social and Economic Progress in Latin America: 1982 Report*, p. 167.

63. Shirley, *Managing State-Owned Enterprises*, p. 15.

64. Ibid., p. 6. See also World Bank, *World Development Report 1983*, p. 49.

65. Calculated from data in Inter-American Development Bank, *External Debt*, pp. 148, 176, 182, 188.

66. Robert Solomon, "A Quantitative Perspective on the Debt of Developing Countries," in Franko and Seiber, *Developing Country Debt*, p. 18; updated statistics based on data from International Monetary Fund, *International Financial Statistics, 1982 Yearbook*; and (for Brazil) Inter-American Development Bank, *Economic and Social Progress in Latin America: 1982 Report*.

67. International Monetary Fund, *World Economic Outlook* (IMF Occasional Paper No. 21, May 1983), p. 144.

68. "De Larosière Address Before ECOSOC Emphasizes Need to Spur Investment," *IMF Survey* (June 11, 1983), p. 196. See also Cline, *International Debt*, p. 28.

69. The estimate is from the Bank for International Settlements. William Pike, "Teller's Window," *South* 46 (August 1984): 55.

70. World Bank, *World Development Report 1982*, pp. 43–46; Inter-American Development Bank, *Social and Economic Progress in Latin America: 1982 Report*, pp. 38–40.

71. Celso Furtado, *No to Recession and Unemployment: An Examination of the Brazilian Economic Crisis* (London: Third World Foundation, 1984), p. 22.

72. James F. Petras and Morris H. Morley, "Petrodollars and the State: The Failure of State Capitalist Development in Venezuela," *Third World Quarterly* 5,1 (January 1983): 26.

73. Peter T. Kilborn, "Brazil's Economic 'Miracle' and Its Collapse," *New York Times* (November 26, 1983), p. 31.

74. Inter-American Development Bank, *Economic and Social Progress in Latin America: 1982 Report*, p. 58.

75. Larry E. Westphal, Yung W. Rhee, and Garry Pursell, *Korean Industrial Competence: Where It Came From* (Washington, D.C.: World Bank Staff Working Paper No. 469, July 1981), p. 65; and David Goldsbrough, "For-

eign Direct Investment in Developing Countries," *Finance and Development* 22,1 (March 1985): 33.

76. Peter Evans, *Dependent Development: The Alliance of Multinational, State, and Local Capital in Brazil* (Princeton: Princeton University Press, 1979), p. 290.

77. Table 29; Richard Williams et al., *International Capital Markets: Developments and Prospects, 1983* (Washington, D.C.: International Monetary Fund, July 1983), p. 70.

78. Robert E. Wood and Max Mmuya, "The Debt Crisis in the Fourth World: Implications for North-South Relations," *Alternatives* 11 (January 1986): 107–131.

79. Staff team, *International Capital Markets*, p. 12.

80. Dell and Lawrence, *Balance of Payments Adjustment Process*, pp. 95–99. It has been widely noted that the tendency to force adjustment only on deficit countries is rooted in the basic Bretton Woods system.

81. "Capital Inflows to Non-Oil Developing Countries Rose Sharply During 1981, Yearbook Data Show," *IMF Survey* (December 13, 1982), p. 386.

82. Dell and Lawrence, *Balance of Payments Adjustment Process*, p. 124.

83. Richard O'Brien, "Roles of the Euromarket and the International Monetary Fund in Financing Developing Countries," in Killick, *Adjustment and Financing*, p. 150.

84. Makin, *The Global Debt Crisis*, pp. 134, 153.

85. A. W. Clausen, *Third World Debt and Global Recovery* (Washington, D.C.: World Bank, 1983), p. 11.

86. Makin, *The Global Debt Crisis*, p. 162; and International Monetary Fund, *Annual Report 1984*, p. 25.

87. International Monetary Fund, *Annual Report 1983*, p. 4.

88. De Larosière, "The Impact of Interest Rates," p. 360.

89. World Bank, *Annual Report 1984*, p. 32.

90. DAC, *1982 Review*, p. 55.

91. Jacques Cook, "Maintaining the Flow of Loans: The Cofinancing Alternative," *The Banker* 133,687 (May 1983): 55.

92. J. de Larosière, "The Domestic Economy and the International Economy—Their Interactions," *IMF Survey* (December 5, 1983), p. 381. William Cline's estimate of "excess interest payments" is somewhat higher: $41 billion in 1981–82. See Cline, *International Debt*, pp. 22–23.

93. Padma Gotur, "Interest Rates and the Developing World," *Finance and Development* 20,4 (December 1983): 33.

94. De Larosière, "The Impact of Interest Rates," p. 361.

95. Inter-American Development Bank, *Economic and Social Progress in Latin America: 1982 Report*, p. 68.

96. Organization for Economic Cooperation and Development, *External Debt of Developing Countries: 1982 Survey* (Paris, 1982), pp. 15−17.

97. World Bank, *World Development Report 1984*, pp. 22, 24; and "GATT Reports a 2 Percent Volume Increase in Trade in 1983, But a Fall in Value Terms," *IMF Survey* (June 4, 1984), p. 165.

98. "Fund Statistics Show Lower 1984 Price Rise for Basic Commodities," *IMF Survey* (January 21, 1985), p. 17; and "Commodities," *IMF Survey* (February 18, 1985), p. 63.

99. International Monetary Fund, *Annual Report 1982*, p. 18.

100. World Bank, *World Development Report 1984*, p. 24.

101. Anne Koch, "Nicaragua: State of the Nation," *South* 41 (March 1984): 17.

102. Cheryl Payer, "Tanzania and the World Bank," *Third World Quarterly* 5,4 (October 1983): 802.

103. Cline, *International Debt*, pp. 24−25.

104. Inter-American Development Bank, *External Debt*, p. 4.

105. World Bank, *Annual Report 1984*, p. 39.

106. Cline, *International Debt*, p. 88.

107. "Meeting of 11-Nation Cartagena Group Reiterates Call for New Debt Approach," *IMF Survey* (February 18, 1985), p. 55.

108. Melvyn Westlake and Jane Merriman, "The Fire Next Time: Putting off the Day of Reckoning," *South* 30 (April 1983): 11.

Chapter 7

1. Organization for Economic Cooperation and Development, *Development Co-operation: Efforts and Policies of the Members of the Development Assistance Committee, 1983 Review* (Paris, 1983), p. 213. This annual publication is hereafter referred to as DAC, *Review*.

2. Alan Riding, "The New Crisis for Latin Debt," *New York Times* (March 11, 1984), p. 8F.

3. See, for example, World Bank, *World Debt Tables*, 1982−83 ed., pp. vii, xvi.

4. Rudiger Dornbusch, "Dealing with Debt in the 1980s," *Third World Quarterly* 7,3 (July 1985): 534−535.

5. World Bank, *Toward Sustained Development in Sub-Saharan Africa: A Joint Program of Action* (Washington, D.C., 1984), p. 13.

6. Clyde H. Farnsworth, "U.S. Plans Proposal on Aid to Africa," *New York Times* (September 21, 1985), p. 41.

7. M. S. Mendelsohn, *Commercial Banks and the Restructuring of Cross-Border Debt* (New York: Group of Thirty, 1983), p. 3.

8. Quoted in Clyde H. Farnsworth, "Banks' Bid for Aid Stirs Old, Deep Resentments," *New York Times* (February 10, 1983), p. D3.

9. Steven Kinzer, "Venezuela Resisting I.M.F. Rein," *New York Times* (July 25, 1983), p. D8.

10. For details, see Darrell Delamaide, *Debt Shock: The Full Story of the World Credit Crisis* (Garden City, N.Y.: Doubleday, 1984), p. 209; and Michael Moffitt, *The World's Money: International Banking from Bretton Woods to the Brink of Insolvency* (New York: Simon and Schuster, 1983), p. 104.

11. "East European Debt: Turning the Screw," *The Banker* 133,689 (July 1983): 77.

12. Ian Pritchard, "The Mexican Crisis Blurred the Lines Between Public and Private Sector Debt," *Euromoney* (March 1983), p. 28.

13. Staff team headed by E. Brau and R. C. Williams, *Recent Multilateral Debt Restructurings with Official and Bank Creditors* (Washington, D.C.: International Monetary Fund Occasional Paper No. 25, December 1983), pp. 30–34.

14. World Bank, *World Development Report 1985*, p. 64.

15. Calculated from data in Luis Kaffman, "Borrowers Fight a Losing Battle to Keep the Bankers Happy," *South* 33 (July 1983): 63. See also Raymond Bonner, "Banks Gain by Altering Latin Debt," *New York Times* (January 10, 1983), p. D1.

16. Mendelsohn, *Commercial Banks*, p. 8.

17. Luis Kaffman, "Tarred with a Regional Brush," *South* 31 (May 1983): 71; Luis Kaffman, "Asean's Fallen Stars Woo Back the Bankers," *South* 31 (May 1983): 70.

18. International Monetary Fund, *Annual Report 1985*, p. 60.

19. World Bank, *World Development Report 1985*, pp. 5, 22, 23.

20. Richard S. Dale, "Country Risk and Bank Regulation," *The Banker* 133,685 (March 1983): 41.

21. World Bank, *World Development Report 1983*, p. 33.

22. "BIS Reaches Agreement on Financing for Fund," *IMF Survey* (January 9, 1984), p. 1.

23. Pritchard, "The Mexican Crisis," p. 28.

24. Peter Field, David Shirreff, and William Ollard, "The IMF and Central Banks Flex Their Muscles," *Euromoney* (January 1983), p. 35.

25. "Fund Managing Director Outlines Considerable Progress Achieved in Managing Country Debt Problems," *IMF Survey* (June 18, 1984), p. 178.

26. Staff team, *Recent Multilateral Debt*, pp. 12–13.

27. Richard Williams, Peter Keller, John Lipsky, and Donald Mathieson, *International Capital Markets: Developments and Prospects, 1983* (Washington, D.C.: International Monetary Fund Occasional Paper No. 23, July 1983), p. 45. See also Otmar Emminger, "Learning to Live with Stability," *The Banker* 133,690 (August 1983): 31.

28. William R. Cline, *International Debt: Systemic Risk and Policy Response* (Washington, D.C.: Institute for International Economics, 1984), p. 35.

29. Ibid.

30. "World Bank Pamphlet Discusses Efforts to Increase Cofinancing," *IMF Survey* (November 7, 1983), p. 345; World Bank, *Annual Report 1984*, pp. 18–19; World Bank, *Annual Report 1985*, p. 18.

31. World Bank, *Annual Report 1983*, p. 19.

32. World Bank, *Co-Financing: Review of World Bank Co-Financing with Private Financial Institutions* (Washington, D.C., 1980), pp. 5–6.

33. Details of the World Bank's cofinancing policies have been provided in World Bank, *Annual Report 1983*, pp. 38–39; *IMF Survey* (January 14, 1983), pp. 30–31; and "Cofinancing—New World Bank Approaches," *Finance and Development* 20,1 (March 1983): 40.

34. World Bank, *Annual Report 1984*, pp. 23–25.

35. Ibid., p. 24.

36. *IMF Survey* (July 2, 1984), p. 207.

37. *IMF Survey* (June 18, 1984), p. 191.

38. World Bank, *Annual Report 1985*, p. 55.

39. Inter-American Development Bank, *Annual Report 1981*, p. 19; and Inter-American Development Bank, *Annual Report 1983*, p. 22.

40. Asian Development Bank, *Annual Report 1983*, p. 29.

41. "Loans in 1984 Total $2,234.3 Million," *ADB Quarterly Review* (January 1985), pp. 1, 10.

42. Jacques Cook, "Maintaining the Flow of Loans: The Cofinancing Alternative," *The Banker* 133,687 (May 1983): 60.

43. See "New U.S. World Debt Plan Seen," *New York Times* (October 1, 1985), pp. D1, D19; Clyde H. Farnsworth, "U.S. May Back Higher Lending by World Bank," *New York Times* (October 7, 1985), p. A10. See also the proposal by World Bank economist Andrew M. Kamarck that future commer-

cial bank lending be "channeled through consortia headed by the Bank (or one of the other international financial institutions)"; Andrew M. Kamarck, "The World Bank and Development: A Personal Perspective," *Finance and Development* 21,4 (December 1984): 28.

44. For example, see quotations by John T. Basek and Manuel Ulloa in *Wall Street Journal* (June 22, 1984), pp. 35, 36.

45. For example, see Van R. Whiting, Jr., "Financial Populism or Responsible Statism: State Intervention in Brazil and Mexico," paper presented at 1984 annual meeting of the American Political Science Association, Washington, D.C.

46. Jacques de Larosière, speech to International Monetary Conference, June 4, 1984, Philadelphia. *IMF Survey* (June 18, 1984), p. 180.

47. Inter-American Development Bank, *Social and Economic Progress in Latin America: 1985 Report*, pp. 13, 15.

48. International Finance Corporation, *Annual Report 1983*, p. 34.

49. World Bank, *Annual Report 1984*, pp. 28–30; and Roger S. Leeds, "IFC's New Approach to Project Promotion," *Finance and Development* (March 1985), pp. 5–7.

50. World Bank, *Annual Report 1985*, p. 32.

51. For details, see Asian Development Bank, *Quarterly Review* (January 1984), pp. 1, 16; and (October 1983), pp. 10–13; Asian Development Bank, *Annual Report 1983*, pp. 29, 60.

52. For details, see Inter-American Development Bank, *Annual Report 1983*, pp. 1–11; "Shares Allocated for Investment Corporation," *IDB News* (December 1984), p. 1; and *IMF Survey* (December 10, 1984), p. 383.

53. Overseas Private Investment Corporation, *Annual Report 1982*, p. 22; *Annual Report 1983*, p. 26; and *Annual Report 1984*, pp. 2, 6.

54. World Bank, *World Development Report 1983*, p. 17.

55. "A Conversation with Mr. Clausen," *Finance and Development* 19,4 (December 1982): 7.

56. Ibrahim F. I. Shihata, "Increasing Private Capital Flows to LDCs: An Examination of the Proposed Multilateral Investment Guarantee Agency," *Finance and Development* 21,4 (December 1984): 6–9.

57. Ibid., p. 9.

58. Richard J. Meislin, "Mexican Conglomerate's Comeback," *New York Times* (December 3, 1984), p. D10.

59. William Pike, "Putting Debts to Work," *South* 50 (December 1984): 67.

60. World Bank, *World Development Report 1985*, p. 19.

61. Statement by Jack Guenther in "Roundtable: Is Government Intervention or Marketplace Mechanism the Solution to the Debt Dilemma?" *Wall Street Journal* (June 22, 1984), p. 39.

62. Peter Leslie, "Techniques of Rescheduling: The Latest Lessons," *The Banker* 133,686 (April 1983): 24.

63. Manuel Guitián, *Fund Conditionality: Evolution of Principles and Practices* (Washington, D.C.: International Monetary Fund, 1981), pp. 16, fn., 20, fn.

64. DAC, *1979 Review*, p. 96.

65. "Fund Requires Adequate Finance to Underpin Adjustment Efforts and Strengthen Monetary System," *IMF Survey* (October 10, 1983), p. 310.

66. International Monetary Fund, *Annual Reports*, 1980–84; and International Monetary Fund, *World Development Report 1984*.

67. "Decline in Net Use of Credit Continues, SDR Operations Fall Below 1978 Peak," *IMF Survey* (January 21, 1980), p. 28; "Purchases from Fund by Member Countries Total SDR 7.0 Billion in January-June 1983," *IMF Survey* (July 25, 1983), p. 209; and "Use of Fund's Resources Totals SDR 12.6 Billion," *IMF Survey* (February 6, 1984), p. 33.

68. "Success of Adjustment Programs Reduces Use of Fund Resources," *IMF Survey* (February 4, 1985), p. 33. If trust fund loans in earlier years are not counted and SDR, rather than dollar, amounts are used, calendar year 1984 ranks as the third most active year for the Fund.

69. Ibid., p. 45.

70. Ibid.

71. J. de Larosière, "The Role of the International Monetary Fund in Today's World Economy," *IMF Survey* (June 21, 1982), pp. 184–185; International Monetary Fund, *Annual Report 1983*, p. 90; and International Monetary Fund, *Annual Report 1984*, p. 76.

72. J. de Larosière, "Adjustment Programmes Supported by the Fund: Their Logic, Objectives, and Results in the Light of Recent Experience," *IMF Survey* (February 6, 1984), p. 46.

73. "Fund Requires Adequate Finance," p. 309.

74. See, for example, Maria Elena Hurtado, "Chile: The Last Disciple," *South* 38 (December 1983): 384.

75. "Brazil Will Resume Purchases Following Agreement with Fund," *IMF Survey* (December 5, 1983), p. 384.

76. "Formal Approval Given to 1985 Access Limits," *IMF Survey* (November 26, 1984), p. 357.

77. "Revised and Enlarged GAB Approved by Participants," *IMF Survey*

(January 9, 1984), pp. 1, 7; and "Four Fund Borrowings Provide SDR 6 Billion," *IMF Survey* (May 8, 1984), p. 129.

78. U.S. Department of the Treasury, *United States Participation in the Multilateral Development Banks in the 1980s* (Washington, D.C.: Department of the Treasury, 1982), pp. 84–88.

79. Clyde H. Farnsworth, "Discord on Aid to Poor Lands," *New York Times* (September 24, 1983), pp. 29, 37.

80. Inter-American Development Bank, *Annual Report 1981*, p. 13; and Inter-American Development Bank, *Annual Report 1983*, p. 6.

81. DAC, *1983 Review*, p. 105; "Loans in 1984 Total $2,234.3 Million," *ADB Quarterly Review* (January 1985), p. 1. The one exception to this trend is the African Development Bank, whose expanded membership (now including advanced capitalist countries) agreed to contribute $1.5 billion to its soft-loan subsidiary, the African Development Fund, in May 1984, a 50 percent increase.

82. Thomas Hoopengardner and Ines Garcia-Thoumi, "The World Bank in a Changing Financial Environment," *Finance and Development* 21,2 (June 1984): 14.

83. For details, see World Bank, *Annual Report 1983*, pp. 39–40; *IMF Survey* (March 7, 1983), pp. 77–78; and "The Bank's Special Action Program," *Finance and Development* 20,2 (June 1983): 14–15.

84. "Adjustment and Growth," *Finance and Development* 20,2 (June 1983): 13.

85. Clyde H. Farnsworth, "Role Grows for 3rd World's Lenders," *New York Times* (September 29, 1983), p. D9.

86. World Bank, *Annual Report 1985*, p. 54; and "World Bank Disbursements Up by 26 Percent As Special Program Takes Hold, Report Says," *IMF Survey* (September 17, 1984), p. 285.

87. Inter-American Development Bank, *Annual Report 1983*, p. 10; and *Annual Report 1984*, p. 22.

88. "AsDB Lending Exceeds $1.8 Billion in 1983," *IMF Survey* (May 8, 1984), p. 142.

89. World Bank, *Annual Report 1984*, p. 48.

90. DAC, *1983 Review*, p. 124.

91. Ibid., p. 127.

92. DAC, *1984 Review*, pp. 55–56.

93. Ibid., p. 33.

94. Ibid., p. 56.

95. Sheila Meehan, "On the Spot: Fund and Bank Representatives in the Field," *Finance and Development* 21,3 (September 1984): 47–48.

96. World Bank, *Annual Report 1985*, p. 58; and Cheryl Payer, *The World Bank: A Critical Analysis* (New York: Monthly Review Press, 1982), pp. 123, 141.

97. Stanley Please, *The Hobbled Giant: Essays on the World Bank* (Boulder: Westview Press, 1984), esp. pp. 9–12.

98. "Fund's Central Role Is Stressed, with Need for Due Conditionality," *IMF Survey* (October 24, 1983), p. 331; and Peter Kilborn, "Tough Talk by U.S.: New Development for I.M.F.," *New York Times* (September 27, 1983), p. D6.

99. "De Clercq, de Larosière Respond to Questions on Access, Fund Finance," *IMF Survey* (October 10, 1983), p. 300; and "Governors Discuss Fund Resource Adequacy and Reach Agreement on Members' Access," *IMF Survey* (October 10, 1983), p. 296.

100. Ibid.

101. For the text of the summit communiqué, see *IMF Survey* (June 18, 1984), pp. 188–190.

102. John Makin, *The Global Debt Crisis: America's Growing Involvement* (New York: Basic Books, 1984), p. 36.

103. "Successful Resolution of Debt Problem Linked to Future Growth in World Trade," *IMF Survey* (February 18, 1985), p. 51.

104. James Feron, "Speakers at U.N. Stress Economics," *New York Times* (September 25, 1984), p. A12.

Epilogue

1. John White, *The Politics of Aid* (New York: St. Martin's Press, 1974), p. 55.

2. "De Clercq, de Larosière Respond to Questions on Access, Fund Finance," *IMF Survey* (October 10, 1983), p. 305.

3. See, for example, Bela Balassa, *Structural Adjustment Policies in Developing Countries* (Washington, D.C.: World Bank Staff Working Paper No. 464, July 1981); Bela Balassa, "The Adjustment Experience of Developing Economies after 1973," in John Williamson (ed.), *IMF Conditionality* (Washington, D.C.: Institute for International Economics, 1983), pp. 145–174; Parvez Hasan, *Growth and Structural Adjustment in East Asia* (Washington, D.C.:

World Bank Staff Working Paper No. 529, 1982); Vijay Joshi, *International Adjustment in the 1980s* (Washington, D.C.: World Bank Staff Working Paper No. 485, August 1981); Robert Liebenthal, *Adjustment in Low-Income Africa 1974–78* (Washington, D.C.: World Bank Staff Working Paper No. 486, August 1981); Christine Wallich, *An Analysis of Developing Country Adjustment Experiences in the 1970s: Low-Income Asia* (Washington, D.C.: World Bank Staff Working Paper No. 487, August 1981); Barend A. de Vries and Willem Brakel, *Restructuring of Manufacturing Industry: The Experience of the Textile Industry in Pakistan, Philippines, Portugal, and Turkey* (Washington, D.C.: World Bank Staff Working Paper No. 558, 1983).

4. John Gerard Ruggie, "Introduction: International Independence and National Welfare," in J. G. Ruggie (ed.), *The Antinomies of Interdependence* (New York: Columbia University Press, 1983), p. 17, fn.

5. World Bank, *Toward Sustained Development in Sub-Saharan Africa: A Joint Program of Action* (Washington, D.C., 1984), p. 15.

6. In addition to the citations in footnote 3, see Anne O. Krueger, "The Effects of Trade Strategies on Growth," *Finance and Development* 20,2 (June 1983): 6–8; Anne O. Krueger, "Trade Strategies and Employment in Developing Countries," *Finance and Development* 21,1 (June 1984): 23–26; and Bertil Walstedt, *State Manufacturing Enterprise in a Mixed Economy: The Turkish Case* (Baltimore: Johns Hopkins University Press, for the World Bank, 1980).

7. World Bank, *World Development Report 1983*, pp. 57–63; de Vries and Brakel, *Restructuring of Manufacturing Industry*, pp. iv, 20; and Balassa, *Structural Adjustment Policies*, p. 27.

8. "Adjustment Burden is Manageable with Needed Finance and Recovery," *IMF Survey* (May 21, 1984), p. 146.

9. "Bangladesh Acts to Adjust Policies and Is Now Ready to Resume Growth Process," *IMF Survey* (August 22, 1983), p. 250.

10. World Bank, *Sub-Saharan Africa: Progress Report on Development Prospects and Programs* (Washington, D.C., 1983), p. 25.

11. World Bank, *Accelerated Development in Sub-Saharan Africa: An Agenda for Action* (Washington, D.C., 1981), p. 37.

12. G. Russell Kincaid, "Korea's Major Adjustment Effort," *Finance and Development* 20,4 (December 1983): 22.

13. "Korea Maintains Growth, External Adjustment Despite Depressed Condition of World Trade," *IMF Survey* (April 18, 1983), p. 117.

14. Ibid.

15. Ibid.

16. Kincaid, "Korea's Major Adjustment Effort," p. 23.

17. See, for example, Basil Caplan, "Hesitant Liberalisation in Korea," *The Banker* 134,695 (January 1984): 31–35.

18. Roberto Espindola, "Cuba Plays the Field," *South* 32 (June 1983): 71.

19. Andrew Thompson, "Coming Up for Air," *South* 38 (December 1983): 29; "Throwing off the Silken Chains" (interview with Julius Nyerere), *South* 46 (August 1984): 35–36.

20. For recent and pessimistic assessments of the prospects for North-South negotiations, see Jagdish N. Bhagwati and John Gerard Ruggie (eds.), *Power, Passions and Purpose: Prospects for North-South Negotiations* (Cambridge: MIT Press, 1984); and Robert A. Mortimer, *The Third World Coalition in International Politics* (Boulder: Westview Press, 1984).

21. J. de Larosière, "The International Monetary System and the Developing Countries," *IMF Survey* (November 29, 1982), p. 380.

22. "World Economy at Threshold of Recovery: Marked Pickup Anticipated in Second Half," *IMF Survey* (June 13, 1983), p. 166.

23. "GATT Reports a 6 Percent Fall in Dollar Value of World Trade," *IMF Survey* (March 21, 1983), p. 88.

24. World Bank, *World Development Report 1983*, p. 126.

25. Ibid., p. 35.

26. H. Erich Heinemann, "Hope Stirs for World Debt Relief," *New York Times* (April 19, 1983), pp. D1, 20.

27. J. de Larosière, "The Domestic Economy and the International Economy—Their Interactions," *IMF Survey* (December 5, 1983), p. 381.

28. World Bank, *World Development Report 1984*, p. 44.

29. "Global Recovery to Continue in 1984 and 1985, According to Fund's World Economic Outlook," *IMF Survey* (April 23, 1984), p. 123; and "Recent Increases in Public Debt Pose Threat to Economic Recovery, Fund Managing Director Cautions," *IMF Survey*, pp. 261–267.

30. C. Fred Bergsten, "Our Trade Balance: A Growing Crisis," *New York Times* (December 7, 1984), p. A31.

31. "IMF Austerity Prescriptions Could Be Hazardous," *Business Week* (February 21, 1983), p. 112.

32. William R. Cline, *International Debt and the Stability of the World Economy* (Washington, D.C.: Institute for International Economics, September 1983), p. 11.

33. J. de Larosière, "The Challenges Facing the World Economy and the

Role of the International Monetary Fund," *IMF Survey* (March 26, 1984), ·
p. 82; and "Successful Resolution of Debt Problem Linked to Future Growth
in World Trade," *IMF Survey* (February 18, 1985), p. 51.

34. De Larosière, "Successful Resolution of Debt Problem," p. 50;
"GATT's Assessment of 1984 World Trade: Record Volume But Rising Protectionism," *IMF Survey* (April 15, 1985), pp. 114–115.

35. International Monetary Fund, *Annual Report 1983*, p. 2.

36. International Monetary Fund, *Annual Report 1984*, p. 33.

37. World Bank, *Annual Report 1984*, pp. 39–40.

38. Paul Lewis, "A 'Cartel' of Debtors Ruled Out," *New York Times*
(June 19, 1984), p. D19.

39. World Bank, *World Development Report 1982*, p. 33.

40. See Celso Furtado, *No to Recession and Unemployment: An Examination of the Brazilian Economic Crisis* (London: Third World Foundation,
1984), including introduction by Teresa Hayter.

41. Inter-American Development Bank, *Annual Report 1983*, p. 2.

42. World Bank, *Annual Report 1983*, pp. 2, 27.

43. Asian Development Bank, *Annual Report 1983*, p. 91; *Annual Report
1984*, p. 101.

44. World Bank, *Debt and the Developing World* (Washington, D.C., 1984),
p. ix; World Bank, *Annual Report 1985*, p. 43.

45. William R. Cline, *International Debt: Systemic Risk and Policy Response*
(Washington, D.C.: Institute for International Economics, 1984), p. 175.

46. Inter-American Development Bank, *External Debt and Economic Development in Latin America* (Washington, D.C., 1984), p. 20.

47. Lawrence Rout and S. Karene Witcher, "Politics of Nations Are In-
truding in Arena of International Debt," *Wall Street Journal* (October 10,
1983), p. 1.

48. Ibid.

49. Alan Riding, "The New Crisis for Latin Debt," *New York Times*
(March 11, 1984), p. 8F.

50. L. C. Raghavan, "The Buck Stops in Belgrade," *South* 32 (June
1983): 25–26.

51. See, for example, Walden Bello, David Kinley, and Elaine Elinson,
Development Debacle: The World Bank in the Philippines (San Francisco: Institute for Food and Development Policy, 1982).

INDEX